INSTITUTIONS AND REGIONAL LABOUR MARKETS IN EUROPE

Institutions and Regional Labour Markets in Europe

Edited by
LAMBERT VAN DER LAAN
SANTOS M. RUESGA

Routledge
Taylor & Francis Group
LONDON AND NEW YORK

First published 1998 by Ashgate Publishing

Reissued 2018 by Routledge
2 Park Square, Milton Park, Abingdon, Oxon, OX14 4RN
52 Vanderbilt Avenue, New York, NY 10017

Routledge is an imprint of the Taylor & Francis Group, an informa business

A Library of Congress record exists under LC control number:

ISBN 13: 978-1-138-36979-5 (hbk)
ISBN 13: 978-0-429-42843-2 (ebk)

Contents

1 Introduction
Lambert van der Laan & Santos M. Ruesga 1
1.1 Western Europe: the rise and fall of the regulation model 3
1.2 Eastern Europe: changing policies and institutions 5
1.3 The present book 8

Part One: The general framework 13

2 The spatial-institutional perspective on the labour market in Europe
Lambert van der Laan & Santos M. Ruesga 15
2.1 Three trends in economic thinking 15
2.1.1 Humanisation and socialisation 15
2.1.2 Localisation 16
2.1.3 Theoretical integration 17
2.2 The spatial-institutional perspective 18
2.3 Regional labour markets 20

3 Setting the stage: general changes on the European labour market
Lambert van der Laan 27
3.1 Introduction 27
3.2 Quartairisation of jobs and functions 27
3.2.1 Economic, social and cultural capital 30
3.2.2 The information society 32
3.3 Developments in the supply of labour 34

3.3.1 *Ageing* 34
3.3.2 *Migration* 38
3.3.3 *Participation* 40
3.3.4 *Feminisation* 42
3.3.5 *A macro-spatial summary of changes in labour supply* 43
3.4 Macro-institutional structures, policies and labour market performance 46
3.4.1 *Institutional structure and labour market performance* 46
3.4.2 *Policies and labour market performance* 50
3.4.3 *Conclusion* 54
3.5 General conclusions 54

4 Regional and institutional changes in European labour markets
Santos M. Ruesga & Carlos Resa-Nestares 61
4.1 Introduction 61
4.2 Labour markets in Western Europe: convergence and divergence 62
4.3 Labour markets in Eastern Europe 67
4.4 Conclusion 68
Annex I 70
Annex II 76

Part Two: Western Europe 79

5 Regional labour markets and institutions in the United Kingdom
David Armstrong & David H. Blackaby 81
5.1 Introduction 81
5.2 Regional disparities in unemployment in the United Kingdom 83
5.3 The policy context 87
5.3.1 *Labour market policy and the regional problem* 87
5.3.2 *Unions and pay bargaining* 89
5.3.3 *Labour mobility and vocational training* 90
5.4 Labour market adjustments in the United Kingdom 92
5.4.1 *Training* 92
5.4.2 *Labour mobility* 95
5.4.3 *Wage flexibility* 97

5.5 Summary and conclusions 99

6 Institutions and regional labour markets in The Netherlands
Jouke van Dijk & Andries de Grip 105
6.1 Introduction 105
6.2 The Dutch labour market 106
6.2.1 The economic framework and socio-economic background 106
6.2.2 The policy framework 110
6.3 The regional setting 113
6.4 Main policy issues 118
6.4.1 Employment policy 118
6.4.2 Regional policy 119
6.4.3 Labour market policy 121
6.5 Effects of policy measures 123
6.5 1 Employment policy 123
6.5.2 Regional policy 125
6.5.3 Labour market policy 125
6.6 Conclusions 128

7 Institutions and regional return to education in Sweden
Eugenia Kazamaki-Ottersten 133
7.1 Introduction 133
7.2 General characteristics of the Swedish labour market 134
7.3 Regional labour markets 139
7.4 Human and social capital: three hypotheses 145
7.5 An empirical analysis of regional returns to education 146
7.5.1 Data and model specification 148
7.5.2 Results 149
7.6 Conclusions 150

8 Institutions and regional labour markets in Spain
Carlos Álvarez; José M.F. Polanco & Santos M. Ruesga 157
8.1 Introduction 157
8.2 The Spanish labour market 157
8.2.1 General characteristics of the institutional framework 157
8.2.2 Labour policies 159
8.2.3 The recent performance of the Spanish labour market 162
8.3 Regional labour markets in Spain 165
8.3.1 The spatial framework 165

8.3.2 *Regional disparities* 168
8.3.3 *Regional labour policies* 169
8.4 Changing regional imbalances in the Spanish labour market 172
8.4.1 *General changes in regional unemployment* 172
8.4.2 *Analysis of inter- and intra-regional disparities in unemployment levels* 176
8.5 Regional labour supply and demand in Spain: an explanatory model 178
8.6 Summary and conclusions 181

9 Labour market institutions and the North-South divide in Italy
Luigi Bonatti & Carlo Borzaga 187
9.1 Introduction 187
9.2 Increasing North-South dualism 189
9.3 The polarisation of the labour market 193
9.4 The vicious circle perpetuating the disparities between the North and the South 199
9.5 Policy implications 205
9.6 Conclusion 208

Part Three: Eastern Europe 213

10 Institutions and regional labour markets in Bulgaria
Katia Vladimirova & Rossitsa Rangelova 215
10.1 Introduction 215
10.2 The economic and institutional framework of the labour market 217
10.3 Regional labour markets 219
10.3.1 *Impact of demographics on regional labour markets* 219
10.3.2 *Development of the regional employment* 220
10.3.3 *Development of the (regional) unemployment* 223
10.4 Labour market institutions 227
10.4.1 *Labour offices, private job centres and other intermediates* 227
10.4.2 *Local authorities and tripartite cooperations* 230
10.5 Employment policies 231
10.5.1 *Unemployment insurance and benefits* 232
10.5.2 *Active policies* 233
10.5.3 *Effects of the institutional changes* 234
10.6 Summary and future activities 235

11 Institutions and regional labour markets in the Czech Republic
Jaromir Gottvald & Milan Simek 239
11.1 The socio-economic background of the Czech labour market 239
11.2 The regional structure 243
11.2.1 Historical background 243
11.2.2 Administrative regions 245
11.2.3 Main features of the regions 246
11.3 Actors on the regional labour markets 249
11.4 Employment policy 250
11.4.1 Basic objectives 250
11.4.2 Main policies 251
11.4.3 Policy implementation 253
11.5 Future developments of labour market policies and the institutional framework 255

12 Regional labour market institutions in Slovakia
Magdaléna Hiadlovská 257
12.1 Introduction 257
12.2 The general socio-economic setting of the labour market 257
12.3 The regional differentiation of the socio-economic setting 260
12.4 Actors on the labour market 263
12.4.1 Governmental organisations 263
12.4.2 Employer's organisations 264
12.4.3 Trade unions 265
12.4.4 Independent employment services 266
12.5 Governmental labour market policies 266
12.6 Regional actors and policies 269
12.6.1 Regional state administration 269
12.6.2 Local government 269
12.6.3 Regional policies 270
12.7 The results of the labour market policies 271
12.8 Future developments 272

13 Institutions and regional labour markets in Rumania
Constanta Partenie, Dorin Jula, Daniela Constantin, Cornelia Pârlog & Calin Dinga 275
13.1 Introduction 275
13.2 Socio-economic conditions of the labour market 276
13.3 Institutional reform and labour market policies 279

13.4 The negotiation game 283
13.5 Regional disequilibria of the labour market 286
13.6 Regional unemployment 291
13.6.1 New job-searchers on the labour market 291
13.6.2 Regional migration of the unemployed 292
13.7 Regional policy and the labour market 293

About the authors 297

1 Introduction

Lambert van der Laan & Santos M. Ruesga

The central theme of the book is the performance of european labour markets in different regional socio-economic settings. These are compared from an institutional perspective. That means that the strategic behaviour of economic and political actors on the labour markets and how these actors meet in a regional setting are crucial. Moreover, a meso-economic starting point is used to bridge the gap between the micro and the macro-economic perspective on the labour market. Another innovative character of the book is the systematic comparison of the functioning of labour markets in different cultural and economic settings in both Western and Eastern Europe at various spatial levels. This is complemented by the integration of labour market economics and spatial economics. The substantive country and regional diversity allows the reader to understand the role of labour economics in the economic development of countries and regions. Moreover, access is provided to information which was widely dispersed, had high entrance levels or even non-existent up till now. The book permits to get a clear picture on the mosaic of the impressive transformations currently happening in both Western and Eastern European labour markets.

Taking the distinction between Eastern and Western Europe as a starting point, we see in these regions different - although related - developments. Changes in both Western and Eastern Europe have in common, the development from highly institutionalised and regulated markets towards less regulation, as reflected in higher flexibility, more decentralisation and more regionalisation. Next to common changes, we see differences. In *Western Europe* the disappearance of traditional economic activities, the change in the structure of the labour supply and labour relations cause fundamental changes on the labour market. The old regulation model vanishes and is succeeded by a postmodern model comprising several variations of labour market regulation. No specific model of labour market relations is preferred highest. In *Eastern Europe*, the transition from a centralistic system towards capitalism dominates the changes on the labour market. As the capitalistic system of labour market activities and relations itself is on the move, there is also no blueprint for the developments in Eastern Europe. This implies that the developments in both parts of Europe should not be perceived as one where one system follows the other. Eastern european countries are not lagging countries, which still have to copy the western model. The book clearly shows that each country and region, depending on the general social-economic developments, its history, and the actors on the labour market, shares much with others, but has its own characteristics.

Why is it so important to highlight the role of the labour market in these changes and, particularly, its regional diversity? Main reason is that in the general context of redefining productive systems, in this *'new' world of business*, countries, regions and corporations increasingly have to deal with complexity, turbulence and heterogeneity. Corporations counter these by relying increasingly on an integrated business-strategy (Reshef & Murray, 1988). This includes the minimalisation of costs, an increase of the quality of the products, innovation, marketing and the 'control of the unknown' (Fonda & Hayes, 1988). The latter includes major political and economic changes like those in Eastern Europe. The various business strategies all stress the importance of the labour factor. Productivity may show considerable increase as a result of training. The improvement of product or service quality is largely due to better staff. The labour factor is also important for innovations who strongly appeal to human creativity. This also goes for controlling the unknown. Therefore many studies of the differences in competitiveness between corporations, countries and regions underline the importance of labour. This is not only visible in a increasing importance of 'human resource management' at the micro-level, but also for the meso- and macro-economic industrial relations.

Labour becomes even more important due to the development of the knowledge-based society. Strategies of corporations, trade unions and governments are more and more based on the role of knowledge. For new economic growth immaterial aspects like the investment in various kinds of 'soft-technology' becomes increasingly crucial for development. Besides knowledge of the production and logistics, knowledge of markets and organisations is important. The development of these kinds of technology is closely connected to the labour market. This changing concept of technology stresses also the regional environment (van der Laan & Mevissen, 1994; de Jong & Don, 1995; Storper, 1997). Knowledge of the position taken up by a region within the dynamic environment is of vital importance to determine development strategies. Therefore the regional character of the demand, supply and the socio-economic setting have to be taken into account. In this, the active role of actors on the labour market in shaping their environment and the importance of the institutional context is stressed (Grandori, 1987; Boschma, 1994). The institutional network increasingly becomes important for competitiveness. Not only for the relationships between corporations, but also for the relations inside corporations and with other institutions (Cooke & Morgan, 1994). Institutions, like trade-unions, employers and governmental agencies, influence the size and quality of the labour market. This parallels the shift in focus from the regional production structure towards the production environment (NEI, 1993; van der Knaap, 1994). Therefore an accurate characterisation of regions is only possible if it is based on the organisational and regional structure of institutions (Casson, 1991). This is not only relevant for Western Europe, but also for the countries and regions in Eastern Europe.

This chapter introduces some of the main general economic and political changes which happened in Western and Eastern Europe in recent decades. As such it functions as a starter for the more detailed chapters on general labour market changes and on specific countries further on in the book.

1.1 Western Europe: the rise and fall of the regulation model

Increasing economic intervention of public powers accompanied the strong economic growth which the countries of Western Europe experienced in the 1950s and 1960s. Institutional structures were established which, either as direct economic or as regulatory agents, ordered and managed the functioning of markets. Institutions became essential parts of decisions in relation to the allocation of production factors, the production process itself and the distribution of its results. This was particularly intense in the field of labour relations. However, the process was unequal and acquired very diverse intensities according to geographic region, collecting different ideological viewpoints and cultures. These spatial differences created a broad set of models, ranging from corporatism in Nordic european countries to liberal in parts of the Anglo-Saxon world (Boyer, 1989). With all its variations, the general character of this regulation model is articulated around two fundamental cores. On the one hand, it is the institutionalised presence of corporative organisations, brought together by trade unions, business associations and the government. These regulate basic variables on the labour market, like the supply and demand of labour and wages. On the other hand, it is the creation of a legal framework directed at the protection of employment and its stability and at the improvement of work conditions of employees (Ruesga & Resa-Nestares, 1997).

There are at least two key elements which explain the outstanding momentum of the regulation model. One was the increasing political power of social movements, particularly the workers' movement, which hypothetically could constitute, and for many was, a threat for the capitalist system. The other one was that this model was highly functional for the growth in industrial economies with a fordist system of organisation of the production. This functionality was based, on the one hand, on the presence of a *de facto* and permanent social agreement which minimised the underlying social conflict inherent to labour relations. It reduced potential economic losses generated by conflicts. On the other hand, it was based on stabilisation policies which permitted the matching of the growth model to cyclical fluctuations. The model favoured the development of a sustainable process of capital accumulation under conditions of social stability. Moreover, there was theoretical support for the model emanating from the Keynesian paradigm in economics. This made it possible to create instruments, both in the real- and monetary-side of the economic system, for controlling and manipulate aggregate demand to attain economic and social goals. By this, the hypothetically contradictory relationship between economic and social equality and the achievement of economic efficiency was resolved within the framework of a regulated market economy. Implementation of intervention mechanisms was necessary to solve market 'failures'. It resulted in a more equitable income distribution and in general social welfare particularly in those countries where the model was completely developed. To be sure, the development of the model was centred on a limited number of countries, whose strong economic growth was highly dependent on maintaining severe protection schemes against third countries.

The regulation model of economic growth went into a deep crisis in the seventies and reached a high degree of explicit questioning. Increasing prices for raw materials and the successive oil shocks sparked off, and resulted in the decline of the regulation growth-model. The old model's characteristic of constant technological innovation, which favoured a strong process of capital accumulation, evoked its exhaustion. Sectors of the economy, particularly the heavy industry, which supported much of the development until then, run into structural decline. Formerly dynamic sectors reached maturity in the technological cycle. This consequently slowed down the increases in productivity. Demand stagnation in mature industrial sectors, hastened by a supply-side shock, was the central problem of the crisis in the seventies. Stagflation - unemployment plus inflation - was the corollary, in macroeconomic terms, of that stagnation in the development of many productive processes (Ruesga, 1988).

In this context of economic recession, a growing contradiction between the existing institutional framework and the new economic circumstances appeared. Accordingly, and beyond short-term adjustments based on more or less orthodox macroeconomic policies, many factors urged for a redefinition of the institutional framework. This resulted in deregulation, particularly affecting labour relations. Institutional response to new technical developments was necessary to reconstruct capital accumulation put to an end in the 1970s crisis. A new model of economic growth was put to practice. That the labour market constituted an essential obstacle to economic growth became a commonplace. This resulted in terms as 'eurosclerosis', comprising wage-rigidities, employment conditions and quantity and quality of labour (Bagionni & Crouch, 1990).

Almost all the legislative apparatus established to regulate the labour market were questioned. Reform of the labour market was incorporated to the agenda of many political parties and constituted an unprecedented attack on the economic framework of the Welfare State. As reformists pointed out, for significant improvements in economic conditions for countries in an increasing globalising environment, it was necessary to redefine the framework of labour relations. In order to make it more flexible, it should break rigidities preventing recoveries in economic growth.

Reforms were needed to get closer to the ideal of a 'free' style labour market. Therefore, it was thought necessary to revise those elements which resulted in the combined rigidities of the labour market: institutional restrictions, social policies, specific legislation, collective agreements, centralised bargaining, union presence and government directives. This would generate a reduction of high unemployment rates and an improvement of the functioning of the productive system. In other words, it tried to eliminate those prerogatives workers had acquired during the times of regulation and which, paradoxically, were supposed to endanger their future welfare. A comparison between the performance of labour markets in Western Europe and in the United States was often made. While economic recovery in the US meant significant creation of new jobs, european unemployment rates were persistently higher (Reich, 1991).

The need of promoting and spreading technological development urged for greater *flexibility* in allocating production factors. It should create an environment of higher mobility and by this easing the adjustments to quickly changing global circumstances. This constituted the 'flexible specialisation' model, one of whose preliminaries was how to organise informal activities. Theoretical and ideological support was provided by new forms of the classical-marginalist paradigm, in its neo-classical and monetarist versions (Hall, 1992). These emphasised the virtuality of a market without external interventions as an ideal instrument for achieving a higher level of economic efficiency. Together with the search for innovations, this paved the way for a continuous process of deregulation and/or liberalisation of the labour market. Globalisation, induced by national governments and international institutions intensified deregulation. Simultaneously, differentials in the regulatory intensity justified 'productive delocalisation' or 'glocalisation' in various geographical areas (Ruesga, 1997).

In the arena of labour, *labour flexibility,* became the buzz-word and has polarised the debate in labour economics since then. Flexibility has traditionally been applied to the capability of the labour system, and specifically nominal wages, to adapt to the changing economic, social and technological circumstances (Piore, 1986). However, the meaning of flexibility has been subject to different interpretations, mostly coincident with the discourse of some social agents which tried to introduce reforms on national labour legislation to their own benefit (Lagos, 1994). A broad definition leaves way to introduce many nuances. Therefore, every national or regional context gives specific meanings to it (ILO, 1986; OECD, 1986).

1.2 Eastern Europe: changing policies and institutions

The labour market of Eastern Europe has experienced tremendous changes since the collapse of the communist regimes. Also labour market policies changed radically. After a situation of a highly planned employment system, the essential aim was to create a Western-style institutional apparatus on the labour market. The most clear transformation was the change of a system of full employment to a model of market-oriented policies based on effective employment.

Generally, countries showed a decrease in labour demand mainly as a result of a substantial reduction of output. Manufacturing and agriculture have suffered more hardly the common crisis, both in output and employment terms. Although some of the changes have been common for all countries, differences between the transition economies are large. Some - parts of - countries met relatively less obstacles in their adaptive process and currently show good perspectives for employment. This particularly, because of their low wages, they can function as production centres for mature and work intensive industries coming from Western Europe. However, still substantial changes in the infrastructure of various kinds have to come about. In contrast to these countries, other economies are facing an extraordinary crisis in which production has decreased to levels of the early post-Second World War years and where a large part of the population has substantial income and employment problems.

In addition to the decreases in demand, there has been a decrease in participation too. Difficulties to find a job resulted in an expulsion of workers from the labour market. By this, unemployment became lower than could be expected by the reduction in output. However, new measures such as unemployment benefits, in some cases generous, and aimed at protecting incomes of the workers, led in some countries to increases in unemployment.

Various forms of new employment and wage schemes were implemented. These included specifically the establishment of schemes of minimum wage as the income decline was one of the main problems affecting Eastern countries. Moreover, new models of professional training were implemented, both for the new conditions of private enterprises and for readapting old knowledge to the very different economic and production circumstances.Education and training for many people had become completely obsolete. Therefore retraining became a major priority. Different systems of professional training were adopted, ranging from privately managed schemes to models in which the public sector plans and finances them. In relation to this, qualified workers have been more successful both in employment and wage terms. Access for unqualified workers to particularly the private sector was much harder.

Privatisation which ranges from a voucher system in the Czech Republic to simply sell-off in the Hungarian case, could create some employment. The private sector, however, was not able to create enough jobs needed to compensate employment decreases in the public sphere, like governmental agencies and state-owned firms. Privatisation became a pre-requisite for the change towards the market economy. However, the new activities faced several obstacles, particularly because some of them created large problems for the people they were aimed at and which were supposed to support the changes. Accordingly, the development of a market economy in Eastern Europe has suffered slow-downs and showed several characteristics to minimise the consequences of the transformations.

Although theoretically an approach of liberalisation of the labour market was used, large differences have appeared between the objectives of macro-economic policy and the labour policies put to practice. An example for this is that, as time passed and unemployment rates increased rapidly, labour market policies changed from active into passive employment policies. Unemployment benefit payments constitute now the most important part of the labour market funds. This change to passive policies was to a large degree influenced by the reduction of public expenditures. This to adjust to the general economic shocks generated by the new circumstances and particularly to avoid inflation.

A main aim of labour market policy was also the creation of a real labour market through mediation activities and to increase wage flexibility and job mobility in a world characterised up till then by rigidity. From a system of relatively arbitrary labour allocation, it was tried to develop a model which could help the meeting of supply and jobs in the newly established private sector. Different models of mediation between the unemployed and vacancies were created. Labour offices for advise, information and analysis at the district level have been established both for workers and firms. Labour market agencies, where trade unions, business associations and governments are involved, got various functions. This ranges from an active participation in the establishment of new worker laws, the collecting of funds for financing unemployment benefits and active policies, consultative functions and the co-ordinating of national employment policies. However, the results of this concertation have been generally limited. Reasons for this poor performance were the very complicated structure of the transformation and the high dependency on political ups and downs particularly related to the question how to incorporate trade unions and private business in labour policies.

The intended system of collective bargaining has faced additional problems, although again different for each country. A culture of bargaining did virtually not exist. Other problems were the disequilibrium among the negotiators, trade unions themselves engaged in a process of readjustment, and badly structured employers associations. Formerly, the centralized institutional system had a top-down structure. The state or a national department governed labour market policy. There was little manoeuvring space for - regional - actors on the labour market. Related to this was the low degree of involvement of local and regional governments, employers and employees. Although there were genuine attempts to create decentral institutions for collective bargaining between trade unions and business associations at the national, sectoral, regional or district level, bargaining is usually still very centralised. Aims are still established by central agencies who are very reluctant to take specific regional labour market characteristics into account. Regional policies play a marginal role in the transformation towards a market economy. The regional perspective is almost ignored and proposals for a regionalisation of labour market policies have been kept to a minimum. There even was often a paradoxical movement towards larger centralisation.

In countries like those of Eastern Europe, with rapidly changing structures, problems related to institutional vacuum, institutional residuals and the tension between state legimacy and reform quite often dominate the labour market (van der Meer, 1993). The *institutional vacuum* plays a major role. Within the new system, new rules, laws and practises have to be build. The actors in the labour market arena have to find their role and position. Which actors represent which interests? In this phase of transition organisations try to find recognition and legitimacy. In this vacuum *institutional residuals* of earlier times often play a major role. Institutions, persons and rules of the old system influence the development of the new one. This comes about by, on the one hand, the leaning on 'old friends'. Institutions of the old system, sometimes in new clothes, still have an influential role on the labour market. This is sometimes stimulated by disappointing experiences of the early stages of reform. While the old system still offered income, employment and security, the new system has not yet shown positive results. On the contrary, the transition sometimes resulted in a deteoriation of the labour market situation reflected in mass unemployment and income losses. On the other hand, the old system can also 'negatively' influence the efficiency of the new system, in the sense that every possible effort with a more centralistic character is denied. Although for some functions a kind of centralisation might be helpful, political sentiments and the fear for another centralistic system in disguise, inhibit an efficient structuring of the institutional framework of the labour market. The effects of these residuals are reflected in problems with the creation of a new system of labour market institutions.

Related to the institutional vacuum and the institutional residuals is the problem of *state legitimacy and reform*. The changes on the labour market make the question of social stability crucial for economic reform (Establishment, 1992). Although political changes have made possible economic reform, the latter in turn gave rise to large social problems. Rising prices and inflation, growing unemployment, a new social stratification and a marginalisation of large parts of the population come about. These problems undermine public support for economic reform and the legitimacy of the institutional system on the labour market.

1.3 The present book

Within the framework of transformations of the economy and the labour market, this book gives in-depth information on the situation in specific countries and the variation of ways in which countries handle the transformation. By this the book raises knowledge about these changes and this counteracts bad and sometimes misleading information of the labour market of the Eastern and Western European countries. The book is structured in three parts. The first part, the general context, develops a theoretical framework in which subsequent analysis can be inserted (chapter two). Moreover it analyses general changes on the labour markets in Europe (chapter three). This part ends with chapter four which presents a synthetic analysis of major features characterising regional labour markets in Europe. Particularly, problems of con- or divergence of regional labour markets in Western Europe and the regional diversity of the transition in Eastern Europe is discussed. Moreover, this chapter gives for each country the main characteristics of the labour market, the institutional framework, labour policies and regional disparities and policies.

In the other two parts of the book a division is made between the changing social-capitalistic labour markets in Western Europe and the Eastern European markets involved in deep and large-range transformations. Within each sphere country specific studies are presented. Although the approaches differ, it allows the reader to discern clear the tendencies on the labour market at regional and institutional levels.

The second part of the book includes chapters of the labour market in several member countries in European Union. The United Kingdom, the Netherlands, Sweden, Italy and Spain are analyzed as significant cases which reflect the general changes of the social capitalistic labour market. Chapter five on the United Kingdom, examines the paradigm of the liberal changes in economic policy and labour market policy. The effects on the labour market are presented by David Armstrong and David H. Blackaby. The analysis is focused on the institutional aspects of education and its influence on regional development. Professional training has suffered great changes in the United Kingdom during the last decade and some effects produced by its transformation may be applied to other countries who are in similar processes of reform.

Jouke van Dijk and Andries de Grip analyze in chapter six the transformations in the regional labour market within the Netherlands. A small, but highly developed country, central in the European Union and with a very open economy. Institutional changes have been significant here. The analysis emphasises important consequences for the economic development and employment of each region. In their study it becomes clear that policies at the national level, have diverse effects on regions depending on their different starting points and their adaptation to new conditions.

In chapter seven regional disparities are analyzed in the often called 'paradise of the Welfare State', Sweden. With the help of a general analytical model, regional changes are traced in the North, dominated by agriculture and forest activities, and in highly urbanised regions. The analysis is focused on the influence of educational efforts on major macroeconomic and labour aggregates. Eugenia Kazamaki-Ottersten uses an old but rarely used concept, social capital, and relates this to the unequal economic development of regions in Sweden. Regional differences in social capital can have a large influence on wage determination, particularly in those regions with lower levels of development.

The work of Santos M. Ruesga, Carlos Álvarez and José M.F. Polanco on the Spanish case in chapter eight, analyses the deep transformations which happened after the change of political regime and the full membership of the European Union. Existing strong divergencies between different regional markets are described. Moreover, they elaborate an explanatory model focused on the structural and institutional diversity in the country with the highest unemployment rate in the European Union.

Chapter nine analyses one of the most significant cases of regional disparities in income and labour markets in Europe. The example of Italy is important because the very persistent regional differences are a key factor in explaining the birth of political movements which exploit these unequal situations. Luigi Bonatti and Carlo Borzaga explain how institutional factors and rigidities generate difficulties in regional policy and in which ways central policies can help to break down persistent strong spatial differences.

The third part of the book, comprising studies on regional labour markets in Eastern European countries, starts in chapter ten with a contribution by Rossitsa Rangelova and Katya Vladimirova on Bulgaria. This country faces extraordinary obstacles in the transition to the capitalistic oriented model. The country was macroeconomically at a much lower stage in comparison to some other eastern european countries. The reflection on the labour market has been instantaneous. The effects of the economic decline have affected variously the Bulgarian regions, essentially because of different starting situations as a result of territorial specialisation promoted by the central socialist plans.

Among all the countries in the former communist bloc, the Czech Republic, although it faced the splitting from Slovakia, obtained for many years better results in macroeconomic and labour terms during the transition. Consequently, the level of unemployment remained lower in comparison to other countries while carrying out similar economic transformations. Institutional changes inherent to the turnover of the economic model have been relatively efficient and employment policies had strong effects on the transformations. This chapter eleven, written by Jaromir Gottvald and Milan Simek, analyses the introduction of decentralisation in the labour market and its regional effects.

Chapter twelve, by Magdaléna Hiadlovská, is on the Republic of Slovakia, which severely suffered the effects of an industrial development policy during the communist regime. The country became highly dependent on heavy industries whose future in the new economic circumstances is not only uncertain, but also declining. Under the reduction of these industries a rather rigid and excessively structured set of labour relations evolved. This within the context of general high levels of unemployment and a low growth of jobs. Up till now the transformation had very limited effects. Moreover, it faces a labour culture acquired during forty years of communism and an administrative apparatus reluctant to incorporate new procedures.

The analysis of countries in Eastern Europe ends with chapter thirteen on Rumania, where an almost tyrannical communist regime featured by a pseudo-police culture was in existence for many years. Many people and most politicians have faced transformation as the only path to development. While the government tried to introduce as soon as possible a West European-style labour market, some sectors, particularly the heavy industry and mining, have resisted new policies. Regionally, unemployment levels are quite diverse. Some regions show unemployment rates which exceed four times those of other territories. The chapter, written by Constanta Partenie, Dorin Jula, Daniela Constantin, Cornelia Pârlog and Calin Dinga, gives some convincing explanations for this unequal development from an institutional perspective.

In ending this introduction we want to express at first, with special emphasis, our gratitude, to the authors who have offered us their invaluable help when elaborating this book. Next we thank our colleagues of the Spatial Labour Economists Network (SLEN), as part of the European Association of Labour Economists (EALE), who made possible some extensive debates. Some people gave a special contribution in the edition of the texts, partly done in Spain and partly in the Netherlands. In Spain we like to thank Alfonso García-Mora, Ciro Murayama-Rendón and Carlos Resa-Nestares. In the Netherlands we thank Els van Hemert, Emile van Dijk and Gisla Damrie. To all of them, our largest gratitude. We also thank the publisher, who not only showed large patience but also coached the project efficiently during the printing preparation. At the end, we want to anticipate comments and criticism. They will always be welcomed.

References

Baglioni, G. & C. Crouch, (eds.) (1990), *European Industrial Relations: The Challenge of Flexibility*, Sage: London.

Boschma, R. (1994), *Looking through a window of locational opportunity: a long term spatial analysis of techno-industrial upheavels in Great Britain and Belgium*, Tinbergen Institute research series 75, Tinbergen Institute: Rotterdam.

Boyer, R. (ed.) (1989), *The Search for Labour Market Flexibility: The European Economies in the Transition*, Clarendon Press: Oxford.

Casson, M. (1991), *Global research strategy and international competitiveness*. Oxford: Basil Blackwell.

Cooke, P. & K. Morgan (1994), 'The creative milieu: a regional prspective on innovation'. In: M. Dodgson & R. Rothwell (eds.), *The handbook of industrial innovation*, pp. 25-32. Aldershot: Edward Elgar.

Establishment (1992), *Establishment of labour markets mechanisms and institutions in Eastern Europe*, International Centre for Social and Economic Research: Prague.

Fonda, N. & C. Hayes (1988), *Education, training and business performance*. Oxford review of economic policy, 4-3, pp. 108-119.

Grandori, A. (1987), Perspectives on Organization Theory. Cambridge: Ballinger Publishing Company.

Hall, P. (1992), 'The movement from Keynesian to monetarism', in Steinmo, S.et al. (eds.), *Structuring Policies: Historical Institutionalism in Comparative Analysis*, University of Cambridge Press: Cambridge.

ILO (International Labour Office) (1986), 'Labour market productivity', *Report of an Experts Group Meeting*, Geneva.

Jong, A. de & F.J.H. Don (1995), 'Internationale trends en de Nederlandse Econo-

mie'. In: L. van der Geest & J. van Sinderen (eds.), *Kracht en zwakte van de Nederlandse economie*, pp. 1-30. Rotterdam: Barjestek, Meeuwes & Co.
Knaap, G.A. van der (1994), 'Technologie, telematica en regionale ontwikkeling'. In: O.A.L.C. Atzema & E. Wever (eds.), *Economische geografische variaties*. Assen: Van Gorcum, pp. 163-185.
Laan, L. van der & J.W.M. Mevissen (1994), 'Ondernemingen en regionale arbeidsmarkten' in Laan, L. van der & M. Vermeulen (eds.), *Onderwijs en arbeidsmarkt in de regio*, Eburon: Delft, pp. 87-100.
Lagos, B. (1994), 'Labor flexibility: an open debate', *International Labor Review*, Vol. 132, No. 3, pp. 89-101.
Meer, M. van der (1993), 'De spaanse arbeidsverhoudingen in transitie, lessen voor Oost-Europa?', *Tijdschrift voor Arbeidsvraagstukken*, Vol. 9, No. 3, pp. 284-299.
NEI (1993), *New location factors for mobile investment in Europe*. Brussels: Commission of the European Communities.
OECD (Organization for Economic Co-operation and Development) (1986), *Flexibility in the Labour Market. The Current Debate*, OECD: Paris.
Piore, M.J. (1986), 'Perspectives on labour market productivity', *Industrial Relations Journal*, Vol. 25, No. 2, pp. 143-158.
Reich, R. (1991), *The Work of Nations, Preparing Ourselves for 21st Century Capitalism*, Vergara: Barcelona.
Reshef, Y. & A.I. Murray (1988), Towards a neo-institutionalist approach in industrial relations. *British Journal of Industrial Relations*, 26-1, pp. 85-97.
Ruesga, S.M. (1988), *All Otro Lado de la Economía*, Pirámide: Madrid.
Ruesga, S.M. (1997), 'Dumping social y empleo en la fortaleza europea', in Heras, R. & R. Tamames (eds.), *Anuario El Mundo*, Unidad Editorial: Madrid.
Ruesga, S.M. & C. Resa-Nestares (1997), 'Regulación-desregulación de los mercados laborales: el debate eficiencia versus equidad', in Tezanos, J.F., J.M. Montero & J.A. Díaz (eds.), *Tendencias de Futuro en la Sociedad Española*, Editorial Sistema: Madrid.
Storper, M. (1997), *The regional world: territorial development in a global economy*, Guildford Press: New York.

Part One
The general framework

2 The spatial-institutional perspective on the labour market in Europe

Lambert van der Laan & Santos M. Ruesga

2.1 Three trends in economic thinking

The central problem of this book is the analysis of regional labour markets in different socio-economic settings and the comparison of these from an institutional perspective. In this the different kinds of strategic behaviour of economic actors on the labour market and how these actors meet in a regional setting are crucial.

The institutional perspective is a fruitful manner of enhancing existing trends in economic thinking. In this perspective three trends are important (van der Laan, 1991). Firstly there is an increase in the interest for social and cultural aspects of economic and labour market behaviour. Secondly, the regional or local aspects of general economic developments gets a more important role in economic thinking. Thirdly, one can notice an integration of ideas, emerged in other scientific fields, in economics. This book builds on all three aspects and therefore gives it its innovative character. Hereafter the three trends are elaborated.

2.1.1 Humanisation and socialisation

Traditionally, economics regarded those aspects of society which indirectly influence the relation between demand and supply as they meet in the market process, as aspects beyond the economic process itself and therefore, although of interest, no subject for economic study. However, it is increasingly realised that these 'non-economic factors' have a tremendous influence on economic functioning and that they should be incorporated into economic research. This happened at the individual level in, for example, Simon's studies (1957). At a higher level of society also 'non-economic data' were included in economic modelling. Among others, political economists adopted this approach. In these cases there is 'an explicit recognition that the structure of economic processes are not invariant with respect to variations in policy regimes (.....). We will remain forever confronted with a pervasive and ineradicable stochasticity enmeshed in the patterns of social interactions' (Brunner, 1981, p.132). In this broadening of economic interests particularly the transformation and the evolutionary approach are of interest.

The *transformation approach* tries to 'translate' abstract economic terms into concrete concepts which, therefore, become of interest to other social sciences: the abstract entrepreneur becomes a real banker or an industrialist with all his, or her, social aspects. This decision maker is vulnerable and subject to uncertainty and acting in a sub-optimal information field. The concept of 'economic man' was replaced by the concept of economically behaving man within a bounded rationality. The well known human capital approach can also be seen as a way in which cultural concepts such as education can be approached from the economist's viewpoint (Becker, 1965; Kapteijn, Woittiez & Ten Hacken, 1989).

In the *evolutionary approach* economic science as it is today, studies just one phase in western development. In earlier times other economic relationships existed. Transactions were mainly based on reciprocity or redistribution (Polanyi, Arensberg & Pearson, 1956; Harvey, 1972). In these kinds of economic transactions, cultural and/or sociological aspects were as important and integrated into economic behaviour. As in modern capitalistic times exchange relations have become more important, the position of these cultural aspects has changed. Although it may seem that they have disappeared in the economic process, the evolutionary approach considers that they have evolved. Therefore the division between economics and other social sciences is a misunderstanding. Culture or power are still as much 'economic' as are investments or productivity.

2.1.2 Localisation

Besides the broadening of the set of economic factors as related to the transformation and evolutionary approach, the localisation of the phenomena becomes increasingly important too in economic thinking. In traditional economic thinking and labour economics, the spatial aspect was more or less neglected. Labour market models functioned in an a-spatial world (Hampton, 1987; Van der Laan, 1987). The spatial basis for labour markets was a taken-for-granted and largely untheorised tenet of general labour market studies. Only geographical mobility played some role, but was mostly seen in the neo-classical perspective of temporary disequilibriums and processes of market-adjustment. Increasingly studies appear which conceive the labour market as being more than simply an economic exchange between employers and workers within and between localised markets. It is increasingly realised, when considering the motivation behind localised economic activities, the forces of inertia, uncertainty, and market imperfection, that the marginalistic, optimizing theories become partly irrelevant (Eberts & Stone, 1992). In addition, the broad set of economic factors are not only spatially differentiated, but social and cultural aspects play a crucial part in relation to these (Hofstede, 1980). The spatial differentiation of economic growth and stagnation in parts of Europe are related to the regionally different political and social systems.

2.1.3 *Theoretical integration*

A third trend in economics is the integration of market-based perspectives and power-based approaches. Recent developments of labour market theory reflect this trend. For example the micro-economic neo-classical theory has incorporated institutional elements stressing power-relations (agency theory, implicit contract theory and efficiency wage models; see Hartog & Theeuwes, 1989). Important is also, besides the theoretical changes, the development in the institutional viewpoint itself. In the meso- or macro level institutional approach, Moulaert (1987) distinguishes three stages. The first stage of 'old institutionalism' stresses the effort to incorporate institutional controls into conventional economic theory and through this to build an integrated theory of labour. The stage of 'new institutionalism' tends towards an economic reduction of labour problems. Particularly, this stage had its impact on mainstream economics, as illustrated by the development of public or household economics. The third stage, is the 'regulation school' which stresses the 'reciprocal interaction between the dynamics of economic accumulation and social regulation' (p.319). Social regulation is needed to buffer potential conflicts between social groups on the labour market. It is particularly this latter institutional approach which incorporates social and political elements in the analyses. Moreover this approach bridges the gap between economic and sociological inspired viewpoints on the labour market. The structure and developments of the labour market result from the bargaining between employees, employers and the government. The direction in which the labour market will move cannot be predicted, as it all depends on the variable contributions of the organisations and governmental institutions towards negotiations. This close cooperation of institutions representing different interest-groups is often termed as 'neo-corporatism'. The degree of neocorporatism largely influences the presence of labour- and social conflicts and can be linked to theories like the insider/outsider theory (Blanchard & Summers, 1988; van Eijk, 1989).

It is the diversity in supply and demand regulation that creates submarkets embedded in an institutional framework (Addison & Siebert, 1979; van Wezel & Vissers, 1983). On the one hand this results from the fact that institutions link with the existing differences on the labour market (pre-market situations). On the other hand the institutional framework further reinforces the structuring and continuance of submarkets (in-market situations) (Ryan, 1981). As a result of this institutional embeddedness an inversion of the neo-classical short- and long term takes place. The direct relation between for example wage development and the allocation of labour, as assumed in the neoclassical model, does not exist. The feedback between labour market situations and wage-level is less frequent and slower. Related to this process of slackening is the model of 'sticky markets' (Solow, 1979).

The degree of structural division of the labour market has led to various institutional subtheories like the labour-queue model (Thurow, 1975); the segmentation model (Loveridge & Mok, 1979) and the discontinuous model (Cooke, 1983). The degree of regulation is the most important criterion to distinguish market sectors. On the whole 'better' jobs are attended with more institutional proceedings than 'inferior' ones. Examples of this are the presence of collective labour agreements or job-career plans. Related to this is the concept of the internal labour market (Doeringer & Piore, 1971; de Grip, 1985).

A problem of the integration of the changes in the neo-classical market oriented perspective and the institutional power based perspective is that the first is particularly oriented at the micro-economic level and the second at the meso- or macro level. Integration is possible by viewing the relationship between the two such that changes at the higher analytical level changes the structural context of micro-level models. By influencing the chance of individual actors the exogenous context can be incorporated in micro-level models. For example, sectoral employment shifts influence the chance of finding a job for workers with specific characteristics. By this, the macro- and mesostructural context is made endogenous at the micro-level. The relationship also works the other way. Micro level behaviour results in aggregated changes which in turn form the structural meso- or macro-context.

This section discussed some changes in economic thinking and by this framed the general viewpoint of this book. The following section 'translates' this general perspective to the main core of the book: the spatial-institutional perspective.

2.2 The spatial-institutional perspective

What are the general principles behind the spatial differentiation of the labour markets? In our view the regional differentiation of the structure of the labour market is created by the relationship between general labour market processes and the regional arena. The interdependent dynamic between the macro or supra-regional structure of the labour market and the lower meso-regional scale constitutes the evolving character of regional labour markets (van der Laan, 1991). The historical path of both the general processes and the regional arena additionally structures this relationship. Figure 2.1 summarises this view.

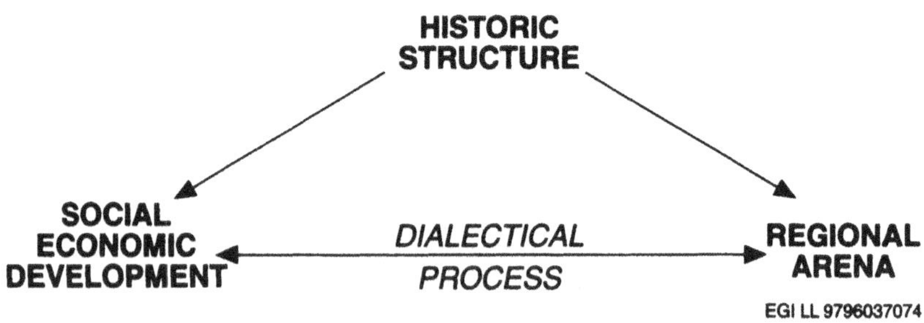

Figure 2.1 Processes creating space

The concepts used in figure 2.1 need some clarification. Social-economic development constitutes all of the changes related to the labour market at the supra-regional scale. It results from evolving production structures and institutional developments. Technological developments, organisational changes and educational upgrading are some examples of these socio-economic changes. Some attribute this development to the processes of the capitalist economy, others to business cycles, 'system-shocks' or a combination of these (Martin, 1989). These are the fundamental underlying socioeconomic processes, which result in a reorganisation of space. Various elements structure the macroeconomic level. We already mentioned technological and educational changes. Important is also the institutional framework: in what manner is the labour market organised? Which public/private organisations play a role and from which starting-points do they proceed?

The macro-economic setting of labour markets evolves in close relationship with the structure and developments of regional arenas. At this lower level, a large differentiation in labour market processes can be found. Similar to the macro level this not only pertains to the efficiency of markets and its distributional effects, but also to the organisational aspect. Groups like trade-unions, employers and governmental agencies, with their specific goals and strategic behaviour, meet each other here. The specific combination and character of the various groups differ by region (van der Knaap & van der Laan, 1989). Green-field locations differ substantially from a service-orientated urban location or a traditional-manufacturing region. The institutional framework is different in various socio-economic areas within Europe. It are particularly these institutional differences which in the future constitutes the heterogeneity of labour market structures and developments. This does not deny the strong influence of, for example, general technological developments or demographic changes. While these show possibly a converging pattern, the way in which institutions in the various areas deal with these general processes remains heterogeneous and sometimes is even diverging. It gives a reason for analyzing labour markets in different socio-economic settings.

Relevant to the structure and development of the labour market is also the manner in which regions not only reflect the general socio-economic development but also influence the latter. This explicitly confronts the general socioeconomic framework of the labour market with the structure and processes in the regions. However, it is not the region itself as a static, reified concept which is of importance here, but the region as an arena. The concept of the arena indicates that the region is the place where groups meet with different strategic behaviour in relation to the labour market (see van Hoof, 1987; Peck, 1992). There is no reason to suppose that political boundaries define the relevant unit in Marshallian terms. In spite that localised units usually overcome political borders, for practical and statistical reasons, regional labour markets are defined in politically-constructed regions, where institutions more frequently works (Krugman, 1991). Particularly interesting are the results of this behaviour, like the efficiency of the allocation process and the distributional effects. These results have to be related to the manner in which demand and supply interact in an institutional framework and the factors influencing this.

2.3 Regional labour markets

The trends of humanisation and socialisation, localisation and theoretical integration point at the importance of an institutional viewpoint. Central is the way in which economic actors (industries, households, etc.) operate within and in relation to an organisational setting. In connection to this the spatial-institutional perspective brings this meso-economic viewpoint 'down to earth': how do economic actors operate in spatially differentiated socio-economic settings?

Economic actors have strategies to attain their goals. For *industries* these are for example profit maximalisation, reducing uncertainty or safeguarding their long-term existence. Labour suppliers aim at parallel goals, be it in the shape of attaining high wages or job-security. In attaining these goals actors choose specific institutional or organisationalstructures. This organisation not only depends on the character of the actors themselves, but also on the surrounding in which they function. These are increasingly becoming important to industry. This finds its origin in increasing complexity and turbulence in the production environment. Growing complexity implies that a corporation cannot but acquire and retain know-how in a limited field. It is not by chance that corporations concentrate on key-activities. An increase in turbulence, resulting from rapidly changing market positions - e.g. as with the integration of Europe - and technological developments, leads to a lower degree of information. In consequence it becomes more and more difficult for corporations to rely on experience gained in the past. The speed at which expertise and skills become outdated has strongly increased. This means that the surroundings in a wider sense becomes more important to the corporation. A thorough knowledge of the position taken up by a company within certain surroundings is of vital importance to determine its strategy. Therefore both the character of the corporation and the socio-economic setting have to be taken into account when analyzing their behaviour. It is specially relevant to point out that the characteristics of the corporation in terms of defining economic goals, is for an adequate labour relations framework (Mueller, 1986). This implies the analysis of organisational structures and their development in relation to the environment they act. For industries this means that the type of organisation like SME, networking, subcontracting or a multi-regional structure have to be linked to the market (see also Scott, 1988; Boekema & Kamann, 1989).

The various strategies which make up the organisational ability of businesses to deal with uncertainty on the market stress the importance of the labour factor. No wonder that many studies of differences in competitiveness between corporations, regions and countries underline the importance of the labour factor (see Roobeek, 1988; Porter, 1990; Koopman-Iwema, 1991). In that sense, in the context of the economic integration and the free movement of productive factors, the heterogeneity at a regional level in such variables as real wages and productivity have important effects on employment. Regions which are more distant from the average levels in these variables are more strongly affected by competition, promoting an acceleration in the inequalities of the present income and unemployment levels. Some theoretical analysis show the risk of a nominal convergence without a true convergence in real variables. In a context of elimination of productive, trade and financial restrictions, it may generate unemployment, losses in competitiveness and even important migrations from some countries to others (Bean, 1992; Emerson, 1991).

The strategic behaviour of *individuals* is approached similar to that of industry. For attaining their goals, individuals choose, in relation to their surroundings, an organisational form adapted to their goals as much as possible. This can be a specific household category. Research on labour market behaviour of newly emerging household-types, like two-earners households, has shown that this behaviour is adapted to specific elements in their surroundings. Childcare facilities or close proximity of services are crucial for these kind of households (Vijgen & van Engelsdorp Gastelaars, 1992). The strategic behaviour of individuals is also reflected in for example whether, and in what trade union, they participate. The socio-economic setting strongly influences this latter behaviour (Bean & Holden, 1992; van der Laan, 1993).

The different kinds of strategic behaviour of economic actors on the demand and supply side are crucial elements in understanding labour market behaviour. Particularly at the level of the region the various actors with different goals and strategic behaviour meet. This book analyses these regional labour markets in different socio-economic settings and the comparison of these labour markets from an institutional perspective. Figure 2.2 summarizes the way of reasoning. Both labour demand and supply show some fundamental changes (see chapter three). On the demand side we see, for example the emergence of the information economy and the growing importance of social capital for production. At the supply side processes like an ageing labour force or a feminisation of the labour supply come about. In regulating and controlling these changes, economic actors can choose various organisational types like a specific kind of production network or a specific household form. These organisational types meet eachother in the institutional market. In this actors try to reach their goals as much as possible. The institutional market can have characteristics like the presence of internal markets, type of wage bargaining, level of governmental intervention, etc. The results are characterised by unemployment rates, level of income-inequality, industrial conflicts or participation-rates. The application of this general viewpoint to specific socio-economic settings in space is particular of interest for this book. How do the behaviour, structure and development of labour demand, supply, institutions and results differ in various socio-economic settings and regional contexts?

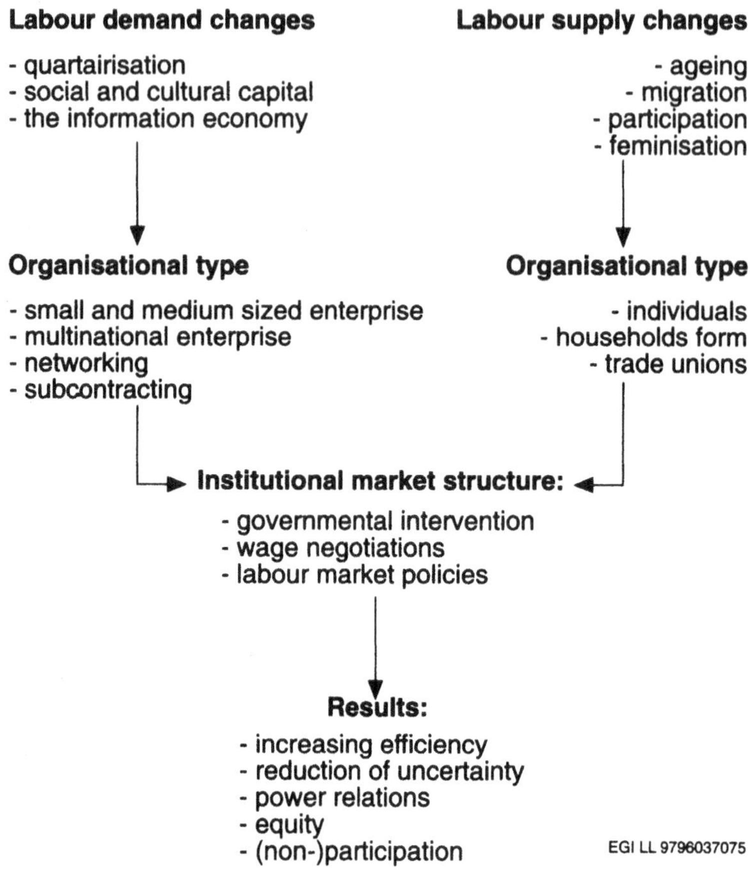

Figure 2.2 A general perspective on the labour market

It is also interesting to analyse in this context the possibilities for institutional actions for promoting the appropriate economic conditions to induce employment (Ruesga & Alvarez, 1992). For example, the growth of stable labour markets for medium and high qualified labour supply appears more and more determined by exogenous factors such as the attraction of new investments from large national or transnational high-technology corporations. This attraction is limited by the dependence on public labour market policies and the strong competence at regional or national level for attracting those investments. As a consequence, in many cases the endogenous instruments available by the regional and local institutions are actually limited to the conditions for firms with sometimes a strong component of low-qualified and unstable employment.

Looking at the regions of Europe, it is therefore important to trace the manoeuvring space of actors in the regional arena. In a centralised institutional system labour market policy is governed by one national department. Institutions related to labour demand or supply are directed to this national platform. The institutional system has a top-down structure. This means there is little manoeuvring space for actors in the regions. In contrast to this, a decentralised institutional system stresses the responsibilities of the actors in the regions. In this bottom-up approach much more manoeuvring space is left to the regional arena. Höcker (1994) suggests that within Europe three kinds of institutional systems exist:

- centralised and integrated systems;
- centralised and fragmented systems; and
- decentralised systems.

In centralised/integrated systems labour market policy is located under one administration. In centralised/fragmented systems policy is implemented by a number of sectoral institutions or by agencies directed at specific tasks. In decentralised systems policies are transferred to regional or regionalised institutions. Table 2.1 shows how, according to Höcker (1994) the various countries of Europe fit in this classification. Of course other classifications are possible or may even be preferable (see chapter three). At this point however, the only aim is to illustrate that countries can be classified according to their institutional system.

Table 2.1
A classification of the institutional system for European countries

centralised/integrated	centralised/fragmented	decentralised
Germany	France	Belgium
Ireland	Greece	Denmark
Luxembourg	Italy	Great Britain
Portugal		the Netherlands
Spain		

Source: Höcker (1994)

Two important aspects underly classifications like this. The first is that more decentralisation goes along with a larger local or regional involvement of the social partners. Quite often there exist tripartite structures at the regional level of the decentralised systems. Secondly, one can note that in countries with rapidly changing institutional structures, like formerly in Spain or Portugal and now in Eastern Europe, national governments dominate the labour market policy. In these countries '.. the state prefers to retain more farreaching supervisory opportunities ...' (Höcker,

1994, p.33). This can be related to some characteristics of transitional systems we already discussed in chapter one: institutional residuals and a institutional vacuum (van der Meer, 1993). The first indicates that in new system rules and processes of the old system still influence the development of the new systems. In Spain, for example, elements of the post-Franco-period of social concertation (1980-1986) like centralistic oriented hierarchical industrial relations, still remain visible. Also the institutional vacuum plays a role. Within the emerging system, new rules, laws and practises have to be build. Moreover, the actors in the arena have to acquire their role.

Within this context it is important to point out that economic reform cannot be loosened from its political context. Due to political changes, economic reforms in countries like Spain, Greece and Portugal could come about. This process went gradually with some political outbursts, but took a rather long time. In the case of Spain it to took more than ten years after Franco's death before foreign investments grew. These problems are also dominant now in Eastern Europe. Here changes have been much radical than in some Southern European countries. These changes made the question of social stability crucial for economic reform. Political changes made possible economic reform, but the latter in turn give rise to large social problems.

After having discussed the main elements of the spatial-institutional perspective, the next chapters subsequently elaborate these elements. The next chapter deals with some of the main changes on the European labour market. It builds the general macro-economic element of the analysis of the regional labour markets in Europe.

References

Addison, J.T. & W.S. Siebert (1979), *The market for labor: an analytical treatment*, Goodyear Publ.Comp.: Santa Monica.

Bean, C. (1992), 'European and Monetary Union in Europe', *Journal of Economic Perspectives*, Autumn, pp. 31-52.

Bean, R. & K. Holden (1992), *Cross-national differences in trade union membership in OECD countries*, Vol. 23, No. 1.

Becker, G.S. (1965), *Human Capital: a theoretical and empirical analysis, with special reference to education*, Columbia University Press: New York.

Blanchard, O.J. & L.H. Summers (1988), 'Hysteresis and the European unemployment problem', in: Cross, R. (ed.), *Unemployment, hysteresis and the natural rate hypothesis*, pp. 306-346, Bais Blackwell: Oxford.

Boekema, F. & D.J.F. Kamann (eds.) (1989), *Sociaal-economische netwerken*, Wolters-Noordhoff: Groningen.

Brunner, K. (1981), 'The problem with what they do and why they do it', in Kmenta, J. & J.B. Ramsey (eds.), *Large scale macro-econometric models; theory and practice*, North-Holland Publishing Company: Amsterdam, pp. 129-138.

Cooke, P. (1983), 'Labour Market Discontinuity and Spatial Development', *Progress*

in Human Geography, Vol. 7, No. 4, pp. 543-565.
Doeringer, P.B. & M.J. Piore (1971), *Internal labour markets and manpower analysis*, Heath: Lexington.
Eberts, R.W. & J.A. Stone (1992), *Wage and Employment Adjustment in Local Labor Markets*, W.E. Upjohn Institute for Employment Research: Kalamazoo, Michigan.
Eijk, C.J. van (1989), 'Concerted action: a remedy against persistent unemployment?', in Muller, F. & W.J. Zwezerijnen (eds.), *The role of economic policy in society*, Universitaire Pers Rotterdam: The Hague, pp. 62-71.
Emerson, M. (1991), 'Aspects of Economic of EMU', *European Economic Review*, pp. 467-473.
Grip, A. de (1985), 'Interne arbeidsmarkttheorieën', *Maandschrift economie*, Vol. 49, pp. 333-345.
Hampton, P. (1987), 'Economics and human geography', *Progress in Human Geography*, Vol. 11, No. 1, pp. 106-125.
Hartog, J. & J.J.M. Theeuwes (1989), 'Ontwikkelingen in de arbeidseconomie', *Economisch Statistische Berichten*, Vol. 74, No. 3691, pp. 83-91.
Harvey, D. (1972), *Society, the City and the Space-Economy of Urbanism*, Association of American Geographers: Washington DC, Resource Paper 18.
Höcker, H. (1994), 'The organisation of labour market policy delivery in the European Union', *InforMISEP 48*, pp. 26-35.
Hofstede, G. (1980), *Culture's consequences: international differences in work-related values*, Sage Publications: Beverly Hills; London.
Hoof, J. van (1987), *De arbeidsmarkt als arena*, SUA: Amsterdam.
Kapteijn, A., I. Wottiez & P. ten Hacken (1989), *Household labour supply in the Netherlands in the eighties and the nineties with specific attention to micro/macro integration, shifting preferences and fiscal incentives*, OSA: Den Haag.
Knaap, G.A. van der & L. van der Laan (1989), 'Spatial implications of unionisation, employment and labour activism', in Linge, G.J.R. & G.A. van der Knaap, *Labour, environment and industrial change*, Routledge: London, pp. 144-166.
Koopman-Iwena, A.M. (1991), 'De vitaliteit van arbeidsorganisaties', *Economisch Statistische Berichten*, Vol. 76, pp. 328-332.
Krugman, P. (1991), *Geography and Trade*, Leuven University Press: Leuven.
Laan, L. van der (1987), 'Causal Processes in spatial labour markets', *Tijdschrift voor Economische en Sociale Geografie*, Vol. 78, No. 5, pp. 325-338.
Laan, L. van der (1991), *Spatial Labour Markets in the Netherlands*, Eburon: Delft.
Laan, L. van der (1993), 'Regional differentiation in labour union density', *Environment & Planning-A*, Vol. 25, pp. 255-272.
Loveridge, R. & A.L. Mok (1979), *Theories of labour market segmentation: a critique*, Martinus Nijhoff: The Hague.
Martin, R. (1989), 'The reorganisation of regional theory: alternative perspectives

on the changing capitalist space economy', *Geoforum*, Vol. 20, No. 2, pp. 187-201.
Meer, M. van der (1993), 'De spaanse arbeidsverhoudingen in transitie, lessen voor Oost-Europa?', *Tijdschrift voor Arbeidsvraagstukken*, Vol. 9, No. 3, pp. 284-299.
Moulaert, F. (1987), 'An institutional revisit to the Storper-Walker theory of labour', *International Journal of Urban and Regional Research*, Vol. 11, No. 3, pp. 309-330.
Mueller, D.C. (1986), *The Modern Corporation: Profits, Power, Growth and Performance*, Wheatsheaf: Brighton.
Peck, J. (1992), 'Labor and agglomeration: control and flexibility in local labor markets', *Economic Geography*, Vol. 68, No. 4, pp. 325-347.
Polanyi, K., C.M. Arensberg & H.W. Pearson (1956), *Trade and markets in early empires; economics in history and theory*, Glencoe.
Porter, M.E. (1990), *The competitive advantage of nations*, The Free Press: New York.
Roobeek, J.M. (1988), *Een race zonder finish*, Vrije Universiteit Uitgeverij: Amsterdam.
Ruesga, S.M. & C. Alvarez (1992), 'Relaciones laborales y competitividad en la economía española', in Ruesga, Santos M., *Economía y Trabajo*, Editorial Pirámide Madrid.
Ryan, P. (1981), 'Segmentation, Duality and the internal labour market', in Wilkinson, F.(ed.), *The dynamics of labour market segmentation*, Academic Press: London, pp. 3-20.
Scott, A.J. (1988), *New industrial spaces*, Pion: London.
Simon, H.A. (1957), *Models of man, mathematical essays on rational human behaviour in a social setting*, Wiley & Sons: New York.
Solow, R.M. (1979), 'Alternative Approaches to Macro-Economic Theory: A Partial View', *The Canadian Journal of Economics*, Vol. XII, pp. 339-354.
Thurow, L. (1975), *Generating Inequality*, Basic Books: New York.
Vijgen, J. & R. van Engelsdorp Gastelaars (1992), *Worlds aparts: social profiles and ways of life in inner city, older city and new town*, The Hague, Paper conference European Cities, Growth and Decline.
Wezel, J.A.M. van & A.M.C. Vissers (1983), *Evenwicht en onevenwicht op de arbeidsmarkt en in de economie*, Van Gorcum: Assen.

3 Setting the stage: general changes on the European labour market

Lambert van der Laan

3.1 Introduction

The spatial-institutional perspective stresses that the regional differentiation of the labour market is the result of the relationship between general labour market processes and the regional arena. Before the latter, regional, view is discussed for various countries of Europe, we at first focus on the general processes on the labour market. These constitute the supra-regional or supra-national developments on the labour market and comprise those of labour demand and supply and various socio-institutional developments. All these changes lead to opportunities, threads and challenges for the countries and regions of Europe. The general processes determine the playground of the actors on the labour market. In a dialectical process the general processes influence the actors on the labour market of the regions but the latter also influence the general processes. Each country or region takes a different position towards these general developments. While some are lagging, others are ahead.

Central in this chapter is how general processes govern demand, supply and institutions of the labour market in different countries. It is about the delineation to which extent corporations, trade-unions and governments can adapt to this. Unfortunately, for reasons of data availability, the empirical parts of the analysis are mostly confined to those parts of Europe which belong to the European Union. This does not imply that the general processes are not relevant for the countries of Eastern Europe. On the contrary, processes like de-industrialisation or the ageing of the labour force are relevant for both the Eastern and Western part of Europe. At first some general processes related to labour demand are discussed.

3.2 Quartairisation of jobs and functions

The employment structure differs in space and time. Both are interlinked. As figure

3.1 shows, most people in the pre-industrial society worked in agriculture and fishery, the primary sector. Labour productivity was low and only a small food surplus was available to feed people outside the primary sector like craftsmen, soldiers and governors. Because of this, only about 10 percent of the population could live in cities. This level was until the nineteenth century standard in societies in different culture realms (Bairoch, 1988). Since the industrial revolution the share of the primary sector decreased, while that of the secondary sector, manufacturing, increased. Besides changes in the kind of input of raw materials and production technology, changes happened in the organisation of production in all sectors. In agriculture there was a privatisation of common grounds and the introduction of artificial fertiliser. Ores became very important in manufacturing as well as the introduction of fordistic production processes and venture capital. Increasingly non-material production inputs became important. Concurrently large scale urbanisation evolved.

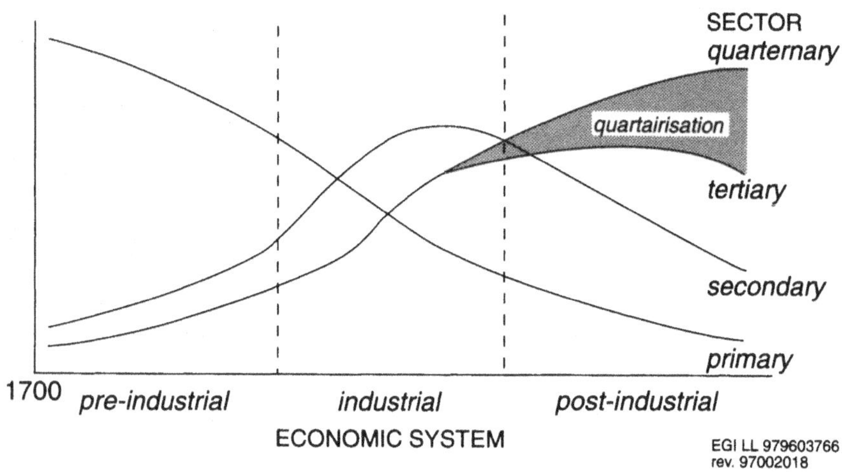

Figure 3.1 The changing sectoral employment structure

In due time the secondary sector made room for the service sector. This sector contains activities related, on the one hand, to the handling of material goods and, on the other, to the generation and handling of information. While the first, the tertiary sector, is related to transport, wholesale and retailing, the information oriented activities contains activities like banking, advising and education. These information activities together can be called the quartairnary sector. The dominant role of this sector for employment leads to the post-industrial or information economy.

Criterium for the structure of the economy is often the size of the employment. However, this should not be confused by the importance of a specific sector for the economy. Because of large changes in the productivity of labour, total production in some sectors rose while employment actually went down. As illustrated in figure 3.2, the relationship between employment and production can change over time.

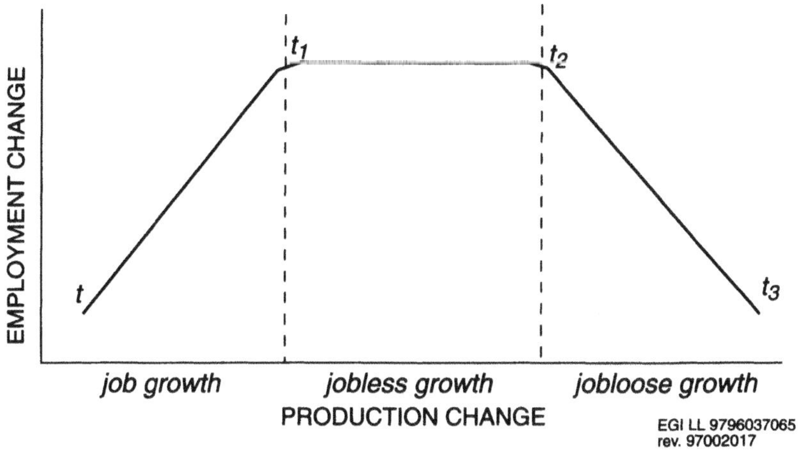

Figure 3.2 The changing relationship between employment and production

Between t and t_1 there is both a growth of production and employment. This is the traditional perspective of a growing economy with additional job creation. This is still happening in the modern sectors of the economy: in high-tech manufacturing as well as consumer oriented services and information services. Figure 3.2 shows that during the period t_1 and t_2 production still increases, but no additional jobs are created: *jobless growth.* The change in the handling of goods in seaports is an example of this. In the following period there is even a negative relationship between economic growth and employment: *jobloose growth.* This process happened in Europe in agriculture and traditional manufacturing. Increasingly also standard activities in the service industry become prone to this process. Fortunately growth in new activities, with a positive relationship between production and employment, was up till now larger than the loss of employment in traditional sectors (Maddison, 1995). Things are more complicated than figure 3.2 suggests. Not only 'traditional' activities like housekeeping or meat-packing still show a growth of employment, also can changes in the business cycle disturb the general development. Moreover joblosses can be counteracted by a reduction in working time. By this the number of jobs can be stabilised. Also can international competitiveness increase the destruction of jobs in some countries and by this speed up the process, while increasing at the same time the number of jobs in other countries.

The processes indicated do not only differ in time but also in space. While countries in Northwestern Europe already saw a change towards the post-industrial society, some Southern and Eastern European countries are still dominated by manufacturing. Countries like Rumania or Albania are still largely oriented at agriculture. These differences in economic structure between countries and regions are important because they point at possible future employment changes. The lagging countries are more prone to economic restructuring and have to reckon with large losses of jobs in specific sectors. This is aggravated if their international competitiveness is less than the countries with which they increasingly have trade relationships.

3.2.1 Economic, social and cultural capital

The sectoral division does not give enough insight into the true character of the changes in people's activities. Besides the sector people are working in, also the kind of work in these sectors has changed tremendously. In all sectors, the number of people which handle or generate information has increased. Economic growth is less based on muscle power and mechanistic production but increasingly on creative and communicative abilities. Particularly the knowledge intensive functions have grown (Woodall, 1996). This caused the emergence of knowledge labourers or symbol analysts as Reich (1991) called them. It is a broad spectrum of functions these people work in: journalists, bankers, software developers, advertisers, consultants, researchers, etc. All these people generate an abundance of information (McCloskey & Klamer, 1995).

By the quartairisation of the economy, both in an inter- and intrasectoral sense, knowledge has become the new production input of the economy (Grossman & Helpman, 1991). By this the concept of labour changes fundamentally. No more work in the traditional material oriented sense, but work based on intangibles (OECD, 1987; Jacobs, 1995). Not only does knowledge become the main production input, also the meaning of knowledge itself has changed. To understand this, it is useful to distinguish between three kinds of knowledge (Klamer, van der Laan & Prij, 1997). Traditionally knowledge is seen as *economic capital*. In this kind of capital, knowledge is directed at economic returns. Knowledge is an investment in the future. It is 'human capital' and comprises the 'know what' and the 'know how': the factual knowledge and the way to use it. More knowledge of this kind, embodied in technological development, means higher competitiveness and higher economic growth. Particular R&D is seen as an investment for generating economic capital.

Besides economic capital, *social capital*, the manner in which to deal with other people and groups, becomes increasingly important. Particularly the communicative capabilities are crucial. The social capital is the capacity to value the behaviour of others. In this 'trust' and consensus play a major role (Putnam, 1993; Fukuyama,

1995; Peyrefitte, 1995). By this the relative value of production-oriented labour decreases, as does the value of economic capital. Important is the positive relationship between the trust in other people and economic growth. Countries with higher levels of trust have shown higher growth. The same also applies to the trust in economic institutions. Also in this case significant positive relationships are present (Bomhoff, den Hartog & Lageweg; 1996). Figure 3.3 shows the differences between countries in the trust in other people on basis of the 'World Values Survey'. It shows that the trust is relatively high in Ireland, Denmark and Norway. Most southern European countries have a low score. Of course social capital is not solely responsible for economic growth. The point is that it becomes more important.

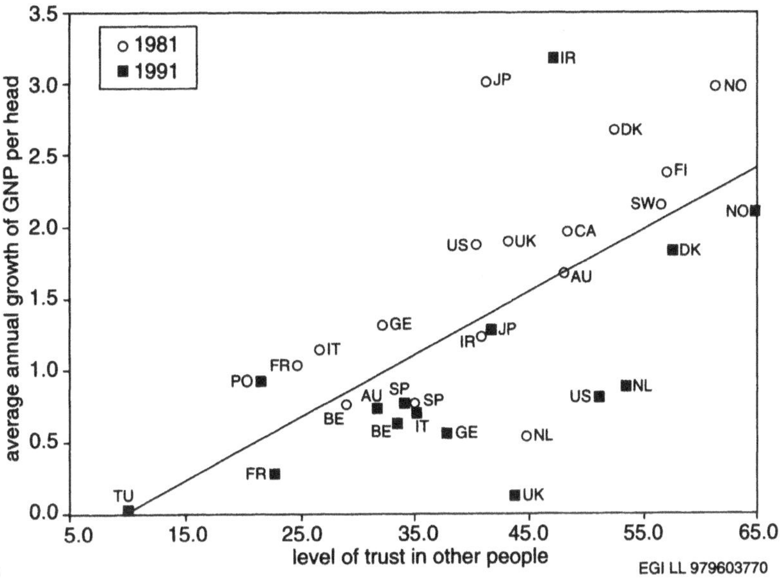

Figure 3.3 Trust in institutions and other people in 20 OECD countries

Source: Bomhoff, den Hartog & Lageweg (1996)

The third kind of knowledge is embodied as *cultural capital*. It represents the ability to get inspired, to give meaning to behaviour: the 'know why'. This is crucial in the information society and for knowledge workers. Particularly this inspiration is important for jobs in which the power of convincing other people is central like for consultants, managers and specialists. It increasingly determines the economic success. It is not the amount of information as such which gains importance in the information society, but in particular the capacity to generate meaningful ideas out of this plentitude of information (Postman, 1986; McCloskey & Klamer, 1995). Although information pro byte becomes increasingly cheaper, the average quality of it decreases too. This is the information paradox (Keuzenkamp, 1996). If the amount of information grows, the incentive to generate and classify information decreases. Skills related to cultural capital are necessary to select out of the mountains of information. Not the reproduction, but the selection and combining of the information becomes important as a defence against the overkill of information.

3.2.2 *The information society*

The change towards the quartainairy sector and the emergence of new forms of knowledge leads to the information society. In this knowledge workers do not produce products but participate in knowledge processes. The content of the jobs is changing. Because of this, it becomes difficult to estimate the exact production output of knowledge workers. Moreover, because it is a process, boundaries between work and not work become unclear. The job is never finished. There is no nine to five. Always things can be done better. Also the usual rewards work different. Of course financial rewards will stay important, but also the appraisal of peers, the feeling to do something right and to work in a stimulating environment is important.

Codified knowledge becomes less important in the information society. Tacit knowledge in which unwritten rules and uses of the professional group and the business environment become important (Polyani, 1958), as does the embeddedness of labour in social networks. This not only pertains to the commutative and creative abilities of workers, but also to the quality of the business environment in which workers operate. By this the role of the price mechanism diminishes. Value depends on the non-tradable recognition of others (Machlup, 1984). Price-making is also difficult because comparison is often not possible (Carter, 1996). If there is a price, this depends on subjective estimations. Results are very different and sometimes exorbitant prices. Examples of this are the fees given to (academic) superstars.

Mostly though, it are not the prices as such which are important, but the accumulation and sharing of knowledge within companies and company networks. In this social and cultural capabilities play a major role. This change is also reflected in the 'new economic growth theory' in which technology is not only endogenous, but in which immaterial investments have an important role too. Examples are the development of software, marketing, designing, customer dedication and quality of products and relations. Increasingly, corporations, regions and countries compete with immaterial investments. In relation to the changing content of technology Amable & Boyer (1995) stress the necessity of a change from a linear concept of technological development towards an interactive. The first is based on a linear relationship between, on the one hand, research and technology and, on the other, competitiveness and economic growth. More research will lead to higher economic growth. However, research and development is often not enough for this growth.

Technology increasingly becomes 'soft' and increasingly depends on the cooperation between people, i.e social and cultural capital. Next to knowledge related to products, processes and logistics, it is the market and organisational knowledge which determines the welfare of regions and countries. In relation to this the organisation of the production and the market need to change. The development of soft technologies needs the networking within and between companies, trade-unions and the government. With the help of these networks, technology is generated, diffused and applied. Particular the elaboration of (regional) networks shows high growth potencies (see Cooke & Morgan, 1994).

Although the immaterial side of economic development is sometimes hard to quantify, table 3.1 gives an indication of the share of it in the GNP in some european countries.

Table 3.1
Immaterial investments in various European countries
(percent of GNP; 1992)

Sweden	11.0
Norway	10.8
The Netherlands	9.6
Belgium	9.4
Denmark	9.4
France	9.2
United Kingdom	8.8
Austria	8.5
Germany	8.2

Source: Minne, Herzberg & Reijnders (1996)

The table shows that the spending for immaterial investments, like for public education, software, licences and marketing is highest in Sweden and Norway. More than 10 percent of the GNP is directed at immaterial investments. Germany and the United Kingdom are among the lowest. Table 3.1 includes public education. Excluding public education results in about a halving of the spending. In this case, although Sweden is still in the lead, Germany now takes the second place. Austria takes the last position.

The change towards the information economy and intangibles means a tremendous change in the structure of labour demand. This general process heavily influences the chances of economic development and recovery for the countries and regions of Europe. It implies, for example, that short-term reindustrialisation based on traditional sectors, will in the longer term be less fruitful. Moreover the increasing importance of social and cultural capital in economic development shows that particular non-tangible investments get higher priority.

3.3 Developments in the supply of labour

Besides changes in labour demand, also major changes in labour supply come about in Europe. Next to ageing, changes in migration, participation and feminisation are important for the - future - labour supply of the countries and regions of Europe.

3.3.1 Ageing

Besides individual ageing, collective ageing has occurred in various European countries. These have various effects for the labour market (Richter, 1992; Winkelmann & Zimmermann, 1993; OECD, 1996[a]). *Individual ageing* means that people live longer. Within Europe differences exist with the highest life expectancy for 1995 for men in Sweden (76.1) and the lowest in Portugal (71.5). For women France has the highest life expectancy (81.9) and Denmark the lowest (78.0) (CPB, 1997). A longer life span implies, given the existing behaviour and regulations on the labour market, that over the life cycle less time is spent relatively on the labour market and more on 'retirement'. The working years shrink correspondingly (OECD, 1996[b]).

As far as *collective ageing* is concerned, European countries increasingly show signs of what is often called the second demographic transition (van de Kaa, 1987). Characteristics of it are a declining but ageing population, a fall of the fertility rate below the replacement rate and an increase in the relative importance of migration for total population change. Although causality is difficult to proof, quite often various other demographic and cultural changes, such as individualisation, are related to it (Cruysen, 1991; Lesthaeghe & Verleye, 1992). The EU-population increase has declined steadily since the second half of the sixties. Particularly the natural increase shows a stable, but declining pattern. This can be related to the decreasing number of children per woman. Because of this, and particularly the increase of the life expectancy formerly due to lower infant mortality, but now to lower old age mortality, the proportion of younger aged people has steadily declined while that of older people has risen (European Commission, 1996). Kessler (1993) estimates that the increasing life expectancy due to a lower mortality is responsible for two-thirds of the ageing population, while the lowering of the fertility rate is responsible for one-third.

Ageing will certainly influence the future size and structure of the population. Gonnot (1995) gives an indication of the range of possible changes. In this study four scenarios are designed. They assume different changes in various demographic aspects. It must be stressed that these scenarios do not reckon yet with changes in behaviour, like an increase of the participation of women on the labour market. The following scenarios can be distinguished:

- *A constant rates scenario* with rates remaining constant at their 1980-1985 level.

- *A replacement fertility scenario* which assumes that fertility will gradually reach replacement level.

- *A low mortality scenario* under which age specific mortality rates decrease by 30 percent for women and 45 percent for men.

- *A western low rates scenario* which combines the most extreme demographic rates observed in Western Europe: Low German fertility rates; Swedish marriage and divorce rates; and Swiss low mortality rates.

Table 3.2
Changes in the old-age dependency ratio between 1985 and 2030 (percent-points)

	Scenario[1]			
	Constant Rates	Replacement Fertility	Low Mortality	Western Low Rates
30+			Germany Netherlands	
25-30			Finland Italy Austria	Germany Netherlands Finland
20-25	Netherlands Germany		France Norway Sweden	Italy Austria Hungary
15-20	Finland Italy	Netherlands	France	Poland
10-15	Austria France Norway France	Germany Finland Italy	Poland Hungary	Sweden CSFR
5-10	Sweden Poland Hungary Poland Hungary	Austria Norway Sweden Poland Hungary	CSFR	
0-5	CSFR	CSFR		

[1] (see text for an explanation)

Source: after Gonnot (1995)

Table 3.2 shows the results of the various scenarios for the changes in old-age dependency ratio (OADR): the number of persons of 65 years and older per 100 persons between 15 and 64 years. For all countries there will be ageing between 1985 and 2030. While some eastern european and nordic countries are on the low side, Germany and the Netherlands are top-ranking countries. Particularly the low mortality scenario foresees a large growth of the dependency ratio for these countries. Also in case no changes occur in fertility, mortality and migration, like in the constant rates scenario, a large growth of the OADR is expected in these countries. This implies that much change is already embodied in the present population structure. Gonnot (1995) furthermore concludes that changes in fertility and immigration will not affect the ageing process very much. In contrast to this, changes in mortality can have a large effect. The OADR will increase to very high levels. Under the assumptions of the constant rates scenario ageing will occur between 2015 and 2030. Taking 1985 as a base year, the index of OADR will be for the Netherlands 184 in 2030 and for Germany and France respectively 125 and 150. After 2030 the OADR will decrease to 163 (the Netherlands), 92 (Germany) and 141 (France) in 2050. If the fertility rate drops, as is assumed in the western low rates scenario, ageing will continue in all countries.

In an ageing society, with relative more elderly potential employees, the participation rate of the total labour force will drop: the demographic effect. This is because, in general, the age-specific participation pattern of the labour force has an inverse U-pattern. The degree in which total participation will decrease depends on the size of the various age groups. If the size of the older groups is relative large, the effect on the total participation rate is also large. This will happen in the coming years, for example, by the vertical rise of the post second World War 'baby-boom generation' in the age pyramid. Particularly this age cohort effect has elicited much discussion about the future problems related to ageing. The effects of demographic changes on the total labour force for various countries are depicted in figure 3.4.

Three of the demographic trends, as mentioned earlier are used. For some countries some existing 'national' scenarios are added. The figure shows that the total labour force will decrease in the Netherlands and Germany. For France the situation is different. In this country only the 'western low scenario' shows a decrease. For Germany and the Netherlands a change to the replacement level by 2005 would make some, but not very much difference for the year 2030. A larger effect can be expected at 2050.

It is sometimes assumed that, because of ageing, less people will be available. This leads to a tightening of the labour market and therefore to less unemployment. Suppose that this mechanism works we still have to reckon with the time needed to find an equilibrium and with the age selective aspects of the process. In European Commission (1996) a cursory simulation shows that due to different initial unemployment levels, unemployment for the youngest group would fall substantial but still be high in 2005. For the middle aged and older groups unemployment would be significantly lower or disappear.

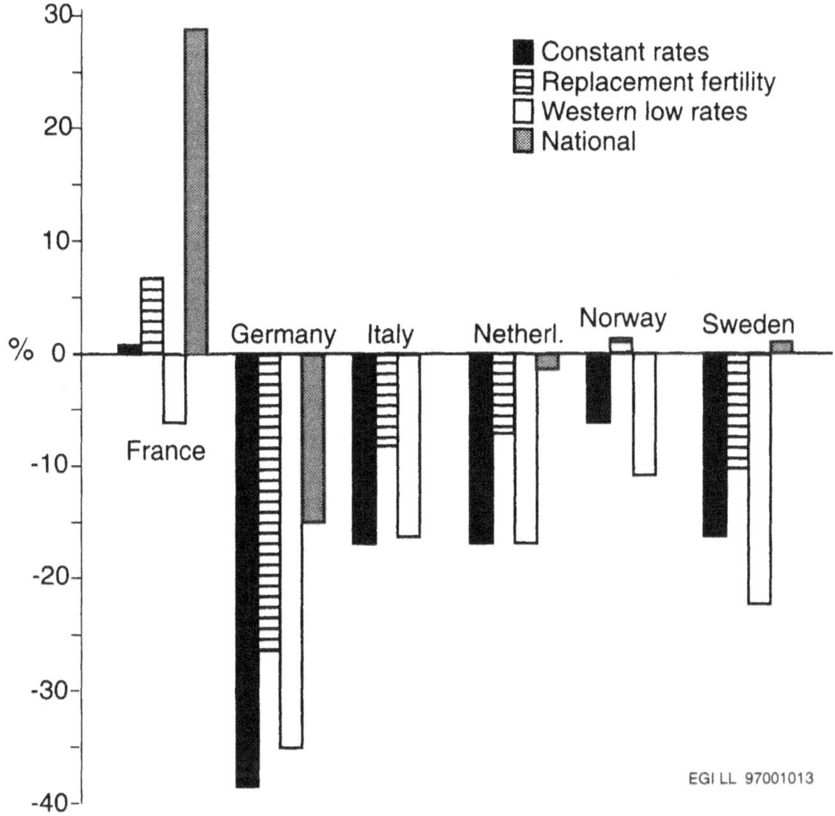

Figure 3.4 Change in the total labour force in various countries assuming various demographic trends (1985-2030; percent)

Source: Gonnot (1995)

Whether the mechanism indicated works is however also questionable. Many countries already experienced a substantial ageing of the population. The Netherlands for example had, in the last 20 years, an increase of 43 percent in the number of retired persons (de Vries & Dur, 1996). In this 20 years much happened with unemployment. Sometimes rates of unemployment went down, but also often remained high or increased. This means that 'other factors are clearly more important' (OECD, 1996[b], p.8). A mechanistic interpretation of the relationship between ageing and employment therefore should be rejected. Among the other factors which play a role are changes in the level of migration and participation.

3.3.2 Migration

Besides that the population changes by natural growth and by changes in the age structure, migration will change its size and structure too. At this moment migration largely depends on policy regulations. This not only pertains to the number of migrants, but also to its composition. Political and ethical causes are far more important than economic ones (Johnson & Zimmermann, 1993). Migration becomes relatively more important for the population changes in Western Europe. Net migration rose considerably during the second half of the 1980s (Böhning, 1991; van der Knaap & Odé, 1994). That migration becomes more important for total change, does not imply that this is *because* natural growth declined or stagnates. Migration becomes relative more important due to the statistical effect of less high natural growth, and in an absolute sense because of external pressures (Zimmermann, 1996). Migration will become the main source of population change in the future. This will, however be accomplished at a lower absolute level than before.

There are, however, considerable differences in the importance of migration between the European countries. Although all countries show a net population increase, a distinction can be made between the North and the South of the European Union as far as demographic changes and migration are concerned. The North reflects a migratory population regime, i.e. population shows a net increase, mainly because of positive net migration figures. This northern region includes countries like Denmark, Germany, the United Kingdom and the Netherlands. The population in the South of the EU is expanding as well, but natural increase more than migration is still responsible for this. The South includes countries like Greece, Portugal and Spain.

Some main types of migration flows can be distinguished within Europe. These are return migration, family reunification, asylum seekers and migration of highly skilled employees (van der Laan & van der Knaap, 1995; Odé, 1996). The rise and fall of these various types of international migration flows resulted in a specific spatial pattern. The traditional 'core-periphery' pattern has partly vanished. Traditional emigration countries of Southern Europe, particularly Greece and Italy, are now net immigration countries as well. Spain and Portugal face net small losses of migrants, while only the Republic of Ireland has persisted in its large outflow of population.

Parts of the - perceived - problems of an ageing economy for the labour market are quite often expected to be resolved by pointing at possibilities of (selective) immigration. The inflow of, especially young people, from abroad might fill the hole in the labour supply caused by ageing. By this, large necessary efforts of trying to increase participation and/or social security measures, possibly can be avoided. Hypothetically, for countries which face a rapid ageing of the population, young migrants could be important for the relative size of the potential labour force (Steinmann, 1991; Long, 1991). Given the present situation and even under the most optimal conditions, the contribution of migration in alleviating the problems of an ageing society will be very limited however (de Jong Gierveld, 1993; United Nations, 1994; European Commission, 1996). In this perspective, net migration in the European Union should rise from the present half million to 5 or 7 million in order to counteract the 'baby boom effect' in the year 2025 (European Commission, 1996). Also, in a more general sense, demographic 'efforts' will not be able to counteract the process of ageing. Only an average number of 3 or 4 children per women or a migration equivalent of that number of new people might help. Obviously these numbers are, given the present economic and social framework, rather unrealistic (see also Keilman, 1989; Kessler, 1993; OECD, 1996[a]).

Besides these quantitative relationships between ageing and migration, also *qualitative aspects* of the labour market play a role. These are particularly related to labour market mobility, unemployment and the sectoral/occupational structure. The distribution of the immigrants in Europe is not random but directed at specific sectors (OECD, 1993). Traditionally most -non-European- mediterranean migrants were directed at manufacturing. The United Kingdom deviates from this general pattern. Here migrants are much more oriented at the service industry. Odé (1996) gives a detailed and more recent picture of the sectoral orientation of - legal - migrants. He concludes that non EU migrants are mostly oriented at mining, distributional activities, trade and catering. Also manufacturing stays important. Next to agriculture, banking and other services are underrepresented in the northern countries of the EU. In contrast to this, in Spain, Greece and somewhat less in Portugal, migrants are directed at the service industry and particularly at the less qualified jobs (Odé, van der Knaap & Nijsse, 1993). In general the picture emerges that non-EU migrants take part in those sectors, like trade or manufacturing, which show a relative stabilisation or decline in their share of jobs. For growing sectors, like catering or banking, migrants are oriented at the lower qualified jobs.

Important is whether changes in the number of jobs among the national and foreign work force in a country have a *substitution* or *complementary* character. Substitution indicates a divergent development in employment between both categories, whereas complementarity illustrates a convergent pattern. The OECD (1993) studied both effects for a number of Western European countries. Between 1982 and 1991 the labour market position of foreigners has become more vulnerable in most manufacturing industries. However, for services and agriculture no clear pattern could be traced. 'Although it is true that in some countries foreigners are concentrating in declining sectors, there does not appear any systematic trend towards substitution of nationals for foreigners' (OECD, 1993[b], p.36). Zimmermann (1996) and de New and Zimmermann (1994) studied complementary and substitution effects by concentrating on wages and employment. If substitution exists, immigration would affect the wages of natives negatively. In a complementary relationship the opposite would happen. The overall evidence for Europe is that substitution effects are rare and at best weak. This is in line with findings elsewhere and with different methods. With the exception of manual labour in agriculture, most occupational categories show a more or less complementary development of total employment change and the number of employment permits issued. However, increasingly migration is upgrading (Odé, 1996). More and more migrants have a higher education. This counteracts the stereotype of migrants oriented at the lower parts of the labour market.

Migration changes the ethnic population structure. The proportions of foreign residents in each country reflects the migration pattern of a few decades ago. North-Western and Central European countries have comparatively high shares of foreigners. For Belgium this was in 1993 about 9.0 percent of the population, in Germany 8.0 percent, France 6.3 percent and for the United Kingdom 3.5 percent. Most countries on the fringe of Europe show, except for Sweden, only small shares. For Spain it was about 1.0 percent, Portugal, 1.2 percent, Italy 1.6 percent and Ireland 2.5 percent. Most of the 'older industrial' countries reveal very high proportions of foreign residents coming from the Maghreb and Turkey. Recent migration patterns will become important for the future composition of foreign citizens. These patterns refer more to political and humanitarian reasons, rather than economic motives (see Appleyard, 1991; King, 1991).

Due to migration the labour market underwent a process of *multicolourisation*. On the one hand this led to labour supply with mostly a lower educational level. On the other hand it also resulted in a growing demand for specific 'multicoloured' goods and services. Whole new activities arised, particularly in the larger cities where ethnic groups are concentrated in specific neighbourhoods. This growth in turn led to new labour demand often oriented at the ethnic group involved.

3.3.3 Participation

Changes in the labour supply are next to natural changes and migration, also caused by changing participation rates (van der Laan, 1995). For example, in 10 years time not only the population cohorts of different sizes will shift to another age bracket (the demographic effect), also the participation rate of that age bracket itself may change (the participation effect). Important is whether the participation effect will amplify or counteract the changes caused by demographic changes. One expects that the increase in the longevity of the population is reflected in a more active elderly group, also on the labour market. This would result in an increase of the participation rate of the older age brackets of the labour force. In contrast to this, empirical findings show there has been a steady decline in the participation of the labour force above 55 years (Rein & Jacobs, 1992). Although there are differences in the most important exit-year or the slope of the exit years, most countries show this pattern. The decline happened in countries which *differ substantially* in the scope and level of exit, the industry-mix and legislative structures for the exit-process or employment alternatives for older workers. In comparing the development in Germany, Japan, Sweden, the United Kingdom and the United States, 'early exit of older workers is a general phenomenon of the labour market rather than a strategic measure of coping with specific problems of certain industries' and 'the expectation of reversing this trend does not appear to be very realistic since the trend of early exit is primarily driven by labour market dynamics rather than by old age pensions arrangements of the state' (Rein & Jacobs, 1992, p.115). Notwithstanding industrial differences, the overall result is a decrease of the activity rates of people aged 55-64 years. The growing absolute number of older people on the labour market due to the demographic effect and the lowering of the participation of those older groups leads to changes in the share of older people in the labour force. For example, in Sweden and the United Kingdom, demographic and participation changes result in a lowering of the employment shares of the older groups.

The major trends in the age-specific participation change are a stabilisation of the participation of the younger group, an increase of the middle age group and decreasing levels for the elderly. Result is a potential increase of the middle age-groups in the labour force. These trends differ, however, for each country and depend on the level of participation of each age category. In 1990 high levels of *total* participation were in the northwestern part of the EU and low levels in the South (Dickmann & van der Laan, 1989; Van der Laan, 1995). This dualistic pattern is however by no means a standard one. Both within the North and in the South there are regions which deviate from the general pattern. In 1990 the North of the European Union also had higher levels of participation of the younger groups. The South had lower levels. Also this is no standard regional pattern. For the oldest age-groups high rates exist in the South as in some northern countries.

What are the effects of existing trends in the participation on the future labour supply of regions? We discuss these trends for 12 countries of the EU onwards to the year 2020 (Eurostat, 1991; IFO, 1993 and Report, 1994). The projections are made from the perspective of a so-called high scenario. Next to ongoing developments, this scenario includes the effects of additional positive policy measures on participation of the labour force. The scenario presupposes moreover a tendency towards regional convergence. This is based on the assumption that the labour market in different regions of a country tends to evolve towards a convergence of their socio-economic and cultural patterns. The participation rates for the scenario are multiplied by the corresponding estimated population figures to obtain the labour force.

Although the participation and demographic effect have a substantial regional variation, there is, however, no significant regional correlation between both at the level of 156 regions. Changes due to *real participation* are high in, on the one side, the mediterranean parts of the EU and, on the other, in the Benelux countries and in the western part of Germany. Lower changes happen in Ireland, the United Kingdom, France and the former East-German regions. The *demographic effect*, generally negative, is only slightly negative or even positive in Ireland, Germany and Spain. In other parts of Europe, and particularly in Northern Italy and parts of France, the demographic effect is in a negative sense much stronger, implying a negative effect on total activity rates. The regional variation of both the demographic and participation effect is substantial. Within Europe, two spatial belts of high growth due to higher participation changes and, at the same time, low negative demographic effects can be traced. On the one hand we have the Benelux/ Western Germany belt, and on the other, Mediterranean Europe.

If these general changes are analysed by age, the integration of demographic and participation changes shows that the share of the age-category 15-24 years in the labour force decreases in the period 1990-2020. While in regions like Ireland and southern Spain a quarter of the labour force was less than 25 years old in 1990, this will decrease to about 17 percent in 2020. The regional variation in the share of the younger group though will not change very much in the EU: the decrease is a general phenomenon. On average the share of the oldest age-category (50-64 years) increases. In contrast to the decrease of the youngest group, this increase shows a more clear regional variation. Particularly many regions of Germany, northern Spain and Italy come to the fore, as the share of the oldest group in these regions increases from about a fifth in 1990 to a third in 2020. On basis of these regional differentiated changes by age, we conclude that the youngest group shows only changes in the *general* share. The oldest group shows besides the general effect a much clearer *regional* effect.

3.3.4 Feminisation

In many countries there was a large growth in the participation of women on the labour market. By this the gender structure of the labour force changed and lead to a feminisation of the labour force: a higher share of females in the total labour force. Besides the changes in the female labour force this also depends on the changes for men. In 1991 41 percent of total employment in the European Union consisted of female workers. Men dominated the labour market particularly in peripheral Europe, the Netherlands, Luxembourg and the Northwestern part of Germany. The female participation rates show a rather dispersed spatial pattern. Although many regions in Spain, Italy and Greece are in the lower categories, also in this case, the 'standard' pattern of high levels in the North and low in the South does not apply. Parts of Belgium, the Netherlands and Germany are below the average of the EU-regions. In contrast to this, parts of Portugal and Greece are quite well above the average.

Women work mostly in specific occupations. For example, about two-thirds of all clerical workers are female. For production related workers this is only about 12 percent. There are, however, quite large differences in the occupational bias between the countries of the Union (Hoevenberg & de Grip, 1994). Using the high scenario forecasting method, as described above, we see, as far as the change in real participation of females in the period 1990-2020 is concerned, that the average participation rate rises from 40.5 percent in 1990 to 50.5 percent in 2020. In this, changes in the participation are much more important than demographic changes. Most regions in Southern Europe see their female participation levels rising. This is also the case in the less central regions of the Netherlands and the Northwestern part of Germany. The decrease of female participation in France, already existent before 1990, becomes spatially more extensive.

There is a catching-up effect in female participation. Regions with lower levels of participation are growing more quickly than those with higher levels. For men two groups of regions can be distinguished. On the one hand, there are regions with still growing male participation levels. For this category there exists a saturation effect: higher level regions grow less than low level regions. On the other hand there are the regions with decreasing levels. In this case higher level regions show larger decreases. Although women increasingly become more important, men still dominate the labour market in 2020, albeit at a lower level. The various changes result in a complex spatial pattern with regions with high ratios next to regions with low ratios. Many regions get a more gender balanced pattern. Still men dominate statistically the labour market in many regions of Southern Europe, Ireland, parts of France, Belgium and the Netherlands. This domination is even larger if one takes part-time work into account (Hoevenberg & de Grip, 1994). Part time work is rather popular in countries like the United Kingdom, Denmark and, above all, the Netherlands. In the first mentioned two countries a fifth of total employment is a part-time job. For the Netherlands this is about a third. For women these figures are much higher. In the Netherlands more than 60 percent of all employed women work part-time. In countries like Greece or Spain only 3 or 4 percent of total employment is part-time. In the countries with much part-timing it is particularly the women who do so, mainly in service and sales work.

3.3.5 A macro-spatial summary of changes in labour supply

Natural change, migration and changes in the participation have a distinct spatial structure in Europe. This spatial structure can be described as a central region surrounded by peripheral areas. The central region encompasses the old industrial zone ranging from Birmingham (UK) towards Milan in Italy and new growth areas at its outskirts. The latter includes regions like the Third Italy and Southern France. The periphery consists of the less developed countries of the EU lying at the West and South side. Ireland, Portugal and Greece are within this group. This is not to say that the causes of labour supply changes of Europe are confined to these central and peripheral regions. Changes are also influenced by developments elsewhere, like in the countries still outside the EU, but which have growing trade and political relationships with it. Some of these countries are in the EU-waiting room, like the Czech Republic, Hungary and Poland, which already have strong ties with the EU. Whether these countries, for example, will be a major source of migration depends to a large degree on the success of trade-and-aid agreements with the EU. Economic aid to Eastern Europe partly has the objective to reduce the propensity to migrate. The high and growing unemployment rates which are particularly high for younger people, can play a role in this. Also countries with quite often old colonial and cultural ties with Europe play a role for the European labour market. The Maghreb countries and Pakistan are examples of this. A major share of the asylum seekers and refugees come from the Third World, in particular from the Middle East, Central and North Africa and some countries in the Far East.

Table 3.3 summarises the main supply differences between the economic centre and the peripheral parts of the EU. For the *economic centre* demographic changes imply an increasing importance of migration and participation. As far as migration is concerned, particular labour migrants from non-Union countries become important. These migrants form a heterogeneous group. Contrary to the traditional massive and low-skilled labour movements from the Mediterranean regions to the industrial heartland of Europe, international labour mobility becomes much more segmented. This with regard to the socio-economic characteristics of the migrants, the employment structure and the regions of origin.

Table 3.3
A summary of spatial differences in natural change, migration and participation within the EU

	Economic centre	EU periphery
- demographic changes	- low increase/decrease	- increase
- migration	- family reunification - highly skilled employees - asylum seekers	- outmigration (Ireland) - return migration - asylum seekers
- participation	- higher levels - stabilizing growth or decrease	- lower levels - catching-up regions (Portugal, Spain) - lagging regions (Italy, Greece)

A dual structure with a low and high segment exists in the central countries. As far as the lower segment is concerned, the immigration of workers from non-Union countries during the last two decades has ended filling up some qualitative imbalances of demand for labour, rather than responding to the structural needs of expanding industrial economies. To the group of legally employed migrants, we must add the illegally employed. There is, of course, little evidence about the exact number and nature of these migrants. The marginal position of these groups reflects demand, supply, and various institutional conditions. These workers are particularly concentrated in labour intensive, small scale industries with quite open, quickly changing demand, like seasonal work in horticulture, auxiliaries in manufacturing and self-employed services (Appleyard, 1991). These illegal workers are profitable for employers because pay-roll taxes can be avoided and flexibility is guaranteed. The suppliers of labour, because of their legal status, are compelled to take the marginal job.

The second part of the dual migration structure related to the economic centre consists of highly skilled employees directed at high level manufacturing and business services. As far as manufacturing is concerned these jobs, mostly within large companies and modern specialised industries, need skilled employees and are mainly concentrated in the newly industrialised regions like Southern-Germany and South-Eastern France or in large metropolitan areas. High level business services include the financial world, advisory services and institutes for training and/or research. This group is supported by additional services. Among them are, for example, the building industry, brokers, luxury shops and cultural activities. The high-grade urban tourist infrastructure is linked with this too. In this case particularly metropolises included in the international system of world cities are most strongly affected. Because international companies or organisations are most important as recruiting channels, the spatial effects will be on those regions where most of these are located. Again, particular the metropolitan areas in the economic centre are affected.

The natural growth rates in *the periphery* are mostly above the EU-average. Migration shows a varied picture. Besides Ireland which had relatively large migration losses, migrational changes are less important than natural changes. However, return migration, and increasingly, flows of asylum seekers play also a role in these countries. In this periphery the participation levels and changes are below average. Of course this is a general pattern. In many Portuguese and Spanish regions, for example, there was a strong increase of the participation. The Iberian regions mostly catch up with the economic centre, while countries like Greece stay in the peripheral group. The EU-integration makes it easy for the inhabitants of the periphery to migrate towards other EU-countries. Whether this happens, depends partly on the economic development of these countries. The countries in the periphery show a diverging pattern as far as economic development is concerned. GDP-growth of Greece was below the EU-average, while those of Spain and Portugal were well above that average. By this the latter countries help to the convergence of the levels of development within the EU. As with the changes in the participation, also for migration, Spain and Portugal are in more favourable position to absorb their growing population than Greece. On the other hand particularly these countries increasingly attract migrants from 'third countries'. Quite often these EU-peripheral countries act as the first (informal) stepping stones.

3.4 Macro-institutional structures, policies and labour market performance

Besides demand and supply, institutions influence the behaviour of economic actors and by this the structure of the labour market and its performance. Demand and supply changes are embedded in a macro-institutional framework. This framework can be crucial for the future development of regional labour markets (van der Laan, 1996). Institutions structure the relations of economic actors in such a way to protect them from undesirable behaviour of others. At the same time the institutional structure may show slowness and prevent changes on the labour market. Moreover, the institutions are related to parts of the economic actors on the labour market. Not all groups are inside the game. It is, however, quite difficult to quantify the various institutional relationships in a comparative sense for all european countries. Quite often data are not present or hardly comparable. Notwithstanding this, in this section a tentative attempt for such a comparison is made. We, at first, analyse the differences in the macro-institutional structure of some countries of the European Union. These countries are Belgium, the United Kingdom, Germany, Denmark, Sweden and the Netherlands. Unfortunately, at this stage, no comparative data were available for other european countries. This implies, of course, that the results are biased towards the countries included. Notwithstanding this, the results are of interest for other countries because they show how general institutional processes influence the performance of the labour market. Furthermore we relate the institutional differences between the countries to differences in the performance of the labour market. The latter is indicated by, on the one hand, volume related aspects like the level of unemployment and participation, and, on the other hand by price related aspects like labour costs, labour productivity and wage flexibility. By comparing the performance of individual countries with the average performance (bench-marking), an indication of possible institutional change is given.

Secondly, we give an overview of the intensity of labour market policies in the six countries and analyse how the situation on the labour market provokes more or less institutional activities like measures for preventing or curing unemployment.

Before we analyse the relationship between, on the one hand, institutional structure and market performance and, on the other, between policies and performance, we have to state that the *direct* relationship between the kind of institutional structure and policies is very weak. The number of policies taken does not depend on whether countries have, for example, a more or less centralised structure, a higher level of corporatism or a higher level of unionisation. As the following will show, however, some *indirect* links between labour market performance, institutional structure and policies can be traced.

3.4.1 Institutional structure and labour market performance

Table 3.4 shows that countries differ in the macro-institutionalisation of the labour market. In the table, countries get more points if their institutional structure is highly centralised, if there is more corporatism, more coordination of collective agreements, a central level of labour negotiations, a larger coverage of the labour agreements, a higher level of unionisation and more judicial regulations. Although the selection and weighting of these characteristics is somewhat arbitrary, the table shows that the United Kingdom is clearly less institutionalised than the other countries. Here central level interference with labour negotiations is less extensive. Potentially there is more room for lower level institutions like individual corporations and regions. In contrast to the United Kingdom, Belgium and Sweden have the most heavily institutionalised structure. These countries have an intensive governmental interference with negotiations and tripartite agreements. The other countries are more similar to Belgium and Sweden than to the United Kingdom.

Table 3.4
Differences in the institutional influences on the labour market

	UK	B	D	NL	DK	S
- centralisation[a]	1	2	2	2	3	3
- corporatism[b]	1	3	3	3	3	3
- coordination of collective agreements[c]	1	2	3	2	2	2
- level of negotiation[d]	1	3	2	2	2	2
- coverage of collective agreements[e]	2	3	3	3	3	3
- unionisation[e]	1	2	1	1	3	3
- judicial regulations[f]	2	3	3	2	1	2
total	9	18	17	15	17	18

a = low = 1; high = 3
b = low = 1; high = 3
c = absent = 1; limited = 2; high = 3
d = corporation level = 1; sectoral = 2; central = 3
e = <33.3 percent = 1; 33.3-66.6 = 2; >66.6 = 3
f = low = 1; high = 3

Source: Based on Verzorgingsstaat (1996), p.61 and 112

Table 3.5
Price and volume related labour market performance in various European countries

	B	UK	D	DK	NL	S
prices	1	3	1	2	2	2
- labour costs per hour[a]						
- labour costs per unit product[a]	2	1	1	2	2	2
- minimum wages[b]	1	3	2	1	1	2
- short term wage flexibility[c]	-	1	2	2	3	3
- long term wage flexibility[c]	2	2	1	2	1	3
- labour productivity[d]	3	1	3	2	3	1
- social climate[e]	2	1	3	2	3	2
average price performance	1.83	1.71	1.86	1.86	2.14	2.14
volume	1	2	1	3	1	3
- participation[f]						
- unemployment[g]	1	1	2	1	3	2
- long term unemployment[h]	1	1	1	2	1	3
- corporate training[i]	1	1	3	2	2	2
- flexibility[j]	1	2	2	3	3	3
- unemployment low educated[k]	1	2	3	2	3	3
- participation low educated[k]	1	1	1	2	1	3
average volume performance	1.00	1.43	1.86	2.14	2.00	2.71
total	18*	22	26	28	29	34
average total performance	1.38	1.57	1.86	2.00	2.07	2.43

a = high = 1; low = 3 (manufacturing)
b = high = 1; low = 3
c = low = 1; high = 3; - = n.a.
d = low = 1; high = 3 (per hour)
e = bad = 1; good = 3 (average of strike intensity and educational possibilities)
f = low = 1; high = 3 (in persons)
g = high = 1; low = 3 (average 1990-1995)
h = high = 1; low = 3 (share of long term unemployment of the total)
i = low = 1; high = 3 (world competitiveness)
j = low = 1; high = 3 (net job creation and job mobility)
k = low = 1; high = 3
* = Belgium N = 13; other countries N = 14

Source: Calculations based on Verzorgingsstaat (1996)

What does the level of institutionalisation mean for the performance of the labour market? Table 3.5 shows some indicators of labour market performance. Two categories are distinguished. On the one hand, there are various price related variables, like labour costs or labour productivity. On the other, volume related variables like the unemployment rate or flexibility (job creation and mobility) are distinguished. The table shows that, for the total, the labour markets of Belgium and the United Kingdom perform on average less well than those of the other countries. They have an average score of 1.38 and 1.57 respectively. Sweden performs with 2.43 best. If only the price indicators are taken into account, the table shows smaller differences between the countries. Also in this case the United Kingdom scores quite low. Sweden and the Netherlands, rank highest. As far as the volume aspects are concerned, Belgium is last on all indicators. Again Sweden ranks highest.

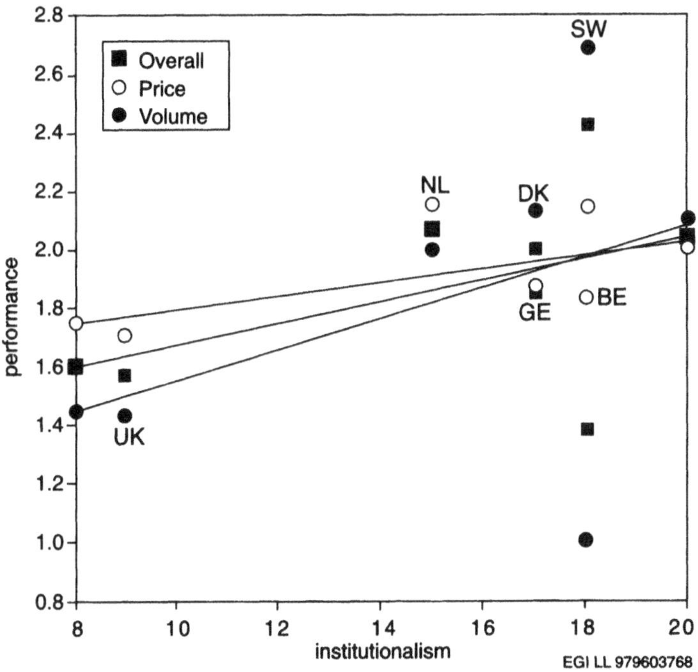

Figure 3.5 **The relationship between institutionalisation and labour market performance (lines indicate regression)**

Figure 3.5 shows that the relationship between the level of institutionalisation and labour market performance. In this, table 3.4 is related to table 3.5. In general, as the regression lines show, a higher level of institutionalism has a positive effect on labour market performance. The relationship is however not very clear. The level of institutionalism explains only 12 percent of the overall average performance. The price related indicators of labour market performance are, with 21 percent, explained somewhat better. The volume aspects of economic performance only reach to 9 percent. As, figure 3.5 shows, these low scores are largely influenced by the broad range in the values of the various countries. Most extreme, Sweden and Belgium illustrate this. They have the same level of institutionalisation but clearly different levels of performance. The figure shows that particularly the volume related performances cause these large differences.

Figure 3.5 also shows that the relationship between institutionalisation and - different kinds of - labour market performance differs clearly by country. The United Kingdom, the Netherlands and, particular, Belgium perform relatively better on the price variables. Given their level of institutionalism, price performance is higher than their overall performance. Countries like Sweden and Denmark perform better on the volume side of labour market. In these cases volume performance is above the overall performance. Germany shows for both the price and the volume aspects figures similar to those for the total. The negative deviations on price and volume performance from the average, point to opportunities for institutional change. Countries like Sweden and Denmark could, by international standards, do better on their price performance. The United Kingdom, the Netherlands and particularly Belgium could do better on the volume aspects.

3.4.2 Policies and labour market performance

Two main fields of institutional interference in the labour market are related to participation and employment. A distinction can be made between measures directed at the prevention of unemployment and non-participation and curative measures. The latter try to re-employ the unemployed and increase the participation rate of specific groups. Next to general economic policies directed at, for example, the wage level and labour taxes, particularly group related policies are important. Examples of these are employment policies for women, young or old age categories, disabled persons or ethnic groups. Within Europe these group related policies play a major role.

Table 3.6 gives a general overview of the various policy areas aimed at the group related determinants of employment and participation. The position of each country is deduced from the number of measures for three main policy fields: measures directed at young people, old people and specific groups (women, ethnic groups and disabled). To give an example, table 3.6 shows that Belgium has 7 different measures aimed at the integration of young people into the labour market. Measures of this kind are the temporary employment in the public sector, the supply of trainerships or training in application.

Table 3.6
The quantitative intensity of labour market policies in six countries of the European Union

Policies	B	UK	D	DK	NL	S	total
* *young people*							
- integration into market	7	5	4	3	3	4	26
- vocational training in education system	5	5	5	5	6	4	30
- transition school→work	2	2	2	1	3	4	14
- parity of esteem vocational training	0	2	4	0	2	0	8
- second change	0	2	3	1	2	0	8
- job training apprenticeships	2	2	3	2	1	2	12
- initial training	5	2	4	5	1	1	18
total	21	20	25	17	18	15	
* *older people*							
- protection and increasing employment	2	1	1	1	1	1	7
* *specific groups*							
- child care services	9	8	6	6	5	8	42
- unemployed women	2	2	3	2	1	2	12
- equal pay and treatment	6	3	2	5	5	5	26
- positive action	3	1	0	3	1	1	9
- equality audits	1	1	0	1	0	0	3
- disabled	5	5	5	4	4	3	26
total	26	20	16	21	16	19	
Total general	49	41	42	39	35	35	

Source: Calculations on basis of EOT (1994-'96); Employment (1994-'96); OECD (1995); Schmid et al (1996)

In total Belgium has 21 different measures aimed at young people, 2 for older people and 26 for specific groups. It should be stressed that the table and the following interpretation are is related to the number of measures, or, in other words, to the quantitative dimension. The quality of the measures existing in the various countries is not analysed.

If one looks at the general picture of the quantitative intensity of labour market policies in relation to participation and employment, it is Belgium with 49 measures which is most active. Sweden and the Netherlands with 35 have the lowest number of measures. The table shows that for the policies aimed at *young people* Sweden has the lowest number of measures, while Germany ranks highest. Over all countries, the integration of vocational courses into the general curricula is important. The number of such measures is about the same in the various countries. Next to this, the integration of young people into the job market is important. Usually various types of 'sandwich training', employment and training grants are used. In relation to these measures, there is more variation between countries. Denmark and the Netherlands have relatively few measures. In these countries, however, there is a guarantee of (temporary) employment. The least popular measures are those, aimed at the parity of esteem of vocational training and second chance programmes. Table 3.6 shows also that there are few active measures for *older people*. Most measures are not aimed at increasing the participation and employment of older people, but in contrast, at reducing the demand for work. Early retirement schemes and easy access to disablement programmes are examples of these kind of policies.

Measures for promoting equal opportunities for *specific groups* are rather well used. In this field Belgium, again, is the most active. The Netherlands and Germany have the lowest score. Child care services are popular in Europe. The number of measures in this particular field is highest in Belgium and lowest in the Netherlands. Next to this, measures aimed at equal pay and treatment in the legislative field and in collective agreements together with measures for the disabled are popular. Remarkably, equality audits aimed at the assessment of the extent to which policies have progressed are used quite scantly.

Figure 3.6 shows the relation between the number of measures and the average performance. In this figures the results of table 3.5 are related to those of table 3.6. For the six countries there is a clearly negative relationship: more measures go hand in hand with a lower average performance. As table 3.7 shows, the performance level explains significantly about 80 percent of the number of measures taken. In a more worse labour market situation, countries try harder to combat this. Given this general relationship, one would expect in the United Kingdom and the Netherlands, given their performance, a larger number of measures. Belgium, Germany and Sweden take relatively more measures then could be expected from the average relationship over the countries. The relationship with the volume performance shows about the same picture. Also in this case the explanatory level is, with 75 percent, high. Price performance also induces policy measures. However, it explains only half of the number of measures. In this case, given the general relationship, the United

Kingdom and Denmark are somewhat 'reluctant'. Again, in Belgium, the number of measures is larger than could be expected from the average.

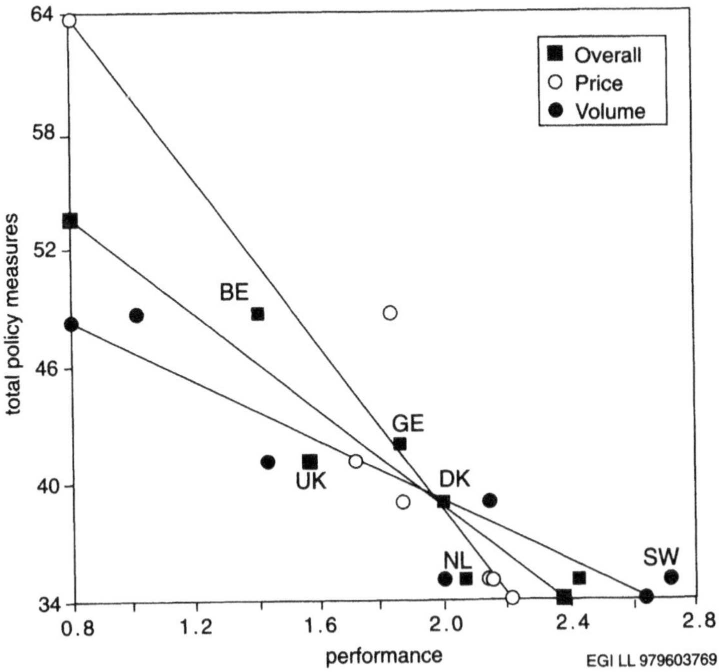

Figure 3.6 The relation between the number of measures and the average performance (lines indicate regression)

Table 3.7 furtheron shows whether the inducement of policy measures by the labour market are biased towards policies concerning young people or specific groups. The table shows that there is no real bias. Moreover the relationship between the number of policy measures and labour market performance is less clear and less significant for these specific groups. Only about 20 or 40 percent of the number of measures for these groups are explained by the market performance.

Table 3.7
The effect of various kinds of labour market performance on the number of policy measures (B's; t-values in brackets)

policies	overall	price	volume
all	.79 (-3.8)	.50 (-2.0)	.75 (-3.5)
young people	.39 (-1.6)	.31 (-1.4)	.36 (-1.5)
specific groups	.35 (-1.5)	.20 (-1.0)	.33 (-1.4)

3.4.3 Conclusion

This macro-analysis of the differences of the general institutional structure shows that countries differ substantially in the level of institutional influence on the labour market. A country like the United Kingdom has a low level of centralisation of labour market policies, a low level of corporatism, coordination of collective agreements, a low level of unionisation and corporation bound level of negotiations. In contrast, countries like Sweden score high on these aspects. There is a positive relationship between the level of institutionalism and performance of the labour market. However, the institutional differences between countries explain only to a small degree the overall economic performance of the labour market in the various countries in terms of price and volume. In this there are large differences between the countries. Although 'other factors' thus play a major role, one can notice that countries like Sweden or Denmark perform better on the volume side, while countries like the Netherlands, the United Kingdom or Belgium do better on the price side.

Important is also how institutional activities like measures for the unemployed are provoked by the situation on the labour market. The performance level explains significantly the amount of measures for preventing and curing unemployment. However, some countries like the United Kingdom and the Netherlands stay behind the general pattern, while Germany and Sweden are on the lead. The measures provoked are particularly on the volume side; price measures react less to the situation on the labour market. The measures taken are rather evenly directed at specific groups on the labour market like young people or women.

3.5 General conclusions

Regions react to general changes on the labour market. In turn, changes in specific regions induce general changes in labour demand, supply and institutions. This chapter dealt with some main changes in the European labour market which not only frames the specific position of countries and regions, but also determines their future. At the *demand side* the most important change is the quartairisation of the employment. Increasingly production is directed at services and information oriented functions. Next to an intersectoral change towards the service industry, intrasectoral changes come about. Both stress the generation and handling of information. Concurrently the meaning of knowledge changes. There is a development from traditional knowledge reflected in the *know how*, towards social and cultural capital. In this the relationship with other people is important. Trust and the giving of meaning to information is crucial for economic progress. Tacit knowledge becomes a main factor of economic success. By this the importance of the embeddedness of labour in social networks and immaterial investments increases.

Also major changes on the *supply side* restructure the labour market. Ageing will influence to a large degree the future size and structure of labour supply. Not only do the old age dependency ratios change, also a 'greying' of labour supply will appear. However, this will not influence the labour supply or unemployment rates in a mechanical sense. Behavioral developments will interfere with the relationship between ageing and labour supply. The same applies to the influence of migration on labour supply. Migrational flows like return migration, family reunification, asylum seekers and migration of highly skilled employees, change the quantity and quality of the supply of labour in regions. Migration, depending largely on policy regulations will become more important for Europe. This particularly, although at a lower absolute level, pertains to the North of the EU. Migration will, however, not be able to balance the national population decrease. Migrants do not substitute labourers in the host countries. Increasingly migration is upgrading, counteracting the stereotype of migrants working only at the less qualified end of the labour market. Moreover, changes in the participation will influence the supply of labour. In some european countries the gender structure of the labour force will change particularly due to developments of male and female participation rates. The latter is expected to rise greatly. There will be particularly an increase in some regions of Southern Europe, the less central regions of the Netherlands and the Northwestern part of Germany. Other regions like in France see their rates decreasing. In general catching-up effects are noticeable. Regions with lower levels of participation are growing more quickly. Although women become more important, men continue to dominate the labour market. More regions, however, will have a more gender balanced pattern. The regional variation of both the demographic and participation effect is substantial. Within Europe, two spatial belts of high growth due to higher participation changes and, at the same time, low negative demographic effects can be traced. On the one hand we have the Benelux/ Western Germany belt, and on the other, Mediterranean Europe.

A third important factor possibly causing changes in the labour market is the *institutional structure* of countries. Some countries, like the United Kingdom, have a low level of centralisation of labour market policies, a low level of corporatism, coordination of collective agreements, a low level of unionisation and corporation bound level of negotiations. In contrast to this, countries like Sweden score high on these aspects. Institutional differences explain only little the performance of the labour market. Still some countries perform better on the volume side, while others do better on price aspect. The performance of the labour market influences the number of measures for preventing and curing unemployment. In a comparative sense some countries stay behind, while others are on the lead. The measures are particularly volume oriented and evenly directed at specific groups on the labour market.

What do the general changes on the labour market mean for the various countries and regions of Europe? Starting from the observation that a specific evolutionary pattern in the direction of the information society can be traced, regions can react passively or actively (van der Laan & Mevissen, 1994). A *passive* attitude leads to an continuation of the existent differences where some countries and regions take the lead while others stay behind. For Europe this means that the highly developed - urban - regions of western Europe control the developments. Peripheral regions, including the countries of Eastern Europe will lag behind. Due to the intensification of the integration some may even loose. There is a chance that highly competitive products from the core of Europe will overtake their markets. Although some reallocation of the production can be expected, this will have a lower quality. While the traditional activities with less growth potential which will be located in these regions, modern high-tech manufacturing activities and other knowledge based activities will be tight to the core areas (NEI, 1993). Labour market policies in the lagging regions then can only focus at the curing of unemployment. Although this will already demand huge institutional efforts, it results in a situation of stabilizing or increasing arrears. The analysis of the influence of institutional efforts has shown that this only effects market performance to a small degree. The copying of standard models of labour market policies of the core countries and core regions will only marginally improve the labour market situation elsewhere.

Although in regions with high unemployment levels every job is a job, more promising is an *active* attitude which stresses the new economic base of regional growth. In this, besides economic capital, also social and cultural capital becomes important. This means a stress on knowledge and trust and on the production environment in stead of only the production structure. Although policies based on a technopole or bottom-up perspective could be used, particularly regional networks can play a major role in this. In this perspective not only the relations between institutions are stressed, also and at the same time, the relationships within institutions of various kinds get priority. By the creation of formal and informal relationships between, for example, companies, trade unions and governmental institutions, there is an active involvement and reshaping of the labour market. The regional network itself becomes an important competitive asset. Strategic regional cooperation makes it possible to induce competitive advantages. In contrast to a passive inventarisation of regional characteristics, action research and policies are preferred. This is not only directed at the traditional 'know how', but also at organisational and institutional knowledge in which social and cultural capital plays a major role.

The following chapters analyse more in detail the regional institutional structure of the labour markets in Europe. Within the spatial institutional perspective, described in chapter two, we change the level of general labour market processes for that of the regions themselves. How do regions, institutions and policies react to the general changes? Before we treat the regional situation of various European countries themselves, the next chapter discusses some regional differences of the labour markets within Europe.

References

Amable, B. & R. Boyer (1995), 'Europe in the world technological competition', *Structural Change and economic dynamics*, Vol. 6, pp. 167-183.

Appleyard, R.T. (1991), *International Migration Challenge for the nineties*, International Organisation for Migration: Geneva.

Bairoch, P. (1988), *Cities and economic development*, Mansell Publishing: London.

Böhning, W.R. (1991), 'Integration and immigration pressures in Western Europe', *International Labour Review*, Vol. 13a, No. 4, pp. 445-448.

Bomhoff, E.J., R. den Hartog & I. Lageweg (1996), *Instituties, waarden, normen èn groei* (mimeo), Nyfer: Breukelen.

Carter, A.P. (1996), 'Measuring the Performance of a Knowledge-Based Economy', *Employment and Growth in the Knowledge-based Economy*, OECD: Paris, pp. 61-68.

Cooke, P. & K. Morgan (1994), 'The creative milieu: a regional perspective on innovation', in Dodgson, M. & R. Rothwell (eds.), *The handbook of industrial innovation*, Edward Elgar: Aldershot, pp. 25-32.

CPB (1997), *Bevolking en arbeidsaanbod: drie scenario's tot 2020*, Centraal Planbureau en Centraal Bureau voor de Statistiek, SDU-uitgevers: Den Haag.

Cruysen, H. (1991), *Fertility in the European Community. Main trends, recent projections and two future paths*, Background papers on fertility, mortality and international migration under two long term population scenarios for the European Community: 1-30, Eurostat: Luxembourg.

Dickmann, A. & L. van der Laan (1989), 'Arbeidsmarktparticipatie in de Europese Gemeenschap', *Tijdschrift voor Arbeidsvraagstukken*, Vol.5, No. 3, pp. 66-76.

Employment (1994, 1995, 1996), *Employment in Europe, Directorate-General for employment, industrial relations and social affairs*, European Commission: Brussels.

EOT (1994, 1995, 1996), *Employment Observatory Tableau*, European Commission: Brussels.

European Commission (1996), *The demographic situation in the European Union*, Office for Official Publications of the European Communities: Luxembourg.

Eurostat (1991), *Two long term population scenarios for the European Community*,

Eurostat: Luxembourg.

Fukuyama, F. (1995), *Trust, the social virtues and the creation of prosperty*, Free Press: New York.

Gonnot, J.-P. (1995), 'Demographic changes and the pension problem: evidence from twelve countries', in Gonnot, J.-P., N. Keilman & C. Prinz (eds.), *Social Security, Household, and Family Dynamics in Ageing Societies*, Kluwer Academic Publishers: Dordrecht, pp. 47-110.

Grossman, G.M. & E. Helpman (1991), *Innovation and growth in the global economy*, MIT Press: Boston.

Hoevenberg, J. & A. de Grip (1994), *Indicators of occupational employment in the European Union.* ROA-R-1994/3E, Research centre for education and the labour market: Maastricht.

IFO (1993), *Labour force scenarios for the European Economic Area*, IFO-institute for Economic Research: Munich.

Jacobs, D. (1995), 'Gebakken lucht- waardetoevoeging in de kennismaatschappij', in Geest, L. van der & J. van Sinderen (eds.), *Kracht en zwakte van de Nederlandse economie*, Barjestek, Meeuwes & Co.: Rotterdam, pp. 119-142.

Johnson, P. & K.F. Zimmermann (1993), 'Ageing and the European labour market: public policy issues', in Johnson, P. & K.F. Zimmermann (eds.), *Labour markets in an ageing Europe*, Cambridge University Press: Cambridge, pp. 1-25.

Jong Gierveld, J. de (1993), 'Ontgroening en vergrijzing: een bevolkingsvraagstuk op mondiaal niveau', in Nimwegen, N. van & J. de Jong Gierveld (eds.), *De demografische uitdaging*, Bohn Stafleu Van Loghum: Houten.

Kaa, D.J. van de (1987), 'Europe's second demographic transition', *Population Bulletin*, Vol. 41, No. 1, Population Reference Bureau: Washington DC.

Keilman N.W. (1989), 'Het Münchhausen dilemma', *Demos*, Vol. 5, No. 2, pp. 9-11.

Kessler, D. (1993), 'Kanttekeningen IV. De vergrijzing van de bevolking een europese uitdaging', *Belgisch Tijdschrift voor sociale zekerheid*, pp. 969-983.

Keuzenkamp, H. (1996), 'Leve de hedonist', *Economisch Statistische Berichten*, Vol. 81, No. 4085, pp. 1005.

King, R. (1991), 'The social and economic geography of labour migration: from guestworkers to immigrants', in Pinder, D. (ed.), *Western Europe, challenge and change*, Belhaven Pres: London & New York, pp. 162-178.

Klamer, A., L. van der Laan & J. Prij (1997), *De illusie van de volledige werkgelegenheid*, Assen: Van Gorcum.

Knaap, B. van der & A. Odé (1994), 'Population dynamics and interregional migration in Western Europe', in Hooimeyer, P., G.A. van der Knaap, J. van Weesep & R.I. Woods (eds.), *Population dynamics in Europe: current issues in population geography*, Netherlands Geographical Studies, Royal Netherlands Geographical Society: Utrecht, pp. 38-52.

Laan, L. van der & J.W.M. Mevissen (1994), 'Ondernemingen en regionale arbeidsmarkten', in Laan, L. van der & M. Vermeulen (red.), *Onderwijs en arbeids-*

markt in de regio, Eburon: Delft.

Laan, L. van der (1995), 'Participation and regional disparities in the European Union, *Tijdschrift voor Economische en Sociale Geografie*, Vol. 86, No. 1, pp. 88-92.

Laan, L. van der & G.A. van der Knaap (1995), 'Labour supply changes within Europe: a regional sensitivity analysis', in Knaap, B. van der & R. LeHeron (eds.), *Human resources and industrial spaces*, John Wiley & Sons: Chichester, pp. 83-101.

Laan, L. van der (1996), 'A review of regional demand and supply forecasting in the European Union', *Environment & Planning A*, Vol. 28, pp. 2105-2123.

Lesthaeghe, R. & G. Verleye (1992), 'De tweede demografische transitie; conceptuele basis en recente evolutie', in Nimwegen, N. van, de Jong-Gierveld, J., (eds.), *De demografische uitdaging*: Vol. 15, No. 49. Bohn Stafleu Van Loghum: Houten.

Long, J.F. (1991), 'Relative Effects of Fertility, Mortality and Immigration on Projected Age Structure', in Lutz, W. (ed.), *Future Demographic Trends in Europe and North America*, IIASA: Laxenburg. pp. 503-522.

Machlup, F. (1984), *Knowledge; Its Creation, Distribution, and Economic Significance*, vol 3: The Economics of Information and Human Capital, Princeton University Press.

Maddison, A. (1995), 'Monitoring the world economy 1820-1992', *Development Centre*, OECD: Paris.

McCloskey, D.N. & A. Klamer (1995), 'One Quarter of GDP is Persuasion', *American Economic Review*, Vol. 85, No. 2, pp. 191-195.

Minne, B., V.P. Herzberg & J. Reijnders (1996), 'Immateriële investeringen', *Economisch Statistische Berichten*, Vol. 31, No. 1, pp. 106-107.

NEI (1993), *New location factors for mobile investment in Europe*, Commission of the European Communities: Brussels.

New, J.P. de & K.F. Zimmermann (1994), 'Native Wage impacts of foreign labor: a random effects panel analysis', *Journal of Population Economics*, Vol. 7, pp. 177-192.

Odé, A.W.M. (1996), *Migrant workers in the Dutch labour market today*, Tinbergen Institute Research Series 126, Thesis Publishers: Amsterdam.

Odé, A.W.M., G.A. van der Knaap & P. Nijsse (1993), *Internationale migratie en arbeidsmarkt in de Europese Gemeenschap en Nederland*. Erasmus University: Rotterdam, EGI-Onderzoekspublicatie 10.

OECD (1987), *Intangible investments. An essay at international comparison*. Organisation for Economic Co-operation and Development: Paris.

OECD (1993), *Structural Changes and Employment of Foreigners in some OECD Countries*, Organisation for Economic Co-operation and Development: Paris.

OECD (1995), *The labour market and older workers*. Social Policy Studies 17, Organisation for Economic Co-operation and Development, André-Pascal: Paris.

OECD (1996[a]), *Ageing in OECD countries; a critical policy challenge*, Social Policy

Studies no. 2, Organisation for Economic Co-operation and Development: Paris.
OECD (1996[b]), *Ageing populations, pension systems and government budgets: simulations for 20 OECD countries*. Economics department working papers, 168, Organisation for Economic Co-operation and Development: Paris.
Peyrefitte, A. (1995), *La société de confiance. Essai sur les origines et la nature du développement*, Éditions Odile Jacob: Paris.
Polyani, M. (1958), *The Tacit Dimension*, Garden City, N.Y. Doubleday, Anchor.
Postman, N. (1986), *Amusing ourselves to death: public discourse in the age of show business*, Penguin: New York.
Putnam, R.D. (1993), *Making democracy work, civic traditions in modern Italy*, Princeton University Press: Princeton, New Yersey.
Reich, Robert (1991), *The Work of nations, preparing ourselves for 21-st century capitalism* 1991.
Rein, M. & K. Jacobs (1992), 'Employment trends of older workers in Western Countries' in Heuvel, W. van den, R. Illsley, A. Jamieson & C. Knipscheer (eds.), *Opportunities and challenges in an ageing society*, Verhandelingen, Nieuwe Reeks 151, KNAW: Amsterdam, pp. 12-25.
Report (1994), *Regional population and labour force scenarios for the European Union; part II: Two long term labour force scenarios*, Netherlands Economic Institute/ Economic Geography Institute of the Erasmus University, Rotterdam.
Richter, J. (1992), 'Economic aspects of ageing: review of the literature', in Stolnitz, G.J. (ed.), *Demographic causes and economic consequences of population ageing*, United Nations Economic Commission for Europe/ United Nations Population Fund, Economic Studies 3, United Nations: New York, pp. 171-186.
Schmid, G., J. O'Reilly & K. Schömann (eds.) (1996), *International handbook of labour market policy and evaluation*, Edward Elgar: Cheltenham.
Steinmann, G. (1991), 'Immigration as a Remedy for the Birth Dearth: The Case of West Germany', in Lutz, W. (ed.), *Future Demographic Trends in Europe and North America*, IIASA: Laxenburg, pp. 337-357.
United Nations (1994), *Ageing and the family*. Proceedings of the United Nations international conference on ageing populations in the context of the family, United Nations: New York.
Verzorgingsstaat (1996), *De Nederlandse verzorgingsstaat in internationaal en economisch perspectief*, SDU Uitgevers: Den Haag.
Vries, B. de & R.A.J. Dur (1996), *Verzilverend vergrijzen*, OCFEB research memorandum 9608, Erasmus University: Rotterdam.
Winkelmann, R. & K.F. Zimmermann (1993), 'Ageing, migration and labour mobility', in Johnson, P. & K.F. Zimmermann (eds.), *Labour markets in an ageing Europe*, CUP: Cambridge, pp. 255-283.
Woodall, P. (1996), 'The Hitchhiker's guide to cybernomics', *The Economist*, September 28.
Zimmermann, K.F. (1996), 'European migration: push and pull', *International Regional Science Review*, Vol. 19, pp. 95-128.

4 Regional and institutional changes in European labour markets

Santos M. Ruesga & Carlos Resa-Nestares

4.1 Introduction

European labour markets have changed deeply (Morgan, 1996). Starting point was, the division between two absolutely different production systems in the East and West since the Second World War which, in fact, were in total confrontation. Many transformations in the East have been a by-product of the collapse of the former planned economies and the subsequent transition towards capitalism. These large changes have been surrounded by substantial obstacles and have generated deep changes in these countries' productive and social structures. In the labour market there was a transformation from a extremely controlled, regulated and structured labour system with a state taking upon itself to act as the major and almost unique employer in the whole economy to a system where, yet stuttering and unequal according to different countries and regions, private initiative must start playing a major role as employer.

Changes in West European countries, at a different degree, have not been less meaningful (Ruesga & Resa-Nestares, 1997). As discussed in chapter one, during recent decades, a discourse favouring the Welfare State has been partly abandoned and policies trying to provide greater hegemony for market forces have been carried out. In the context of these overall policies, the labour market and institutions related to it, have been a major target. Annex I of this chapter shows how this general change in policy was elaborated in the institutional system of various countries of Western Europe. The main institutions, based on fordist production, have passed through a deep crisis and an update in which new forms of employment have emerged. In this line of reforms of the regulation framework, institutions at a regional and even local level have acquired a prominent role as agents of active labour policies and, to a lesser extent, of managing labour regulation instruments.

In this chapter, some main dimensions of regional labour market dynamics, to be analysed in the following parts of the book, are traced. Annexes I and II give some factual data on which some of the main findings of this chapter are based. In turn, these annexes are based on some of the chapters in the second and third part of the book.

4.2 Labour markets in Western Europe: convergence and divergence

Table 4.1
Activity, employment and unemployment rates and per capita GDP in European Union countries

	Activity rate[1]			Employment rate[2]			Unemployment[3]			Per capita GDP		
	1980	1988	1993	1980	1988	1993	1980	1988	1993	1980	1988	1993
Austria	68.4	66.8	59.6	67.3	64.5	66.6	1.6	3.6	4.2	102	112	112
Belgium	64.3	61.8	63.4	59.3	55.4	55.7	7.7	10.3	12.2	105	102	113
Germany	66.7	68.9	69.4	64.5	63.7	63.3	3.3	7.6	8.8	116	114	108
Denmark	80.3	83.8	82.6	75.1	78.3	73.9	6.5	6.5	10.7	104	107	112
Finland	76.4	76.9	73.9	72.9	73.5	60.8	4.6	4.5	17.7	110	111	91
France	68.1	65.3	66.7	63.8	58.8	59.0	6.3	10.0	11.5	112	110	110
Greece	55.9	59.5	58.6	54.3	54.9	53.0	2.8	7.7	9.7	62	58	63
Ireland	62.3	61.0	62.3	57.8	50.8	52.4	7.3	6.7	15.9	59	63	81
Italy	60.8	60.9	58.9	56.2	53.7	52.6	7.5	11.8	10.8	101	102	102
Luxemburg	64.4	68.1	72.6	63.9	67.1	71.7	n.a.	2.0	2.3	114	136	160
Netherlands	57.7	65.2	67.4	54.3	59.2	63.2	6.0	9.2	6.2	106	99	103
Portugal	73.9	70.7	71.7	65.0	66.7	67.6	7.7	5.7	5.7	59	61	69
Spain	56.9	58.4	58.6	50.5	47.2	45.5	11.2	19.1	22.4	70	72	78
Sweden	81.0	82.3	77.6	79.4	81.0	71.2	2.0	1.6	8.2	103	120	98
U. Kingdom	74.4	75.5	74.7	70.2	69.2	67.4	5.6	8.3	10.2	94	102	99

[1] Total labour force as a percentage of population from 15 to 64 years-old
[2] Total employed as a percentage of population from 15 to 64 years-old
[3] Unemployed as a percentage of total labour force

Source: OECD, (1995) *Statistics in retrospective* and own elaboration

As table 4.1 shows, there exist strong national differences in the performance of the labour market in Western Europe. No matter which variable for labour analysis one chooses, large disparities between the European Union countries can be observed. Activity rates, occupation and unemployment rates and GDP per capita clearly show this divergence.

These disparities in the labour market, evident at the national level, are also strongly present in the regional sphere. For example, activity rates varies by regions from eighty to forty per cent within the European Union. Dispersion in any other variable are not lower. The remark of Fisher & Nijkamp (1987) still holds: 'It is clear that structural transformations in recent fifteen years have triggered a lot of problems for the efficient functioning of regional labour markets. Among the most important ones seem to be remarkable the persistent existence of spatial asymmetries (specially lacking of opportunities for women and young people in rural and peripheral markets)'. Besides large regional variations, it is also possible to identify a growing dualisation on the European labour market. This is reinforced by the gradual deregulation (Marsden, 1995).

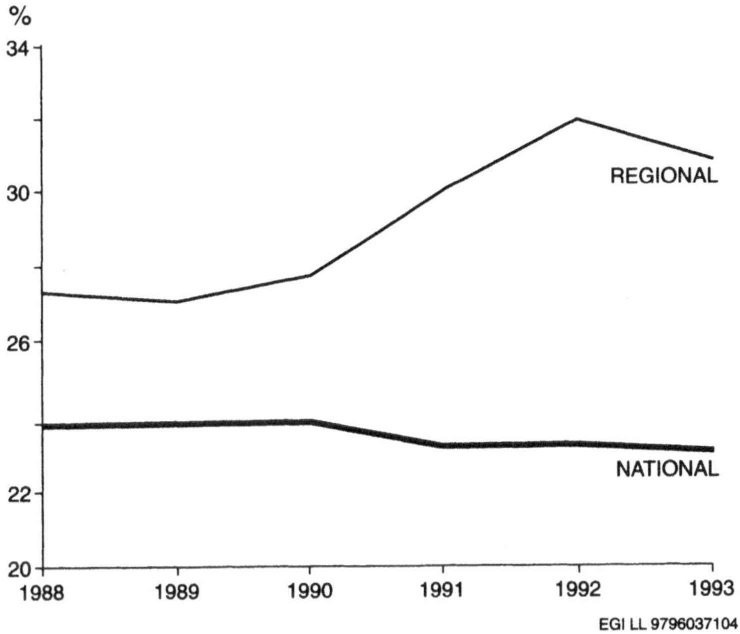

Figure 4.1 Per capita GDP dispersion index

Within the European Union no large changes in the dispersion of economic development have been observed. The changes in the national dispersion of per capita GDP for the period 1988-93 are shown in Figure 4.1. Only small variations have happened. If the reference period is enlarged, the conclusion remains the same. Figure 4.1 also shows that fluctuations are larger at the regional level. An anticyclical component in development of the dispersion index may be observed, as more developed regions suffer more during recession. Nevertheless, long time analysis shows no large changes in relative positions.

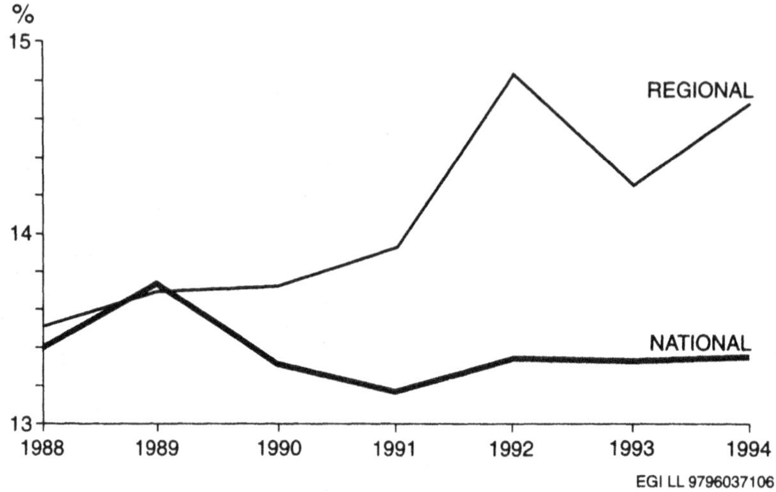

Figure 4.2 Employment rate dispersion index

In relation to employment and unemployment some larger changes in relative position between countries may be observed (see figures 4.2 and 4.3). The deterioration in labour market equilibrium has been more intense in the Nordic countries (Sweden and Finland), in the South (specially Spain), as well as Ireland and France, during the 1980s and 1990s. Other countries show a more moderate behaviour, although there are some differences among them. The Netherlands, Luxembourg and, to a lesser extent, Portugal showed, at least until 1994, an upward trend in unemployment rates. Lower increases are found in other countries since 1980. Because of this, countries like France, the Netherlands and the United Kingdom have implemented intensive adjustment wage mechanisms (Bowles & Boyer, 1992).

Some general patterns exist in Western Europe. On the one hand, it can be observed that reservation salary is relatively high in the poorest regions. This may explain higher long-run unemployment rates there. On the other hand, the less demand, the lower the level of job search, especially among women. Finally, it seems to be evident that in regions where employment levels are lower, the so-called *social capital* has a stronger influence in determining wages. When job search is difficult, social networks tend to play a more important role in setting up wage and employment opportunities. In addition, while unemployment in the poorest regions seems to be more sensitive to business cycle fluctuations, macro-economic and labour movements at aggregate level are more autonomous with respect to changes in economic growth in the rich regions.

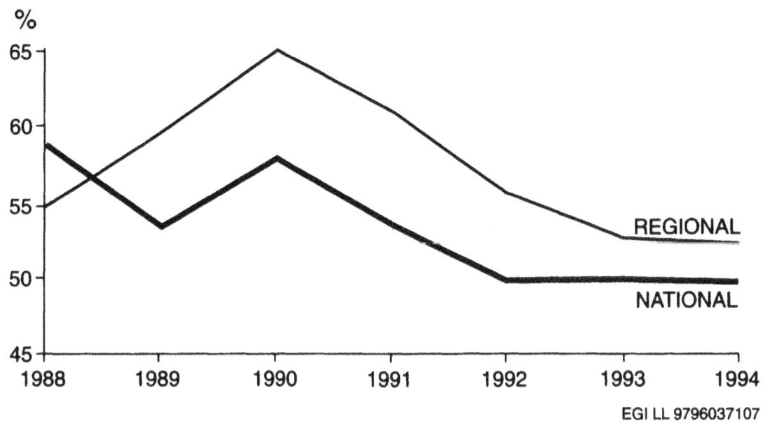

Figure 4.3 Unemployment national dispersion index

Causes for the divergences, both regionally and nationally, are many and are concentrated around a set of institutional variations all over Western Europe. Under any consideration, regions with the best behaviour in employment terms are located in a spatial centre composed by Denmark, the Benelux, Northern France, Italy and the western part of Germany. Elsewhere differentials are higher. For all labour variables concentric lines of long-standing different activity and unemployment rates are observed. Differentials cannot be found only at the inter-regional but also at the intra-regional level. 'If not managed properly, market mechanism will simply accentuate polarisation towards a control area (a *Central European metropolis*) that already exists in the European Union' (Bruneta & Tronti, 1995, p. 152). The economic and sectoral structure in peripheral regions, a low orientation to export, a greater presence of the public sector and strong productive hindrances, even socially produced, have been factors explaining significantly higher unemployment rates (Ruesga & Álvarez, 1992).

Although sometimes, like in the Netherlands, a direct correlation between the size of the active population and employment can be found, it is impossible to obtain a conclusive relation between the activity rate, employment and unemployment. There even is sometimes a negative correlation between education and unemployment. Likewise, quite in contrast to the classic economic theory, there is a negative correlation between wages and unemployment.

After the Second World War, as discussed more in detail in chapter three, some important migratory movements were observed within Western Europe. This migrations mitigated unemployment for some regions and avoided impoverishment to a large extent. In net-receiver regions migrations permitted a significant control of industrial wages. In more recent decades, growing regional disequilibria have not triggered an increase in migration, rather the opposite. There is no sign that this trend to lower migration is reversed in the foreseeable future (Ruesga, 1989). In some countries a theoretically paradoxical movement from regions with relatively higher wages and lower unemployment rates to regions with lower wages and higher unemployment rates can even be observed. However, intra-regional migration showed a constant increase during recent years and, particularly was the result of desurbanisation. As a consequence, the number of people with a job in another city, or even region, increased. In this, improvements in public and private transport played an important role.

Evidence shows that migration is more likely for both the better educated and younger individuals. In general, that those with a better education show a larger tendency to migrate may contravene conventional wisdom, as regional wage dispersion is lower for qualified jobs. The educational level seems to be less relevant for women. One explanation for this is the family burden. At any case, in recent decades migration has demonstrated almost no correlation to wage levels and a very low one, but positive, in respect to unemployment for most countries. Therefore, the role of migration as balancing regional disparities has been very limited. If any, its role has been that of constricting development in the home regions at an international and interregional level because of the 'brain drain'.

Labour market policies in Western Europe have shown some common transformations. Annex I shows these changes more detailed for the various European countries. Firstly, there has been a transition of employment policy instruments from the supply side to the demand side, particularly at the local level. Secondly, the approach has changed from specific instruments to general mediation tasks. Thirdly, correction and adjustment policies have been largely abandoned and policies oriented to indirect employment generation was given priority. Fourthly, greater support was given to job creation projects (active labour market policies) and lower emphasis on unemployment protection. And fifth, there has been an increasing regionalisation of labour market instruments. Result of this was a widespread growth in regional employment agreements among governments, trade unions and employers associations.

Regional policies also showed deep transformations within the European Union (see Annex II). The most essential change has been the growing importance of the European Union as a promotor of regional development. From 1950s to 1970s, regional policies were fundamentally aimed at achieving regional equity. As a consequence, industrialisation policies were implemented in less developed regions through public and private investments, particular in infrastructure, and special fiscal policies. During the two last decades, however, an essential change in approach came about. With the help of arguments coming from classic economics, policies attempting to favour endogenous development in poorest regions and to improve efficiency of each region's potentialities in a increasingly borderless environment have been implemented (Garofoli, 1978). Measures were aimed at adjusting supply and demand plus active employment policies and laws promoting wage bargaining at regional levels. Moreover, income transfers to families have been restricted as they produce larger interregional dependence and were not in line with regional efficiency.

In spite of all efforts, made by politicians at every level of government, to eliminate regional diversity in terms of per capita income and employment within European Union, results have been very limited. Significant regional differences stayed and persisted. In this sense, research has shown great failures in communitary policies in respect to social cohesion, in particular adjustment policies given birth in the Maastricht (European Union) Treaty oriented to achieve a nominal convergence (Bruneta & Tronti, 1995).

4.3 Labour markets in Eastern Europe

Table 4.2 shows large differences in unemployment between the countries of central and eastern Europe. Rates have been particular high in Albania and Poland. In contrast to this, the Czech Republic and the countries of the former Soviet Union, have a much lower level. The table also shows that particularly after the 'fall of the wall' in 1990-1991, unemployment levels rose sharply (more detailed information on each country can be found in Annex I). Variation in these general unemployment rates according to regions, economic sectors and demographic segments are substantial. Moreover, after the collapse of real socialism, under which government jobs were arbitrarily allocated from a completely centralised plan, regional divergences have deepened. Inter-regional differences in unemployment, however, was quite irregular. In recent years a slow-down of regional diversion has appeared in some countries.

Regions suffering more acutely from the transformations have been those which were strongly dependent on a set of large heavy firms or those where agriculture played an important role. In contrast to these regions, large and medium sized cities, presenting a more diversified productive structure, a better infrastructure and better facilities for exporting goods and services, have received an overwhelming majority of foreign investment. Accordingly, those regions frequently did better. Their unemployment rate is significatively lower than the national average. Also some new industrial regions concentrating on expanding sectors and those at the border of the European Union did better.

Next to the different starting point of regions, causes of these labour disequilibria could be found in a diversified development of labour supply. This has affected particularly those regions specialised in goods or services whose output reduction have been larger. Moreover, both professional and territorial mobility stayed at very low levels. If any, there have been movements to foreign countries, in particular to the European Union or to the United States and from rural regions to the cities. However, this latter migration was, in some cases, the consequence of the official regularisation of the illegal workers previously resident in large cities. Regional policies have played an almost marginal role in the extraordinary efforts generated by the transformation from an socialist economy to a market one (see Appendix II). Regional perspectives have been almost ignored in policies and proposed movements towards regionalisation have been limited to a minimum. In fact, there has been a paradoxical movement to even greater centralisation of many general policies. Labour policies has not been kept out of that overall trend.

Table 4.2
Unemployment rates in Central and Eastern European countries, 1990-1994

	1990	1991	1992	1993	1994
Albania	9.5	9.1	24.2	19.5	17.0
Poland	3.5	9.7	13.3	15.7	16.9
Slovakia	1.5	11.8	10.4	14.4	14.4
Slovenia	4.7	8.2	11.5	14.4	14.3
Bulgaria	1.7	11.1	15.3	16.4	13.3
Hungaria	1.7	8.5	12.3	12.1	11.0
Rumania	n.a.	3.0	8.4	10.2	10.8
Latvia	0.0	0.1	2.3	5.8	6.2
Lithuania	0.0	0.3	1.0	4.4	3.8
Czech Republic	0.8	4.2	2.6	3.5	3.1
Estonia	0.0	0.1	1.7	1.9	2.3
Russian Federation	0.0	0.1	0.8	1.1	2.0
Belarus	n.a.	n.a.	0.5	1.4	1.8
Ukraine	0.0	0.0	0.3	0.4	0.4

Source: ILO (1995)

4.4 Conclusion

In characterising the general performance of regional labour markets in Europe during recent periods, some main conclusions can be drawn. Firstly, national labour markets in Western Europe show the common feature of high regulation but with important disparities in their dynamics and potentiality for adjustment and equilibrium. The same applies to Eastern Europe countries, although differences are generated, in this case, by higher or lower development levels in the transition to the market economy. Secondly, large regional disparities are dominant within countries and in Europe in general. Regional unemployment rates range from under five per cent to more than thirty per cent. Such disparities seem to be quite stable, while regional ranking in unemployment levels show some changes. Thirdly, in European

Union countries a trend to implement more active labour policies at the cost of passive ones can be observed. Actions on productive sectors with stagnant or recessive demand have been gradually abandoned. In Eastern European countries, trends in labour policy are not so homogenous, and they are not very well defined as the building of a new institutional framework is not yet consolidated. Last, labour policies oriented to demand side seem to be more effective when they are implemented at the local and/or regional level. Such experiences are almost unprecedented in Eastern Europe, where political and economic decentralisation is hardly yet applied.

References

Bowles, S. & R. Boyer (1992), 'Wages, aggregate demand and employment in an open economy: a theoretical and empirical investigation', in Epstein, G. & G. Herbert (eds.), *Macroeconomic Policy after the Conservative Era: Studies in Investment Saving a Finance*, Oxford University Press: Oxford.

Bruneta, R. & L. Tronti (1995), 'Italy: the social consequences of Economic and Monetary Union', *Labour*, special issue, pp. 149-202.

Fischer, M.M. & P. Nijkamp (1987), *Regional Labour Market Policies. A Cross-National Overview*, mimeo.

Garofoli, G. (1978), 'Decentramento produttivo, mercato del lavoro e localizzaciones industriale', in Several Authors, *Ristrutturazioni industriale e territorio*, Franco Angeli, Milano.

Hall, P. (1992), 'The movement from Keynesian to monetarism', in Steinmo, S. et al. (eds.): *Structuring Policies: Historical Institutionalism in Comparative Analysis*, University of Cambridge Press: Cambridge.

ILO (1995), International Labour Office: *Employment in the World*, International Labour Office: Geneva.

Marsden, D. (1995), 'Deregulation or co-operation: the future of Europe's labour market', *Labour*, special issue, pp. 67-92.

Morgan, J. (1996), 'Structural Changes in European Labour Markets', *National Institute Economic Review*, February.

Ruesga, S.M. (1989), 'El trabajo: los trabajadores se mueve por Europa', in Ruesga, S.M. (coord.), *1993. España ante el Mercado Único*, Editorial Pirámide: Madrid.

Ruesga, S.M. & C. Álvarez (1992), 'Desequilibrios espaciales en la distribución del desempleo y política de empleo', in Ruesga, S.M. (coord.), *Economía y Trabajo*, Editorial Pirámide: Madrid, pp. 147-79.

Ruesga, S.M. & C. Resa-Nestares (1997), 'Regulación-desregulación de los mercados laborales: el debate eficiencia versus equidad', in Tezanos, J.F., J.M. Montero and J.A. Díaz (eds.), *Tendencias de Futuro en la Sociedad Española*, Editorial Sistema: Madrid.

Annex I — A characterisation of the labour market, the institutional framework and labour policies of the countries of Europe

COUNTRY	LABOUR MARKET
Bulgaria	• Starting point: very centralised system, public ownership, inefficient productive structure, irrational employment structure, unilateral trade orientation, high public and external debt. • Agriculture and industrial crisis from 1990 to 1996. • Economic depression. • employment reduction, high rates of unemployment and reduction of labour demand. • Demand increases of skilled workers. • Demand increases in private sector. • Discouraged people leave working population. • High unemployment: 38% in agriculture sector and 40% in some regions. • Decrease in unemployment rate in workers with studies and increase in women. • Decrease of 52% in the real wages average.
Czech Republic	• 1990s: low inflation and macroeconomic equilibrium. • The transition beginning: decrease in labour demand few dismissals and absorption for private sector (specially skilled workers). • Very good labour performance: quick privatisation, private sector growth, growth in services, low unit labour costs, active employment policies, unemployment insurance restrictions, liberalisation and economic growth.
Italy	• Low women participation. In the 80s their incorporation absorbed the employment creation. • Few part time employment. • Delocalization: using small firms rather than big ones
The Netherlands	• High activity rate. • Low women participation (specially part-time). • High part-time employment participation. • Different unemployment definitions. • Unemployment higher in women, foreigners without studies and young people.
Rumania	• Sharp productive fall. • Fall in employment, specially in industry, transport and increase in agriculture and trade. • Higher unemployment rate due to the incorporation of working population: 1992: 8.4% - 1994: 10.9%. • Great participation of long time unemployment. • Low unemployment rates are in areas with higher activity. • Decrease in investment opportunities. • Increase in agriculture employment and in opportunities in rural areas.
Slovakia	• Transition to market economy. • Prices liberalisation. • Stabilisation. • Secede from Czech Republic. • unemployment growth: 10.2 %.

- stabilisation.
- unemployment growth.
- decrease of 13.1%.
- Important costs of overlapping which it worsens some questions.

Spain

- High unemployment rates, larger than in the European Union.
- Low activity rate.
- Reduction of Unit Labour Cost during last decade.
- Increasing duality between employed and unemployed since 1980s.
- Higher women incorporation to labour markets, but its activity rate is still very low.
- Significant presence of long-run unemployment.
- Low unionisation rate.

Sweden

- High rate of participation mainly women.
- Low unemployment until 90s.
- Low mobility until mid 80s and high degree of stability.
- In last years the employment have sharply deteriorated.

United Kingdom

- 80s: bad performance in old professional education scheme.
- General education and a successful professional education are closely bound together. Thus, it is important to promote general education.
- 70s: it was observed that the inflexibility constraints not only macroeconomic performance but also competitiveness.
- Long time unemployment do not press down on wages.

INSTITUTIONAL FRAMEWORK

Bulgaria

- Abolition of old institutions.

New institutions

- Unemployment register.
- Unemployment insurance, managed by private firms.
- Subsidised education and guided by the state.
- State intervention in labour market.
- Higher flexibility in contracts, mainly in private sector.
- Higher and personal wages in private sector.
- Until 1989 there is only salaries modifications by age, not for employ or skill.
- Trade union and manager associations with low representation and bad performance.
- From 1991 started bargaining mainly for minimum wages.
- In 1990 started a tripartite co-operation between trades union, public and private managers and government.
- Bargaining in different levels: national, sectoral, regional and local. Different structure bargaining.
- Bargaining system reached crisis point due to the lack of bargaining culture, disequilibrium between parts and bad performance agents.
- Restrictive policies in public sector and skilled employees went to the private sector.

Regulation steps:

- It starts the reforms, public sector dismissals and official unemployment register.

- Economic reform becomes more acute.
- Stop in reforms and public sector dismissals.
- To retrieve the reform.

Czech Republic

- Important expansion of private sector.
- Decrease in eight points of the participation rate.
- Low power of regional politics institutions.
- The collective bargaining concentrates in consulting institutions that is composed by trades union, managers, and administrative departments which coordinate the national employment policy in neighbourhood.
- Trade union influence has been positive (in finding solutions in the bargaining process) or negative (to press for advantage positions).

Italy

- Cassa de Integrazione Guadeni: institution charged of premature retirement management in big firms.
- Labour market high regulated during the 60s and 70s due to worker mobilisations.
- Regulation protects mainly men with stable employment in big firms.
- 80s: increasing deregulation.
- It maintains high labour costs which are not sensitive to labour market conditions.

The Netherlands

- Regulation in collective and wage bargaining.
- Bargaining at sectoral level, at firm level and sometime at national level.
- Decentralised bargaining model.
- Regulation of minimum wage, labour conditions and hours.
- More regional and nationals agreements between government, trades union and employers.

Rumania

- Creation of unemployment subsidy.
- Change to "full employment" policy to a market policy focus on effective employment.
- Regulation about retirement, pensions, labour working hours and more than one employment.
- Agriculture reform which returns land.

Slovakia

- **Labour Ministry functions:**
- To propose and implement labour policy.
- To look after the distribution of labour forces.
- To value the labour market position.
- To control the Employment Services Administration.
- Responsibility of local offices.
- To analyse and give information about labour markets.
- Workers supply consulting.
- Education.
- Support for employment creation.
- To pay unemployment subsidy.
- To pay and organise support for handicapped people.
- Employers association created in 1991.
- Trade unions with higher bargaining independence and active participation in the creation of Workers Statute.
- Decrease in unionisation as a result of politics changes.

- Employment Fund created in 1993, it is a tripartite institution controlled by employers, workers and the state with regional branches. The objective: to collect funds and finance unemployment insurance and active market policies paid by managers and workers contributions.
- In the Social and Economic Agreement created in 1991, are represented by government, trades union and managers for advising the government and parliament.
- Main economic policy: to adjust to the transition shock and avoid inflationary processes.
- Generalised reliance to the multiplier effect of infrastructure policies.

Government organisms:

- Labour Ministry, Social and Family Affairs: 1990.
- Employment Fund: created in 1993.
- Employment Services Administration: 1994.

Spain

- From mid 20th Century to 1975 a strongly interventionist regulation model which suppressed effective bargaining between employers and employees.
- In 1980, labour relations are normalised (democratised) by recognising worker rights and collective bargaining.
- From 1994 regulating framework is oriented to increase flexibility and mobility. Model has been very flexible in respect to contract forms.
- Collective bargaining is still in power acting on wages, productivity, mobility and so on.

Sweden

- Trade unions with high influential in wages determination. Increasing unionisation in white and blue-collars.
- Labour market very institutionalised: centralised bargaining and too much legislation.
- Regional and sectoral egalitarian salary distribution.
- Guarantee of employment for all the life.
- Changes for labour market liberalisation.

United Kingdom

- Semiautonomous and local institutions with professional education programs guided to the market and represented by managers (2/3) and trades unions (1/3).
- 80s: legislation which make difficult to join a union and the strikes. Objective: to adjust locally the wages without national bargaining.
- Sharp fall in joining to unions (from 55% in 1979 to 31% in 1993)
- Increase wage dispersion.
- Flexibility in wages related to local conditions.
- Flexible wages is an important way for labour adjustments.

LABOUR POLICY

Bulgaria

- Contradictory institutional trends: decentralisation of the functions and effective centralisation.
- Creation of a national labour market.
- Economic aid to unemployed.
- Information and analysis system.
- Stabilisation measures.
- Objectives: to assure life level to unemployed.

- Mediation between supply and demand.
- Until 1996 there is not clear employment policies.
- Active policies: professional education, aid to private initiatives and promote the contracts for specific groups.

Czech Republic

- **Active policies aims**:
- Assessment of labour market performance.
- Informative aim at neighbourhood level.
- Subsidised and public employment.
- Reclassifications of workers.
- To help to handicapped people.
- Unemployment registration and vacancies.
- Intermediate activities.
- To favour the increase of professional flexibility.
- To promote premature retirement.
- Economic aid to young people.
- Active employment policies are carried out at neighbourhood levels but 62 % of total funds are for unemployment subsidies.

Italy

- Generous help to unemployed. There is not an active policy.
- 80s and 90s: young professional contracts due to difficulties for come in to the labour market.
- Incentives for coming up informal economy.
- 1980s: deregulation increases benefits but not employment creation.

The Netherlands

- Objective: to create employment.
- Wage control policies.
- Changes in employment policy.
- From the supply to the demand side.
- From specific instruments to general intercession processes.
- To preventive policies.
- Regionalisation of instruments.
- Higher support to employment projects.
- Regional and national tripartite agreements.

Rumania

- It generates additional amounts of unemployment.

Slovakia

- Labour policy objective: to reduce the inflation and recession impact.
- Weak links between labour and macroeconomic policies.
- Decreasing amount of money spent to labour policies mainly active ones.
- Special benefits for handicapped people.

Spain

- Institutional reforms and social bargaining policy with reduction of government intervention on labour regulation.
- Active policies oriented to reduce labour costs.
- Fix-time contracts have been favoured.
- Promotion of contracts to discriminated collectives.
- Formation and recycling of labour force.
- Passive policies aimed at relating unemployment benefit to employment promotion programmes.
- In last twenty years, no significant result of government policies.

Sweden	• Objective: full employment. • Stabilisation policies (sectoral, demographic and also distributive). • Labour market policies specifics for forestall regions specially the poorest ones.
United Kingdom	• 1980s: policies guide to wages flexibility, labour mobility and to adjust education to local conditions. • 80s: measures for facilitating the mobility not only territorial but also sectoral.

Annex II Regional disparities and regional policies of the countries of Europe

COUNTRY — **REGIONAL DISPARITIES**

Bulgaria

- Higher growth in employment more in industrial centres, in cities and regions with big firms than in agriculture regions and villages.
- Low mobility due to insufficient education and formation, lack of housing and other infrastructures and lack of money for assuming the change.
- The unemployment tends to converge regionally.

Czech Republic

- Strong sectoral and unemployment differences between regions. It is lesser in cities and in border regions with European Union, and it is bigger between young people and non-skilled workers.
- More private sector in Prague and in the west.

Italy

- Differences exist before the Second World War.
- differences became more noticeable. Growth limited to north-west.
- 1963-80s: growth less limited and more unequal, specialisation (Terza Italy).
- In the south of Italy:
- 50-60s: emigration to the north.
- 70s: minimum differences.
- 80s: increasing differences inside south, better if less Mafia and less public firms, the growing disequilibria do no provoke emigration.
- Vicious circle due to infrastructure lack, low quality of social capital and a waste of human resources.
- It decreases of people seeking after a job (mainly in women), the students tend to public employment and the reserve wage is relatively high.
- Construction as a motor of growth in some regions.

The Netherlands

- There are no essential differences between per capita income: it is worse in north than east.

Unemployment dispersion:

- High and persistent differences.
- decrease in dispersion.
- From 1981: increase.
- Higher increase in employment growth and labour force in regions close to cities.
- Strong correlation between increases in employment and labour force.
- Null correlation between education and employment, unemployment (a bit negative) and working population.

Rumania

- Disequilibria in labour market in all country.
- Unemployment goes from 4.1% to 24.7%, low in the west and south east and higher in east and north-east, with an average area in south and south-east.
- The unemployment is lower as more long time unemployment.
- There is no correlation between the percentage of people seeking after an employment for the first time and the unemployment and long time unemployment.
- The lower unemployment rates are in areas where economic activity is concentrated in powerful autonomous authorities.
- The regions more developed are those in which population is more educated.

	• Few professional and territorial mobility of labour force. • Destination of migrations: • From areas with high unemployment to areas with more opportunities in employment and better social conditions and with social security for unemployed. • From industrial areas to their birth places, as a result of the agrarian reform. • From the countryside to the city.
Slovakia	• Important regional differences in social potential, infrastructures, territorial possibilities of development and modernisation dynamic. A lot of regions dependent of old industries. • The socialist model registers creation of heavy and intensive industries in energy and raw materials in rural regions. • Higher unemployment in agriculture regions or with concentration of heavy industry and less in big cities (more diversified and with better infrastructure).
Spain	• Higher regional disparities in the European Union, as well as Italy. • Per capita income in richest region more than double the one of the richest region. • In 1994 difference in unemployment rate between higher and lower region is 19,8 percentage points. • Relative dispersion increases in regional unemployment rates.
United Kingdom	• 70s-80s: increase in disparity and unemployment. • 8% in Northern England, Scotland and Northern Ireland, 4% in the Southern England. • 90s: north, it maintains unemployment, it decreases the level of labour force desertions; south, it increases the unemployment, the labour supply and the employment level. • Causes of these tendencies: factors referred to financial markets and of housing. • Futures: a possible revival of differences. • Intraregional disparities in unemployment rates. • High correlation between regions with high unemployment and poor levels of education. • Geographical mobility is very low in the 80s. Migration from cities to countryside. • There is correlation between unemployment differences and migration, but not with wages differences. • Negative relation between wages and unemployment at local/regional level. 80s: wages are more flexible and they respond to local conditions

COUNTRY	**REGIONAL POLICIES**
Bulgaria	• no regional policies.
Czech Republic	• There is not regional institutions of labour market, only territorial ones in national centres. Prague concentrates all the economic activity, the investment, the employment and the power centres. • The government has not the purpose of carrying out regional policy. • This regional policy when it is carried out is characterised for being ex-post policy, not preventive, with support measures to the small firms, support to

infrastructures development and active employment policies.

Italy

- Public polices to the south.
- 50s-70s: infrastructures, public firms intensive in capital, subsidies to firms and investment and especial inspections.
- 80s: end of public policies due to the difficulty of attracting investment and it starts the income transfer to families.
- end of income transfer policies.
- Different territorial impact due to the medium and small firms growth and in some areas in order to avoid rigidities (Third Italy).

The Netherlands

- 70s: equity objective.
- 80s: efficiency objective.
- Increasing regionalisation of labour market instruments.
- More regional and national agreements between government, trades union and employers.

Rumania

- Trend to decentralised politics questions.
- Deficiencies in non intervention policies in regional questions.
- Objective of regional labour policy: improvement of situation in areas with difficulties.
- Conflicts between general regional policy objectives and labour market.

Slovakia

- no regional policies

Spain

- Due to large inequality, internal redistribution mechanisms are very important, particularly through Social Security system.
- Passive labour possible is an exclusively national competence until now.
- Development of regional policies depends to a great extent on degree of financial autonomy obtained by regions. Regions with lower revenues practices policies highly dependent on European Union structural funds.
- Qualification policies, rural employment plans, funds to contracts and private employment firms regulation are practised at the regional level.

United Kingdom

- Important division north-south in wages, education, economic growth and labour institutions.
- Important disparities north-south related to labour institutions.
- 60s-70s: it is obligatory to direct a part of the investments (internal or external) to the north and subsidies to the north investment.
- 80s: flexibility in wages, labour mobility and adjustment in education and wages to local conditions. Objective: to facilitate endogenous development.

Part Two
Western Europe

5 Regional labour markets and institutions in the United Kingdom

David Armstrong & David H. Blackaby[1]

5.1 Introduction

During the 1970s the labour market in the United Kingdom was increasingly characterised as being inflexible and, in particular, operating in a variety of ways which constrained macroeconomic performance and international competitiveness. For example, the rate of unionisation was high for a capitalist country, the strike record was poor, nominal wage inflation was high even with rising unemployment and standards of education and training were judged to be lower than in many other industrialised countries. Coupled with this, there was an increasing perception of worsening regional economic disparities, with southern regions generally experiencing significantly higher economic growth and lower unemployment than the northern regions. Throughout most of the post-war period, the government's response to such disparities was to try to divert investment into economically depressed areas from more prosperous regions and from overseas. During the 1980s, however, government became increasingly convinced that one of the most important ways in which both regional and national economic performance could be improved was to reduce labour market rigidities by, for example, increasing wage flexibility and labour mobility and improving the responsiveness of the training sector to local economic conditions. This had led to major changes in a number of key labour market institutions, particularly those relating to pay bargaining and the provision of vocational training. Indeed, there is a sense in which the reform of labour market institutions became one of the main government responses to the existence of spatial economic disparities in the UK.

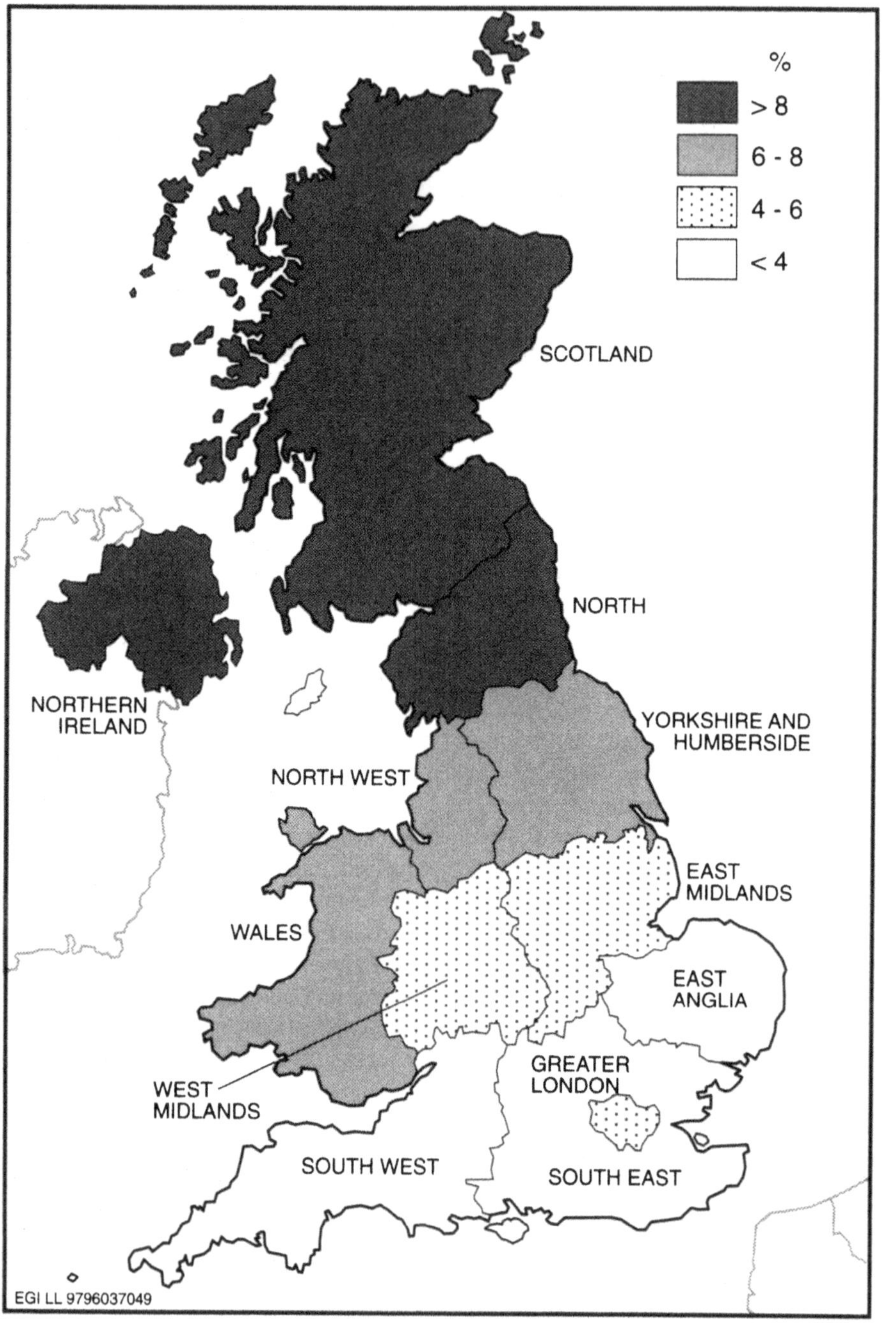

Figure 5.1 **Unemployment in the standard planning regions of the United Kingdom (April 1995)**

At the outset it is important to note that the scope of this chapter is broad. The main purpose being to highlight some of the broad themes which have been pertinent in the UK, particularly since the beginning of the 1990s. The outline of the chapter is as follows: Section 5.2 provides an overview of labour market disparities in the UK during the past 20 years focusing, firstly, on the so-called 'North-South Divide', secondly, on the regional labour market convergence which has taken place since the late 1980s and, thirdly, on differences in unemployment between small local areas. Section 5.3 provides a brief discussion of the policy context, highlighting the main reforms to regional policy and labour market policy which were made during the 1980s. Section 5.4 discusses some broad issues relating to three of the main areas which have been the focus of the Government's labour market reforms, namely vocational training provision, labour mobility and pay bargaining. Section 5.5 reviews the broad themes and conclusions.

5.2 Regional disparities in unemployment in the United Kingdom

It has traditionally been the case that economic prosperity in the northern and so-called 'peripheral' regions of the UK has tended to be significantly lower than in the southern regions. For example, in 1990 unemployment in the North of England, Scotland and Northern Ireland was more than 8 per cent, whereas in the southern regions of East Anglia, the South West and the Rest of the South East it was less than 4 per cent (Figure 5.1). Between the mid-1970s and the mid-1980s, the differences in unemployment between the northern and southern regions increased as aggregate unemployment rose steeply (Figure 5.2), and a lively academic debate ensued, which dominated much of UK regional economic analysis, about the existence and persistence of this so-called 'North-South divide', (see, for example, Gudgin & Schofield, 1993; Blackaby & Manning, 1990).

During the most recent recession, which was more broadly based than that of the early 1980s, the difference in official unemployment between northern and southern regions in Britain practically disappeared. Between 1990 and 1993, for example, unemployment increased by more than 150 per cent in most of the southern counties, whereas in the 'peripheral' regions of Scotland and Northern Ireland it increased by less than 50 per cent (Figure 5.3). Although the apparent convergence in unemployment followed a time of major institutional reform in the labour market, discussed below, there is widespread agreement that it can be attributed mainly to factors relating to the financial and housing markets (see Armstrong, 1994 for a discussion of the main factors at work).

It is too early to judge with certainty, however, whether the most recent recession has altered permanently the geography of regional differences in unemployment.

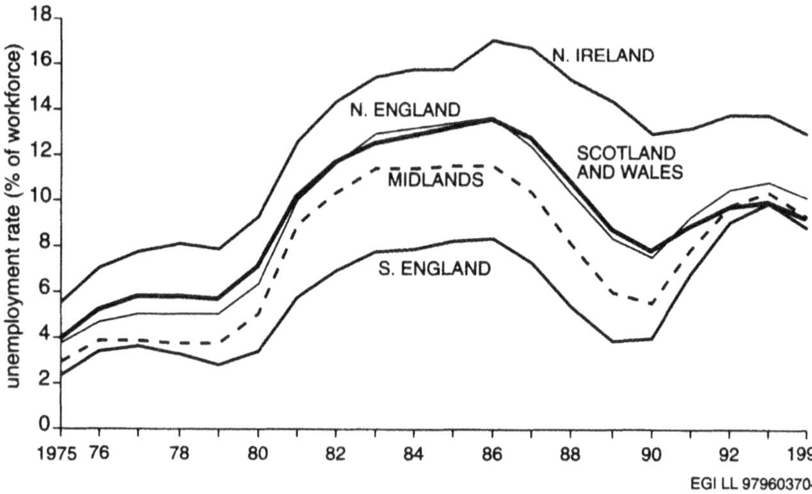

Figure 5.2 Unemployment in the standard planning regions of the United Kingdom (1975-1994)

On balance, most recent studies have suggested that there will be some re-emergence of traditional disparities. For example Wilkinson (1992) and Martin (1993) argue that since the economic prospects in the second half of the 1990s are healthier in the South-East than in any other region, then the effect of the most recession on regional unemployment differentials is unlikely to be permanent. Similarly Swales and Gudgin (1996) suggest that traditional disparities are likely to re-emerge, although they are unlikely to be of the same magnitude as they were during the 1980s.

It is important to note that most studies which have examined regional convergence in unemployment rates have done so using the official 'claimant count' measure of unemployment. According to this measure, unemployment has been falling in all regions since January 1993, although many of those leaving the claimant count register are becoming economically inactive. It is therefore likely that a large part of the recent falls in unemployment are explained by the tougher administration of benefits for the unemployed, a trend which is likely to increase with the introduction of the Job Seeker' Allowance.

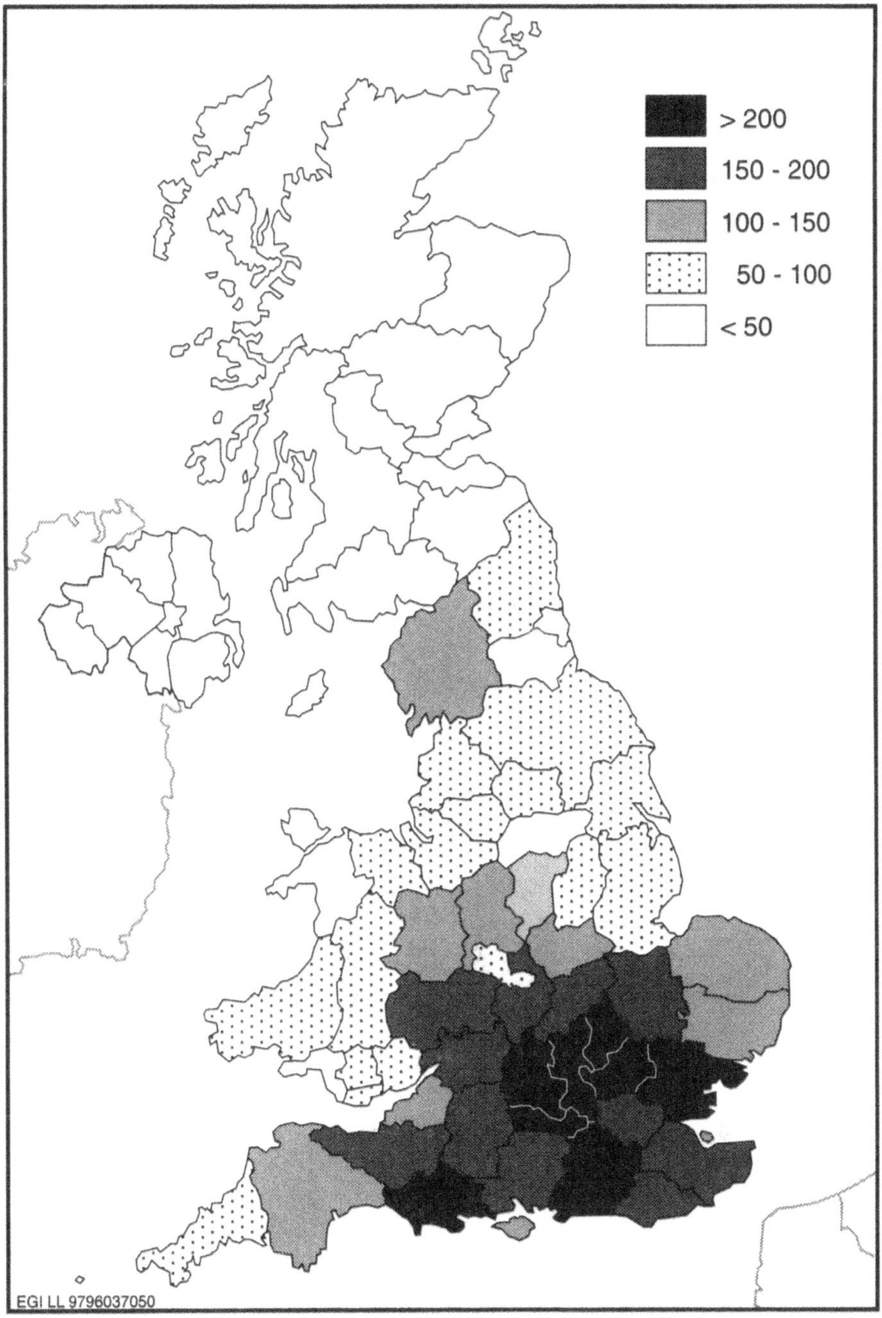

Figure 5.3 **Unemployment change in the counties of the United Kingdom (1990-1993)**

One implication of this is that unemployment may no longer be providing a true indication of the degree of slack in the labour market. For example Gregg and Wadsworth (1994) and Beatty and Fothergill (1996) argue that much of the convergence in regional unemployment rates can be accounted for mainly by differential responses of labour force participation. Unemployment rose in prosperous regions because labour supply has grown and employment changed little, whereas in depressed regions it rose less because employment falls have been partially offset by labour force withdrawals.

Variations in unemployment *within* regions have always been an important spatial phenomenon in the UK, although they have begun to receive more attention recently, mainly because of the convergence which has taken place at the broader regional level, discussed above. In April 1995, for example, unemployment in the South West region was nearly 8 per cent which was the second lowest of all regions; in the southern coastal county of Cornwall, however, unemployment was nearly 10 per cent, whereas in the more central county of Wiltshire it was about half this at around 5 per cent (Figure 5.4). Likewise, in the North West region, unemployment in the small, heavily urbanised county of Merseyside was one of the highest at around 13 per cent, whereas in Cheshire to its south and Lancashire to its north, it was much lower at around 7 per cent.

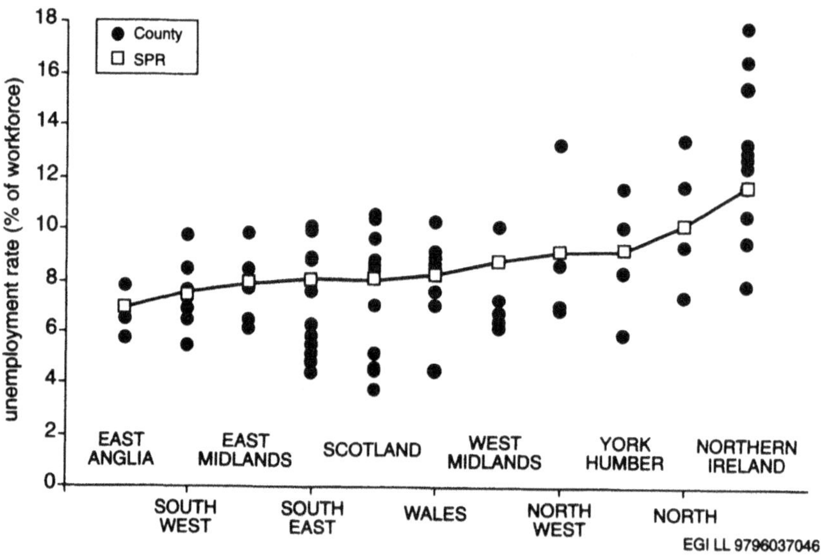

Figure 5.4 Unemployment in the counties and standard planning regions (SPR) of the United Kingdom (April 1995)

Such examples are illustrative of an important point, namely that the dispersion in unemployment rates tends to be higher, the finer is the level of geographical disaggregation. The figures in table 5.1 also show that, although there has been an overall trend towards convergence in regional unemployment rates, this trend has been much less marked for smaller local areas such as counties and Travel-To-Work-Areas (TTWA's).[2] The overall distribution of unemployment shows much less evidence now of the traditional North-South divide. Rather it is the case that within most broad areas of the UK, smaller local areas of relatively high and relatively low unemployment co-exist.

Table 5.1
The dispersion of unemployment rates for the regions, countries and Travel-To-Work Areas of Great Britain

		1984	1986	1989	1993	1995
Regions (n=11)	Mean	11.7	12.3	6.7	10.5	8.4
	Standard Deviation	2.8	2.9	2.5	1.0	1.2
	Range	8.3	8.8	7.6	3.5	4.1
Countries (n=67)	Mean	11.1	11.6	6.4	9.8	7.8
	Standard Deviation	3.4	3.7	3.0	2.3	2.1
	Range	15.8	16.2	12.6	11.3	9.7
TTWA's (n=332)	Mean	11.0	11.6	6.3	9.7	7.8
	Standard Deviation	3.9	4.1	3.2	2.8	2.6
	Range	19.4	21.1	18.8	15.6	14.4

Note: The mean is calculated as the simple arithmetic mean across regions, counties and TTWA's. Figures relate to claimant unemployment in April of each year and they are not seasonally adjusted.

Source: National On-line Manpower Information System

5.3 The policy context

5.3.1 Labour market policy and the regional problem

Throughout the 1960s and the 1970s economic development in the less prosperous northern and peripheral regions of the UK was understood as being primarily dependent on the flow of inward investment from more prosperous central and southern regions and from overseas. The main emphasis of regional policy, therefore, was on measures such as location controls and investment subsidies which attempted to divert investment into economically deprived areas. For example, if manufacturing firms wanted to build new factories over a certain size in the South East or the West Midlands they had to apply for Industrial Development Certificates (IDC's). During the 1960s, when the use of location controls was at its peak, approximately one fifth of all applications for IDC's were refused. In terms of capital investment, the main subsidy during the 1960s and 1970s was the Regional Development Grant, under which all new investment in plant, machinery and buildings in the designated assisted areas was eligible to receive an automatic subsidy of up to 22 per cent of the total outlay.

In the 1980s there was a distinct shift in thinking about the nature of the regional problem and how it might be most effectively addressed by policy. This led to a shift in policy away from the traditional aim of diverting investment and towards a range of measures aimed at facilitating indigenous regional development. For example, in the 1983 government White Paper on regional industrial policy it was argued that, in contrast to earlier policies, the main aim of regional policy in the 1980s would be to 'encourage the development of indigenous potential within the Assisted Areas with the long term objective of self-generating growth in these areas' (DTI, 1983, p. 4). This emphasis on facilitating indigenous development has generally received widespread support amongst academics in the United Kingdom and elsewhere, although there remains an on-going debate about how it can best be brought about (e.g. MacKay, 1993).

One of the most important implications of the change in thinking about the regional problem was that measures aimed at enhancing labour market performance began to assume a much more prominent position in the overall package of measures used by government to promote regional development. For example, in the 1983 government White Paper, which set out the details of a range of new regional policy instruments, it was made clear at the outset that:

> *Imbalances between areas in employment opportunities should in principle be corrected by the natural adjustment of labour markets. In the first place, this should be through lower wages and unit costs than comparable work commands elsewhere. Wage flexibility, ..., would increase the attractiveness to industry of areas with high unemployment.' (DTI, 1983, pp. 3)*

Likewise, in the 1988 White Paper which described a broad range of labour market policies, it was argued that the existing institutional framework for the provision of vocational training was not responsive enough to the needs of small local areas, and that this was hindering the process of indigenous development:

> *A key requirement is that the delivery of training, and its links with small firms and enterprise, must relate closely to the circumstances of each local area. The best way of achieving economic improvement differs from area to area. By tailoring approaches to their own circumstances, localities are more likely to find solutions that work.' (ED, 1988, pp. 39)*

During the 1980s, therefore, it was increasingly accepted by government that enhanced labour market performance was the key to facilitating indigenous regional development and, by implication, reducing regional and local economic disparities. Indeed, there is a definite sense in which the subsequent labour market reforms were seen as one of the key responses by government to the existence and persistence of regional and local economic disparities.

5.3.2 Unions and pay bargaining

In 1984 Nigel Lawson, then Chancellor of the Exchequer, stated that evidence suggests that in Britain a 1 per cent change in the average level of real earnings will in time make a difference of between 0.5 percent and 1 percent to the level of employment - between 150,000 and 200,000 jobs (Hansard, 30 October 1984). Since workers had 'priced' themselves out of jobs, and trade unions played a major role in this,[3] legislation was consequently introduced making it difficult for trade unions to retain and recruit members. Trade unions' bargaining power was reduced by for example impairing their capacity to call strikes and effectively prohibiting the closed shop. In the past, wage increases gained by one group of employees would encourage others to seek a similar wage rise, irrespective of local labour market conditions, and negotiations emphasised 'comparability', 'fairness' and 'established relativities'. Wage inflationary pressures were also transformed across regions through national collective bargaining, even though local labour market conditions may not have justified such an increase (Brown, 1993).

Attempts were made to reduce such 'institutional transmission' of wage increases by repealing aspects of the Employment Protection Act of 1975 and by rescinding the Fair Wages Resolution of 1946. Deregulation also took the form of reducing the influence of and eventually abolishing Wage Councils which had previously enjoyed the statutory ability to set terms and conditions and minimum rates of pay for some three million employees working in some of the poorest paid industries. Encouraged by earlier statutory and government recognition, trade union membership in Britain peaked at 13.3 million in 1979 (covering 55 percent of the potential work-force). Since then, partly as a result of the legislation outlined above, trade union membership has fallen every year. Figures from the 1993 Labour Force Survey suggest that union membership stood at 8.7 million (a density of 31 percent), the lowest figure since 1946 and 4.6 million below the peak.

Wales is the region with the highest level of trade union membership, being 11 percentage points above the national average and 18 percentage points above that found in the South East (Table 5.2). Union membership is always above the average in the less prosperous Northern regions and at or below average in the Southern more prosperous regions. When union membership is measured separately for the public and private sectors all the Northern regions have union membership levels above the national average.

Wage levels in the public sector have been shown to be largely determined by national agreements and, as a result, union membership may have a smaller pay-off. Similar broad patterns are revealed in Table 5.2 with respect to union recognition. Generally speaking the figures suggest that the levels of trade union membership and recognition do not appear to provide an explanation for the relatively low wage levels found in Northern regions. Other things being equal wage levels, it would seem, should be higher.

Table 5.2
Percentage of employees who are Union members or work in workplaces in which Unions are recognised in 1993

	Trade Union Membership			Workplace with recognised union		
Regions	*All employees*	*Private Sector*	*Public Sector*	*All employees*	*Private Sector*	*Public Sector*
South East	27	17	53	45	29	83
East Anglia	28	20	48	46	34	78
South West	28	19	53	45	32	81
West Midlands	34	25	62	51	39	88
East Midlands	34	24	61	49	37	85
Yorks/Humb	37	25	67	51	38	87
North West	40	29	69	54	41	89
North	44	31	71	58	43	91
Scotland	39	24	67	53	37	85
Wales	45	32	70	58	42	88
Great Britain	**34**	**23**	**61**	**51**	**35**	**85**

Note: Figures are taken from the 1993 Labour Force Survey

Source: Department of Employment Gazette December (1994)

5.3.3 Labour mobility and vocational training

Measures to ensure that labour is sufficiently mobile, such as company relocation schemes, have long been supported by government in the UK. During the 1980s, however, further steps were taken to enhance labour mobility. It could be argued, for example, that the above-mentioned reforms to pay bargaining institutions would facilitate mobility by ensuring that wages were responsive to local labour market conditions and so provided both the correct signals to workers about labour shortages and appropriate incentives to motivate migration. Similarly, following the 1986 Social Security Act, employees were given the freedom to opt out of company pension plans and take out personal pensions from a range of providers. Such personal pension plans were intended, amongst other things, to enhance labour mobility by ensuring that employees would not be penalised for career changes.

Throughout the 1980s it was becoming increasingly apparent that the quantity and quality of vocational training in Britain was lower than in many other industrialised countries. For example, such findings were made in of a number of studies conducted during the 1980s by the National Institute of Economic and Social Research (NIESR), based on a series of studies of matched plants in Britain and other Continental countries (e.g. Steedman, Mason & Wagner, 1991) and information from other administrative sources on education and training (Green & Steedman, 1993). During the 1980s, therefore, there was a growing consensus in the UK that many of the institutional arrangements for the provision of education and training in Britain were not producing the desired outputs and that some major changes were necessary if the UK economy was to begin to compete at all levels with the leading industrialised nations.

The Government's main response was announced in 1988 and involved establishing a network of Training and Enterprise Councils (TEC's) throughout England and Wales and Local Enterprise Companies (LEC's) in Scotland.[4] The TEC's and LEC's were set up as independent companies limited by guarantee and funded by central government according to local economic conditions and population size. They are run by boards of directors which comprise two-thirds local business leaders and one third representatives from trade unions, education and voluntary bodies and other organisations involved in local economic development. Their main functions are 'to plan and deliver training and to promote and support the development of small businesses and self-employment within their areas' (ED, 1988, p. 40). In addition, the TEC's and LEC's are expected to use their influence to attract additional funding for training from the private sector and to act as a local forum for discussing more general issues relating to local economic development. The TEC's and LEC's are local bodies. As such it was argued by government that they would be better placed to ensure that existing programs could be adapted more effectively to suit local economic conditions than could be done under the more inflexible arrangements which previously existed at national and industry level. As with the reforms relating to pay bargaining arrangements, outlined above, this move towards a greater degree of localisation in training provision can again be seen within the overall context of efforts to stimulate indigenous economic development.

5.4 Labour market adjustments in the United Kingdom

5.4.1 Training

The emergence of the TEC's has stimulated a large inter-disciplinary literature which has investigated, from a variety of angles, how effective they have been, and are likely to be, at redressing the apparent 'skills gap' which exists between Britain and many other industrialised countries (see, for example, Bennett, 1994; Coffield, 1992; Peck, 1993 and Ploszajska, 1994). It is beyond the scope of this chapter to review or discuss this literature in detail. Instead this discussion focuses on a particular issue which has been raised in the literature but which, it seems, has yet to be fully developed. This relates to the general research finding that there is an important relationship between initial standards of general education and the ability and/or willingness to improve standards of vocational training. For example, the fourth cohort of the YCS shows that the probability of young people with no school-based 'GCSE' qualifications gaining a vocational qualification by the age of 18-19 is significantly lower than for those who have at least one such qualification; in particular, only 36 per cent of those with no GCSE's had gained a vocational qualification by the age of 18-19, compared to 62 per cent for those with GCSE's at grades D - G (Park, 1994). These links between general education and vocational training are important because they suggest that over the longer term one of the more important ways in which standards of vocational training can be improved is to raise standards of general education, particularly at the schooling stage. This is particularly important for the UK because standards of general education amongst young people have tended to be much lower than in many other industrialised countries (see, for example, Armstrong, 1996).

There is an important regional dimension to such arguments because, generally speaking, high unemployment regions in the UK tend to have relatively poor standards of general education amongst young people and *vice versa*. For example, in the relatively low unemployment area of the Rest of the South East, 9.6 per cent of 16 year old males have no graded results, and this compares to 14.1 per cent in the high unemployment urban area of Greater London (Table 5.3).

Similarly, more than one half of 17 - 19 year olds in the Rest of the South East have 2 or more A Levels, compared to less than one-fifth of 17-19 year olds in Greater London. Simple correlation coefficients between ILO unemployment rates and a range of general education outcomes amongst young people confirm that, particularly within England and Wales, this has been the case at least since the beginning of the 1980s (Table 5.4).

Table 5.3
Unemployment rates and educational outcomes amongst young people in the standard planning regions of Great Britain: 1992/93

	ILO unempl. rate	Per cent of 16 year olds with no graded results		Per cent of 16 year olds with 5+ GCSE's		Per cent of 17-19 year olds with 2+ A-Levels	
		M	F	M	F	M	F
North	11.2	12.7	9.3	32.4	40.8	12.6	14.8
Yorkshire & Humberside	9.8	12.4	9.4	31.6	40.1	14.3	15.5
East Midlands	9	9.6	6.9	34.9	43.4	18.3	20
East Anglia	8.3	8.7	6.5	38	49.7	18.8	22.4
South West	9.2	8.3	6	40.3	50.5	20.6	23.6
West Midlands	11.6	11.6	8.1	32.8	41.9	15.4	16.5
North West	10.9	12.8	9.5	36	44.1	13.1	13.5
Greater London	13.2	14.1	11.3	33.4	41.8	17.6	18.7
Rest of South East	8.5	9.6	6.7	41.3	50.4	50.5	52.8
Wales	9.5	13.5	8.5	31.8	41.5	26	33.5
Scotland	10.1	6.4	4.6	42.8	54.1	24.1	28.6
Mean	10.12	10.88	7.89	35.94	45.3	21.03	23.63
Maximum	12.2	14.1	11.3	42.8	54.1	50.5	52.8
Minimum	8.3	6.4	4.6	31.6	40.1	12.6	13.5
Range	4.9	7.7	6.7	11.2	14	37.9	39.3
Standard Deviation	1.41	2.37	1.85	3.87	4.68	10.17	10.91
Coefficient of Variation	13.93	21.78	23.45	10.77	10.33	48.36	46.17

Note: For Northern Ireland, separate figures for males and females are not available and so have not been included.
M = male; F = female

Source: Regional Trends

Table 5.4
Correlation coefficients between regional unemployment rates and educational outcomes

		1981/82	1985/86	1988/89	1992/93
% of School Leavers with no graded results	All Regions	0.65	0.67	0.78	0.60
	Excluding Scotland and Northern Ireland	0.63	0.60	0.65	0.75
% of School Leavers with at least 5+ GCSE's	All Regions	-0.20	0.04	-0.11	-0.46
	Excluding Scotland and Northern Ireland	-0.83	-0.59	-0.71	-0.55
% of School Leavers with 3+ A-Levels	All Regions	-0.35	0.05	-0.61	-0.48
	Excluding Scotland and Northern Ireland	-0.64	-0.50	-0.75	-0.48

Note: Figures relate to males. Data upon which calculations are based were taken from Regional Trends, various issues

These findings are important because they suggest that many of the local areas which are most economically disadvantaged and, therefore, which are in most need of improvements in training standards, are unlikely to achieve such improvements because they have low standards of general education amongst school leavers. This problem has been highlighted in a number of case studies of the activities of the TEC's. For example, in a qualitative research project carried out by the Policy Studies Institute for South Thames TEC in London, one aspect of inner city policy which was highlighted as deserving attention by TEC's was the need for training to be broad based and include training in pre-vocational skills such as, for example, literacy and numeracy. This was attributed to the fact that in many inner city areas, high early school leaving rates and low levels of qualifications amongst school leavers are one part of a complex web of socio-economic disadvantage which includes poor employment and training opportunities and high levels of crime and unemployment (Christie & Rolfe, 1992). Likewise, in a qualitative study of the five TEC's in the north east of England it has been argued that since this region has traditionally had one of the lowest proportion of young people staying-on in post-compulsory full-time education, this would act as a significant constraint on the north eastern TEC's in terms of their ability to meet the national education and training targets (Coffield, 1992).

The regional pattern of standards of general education, outlined above, has become particularly important since the emergence of the TEC's because their funding arrangements are partly output-related, i.e. funding for TEC's is positively related to the extent to which they meet specified targets such as the proportion of trainees reaching certain levels of attainment and the proportion of trainees who enter employment upon completion of training. Generally, this has led to fears that a process of 'creaming' might take place, whereby, in order to attract adequate funding, TEC's organise training provision around the needs of the most able young people, who are most likely to succeed in training and meet the specified targets. Therefore, it has been argued that the market-based approach to training provision might lead to a process of 'institutionalised marginalisation' in which, mainly because of financial constraints, the training needs of less able young people are largely ignored (Peck, 1993). When the regional profile of educational outcomes is taken into account, such fears become all the more pertinent. In particular, it has been shown above that in high unemployment regions, which are in most need ofimprovements in training standards, there is generally a higher proportion of less well qualified young people who will be more difficult and more expensive to train, and less likely to enter employment subsequently. This suggests that at a regional level, linking funding to training outputs is likely to impose significant financial constraints on TEC's operating in high unemployment areas. Thus there is a danger that over the longer-term this aspect of the funding arrangements may exacerbate spatial economic disparities.

5.4.2 Labour mobility

For most UK regions, net migration flows are relatively small at around 0.5 per cent of the population, and for this reason the importance of migration for regional labour markets is often overlooked. However, although annual net flows are small, it is important to recognise that their effect is cumulative and so, in the longer term, their overall impact can be quite large. International comparisons suggest that the level of labour mobility in the UK is around the average for a number of OECD countries (Beatson, 1995).

Standard human capital models of migration predict that migration flows will tend to be from low wage/high unemployment areas into high wage/low unemployment areas. At a very broad level, regional migration in the UK has followed such a pattern, e.g. the northern regions of England, Scotland and Northern Ireland, which have traditionally had relatively high unemployment and low wages, have tended to experience net outward migration, whereas their more prosperous southern counterparts such as East Anglia and the South East have experienced net in-migration (Figure 5.5). Net in-migration to the South West of England is particularly large mainly because it contains a large number of popular retirement locations. Time-series econometric studies of regional migration in the UK generally provide broad support for the conventional relationships between regional unemployment differentials and net migration, although the evidence on the effects of wage differentials is less convincing (Pissarides & Wadsworth, 1989; Muellbauer & Murphy, 1991).

It is important to note that, in addition to overall migration flows from northern to southern regions, there have also been large movements of people from urban into rural areas. For example, although the South East region as a whole experienced net inward migration during the period 1981-91 of nearly 100,000 people, disaggregated data show that there were large net movements out of Greater London and large net movements into the Rest of the South East. Similarly, between 1991 and 1994 Greater London and the other metropolitan counties in England and Wales experienced net outward migration of nearly 100,000 people whereas the non-metropolitan counties experienced net inward migration of 264,000 (OPCS, 1995).

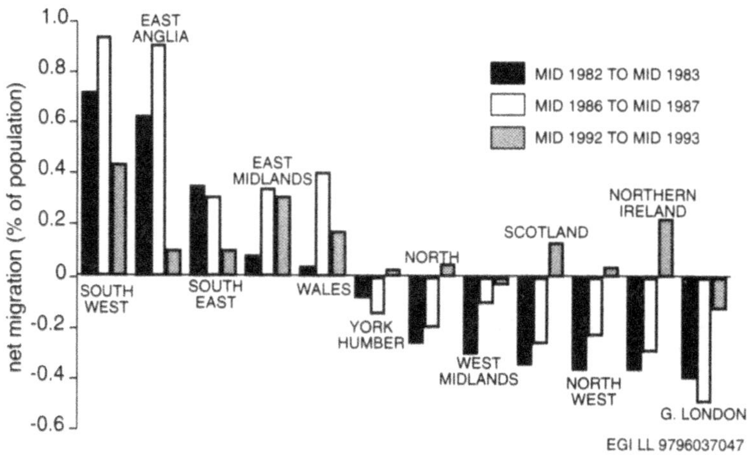

Figure 5.5 Net regional migration in the United Kingdom

The conventional wisdom is that regional migration during the 1980s kept regional economic disparities in the UK lower than they might otherwise have been. The equilibrating role of migration is limited, however, mainly because it tends to take place mostly within the non-manual sector amongst well educated members of the workforce (Hughes & McCormick, 1994; Pissarides & Wadsworth, 1989; McCormick, 1991). This has two main implications: firstly, Hughes and McCormick (1994) have shown that regional unemployment differentials in the UK are important for manual workers but virtually negligible for non-manual workers. Therefore, purely in terms of labour market accounting, the sectors of the economy in which labour mobility is most required are least likely to benefit from it. Secondly, given the links between education and economic development, the net out-migration of well qualified young people from high unemployment areas, is likely to act as a constraint over the longer-term on the development potential of economically depressed areas.

5.4.3 Wage flexibility

As outlined above, one of the main aims underlying the reforms relating to pay bargaining which were introduced during the 1980s was to enhance the flexibility of wages and, in particular, to ensure that they became more responsive to local economic conditions. A common way of evaluating whether or not wages have become more flexible during the 1980s, has been to calculate standard measures of dispersion for regional earnings (e.g. Walsh & Brown, 1991; Beatson, 1995). *A priori*, we would expect that the institutional reforms described above would have resulted in increased dispersion as wages were able to adjust more readily to local economic conditions and, in particular, to local unemployment rates. When standard measures of dispersion are calculated they suggest that, on the whole, there was some increase in regional wage dispersion during the 1980s (Figure 5.6). However, it is important to make a number of points about this basic finding. Firstly, it is the case that the dispersion of earnings tends to be greater for non-manual workers than for manual workers. This is important because, as discussed above, unemployment rates and regional unemployment differentials are significantly higher for manual workers, and so it is within the manual sector that increased wage flexibility is most needed. Secondly, however, it is important to note that a large part of both the overall increase in dispersion and the difference between manuals and non-manuals can be accounted for by the relatively faster growth of non-manual earnings in the South East of England. The expansion of the late 1980s had a much stronger impact on the South East than on any other region of the UK, and one manifestation of this was that the growth of wages in the South East began to outstrip that in the rest of the country.

Standard measures of dispersion such as those presented in Figure 5.6, can only provide a partial analysis of the extent of regional wage flexibility. In particular, even in the absence of an increase in overall dispersion, the ordering of many regions with respect to earnings levels has changed substantially during the 1980s. For example, in 1979 nominal wages amongst manual males in the North of England were higher than in any other region in the UK, whereas by 1982 they were the third highest; similar slippages in ranking took place in Yorkshire and Humberside and the West Midlands. Such a relative decline in the wages of manual workers in these regions is consistent with the large increases in unemployment which took place in the North over this period, largely as a result of industrial restructuring. Similarly, during the most recent recession in which the southern regions were most affected, many of the northern regions regained their position, and some of the southern regions, particularly East Anglia, lost ground. Such changes in the ordering of the regions is consistent with the changes in demand which have taken place in the regions, and they are not something which will be necessarily picked up by measures of overall wage dispersion, such as those illustrated in Figure 5.6.

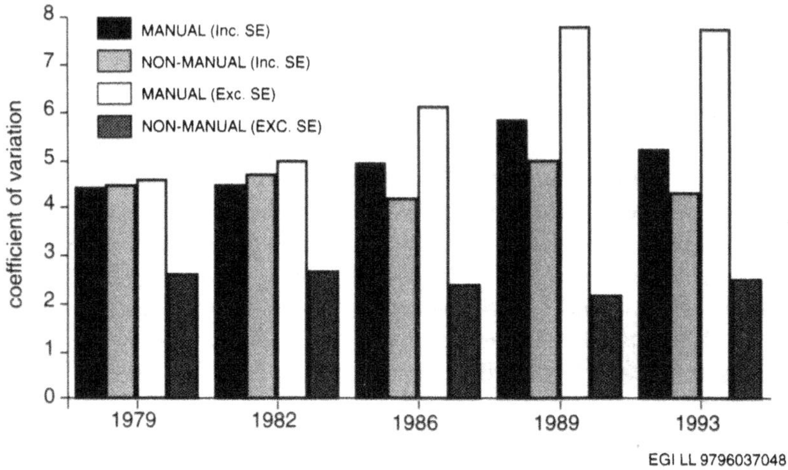

Figure 5.6 Regional earnings dispersion in the United Kingdom - males

The most satisfactory way of evaluating the responsiveness of wages to local economic conditions is to estimate regional Mincer earnings functions. A number of econometric studies have found that earnings are negatively related to unemployment at a regional or local level after controlling for a range of other related factors (e.g. Blackaby & Manning, 1990, 1992; Jackman & Savouri, 1991; Blanchflower & Oswald, 1993; Blackaby & Murphy, 1995). It is difficult for studies such as these, based on aggregate time-series or micro data, to adequately assess whether or not wages have become more responsive in recent years to local economic conditions. Nevertheless, two studies (Jackman & Savouri, 1991; Blanchflower & Oswald, 1993) have attempted to do this and they find some, albeit tentative, evidence of increased responsiveness. For example, Blanchflower and Oswald used micro data from the General Household Survey for the period 1973-90 to investigate the determinants of gross weekly earnings for male and female employees. In the pooled sample they found a negative and significant relationship between regional unemployment and earnings (the wage curve). However, they also split their sample into two sub-periods 1973-80 and 1981-90 and found that in the latter, the coefficient on the regional unemployment variable was larger. Although this provides tentative support for the idea that wages become more responsive to local economic conditions during the 1980s, further econometric testing would be required in order to be confident about such a conclusion. Nevertheless, it seems to be broadly consistent with the changes in the simple measures of dispersion presented in Figure 5.6 above.

Unemployment duration has also featured in a number of explanations for the apparent inflexibility of the wage-rate response to unemployment over the 1970s and 1980s. This approach typically emphasises the deficiencies of aggregate unemployment as a measure of excess supply within the labour market. Interestingly, Layard and Nickell (1986) argue that official figures on aggregate unemployment are an inadequate measure of excess labour supply, and that figures on long-term unemployment are better for use in wage equations. The essence of their argument is that the long-term unemployed represent a less effective supply of potential labour than their short-term counterparts.[5] Similarly, Nickell and Wadhwani (1990) and Blackaby and Manning (1990) using regional unemployment duration rates in wage equations find that the long-term unemployed do not put downward pressure on wages. These findings are important because they suggest that the government can intervene directly in the labour market and improve the outlook for the long-term unemployed without increasing wage inflationary pressures.[6]

5.5 Summary and conclusions

This chapter provided an overview of the nature of spatial labour market disparities in the UK, and discussed the extent to which institutional reform in the labour market might help to alleviate them. The main purpose was to highlight the most important issues, and not to discuss any particular issue in great detail. The main findings can be summarised as follows: Firstly, the traditional profile of regional labour markets in the UK has been characterised as a 'North-South Divide'. In recent years, official figures suggest that the unemployment differential has more or less disappeared and, instead, attention has focused on differences between small local areas which, within most regions, remain significant. It should be stressed, however, that much of the current convergence in regional labour markets can be explained in terms of increased inactivity rates in traditionally high unemployment areas, and not in terms of increases in economic growth and employment. Secondly, the 1980s saw a major shift in emphasis in regional policy away from the traditional aim of divesting inward investment to less prosperous areas and towards a variety of measures which could facilitate indigenous growth. Central to such measures were a series of reforms to labour market institutions, particularly those relating to pay bargaining and vocational training. Potential synergies were understood to exist between regional policy and labour market policy and, indeed, labour market reform was one of the main responses by government to regional and local economic disparities. Thirdly, the pattern of education standards amongst young people is a 'mirror image' of the aforementioned North-South divide, with more prosperous regions generally having higher standards. This is likely to act as a constraint on the growth potential of economically depressed regions, particularly since there is such an important link between standards of general education and the ability and/or willingness to improve standards of vocational training. Such constraints are exacerbated, firstly, by the output-related funding arrangements of the TEC's and, secondly, by the net out-migration from economically depressed areas, of well-education members of the workforce. Fourthly, regional migration in the UK during the 1980s, kept regional unemployment differentials lower than they otherwise would have been. Nevertheless, migration is limited as a labour market adjustment mechanism because it tends to take place amongst well-educated members of the workforce amongst whom spatial labour market disparities in the UK are very low. Finally, wage flexibility remains an important source of labour market adjustment in the UK. There is limited amount of evidence to suggest that regional wages become more flexible during the 1980s, and this is consistent with the major reforms which have been made to pay bargaining institutions.

This chapter has shown that evidence exists to support the notion of a broad divide in earnings, education, economic growth, and labour market institutions between the north and south of the country, although there are some doubts about the ability of official figures to accurately reflect this. Success as a nation in the Single European Market will only be achieved if we can operate as a conglomerate of successful regional economies : a two-tier Britain can expect little more than second - or third-division status in Europe. To avoid this a more broadly based development policy is required which integrates industrial infrastructure and education and training policy more fully into an overall strategy for growth.

Notes

1. This paper draws on work conducted at the Northern Ireland Economic Research Centre (NIERC). The authors would like to thank Stephen Roper of NIERC, Paul Teague of the University of Ulster and Boyd Black of The Queen's University, Belfast for helpful discussions. Excellent research assistance was provided by Neil Gibson and Connor McCarron. The usual disclaimer applies.

2. It is also worth noting that *within* the southern regions (i.e. the South East, the South West and East Anglia) the overall dispersion of unemployment rates tended to increase at the beginning of the 1990s. For example, within the South East region between 1989 and 1993, the standard deviation of TTWA unemployment rates increased from 1.8 to 2.8 and the range increased from 7 percentage points to 11 percentage points.

3. The standard argument is that trade unions raise wages by restricting the entry of labour into firms. By raising union members' wages above the competitive levels, unions may reduce the level of employment and create efficiency losses through a misallocation of resources. However, under certain labour market conditions trade unions may increase both wages and employment. In a review of the existing UK literature Booth (1995) found evidence that the differential is small and positive and larger for manual than non-manual workers. Estimates place the manual wage differential at between 7 percent and 13 percent and non-manual wage differential at between 4 percent and 5 percent.

4. The institutional framework for vocational training provision which existed before the TEC's and LEC's were established as described in Ploszajska (1994).

5. Two main explanations have been put forward for this: firstly, in response to feelings of frustration and hopelessness, many of the long-term unemployed may spend less time looking for work than do individuals who have only recently become unemployed (Moylan, Miller & Davies, 1984; Jackman & Layard, 1991). Secondly, there may be reticence on the part of employers to employ individuals who have experienced a long spell of unemployment, owing to the fact that their human capital may have depreciated. Moreover, employers screen job applicants on the basis of their unemployment duration, using this as an indicator of worker's quality (Meager & Metcalf, 1987).

6. Note that Blanchflower and Oswald (1990) find little support for the Layard-Nickell hypothesis, but instead favour a specification for the relationship between wages and unemployment which emphasizes the role of non-linearities. Blanchflower and Oswald do not draw out the explicit policy implications of their research but note that at high levels of unemployment 'the equilibrating forces of the labour market can break down' (Blanchflower & Oswald, 1990, p. 216).

References

Armstrong, D.M. (1994), 'Unemployment in Northern Ireland: Causes, Characteristics and Cures' in White, M. (ed.), *Unemployment, Public Policy and the Changing Labour Market*, Policy Studies Institute: London.

Armstrong, D.M. (1996), *Education and Economic Development: Empirical Evidence and Regional Perspectives*, Department of Education for Northern Ireland (DENI), DENI Research Series No. 2, Bangor.

Beatson, M. (1995), *Labour Market Flexibility,* Employment Market Research Unit, Employment Department, Research Series No. 48.
Beatty, C. & S. Fothergill (1996), 'Labour Market Adjustment in Areas of Chronic Industrial Decline: The Case of the Coalfields', *Regional Studies*, Vol. 30, No. 7, pp. 627-640.
Bennett, R.J. (1994), 'New Training Institutions at the local level', in Layard, R., K. Mayhew & G. Owen, *Britain's Training Deficit*, Chapter 7, pp. 173-195, Avebury: Aldershot.
Blackaby, D.H. & D.N. Manning (1990), 'The North-South Divide: Questions of Existence and Stability?', *The Economic Journal*, Vol. 100, pp. 510-527.
Blackaby, D.H. & D.N. Manning (1992), 'Regional Earnings and Unemployment - A Simultaneous Approach', *Oxford Bulletin of Economics and Statistics*, Vol. 54, No. 4.
Blackaby, D.H. & P.D. Murphy (1995), 'Earnings, Unemployment and Britains North-South Divide : Real or Imaginary', *Oxford Bulletin of Economics and Statistics*, Vol. 57, pp. 487-512.
Blanchflower, D.G. & A.J. Oswald (1990), 'The Wage-Curve', *Scandinavian Journal of Economics,* Vol. 92, pp. 215-36.
Blanchflower, D.G. & A.J. Oswald (1993) 'Estimating a Wage Curve with Fixed Effects Cell Means', Dartmouth College, Mimeo, January.
Booth, A.L. (1995), *The Economics of the Trade Union*, Cambridge University Press.
Brown, W. (1993), 'The Contraction of Collective Bargaining in Britain', *British Journal of Industrial Relations*, June, Vol. 31, No. 2, pp. 189-200.
Christie, I. & H. Rolfe (1992), 'The TEC's and Inner City Regeneration', *Policy Studies*, Spring 1992, Vol. 13, No. 1, pp. 54-63.
Coffield, F. (1992), 'Training and Enterprise Councils: the Last Throw of Voluntarism?', *Policy Studies*, Winter 1992, Vol. 13, No. 4, pp. 11-32.
DTI (1983), *Regional Industrial Development,* HMSO.
ED (1988), *Employment for the 1990s*, Employment Department, Employment Department Group.
Green, A. & H. Steedman (1993), *Education provision, educational attainment and the needs of industry: a review of research for Germany, France, Japan, the USA and Britain*, Institute of Education, University of London and National Institute of Economic and Social Research.
Gregg, P. & J. Wadsworth (1994), 'Nowt Doing in Crawley?', Regional Labour Market Evolutions in Britain 1975-93, mimeo.
Gudgin, G. & A. Schofield (1993), 'The Emergence of the North-South Divide and its Projected Future', *Regional Policy and Development 2: Spatial Policy in a Divided Nation*, (eds.) Harrison, R.T. and M. Hart, Regional Studies Association.
Hughes, G. & B. McCormick (1994), 'Did Migration in the 1980s Narrow the North-South Divide?', *Economica*, Vol. 61, pp. 509-528.
Jackman, R. & S. Savouri (1991), *Regional Wage Determination in Great Britain,*

Centre for Economic Performance, Discussion Paper, No. 47, July.
Jackman, R. & R. Layard (1991) 'Does long-term unemployment reduce a person's chance of a job? A time series test', *Economica*, Vol. 58, pp. 93-106.
Layard, R.E. & S. Nickell (1986), 'Unemployment in Britain', *Economica*, Vol. 53 Supplement, pp. S121-S169.
MacKay, R. (1993), 'Local Labour Markets, Regional Development and Human Capital', *Regional Studies*, Vol. 27, pp. 783-795.
Martin, R. (1993), 'Remapping British Regional Policy : The End of the North-South Divide?', *Regional Studies*, Vol. 27, No. 8, pp. 797-806.
McCormick, B. (1991), 'Migration and Regional Policy', in Bowen, A. & K. Mayhew (eds.), *Reducing Economic Inequalities,* Chapter 5, National Economic Development Office, Policy Issues Series.
Meager, N. & S. Metcalf (1987), *Recruitment of the Long-Term Unemployed,* Institute of Manpower Studies Report No. 138.
Moylan, S., J. Miller & R. Davies (1984), *For richer, for poorer? DHSS Cohort Study of Unemployed Men*, Department of Health and Social Security Research report No. 11.
Muellbauer, J. & A. Murphy (1991), 'Regional Economic Disparities: The Role of Housing', in Bowen, A. & K. Mayhew (eds.), *Reducing Regional Inequalities*, Kogan Page: London, pp. 246-271.
Nickell, S. & S. Wadhwani (1990), 'Insider Forces and Wage Determination', *Economic Journal*, Vol. 100, pp. 391-439.
OPCS (1995), *Mid-1994 population estimates for England and Wales,* Office of Population and Censuses and Surveys.
Park (1994), *Cohort 4: Young People 18-19 years old in 1995. Report on Sweep 3,* ED Research Series, Youth Cohort Report No. 29, April.
Peck, J. (1993), 'The Trouble with TEC's... a critique of the Training and Enterprise Councils initiative', *Policy and Politics*, Vol. 21, No. 4, pp. 289-305.
Ploszajska, T. (1994), 'Training and Enterprise in England and Wales: A Critical Review', *British Journal of Education and Work*, Vol. 7, No. 3, pp. 43-62.
Pissarides, C. & J. Wadsworth (1989), 'Unemployment and the Inter-Regional Mobility of Labour', *Economic Journal*, Vol. 99, pp. 739-755.
Steedman, H.; G. Mason & K. Wagner (1991), 'Intermediate Skills in the Workplace: Deployment, Standards and Supply in Britain, France and Germany', *National Institute Economic Review*, No. 136, May, pp. 60-77.
Swales, C. & G. Gudgin (1996), *Regional Economic Outlook: Analysis and Forecasts to the year 2005*, NIERC and Oxford Economic Forecasting.
Walsh, J. & W. Brown (1991), 'Regional Earnings and Pay Flexibility' in *Reducing Economic Inequalities,* Chapter 4, National Economic Development Office, Policy Issues Series, pp. 185-215.
Wilkinson, D. (1992), 'Has the North-South Divide Come to an End? Prospects for Regional Unemployment', *National Institute Economic Review,* No. 142, November, pp. 88-98.

6 Institutions and regional labour markets in The Netherlands

Jouke van Dijk & Andries de Grip

6.1 Introduction

This chapter sheds light on the effects of institutional factors on the performance of regional labour markets in the Netherlands. Through various regulations the influence of institutions is rather strong. However, the regional differences in institutional factors are rather small in the Netherlands and the role of regional and local institutions on labour market performance is rather limited. This does not imply that a rather similar institutional structure automatically causes the same type of regional effects with the same magnitude. Stoffelsma (1992) clearly shows that nationwide policy measures can work out quite different for regions with a different economic situation. For example, he shows that the social security system, which does not differ by region, has much larger redistributive effects among regions than regional policy measures with the specific goal of narrowing regional differences. Since the main focus of this paper will be directed to the spatially differentiated effects of similar institutional frameworks, a considerable part of this chapter will consist of a discussion of the national policy measures which affect the regional labour market, viz. employment policy, regional policy and labour market policy.

The organisation of this chapter is as follows. In section 6.2 the socio-economic setting is discussed. First, some general data on labour market developments with respect to employment, labour supply, participation and unemployment are presented. Special attention will be paid to some specific Dutch features like the social security system, female labour market participation, wage determination and the role of unions. The regional setting will be discussed in section 6.3. In this section some basic regional data are presented and regional labour market disparities will be analysed. Section 6.4 focuses on the main policy issues. We successively discuss national economic and employment policies, regional policies and labour market policies. Attention is paid to changes in policy during the last decades and its regional dimension. In particular we focus on the changes in the objectives and instruments of regional economic policy (equity versus efficiency; subsidies on capital or labour) and labour market policy (objectives of the Public Employment Services and the shifts in its organisational structure; active versus passive labour market policies; experience on-the-job-training). Section 6.5 gives an overview of the effectiveness of the policy measures. Finally, section 6.6 summarises the main conclusions of this chapter.

6.2 The Dutch labour market

This section provides some background information for the functioning of regional labour markets. First, an overview of some basic economic and labour market indicators and their development over time on the national level is presented. Moreover, the objectives of macro-economic policy and the wage bargaining process are discussed. Furthermore, the main objectives of employment, regional and labour market policy are analysed.

6.2.1 The economic framework and socio-economic background

As the largest of the smaller countries in the European Union (EU), the Netherlands has about 15 million inhabitants, of which over 10 million are in the working age of 15-64 year. About 65 percent of the working-age population is employed, which is above the EU average of 60 percent (EC, 1994). GDP per capita is still above the EU average, but the difference declined substantially in the 1980s and is now about 10 percent above the EU average. In the period 1983-1995 the labour force increased by 0.9 percent per year. In the same period the annual growth of real GDP was 2.5 percent and the growth of employment 1.7 percent per year (OECD, 1994a). This implies that labour productivity still increases, but much less than in the 1960s when GDP growth of 3 percent hardly increased the number of jobs (jobless growth). In the period 1980-1990 labour costs per unit output increased 1.4 percent annually.

A typical feature for The Netherlands is the traditionally low female participation rate. Although the female participation rate is increasing rapidly, it is still lower than in the surrounding countries, notably among women with young children. Since the 1980s there is a large increase in part-time employment, which effectively meant that total employment was shared among more people. Because most part-time jobs are occupied by women, the share of female workers in full-time equivalents of employment is lower than shown by the participation rates (Pott-Buter, 1994). Part-time working is much more common in The Netherlands than in other European countries (see section 6.5 for more details).

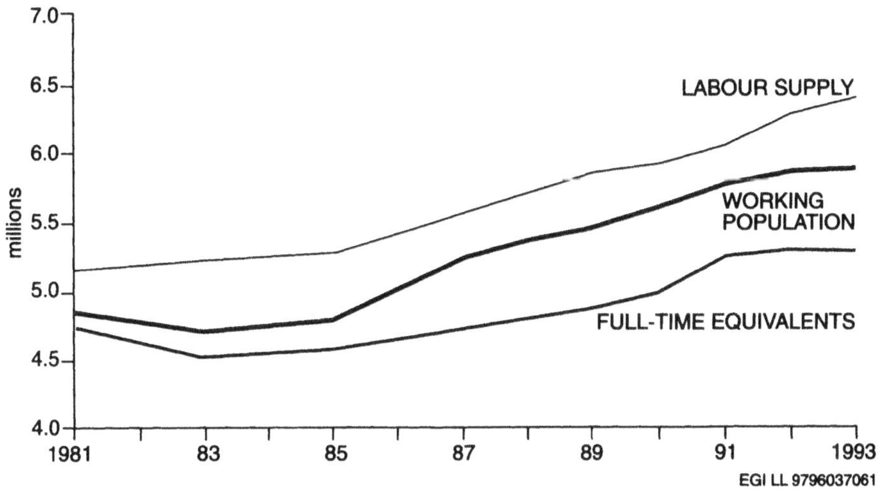

Figure 6.1 Total employment and labour supply, 1981-1993

Source: de Koning et al. (1995)

Figure 6.1 shows the development of total employment and labour supply for the period 1981-1993. The number of people with a job -of at least 12 hours a week- increased with more than one million. As in most other countries the growth of jobs was mainly in the service sector. Measured in full-time equivalents the increase was substantially lower than the growth in the number of jobs. The difference can be attributed to the growth in part-time jobs. Figure 6.1 shows that the increase in labour supply exceeded the increase in employment. About 70 percent of the increase in labour supply is caused by the increased female participation. Another 20 percent is due to the migration of workers of foreign origin. The increasing participation in education, as a result of which young people enter the labour force at an older age, reduced the growth of the labour force. The proportion of individuals with only primary education -the 'unskilled' workers- declined substantially.

Figure 6.2 shows the development of the shares of various groups in the labour force in the period 1981-1993. As the number of people searching for a job is much higher that the number of vacant jobs, the rate of unemployment was rather high in this period. It is, however, difficult to get a clear picture of unemployment in The Netherlands and the development over time. This is due to the fact that several definitions of unemployment have been used during the last 15 years. Moreover, we have to keep in mind that official unemployment figures do not tell the complete story.

According to the official unemployment definition the number of unemployed was almost 500,000 in 1993. When a broader definition is used unemployment is much higher. The number of people who want a paid job and are available in the labour market, but *not* actively searching during the last four weeks is somewhat over 300,000. Furthermore, hidden unemployment among those who receive minimum subsistence or disability benefits is estimated as several hundred thousands. Finally, about 200,000 people participate in all types of labour market policy programmes. Taking all these groups into account, unemployment is twice as high as the official figure.

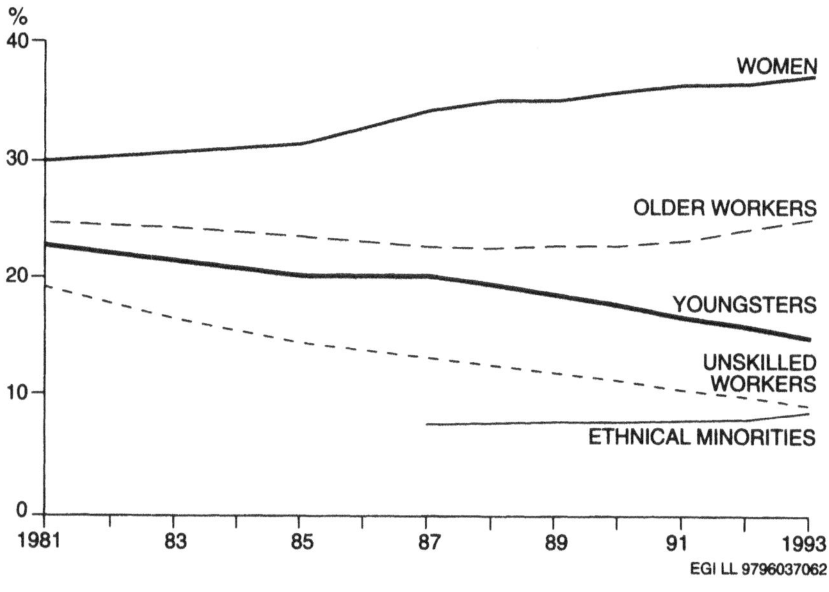

Figure 6.2 Shares of various groups of workers in the total labour force, 1981-1993

Source: Statistics Netherlands; de Koning et al. (1995)

Oosterhaven and Post (1993) used various methods to calculate differences in regional unemployment. Most unemployment measures show a difference in level caused by different definitions in unemployment, but the regional differences are highly correlated. The most striking differences are found if, instead of the actual labour force, the potential labour force is used as denominator. This reflects the differences in participation rates, which can be related to spatially differentiated discouragement effects and differences in the number of individuals receiving disablement benefits (AWW/WAO). The latter benefit system is a well-known source of hidden unemployment. Moreover, commuting between some regions is important. Commuting flows are quite large between certain regions and it is quite well possible that a change in the number of jobs in one region leads to changes in unemployment in (adjacent) regions. Figure 6.3 shows the development of the unemployment rate for the period 1981-1993 according to a definition, which is close to the internationally accepted ILO-definition.[1]

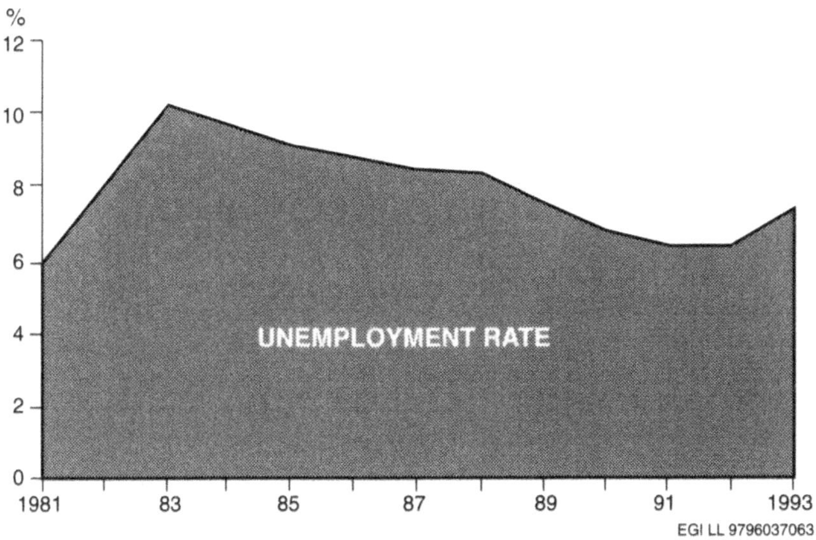

Figure 6.3 Unemployment rate, 1981-1993

Source: Statistics Netherlands; de Koning et al. (1995)

Unemployment is not equally spread among the various supply categories. The unemployment rates of females, people from foreign origin, those with only basic education and youngsters under the age of 25 are above the national average. Apart from the number of unemployed, also the duration of unemployment is of importance. In 1993 about 45 percent is unemployed for more than one year. Long term unemployment is especially high among the workers who only attended basic education, the age group of 45-64 years old and people from foreign origin (see de Koning, 1995).

6.2.2 *The policy framework*

As mentioned in the introduction, the most relevant policy measures for the regional labour market are the regionally undifferentiated policies by the central government. Since World War II the Dutch government has had a rather strong influence on economic and labour market policy. In the 1950s five generally accepted objectives of macro-economic policy were formulated:

1. stable economic growth;
2. full employment;
3. stable price level;
4. stable balance of payments, resulting in stable exchange rates; and
5. a fair income distribution.

With respect to the labour market, the Dutch government has a strong, but mainly indirect, influence. Traditionally, regulations deal with issues like minimum wages, collective bargaining, wage moderation, employment security, working hours and conditions, social policies and taxation.

For the Netherlands, as a relatively small economy, the international competitive position is of major importance. However, since the 1970s the economy showed some structural weaknesses that became manifest by the lack of sufficient employment, which refers to both a high rate of unemployment and a low rate of participation in the labour force. For this reason macro-economic policy focused on three main targets (Miljoenennota, 1995):

1. to increase employment and the labour participation rate;
2. to strengthen the economic growth potential and the functioning of markets; and
3. to diminish the budget deficit of the public sector.

Three types of policy instruments are important for regional labour markets (see also section 6.4).

1. *Employment policy*
   The main objective of employment policy is the stimulation of job-creation by improving the international competitive position of the Dutch economy. Traditionally, wage moderation is one of the main lines in macroeconomic labour market policy. Wage bargaining mainly takes place at the level of economic sectors or large firms. However, trade union federations often negotiate national wage agreements with central employer organisations and sometimes entered into additional agreements with the government. Wage agreements do not differ by region.

2. *Regional policy*
   Since World War II regional policy measures have been used to stimulate employment growth in the lagging regions. Untill 1980 the main aim of regional policy was to achieve a geographically more balanced development of economic activities: the *equity objective*. For that purpose a combination of stimulating measures for lagging regions and restrictive measures for congested areas has been used, although the latter have only been pursued effectively in the mid 1970s. Since 1980, a second objective of regional policy has been introduced: the *efficiency objective*. Its aim was to achieve the maximal contribution of each region to the national welfare (EZ, 1990).

3. *Labour market policy*
   While the aim of the employment policy is to stimulate job creation, the main aim of labour market policy is the improvement of the matching process in combination with the stimulation of the (re-)entry into employment of unemployed workers and new-participants. Labour market policy is supplemented by a social security system aimed at the reduction of the negative financial consequences of not having a job. In the middle of the 1980s substantial changes occurred in the use of active and passive policy measures. Furthermore, there has been a major change in the institutional structure for labour market policies by restructuring the Employment Services from a governmental organisation into a tripartite organisation. Moreover, the reorganisation implied a major regional decentralisation of the Employment Services into 28 relatively independent Regional Boards (RBA's). Another major change was the demonopolisation of labour market mediation, which allows private employment agencies to intermediate. The tripartisation, regional decentralisation and demonopolisation of the employment services all aim at improving the allocation process on the labour market (de Koning et al., 1995).

Local (municipalities) and regional (provincial) authorities do not have special statutory tasks in regional economic policy. Consequently, they are lacking special instruments and budgets. They can use, however national instruments more or less intensive. Furthermore, they can use their statutory tasks in the fields of spatial planning, transport, education and environmental protection to stimulate economic development indirectly. According to Bartels and van Duijn (1981) the local governments are more powerful in this respect than the regional (provincial) governments. This, because of their more important role in spatial policy issues, in particular their right to lay down land use destinations. This still holds for the moment, although an increasing part of the budget for regional policy is decentralised from the central government to the provincial level and to the thirteen so-called 'urban nodes' (stedelijke knooppunten), the biggest urban agglomerations of the Netherlands.

Figure 6.4 Spatial demarkation of the 28 RBA-regions in The Netherlands

In spite of their dependence from national budgets or, better said, their smartness to use such budgets for their own specific goals, especially the local governments in the Netherlands have been very active in the past 10-15 years in creating economic development initiatives. In some of these activities the social character prevails like care for the unemployed, re-education programmes and job-experience plans for youngsters. Others are purely economic like stimulating firm start-ups, improvement of location conditions, active local promotion and acquisition campaigns (van Dijk & Pellenbarg, 1995).

6.3 The regional setting

There are several types and levels of administrative regions in The Netherlands. Below the central government there are twelve provinces, whereas below the provinces there are about 600 municipalities. For specific policy purposes there are other regional subdivisions and cooperations between municipalities. As mentioned before, for the Public Employment Services a regional subdivision in 28 Regional Boards is effective since 1991. Due to some mergers, now 18 RBA's exist. Figure 6.4 shows the spatial demarcation of the 28 RBA-regions. Table 6.1 provides some key figures about some labour market developments. These will be discussed in detail in the rest of this section. The RBA-regions show large differences in size. The regions with the three big cities Amsterdam/Zaanstreek/Waterland (incl. Amsterdam), Rijnmond (incl. Rotterdam) and Den Haag/Delft (incl. The Hague) are the largest RBA-regions, with around half a million jobs, where the smallest have less than 100,000 jobs.

Gross domestic product (GDP) per capita and the regional unemployment rate are the two main indicators to measure regional differences. They are often used to decide whether a region is eligible for assistance. As far as regional production and income are concerned we have to use data at the provincial level. Data by RBA-region are not available. Setting the national average to 100 for 1991, the province of Groningen shows a very high GDP per capita of 135 in official statistics. This is caused by the fact that the production of natural gas is for a very large part attributed to this region. In the recently established province of Flevoland on reclaimed land, GDP per capita is only 74, but this is mainly due to high out-commuting rates. Relying on GDP per capita may lead to misleading conclusions, because the province of Groningen is considered since World War II to be a problem region, whereas Flevoland is not. A better indicator is disposable income per capita. In this perspective regional welfare differences are much smaller and range from 90 to 108 (national average = 100). The lowest values are found in the provinces in the North and East and the highest in the provinces Utrecht, Noord- and Zuid-Holland (see van Dijk & Oosterhaven, 1994). The differences in income per capita between the Dutch provinces are not very substantial.

Table 6.1
Labour market indicators by RBA-region, 1988-1993

RBA region	Empl. (x 1000) 1993	Empl. growth percent 88-93	Labour force 1993	Lab.force growth percent 88-93	percent higher education	RUC percent[1] 1993	Unempl. change 88-93	Vacancies per 100 unempl. 1993
1. Groningen	225.8	5.9	247.6	2.9	22.1	4.1	-1.7	2.7
2. Friesland	223.0	8.7	258.5	5.1	17.6	2.0	-1.2	3.3
3. Drenthe	168.0	8.5	197.8	8.4	18.9	0.0	-2.1	4.1
4. IJssel-Vecht	142.9	12.9	152.0	9.2	17.8	-1.8	-2.1	6.3
5. Twente	221.1	8.6	255.8	6.9	18.1	0.7	-3.3	4.5
6. Midden-IJssel	93.4	10.4	97.7	10.0	21.3	-2.2	-5.0	6.7
7. Veluwe	243.1	7.3	284.5	8.5	18.5	-2.7	-2.4	8.8
8. Arnhem/Oost-Gelderland	275.2	9.5	305.4	8.9	19.4	-0.2	-2.9	8.5
9. Nijmegen/Rivierenland	183.0	15.5	216.5	8.3	25.6	1.8	-2.6	3.8
10. Flevoland	76.7	31.1	106.5	22.4	20.0	-0.9	-1.4	8.8
11. Oost Utrecht	210.7	16.9	229.5	11.7	26.9	-4.2	-3.7	16.1
12. West Utrecht	295.8	13.6	277.7	11.1	29.7	-0.3	-1.1	12.9
13. Het Gooi en Vechtstreek	103.4	0.0	111.1	1.4	31.8	-1.4	0.5	19.1
14. Noord-Holland Noord	199.4	9.7	265.4	7.8	16.8	-2.5	-2.7	19.4
15. Amsterdam/Zaanstreek	528.6	6.1	473.6	5.9	29.3	5.2	-1.0	6.4
16. Kennemer- en Amstelland	316.1	10.2	299.4	8.3	25.3	-3.5	-1.7	19.3
17. Rijnstreek	281.1	12.1	350.5	9.0	25.0	-3.5	-1.6	11.9
18. Den Haag/Delft	467.8	7.0	440.0	5.1	27.0	0.5	0.5	10.9
19. Drechtsteden	150.2	10.9	178.6	8.4	17.3	-2.0	-1.5	22.8

Table 6.1 (continued)

RBA region	Empl. (x 1000) 1993	Empl. growth percent 88-93	Labour force 1993	Lab.force growth percent 88-93	percent higher education	RUC percent[1] 1993	Unempl. change 88-93	Vacancies per 100 unempl. 1993
20. Rijnmond	519.2	5.6	535.1	3.7	19.2	3.4	-0.6	4.1
21. Zeeland	144.1	7.1	161.1	7.0	16.9	-2.2	-1.9	5.8
22. Westelijk Noord-Brabant	94.1	11.9	111.2	9.8	15.3	-1.9	-2.9	5.2
23. Breda	169.9	15.0	181.4	7.6	19.1	-2.0	-2.4	12.0
24. Midden-Brabant	154.8	7.5	185.1	6.8	18.2	0.6	-1.5	6.8
25. Noord-Oost Brabant	252.7	13.7	272.5	9.0	20.8	-1.1	-1.7	9.7
26. Zuid-Oost Brabant	287.6	4.8	316.0	6.2	24.8	1.0	0.3	7.9
27. Noord- en Midden Limburg	202.6	9.5	221.2	5.4	18.6	-2.3	-1.5	10.7
28. Zuid-Limburg	247.2	4.7	285.5	3.1	20.3	2.3	-0.9	6.1
The Netherlands	6,477.3	9.1	7,017.3	7.1	22.0	7.7	-1.6	9.4

[1] RUC = Regional unemployment component: regional unemployment rate minus the national unemployment rate of 7.7 percent.

Source: CBS (1994) and de Koning et al. (1995)

Although the most important indicator for regional policy purposes in The Netherlands is the regional unemployment rate, table 6.1 also shows figures about the dynamics of unemployment, employment and the labour force. The number of vacancies per 100 unemployed is used as an indicator for the extent to which unemployment is due to frictional or structural mismatches or to a lack of jobs. Theoretically, one should expect that a growth in employment will lower unemployment and a growth in the labour force increases unemployment.

In contrast to the small differences in average income between regions, the differences in unemployment rates are considerably larger and persistent. The regional differences decreased in the period 1971-1981, but since than it increased again. Besides the changes over time also the spatial pattern changed. Since World War II the northern provinces show unemployment rates above the national average. Only the northern province of Drenthe has unemployment rates which are in recent years close to the national average. In the beginning of the 1980s, unemployment rates in the eastern provinces Overijssel and Gelderland and the southern provinces North-Brabant and Limburg were also above the national average. The lowest unemployment rates were found in the three western provinces Utrecht and Noord- and Zuid-Holland. Since then, the most striking changes in the spatial pattern occurred in the large cities in the western and in the southern parts of the country.

The large cities of Amsterdam and Rotterdam and, to a lesser extent, The Hague and Utrecht are now regions with the highest unemployment rates. In an absolute sense the majority of unemployed workers is concentrated in the Western part of the country where these cities are located. The number of unemployed in the three largest cities is twice as high than in the three northern provinces. With the exception of Zuid-Limburg, all regions in the South showed a remarkably lower unemployment rate in the beginning of the 1990s than ten years before. In all, except three regions, the unemployment rate decreased from 1988 till 1993. The correlation between the regional level of unemployment and the growth of unemployment is positive ($R = 0.38$), indicating that regional differences are not narrowing.

Table 6.1 also shows the spatial distribution of the number of vacancies in relation to the number of unemployed. The absolute number of vacancies is lowest in the peripheral regions. The number of vacancies per 100 unemployment workers shows substantial differences over time and between regions. For The Netherlands as a whole this ratio decreased from 25.2 to 9.4 over the short period 1990-1993 (de Koning et al., 1995). Especially, in the RBA-regions in the South the decrease was most severe. In 1993 the number of vacancies per hundred unemployed is only 2.7 in the province of Groningen, where in the RBA-region Drechtsteden the ratio is 22.8. This spatial variation implies that the possibility of reducing unemployment by a better matching of unemployed workers and vacancies are in some regions much larger than in others. A negative correlation is found for the relation between the level of unemployment and the ratio vacancies/unemployment ($R=-0.60$). This implies that a high level of unemployment goes together with low vacancies/unemployment ratios. In regions with high unemployment this is not caused by frictional or structural mismatches between demand and supply, but mainly by a lack of job openings.

Besides unemployment some other indicators are relevant for the situation on the regional labour market. Although the working population increased in all regions during the period 1988-1993, there are considerable differences in the growth of employment and the growth of the labour force. The newly established province of Flevoland stands out with an employment growth of over 30percent. The other regions vary between 0 and 17 percent. With the exception of the three northern provinces, which all show relatively low growth rates between 6 and 9 percent, the regions with the highest or lowest growth rates are not located in specific parts of the country. The regions with the lowest employment growth are dominated by the larger cities. Regions located just next to the larger cities show the highest growth rates of employment.

The growth of employment can be related to the growth of the labour force. The most striking results are found for the RBA-regions Flevoland, Breda and Nijmegen-Rivierenland, which all show an employment growth substantially above the national average together with a relatively limited growth of the labour force. In the latter two regions the growth of employment is about twice as high as the growth of the labour force. Although in both regions the decrease in unemployment is larger than the national average, there are quite a number of regions where the difference between employment growth and labour force growth is much smaller and the reduction in unemployment much larger. In only two regions (Veluwe and Zuid-Oost Brabant) the growth in the labour force exceeds the growth in employment. In general the spatial pattern of the growth of the working population is almost similar as for employment growth: the correlation coefficient between the two is 0.92. Both the level of unemployment and the growth of unemployment show a negative correlation (around -0.35) with both the growth of employment as the growth of the labour force. These results imply that an increase in the number of jobs goes together with both an increase in participation and a reduction in unemployment. A possible explanation for the counterintuitive result that a decrease in the growth of the labour force goes together with an increase in unemployment, is that high unemployment lowers participation via discouragement effects.

Between the various RBA-regions the differences in educational level of the labour force are quite large. Table 6.1 shows that in 1993 the percentage of the workforce with a higher vocational or academic education ranges from around 17 percent in the peripheral areas like the three northern provinces to more than 25 percent in the Western provinces (Gooi en Vechtstreek even 32 percent). In a region with a high percentage of well educated workers a higher growth of employment and, hence, lower unemployment can be expected. However, it is well known that the participation rates among higher educated people are higher. This implies that more education also leads to an increase of labour supply. Therefore, the effect of education on unemployment is a priori not clear. The partial correlation coefficients of the educational level with the growth of employment, the growth of the labour force and the level of unemployment are all almost equal to zero. This suggest that there is no relation at all or that the opposing tendencies neutralise each other. Surprisingly there is a weak positive relation between the percentage of higher educated workers and the growth of unemployment (R = 0.39). Probably this is due to the large increase of the inflow into the labour market of graduates from higher education in this period. Moreover, unemployed graduates are often concentrated in the cities where they attended higher education, whereas the greater part of those who found a job moved to other regions.

It is clear that there are important differences in the performance of regional labour markets in The Netherlands. However, there are no clear relations between the spatial patterns and the developments over time of employment growth, labour force growth, education and the level and growth of unemployment.

6.4 Main policy issues

In section 6.2 some introductory remarks have been made about the regional policy framework in the Netherlands. In this section the various policy issues with respect to employment policy, regional policy and labour market policy, are discussed more in detail.

6.4.1 Employment policy

Wage moderation is traditionally one of the main policy lines in the macroeconomic labour market policy in the Netherlands (OECD, 1994a; de Kam et al., 1995). In the period of economic recovery after World War II wages were heavily controlled by the government in order to keep wages low. In the 1950s this policy of direct economy-wide co-ordination was continued, based on central negotiations with the social partners. However, in the beginning of the 1960s this system eroded and wages increased rapidly. Since then, collective agreements on wages became increasingly the exclusive right of the unions and employers' organisations, but the government still had the right to interfere and used this right several times. After 1982 the government did not interfere directly in the wage setting process any longer and wage negotiations were more and more decentralised by economic sector. Unions and employers' organisations still negotiate at a central level, but since 1982 this resulted only four times in a central agreement. The last time was in 1993 due to the threat of the government to freeze wages.

The social partners have the legal monopoly for settling collective agreements (CAOs) and since 1937 these can be extended to non-signatory parties by Ministerial Decree. At the end of 1993 there were about 200 collective agreements for specific branches and 750 for large companies. Although in 1980 only 35 percent of the workers in the Netherlands were union members, the wages of 76 percent of the employees in the private and public sector were determined by collective agreements and their extensions. In 1990 these figures are somewhat lower: 25 percent union members and 71 percent coverage. The extensions mainly concern the small and medium sized firms in the building, trade and the hotel and catering industry (Lever & Marquering, 1995).

A legal national minimum wage exists. In 1991, however, indexation was abolished. In 1993 a minimum rate for 15-year-old workers was set at 30 percent of the adult rate. The number of people actually earning the adult minimum wage is very small, because in most CAOs the lowest wage scales are substantially above the statutory minimum wage. Apart from limiting the annual wage increases, decreasing the wedge between net-wages and the gross labour costs is a main policy focus. The government attempts to decrease the high wedge both by increasing the low labour participation rate ('the volume-effect') and by lowering the spending on social security benefits. In the past, social security payments were rather generous in The Netherlands, but since the 1980s the level of benefits was lowered, the criteria were tightened and the period of entitlement shortened (OECD, 1994b). In particular for low skilled workers the high wedge between net and gross wages, the small difference between wages and unemployment benefits and the inflexibility of the (minimum) wages 'at the bottom of the labour market' are seen as major causes of the high hidden and open unemployment of this group of workers. For this reason the government puts pressure on the collective bargaining process, in the sense that CAOs that do not classify sufficient jobs in the wage scales between the legal minimum wage and the (until than) lowest CAO-wages will no longer be binding for outsiders (Miljoenennota, 1995).

Apart from the policies aiming at a moderation of gross wages, since the 1980s employment policies are aiming at a redistribution of employment by stimulating part-time work (Kloosterman & Elfring, 1991; Borstlap, 1995). Part-time working is stimulated by a lessening of the traditional prejudice against such jobs and the disappearance of cultural barriers. In most cases part-time jobs have the same legal status and conditions as full-time jobs. Moreover, in the 1980s trade unions succeeded to decrease the extent of the full-time working week in the various CAOs.

6.4.2 Regional policy

Dutch regional policy started after World War II. For an extensive overview we refer to van Dijk and Oosterhaven (1994). During the period of rapid economic growth (1959-1975) congestion problems and, in particular, the tight labour market situation in the Randstad -the most heavily urbanised part of the Netherlands- were the main causes for the spread of employment from the Randstad to adjacent regions. To minimise the social costs of the concentration of population and economic activity in the Randstad, regional policy tried to strengthen this autonomous tendency and at the same time tried to extend it from the adjacent, so-called 'intermediate areas', to the peripheral areas. Traditionally the kernel of the toolbox consisted of:

- investment premiums; and
- infrastructural programs.

The main goal of both measures is to stimulate investment in problem regions. Because investment premiums and infrastructural programs make investment more attractive they can be categorised as *stimulative* instruments. These two main types of instruments have an *indirect* effect on the regional economy, in contrast to more *direct* measures.

In the beginning of the 1970s some direct policy measures were introduced, namely.

- Relocation of government offices; a total of 16,000 jobs was relocated to three cities in The North and to one in Zuid-Limburg. This policy was terminated after a few years.
- Regional Development Companies (RDC) were established, of which the NOM for the three northern provinces is by far the biggest (and oldest). RDC have funds to participate financially in new or existing firms. Furthermore, they try to attract (foreign) investors and serve as a regional network for the circulation of knowledge relevant to entrepreneurs.

There was a tendency for regional policy to be directed to more and more regions and more and more policy areas. Since the 1980s regional policies returned to a more purely economic policy for a limited number of regions. This shift could be justified by the decreasing regional disparities. Moreover, there is since 1975, a growing criticism on this 'spreading policy' due to the overall increase in unemployment in all regions. As a result of the criticism this spreading strategy was officially abandoned in 1985. In the 1990s the emphasis is put on the optimal use of the potential of each region to boost the whole Dutch economy. Consequently, regional policy measures are now more directed at improving the performance of the private sector, while using instruments that are more in conformity with market forces. Instead of leaning mainly on subsidies from the central government, regions now have to rely primarily on their own strength.

At the moment the most important problem areas are the big cities Amsterdam and Rotterdam, the northern part of the Netherlands, consisting of the provinces Groningen, Friesland and Drenthe, and Zuid-Limburg, especially because of the high registered and hidden unemployment. For the northern part of the Netherlands the traditional regional policy instruments (IPR, Investment Premium Regulation and ISP, Integrated Policy Programme) are continued, but will be terminated for other regions. Instead, some new policy elements are introduced. The bigger cities get larger budgets for social and employment policies to combat the high rates of unemployment, particularly among ethnical minorities. Financially most important is the new 'Firms Environment Policy' (FEP). The main aim is to create the physical conditions for an internationally competitive production and location environment. This should give all regions the opportunity to contribute maximally to national economic growth (EZ, 1990). Most important for the distribution of the budget of the FEP is the improvement of the international competitive position of the four big cities, the other 'urban nodes', large industrial areas and large distribution nodes. FEP was terminated in 1996 and succeeded by StiREA (Stimuleringsregeling Ruimte voor Economische Activiteit). The main aim is the development of new and restructuring existing industrial zones, because shortages are expected (EZ, 1995).

The budget for regional policy measures has always been rather limited, but decreased further in the 1990s. In 1985 the total budget for regional policies was over 800 million guilders. After 1995 this is reduced to less than 300. For the lagging regions the financial support from the European Structural Funds become increasingly important. Various Dutch regions qualify for Objectives 1, 2 and 5b area as an EU. At the moment the total budget allocated via these funds exceeds the budget of national regional policy substantially (see EZ, 1995).

6.4.3 *Labour market policy*

In the middle of the 1980s there was a general notice that, compared to other countries, the spending on social security benefits for unemployed workers ('passive policy') was much more dominant than the spending on 'active' labour market policies directed to the training and replacement of unemployed workers. Although in the second half of the 1980s the expenses on active labour market policies increased as a percentage of the Gross Domestic Product, the expenses on active labour market policies remained more or less at the same level slightly below the EU-average but still substantially above the level in North-America and Japan (SZW, 1990; OECD, 1994c).[2]

As mentioned, there has been a major change in the institutional structure for labour market policies by restructuring the Employment Services from a governmental organisation into a tripartite organisation. The reorganisation of the Employment Services intended to increase the efficiency as well as the equity of the allocation process on the labour market. The efficiency target refers to a better matching between vacancies and unemployed workers, whereas the equity target is related to the improvement of the labour market perspectives of groups of unemployed workers with a weak labour market position: long-term unemployed, ethnical minorities and women.

In the Employment Services Act ('Arbvo-wet') of 1991 the followings tasks of the reorganised Public Employment Services are mentioned (see also Stanmeyre, 1990):

- to generate and supply information on labour market developments;
- vocational and occupational guidance;
- labour market mediation; and

- to stimulate training activities.

The new organisational structure lead to some important shifts (see de Koning et al., 1995). First, the Employment Services changed its policy focus from a supply-side to a demand-side orientation. The idea behind this policy was the so-called *slipstream philosophy*. In this approach the mediation of the unemployed workers most attractive for employers is seen as an essential mechanism to increase the job placements of workers that belong to target groups with a weak labour market position. This shift towards a demand-side 'market' orientation was probably one of the reasons for the second shift from specific labour market instruments (training and work experience projects) towards the *general mediation task*. This shift is reflected in the increase of the number of mediation consultants as well as in the shift from subsidies given towards staff costs. However, the market orientation of the Public Employment Services did not imply that more emphasis is given to increasing labour market transparency and guidance activities. Probably this is due to the fact that in their 'make-or-buy' decisions the Public Employment Services consider their own mediation task as their core business.

A third shift refers to the tendency towards policies that aim at preventing long-term unemployment instead of the traditional 'curative' policies for unemployed workers with bad job chances due to their long-term unemployment. The rationale behind this shift is that long-term unemployment causes dequalification and demotivation as well as a stigmatisation of these workers, which makes it more and more difficult to find a job (see de Grip, 1987). In particular the labour market policy with respect to youngsters has almost entirely a preventive character. In 1992 the 'Activating labour market policy for youngsters' ('AAJ') started. Youngsters who cannot find a job or apprenticeship on their own, are supported by additional training and/or placement subsidies of the Public Employment Services. If they still fail to get employed within a year, the 'Youth employment-guarantee act' ('JWG') guarantees that they are offered a temporary appointment at the local JWG-organisation. However, this appointment does not necessarily imply that they actually have a job.

A fourth tendency is the increased regionalisation of the labour market instruments. This shift refers to both the character of the instruments applied and the criteria used to define the target groups of the various instruments. A fifth tendency is the increased support for job creation projects and the cooperation with organisations that are responsible for supplying unemployment benefits: the local social benefit organisation ('GSD') and the Industrial (unemployment and disability) Insurance Boards. De Koning et al. (1995) indicated that 19 of the 28 Regional Boards cooperate intensively with the local social benefit organisation, of which 6 state that the effect on job placements is large. Also the local authorities are playing a more important role in job creation for specific target groups. This holds in particular for the prevention of long-term unemployment of youngsters who enter the labour market (the JWG) and the creation of additional temporary jobs (Banen-pool, Melkert-banen) for individuals with labour market characteristics which prevent access to regular jobs.

A last tendency is the rise of national and regional agreements between government and employers organisation and unions (covenants) for several economic sectors. Arrangements are made with respect to training activities, work experience places, the inflow of particular target groups, etcetera. These covenants can be seen as a positive result of the tripartisation of the Public Employment Services' organisation. However, in several sectors it appears that individual firms do not consider the sectoral agreements as binding.

6.5 Effects of policy measures

In this section we look at the effects of the policy measures. As mentioned, regional differences in the institutional framework are very small in the Netherlands, although with respect to regional and labour market policies, the regional autonomy increased to some extent. Therefore, the main effects of the various policy instruments on the performance of regional labour markets must be caused by differences in regional circumstances which lead to different regional outcomes of a similar institutional framework.

6.5.1 Employment policy

The policy to moderate the annual increase in wages was rather successful in the period 1980-1990 when measured in terms of change in unit labour costs. The annual change in The Netherlands was only 0.8 percent, where the averages for the European Union and all OECD countries was 4 to 5 percent. In the beginning of the 1990s the increase in unit labour cost was close to the EU-average (OECD, 1994a). Whether this can be related to changes in the bargaining process and the influence of the government and social partners at the national level is not clear. In a OECD-study (OECD, 1994a) it is argued that the least centralised and the most centralised bargaining structures produce better economic performance than 'intermediate', i.e. industry-level, bargaining. This latter structure is becoming more and more the Dutch case: 80 percent of the CAO-negotiations is at the level of industrial sectors (Lever, 1995). Although the causal relationship between wages, labour costs and employment growth is rather complicated, it can concluded that the relatively small increases in labour costs have been accompanied by a substantial increase in the number of jobs. Lever (1995) estimates that a 1 percent-point lower increase in wages leads to an increase in employment in the range 0.25-0.5 percent. Some disagree with this view. Kleinknecht (1994) argues that a wage increase would improve economic performance in The Netherlands, because it stimulates innovations and leads to higher productivity. The employment effects of abolishing the statutory minimum wage are also questionable (Teulings, 1994; 1995). Lever and

Marquering (1995) estimated that abolishing the extension rules for CAOs increases employment with only 10,000 jobs.

Besides the wage level, collective bargaining can also deal with agreements on the number of jobs, the shortening of the number of working hours and flexible working hours. The latter two may also have positive effects on employment growth, but the precise elasticities are not clear. The Netherlands have by far the highest rate of part-time employment of all member-states of the European Union (Hoevenberg & de Grip, 1994). In 1991 more than 32 percent of all workers was employed on a part-time basis, compared to only 22 percent in the two next-highest countries, Denmark and the United Kingdom. Borstlap (1995) notices that almost half the growth in the number of people employed since 1980 can be attributed to the increase in part-time work (see also Figure 6.1).

Part-time work has expanded the number of people in employment in the Netherlands in the period 1979-1990 by 300 thousand. On average about 5 workers do the equivalent of 4 full-time jobs. Around one-third of all employees work part-time, most of them women, in services especially, and in less skilled positions. The growth of part-time work is also above average for male workers in manufacturing and in high skilled jobs. Even in periods of decline of full-time equivalent employment, the number of persons employed has not fallen because of the continuous growth of part-time working. Especially among female workers a substantial part of the part-timers is employed for less than 10 hours a week. For employers this atypical employment is a way to meet labour needs in peak periods, although to some extent the increase of part-time work is also supply-side induced (see de Grip et al., 1995; Delsen, 1995). The increasing needs of Dutch employers for flexible labour is also reflected in the increasing number of workers (more than 600 thousand) with flexible contracts and the strong increase in the use of labour via temporary employment agencies (SZW, 1994).

As collective bargaining is organised at the national level and only decentralised by industrial sector, the regional labour market situation is not reflected in regional wage differences. Van Dijk and Folmer (1992) estimated that the difference in wages between the central part of the country (Randstad) and the rest is only 3 percent. Others state that wages in the North are 7 to 10 percent below the national average. It is quite likely that this regional difference is mainly caused by the fact that the high paid jobs in the public and private sector are mainly located in the Randstad and not by differences in payment for jobs with the same requirements. With regular intervals there are plans to use differences in labour costs as instrument to increase employment in less favoured areas. To avoid negative effects of lower disposable income, the idea is to lower gross wages instead of net wages by means of lowering the employers' contributions in social security or by the introduction of so-called 'fiscal zones' with subsidies on labour costs (Oosterhaven, 1993).

6.5.2 *Regional policy*

Although several studies dealt with the evaluation of regional policy measures, the results are not unambiguous. Regional differences still exist and although the economic situation in the southern regions improved, it is not clear to what extent this is caused by regional policy. More generally it can be stated that the evaluation of regional policy measures is very difficult due to limitations in the analytical tools, lack of adequate data and the fact that a 'policy off' situation can not be properly specified (Armstrong & Taylor, 1993).

One of the most effective instruments in Dutch regional policy was the direct instrument of relocation of government offices. The multiplier effects for the relocation of the Headquarters of the Dutch PTT from The Hague to Groningen are considerably higher than expected and it improved the regional economic structure (Eekma, 1995). However, for various reasons this direct instrument has only been used for a very short period in the 1970s. In the latest official memorandum on Dutch regional policy (EZ, 1995) positive evaluation results are mentioned for the Firms Environment Policy, the Investment Premium Regulation and the Regional Development Companies.

However, even when the policy measures are effective, both national and European budgets for regional policies are by far to small to achieve a substantial reduction in regional differences. In particular, for the North of The Netherlands it is not very likely that the regional unemployment rate will move closer to the national rate given the weak economic structure and the potential increase in labour supply. Although the effects of regional policy are rather limited, it is interesting to note that Stoffelsma (1992) shows that national policy measures for social security and infrastructure, although *not* targeted to specific regions, have a larger spatially differentiated equalizing impact than specific regional policy measures.

6.5.3 *Labour market policy*

Also the general organisational effects of the restructuring of the Public Employment Services and the effectiveness of the various labour market policy instruments have been evaluated (see Commissie Evaluatie Arbeidsvoorzieningswet, 1995; de Koning et al., 1995). With respect to the organisational structure it was concluded that the Central Board did not fulfil its coordinative task adequately. Two main causes of this failure are mentioned. The first is the inadequate cooperation of the members of the Central Board due to their close connections with the organisation they represent, which turned the Employment Services into an 'insiders instrument' (Scholten & de Groot, 1995). The second is that due to the autonomy of the Regional Boards, the Central Board lost its grip on the entire organisation. Moreover there has been a vicious circle between, on the one hand, the inadequate co-ordination of the generation of information on vacancies, unemployment and the participation in the various training and work experience activities and, on the other hand, the lack of adequate management information required for well-considered management decisions.

As described in section 6.4.3, the reorganisation of the public Employment Services lead also to several major shifts in the labour market policies pursued. Survey results show that both in absolute and relative terms more persons that are searching for a job make use of the Employment Services. In 1992 291,000 persons, i.e. 33 percent of those searching for a job, used the Employment Services. This increased to 422,000 persons, i.e. 46 percent of those searching for a job in 1994. However, the percentage of the vacancies for which firms made use of The Employment Services as a recruitment channel remained more or less the same during this period: 20 percent (de Koning et al., 1995).[3]

Table 6.2
Number of unemployed workers reached by the main labour market policy lines and the number of participants that found a job (1993)

	applications		job finders	
	1991	1993	1991	1993
Guidance	-	68,000	-	21,000
Mediation	181,000	341,000	64,000	83,000
Training	168,000	162,000	101,000	71,000
Job placement	11,000	9,000	10,000	9,000
Work experience	12,000	35,000	ca.4,000	ca. 6,000

- = unknown

Source: de Koning et al. (1995)

Table 6.2 gives an overview of the development of the number of unemployed workers reached by the five main labour market policies and the number of participants that found a job. Altogether about 600,000 'applications' of labour market policy instruments are measured in 1993, whereby several unemployed participate in more activities. The table shows that, as mentioned before, employment mediation is by far the most prominent instrument with a reach of 341,000 persons in 1993, compared to merely 181,000 in 1991. Although the labour market situation worsened, this also resulted in an increase of the number of workers that found a job by Public Employment Services' mediation from 64,000 in 1991 to 83,000 in 1993.

Second in importance are the training activities with a slight decrease in participation from 168,000 in 1991 to 162,000 in 1993. The number of participants who found a job decreased more sharply from 101,000 to 71,000. The three other policies are much less important. Most remarkable is the substantial increase in projects that refer to the work-experience places agreed upon in collective agreements for particular sectors of industry and the JWG and so-called 'Labour pools' ('Banen-pools'), although the latter two policy instruments are not organised by the Employment Services. At the end of 1993 almost 14,000 youngsters participated in the JWG, which is more than 80 percent of the target group, whereas in this year more than 16,000 workers participated in labour pools, i.e. 17 percent of those unemployed for longer than 3 year.

The increased emphasis on employment mediation is reflected in the decrease of the share of subsidies for training, job placement and work experience in the total expenses of the Employment Services from 60 percent in 1991 to 40 percent in 1994. However, the increased demand-side orientation of the Employment Services lead to a debate on the relevance of a publicly financed organisation (Dercksen, 1994; Glebbeek & van Bruggen, 1996). One might wonder if a public organisation is needed in order to improve the efficiency of the allocation process on the labour market, or should be seen as a subsidised competitor of the private employment agencies. In this view the major task of the Public Employment Services refers to the increase of job placements for workers with a weak labour market position. In that case the validity of the slipstream philosophy is of crucial importance.

De Koning et al. (1995) find some evidence on the relevance of the slipstream hypothesis. The regions where the Employment Services have a larger market share in the number of vacancies, show relatively more placements for ethnical minorities, older workers and long-term unemployed. (The adjusted R^2 of the regressions is however small, indicating that more factors play an important role.) Another analysis shows that firms that report more vacancies to the Employment Services, recruit relatively more female workers and workers who belong to an ethnical minority group. However, the recruitment of long-term unemployed in these firms is lower.

The shift from training and job placement subsidies towards employment mediation has unfavourable consequences for the net-effectivity of the policy instruments for some target groups, as training and job placement subsidies have significant positive effects on the employment chances of long-term unemployed, older and low educated workers. For ethnical minorities and women the net-effects of training subsidies is not clear, whereas for youngsters the effects are often small. It is striking that many unemployed workers who participate in vocational training find jobs in other sectors than the sector for which they were trained. This indicates that firms use the participation of unemployed workers in training activities in particular as a screening device, which confirms the hypothesis of Thurow (1975).

De Koning et al. (1995) do not find any effects of the labour market policies of the Employment Services in general on the efficiency of the allocation process on the labour market. Hardly any research has been done on the effectiveness of training activities for the matching process between labour demand and supply, although a study of de Grip (1988a) finds some statistical evidence for a positive effect of the Public Employment Services' training activities on the allocation process on the labour market for the building trades.

6.6 Conclusions

In the Netherlands the working population is still growing. Almost half of this growth is due to the increase in part-time work. At the moment the Netherlands have by far the highest rate of part-time employment of all EU member-states. However, the increase in labour supply mostly exceeded the increase in employment, in particular due to the increased labour market participation of women. For this reason the level of unemployment was for a long time still high. In contrast to the small differences in average income between regions, the differences in unemployment rates are considerably larger and persistent. At the moment the most important problem areas are the northern part of the country, Zuid-Limburg, and the big cities Amsterdam and Rotterdam.

Three types of policy instruments are most relevant for regional labour markets; national employment policies, regional policies and labour market policies. At the national level, wage moderation and regulation, lowering the spending on social security benefits and stimulating part-time work are the major policies. The influence of national policies and institutions on regional development is rather strong. For instance the social security system - which does not differ by region -has in absolute terms much larger distributive effects among regions than specific regional policies that aim to narrow regional differences.

Local and regional authorities do not have special statutory tasks in regional economic policy, although in practice particular local authorities have some power in this respect. The budget for regional policies was further diminished in the 1990s. At the moment regional policies are more directed at the performance of the private sector with a main focus on the improvement of the international competitive position of the big cities and other 'urban nodes', larger industrial areas and large distribution nodes.

In the beginning of the 1990s there has been a major change in the institutional structure for labour market policies by restructuring the Public Employment Services from a governmental organisation into a tripartite organisation, with representatives of the social partners and the government. Apart from this tripartisation the reorganisation implied a major regional decentralisation of the Employment Services into 28 (now 18) relatively independent Regional Boards (RBA's) which also consist of tripartite representatives. A third major change was the demonopolisation of the labour market services, which allows private employment agencies to intermediate between firms and persons searching for a job.

A major policy shift of the Public Employment Services was the change from a supply-side to a demand-side orientation. This shift towards the 'market' was probably one of the reasons for the shift from specific labour market instruments (training and work experience projects) towards the *general mediation tasks*. The idea behind this policy was the so-called *slipstream philosophy*. The mediation of the unemployed workers that are most attractive for employers is seen as an essential mechanism to increase the job placements of workers that belong to the target groups with a weak labour market position. The creation of the Regional Boards increased the regionalisation of the labour market policy instruments to some extent. Moreover, recently the local authorities are playing a more important role in the job creation for particular target groups.

The wage moderation policy was rather successful in the 1980s. However, the increase of part-time jobs also played a major role in the growth of the working population. One of the most effective instruments in Dutch regional policy was the direct instrument of relocation of government offices. There are also positive results of the Firms Environment Policy, the Investment Premium Regulation and the Regional Development Companies. However, even when these regional policy measures are effective, both national and European budgets for regional policies are by far to small to achieve a substantial reduction in regional differences in economic performance and unemployment rates in the Netherlands.

The Public Employment Services considerably increased the number of persons they mediated to find a job. Older unemployed workers, long-term unemployed and ethnical minority groups slightly improved their employment chances. With regard to the target group objectives of the Employment Services, some evidence has been found on the relevance of the slipstream hypothesis. However, no effect could be found on the effect of the labour-market policies on the efficiency of the allocation process on the labour market.

Notes

1. The ILO-definition states that individuals are unemployed when they are without a paid job but are available for work and have been actively seeking work in the past four weeks. This differs from the official definition of Statistics Netherlands, which counts individuals only as unemployed if they search for a job of at least 12 hours. Furthermore, those who have a job for less than 12 hours but want a job for at least 12 hours are also counted as unemployed.

2. In the period 1980-1985, however, the training subsidies were more than doubled (see de Grip, 1988b).

3. If the vacancies registered by the Employment Services are related to the data of the Vacancy Survey of Statistics Netherlands, the Employment Services are much more important as a recruitment channel: 59 percent and 63 percent in the last two quarters of 1994 (SZW, 1995).

References

Armstrong, H. & J. Taylor (1993), *Regional Economics and Policy, Second Edition*, Harvester/Wheatsheaf: New York.

Bartels, C.P.A. & J.J. van Duijn (1981), *Regionaal-economisch beleid in Nederland*, Van Gorcum: Assen.

Borstlap, H. (1995), 'Employment policy: a two-pronged approach', in Jaspers. T., J. Schippers, J. Siegers & I. van Berkel (eds.), *Working Policies? Facts, analyses and policies concerning employment and non-participation in the Netherlands*, Wolters-Noordhoff: Groningen.

CBS (1994), 'De arbeidsmarkt per RBA', *Sociale Maandstatistiek*, No. 2, pp. 7-11.

Commissie Evaluatie Arbeidsvoorzieningswet (1995), *Arbeidsvoorziening in perspectief. Evaluatie Arbeidsvoorzieningswet 1991-1994*, VUGA-Uitgeverij: Den Haag.

Delsen, L. (1995), *Atypical Employment: an International Perspective. Causes, Consequences and Policy*, Wolters-Noordhoff: Groningen.

Dercksen, W.J. (1994), 'Arbeidsvoorziening: mission impossible?', *Economisch Statistische Berichten*, Vol. 79, No. 3969, pp. 633-637.

Dijk, J. van & H. Folmer (1992), 'The impact of personal and regional unemployment on individual wages in The Netherlands', in Verhaar, C.H.A. & L.G. Jansma (eds.), *On the Mysteries of Unemployment*, Kluwer: Dordrecht, pp.110-128.

Dijk, J. & & J. Oosterhaven (1994), 'Past, present and future of Dutch regional policy: with special reference to regional policy indicators', in Verhaar, C.H.A. & P.M. de Klaver (eds.), *The functioning of the economy and labour market an a peripheral region - the case of Friesland*, Fryske Akademy: Leeuwarden, pp. 111-35.

Dijk, J. van & P.H. Pellenbarg (1995), 'Regional problems and regional policy in The Netherlands', in Bandman, M., E. Wever & V. Seliverstov (eds.), *Regional Research and Spatial Development in the Netherlands*, Russian Academy of Sciences - Siberian Branch Institute of Economics and Industrial Engineering, Novosibirsk, pp. 19-39. (in Russian, an english version is available from the authors)

Eekma, K. (1995), *Spreiding KPN naar Groningen. De effecten op de economische structuur van de stad*, FRW/RUG: Groningen.

EZ (1990), *Regio's zonder Grenzen: Het regionaal-economisch beleid voor de periode 1991-1994*, Tweede Kamer 1989-1990, 21571, No. 1-2.

EC (1994), *Employment in Europe 1994*, European Communities: Brussels, Luxembourg.

EZ (1995), *Ruimte voor Regio's, het ruimtelijk economisch beleid tot 2000*, SDU Uitgeverij: Den Haag. Tweede Kamer 1995, nr.24060.

Glebbeek, A. & A. van Bruggen (1996), 'The Regional Employment Board: management or directorship?', in Verhaar, C.H.A. et al, *On the challenges of unemployment in a regional Europe*, Avebury: Aldershot, pp. 283-301.

Grip A. de (1987), *Onderwijs en arbeidsmarkt: scholingsdiscrepanties*, VU Uitgeverij: Amsterdam.
Grip A. de (1988a), 'Causes of labour supply and demand mismatches in the Dutch building trades', *De Economist*, Vol. 135, No. 2, pp. 182-200.
Grip A. de (1988b), *Scholing en werk. Een analyse van de scholingsproblemen op de arbeidsmarkt en het arbeidsmarktbeleid*, SMO-Boek: Den Haag.
Grip, A. de et al (1995), *Atypical employment relations by occupational sector in the European Union*, Maastricht (ROA-RM-1995/5E).
Hoevenberg, J. & A. de Grip (1994), *Indicators of occupational employment in the European Union*, ROA: Maastricht (ROA-R-1994/3E).
Kam, C.A. de, W. van Drimmelen & N. van Hulst (1995), *Loonvorming en loonpolitiek in Nederland*, Wolters-Noordhoff: Groningen.
Kleinknecht, A. (1994), 'Heeft Nederland een loongolf nodig? Een neo-Schumpeteriaans verhaal over bedrijfswinsten, werkgelegenheid en export', *Tijdschrift voor Politieke Ekonomie*, Vol. 17, No. 2, pp. 5-24.
Kloosterman, R.C. & T. Elfring (1991), *Werken in Nederland*, Academic Service: Schoonhoven.
Koning, J. de, P. Donker van Heel, A. Gelderblom, P. van Nes & C.TH. van Zandvliet (1995), *Arbeidsvoorziening in perspectief. Evaluatie Arbeidsvoorzieningswet 1991-1994, Deelonderzoek B: Resultaten en kosten*, VUGA-Uitgeverij: Den Haag.
Lever, M.H.C. (1995), 'Cao's en werkgelegenheid', *Economisch Statistische Berichten*, Vol. 80, No. 4003, pp. 300-303.
Lever, M.H.C. & W.A. Marquering (1995), 'Effect avv op werkgelegenheid blijkt beperkt', *Economisch Statistische Berichten*, Vol. 80, No. 4011, pp. 484-488.
Miljoenennota (1995), Tweede Kamer der Staten-Generaal (1994), SDU Uitgeverij: Den Haag.
OECD (1994a), *Employment Outlook 1994*, OECD: Paris.
OECD (1994b), *The OECD Jobs Study*, OECD: Paris.
OECD (1994c), *The OECD Jobs study, Evidence and Explanations, Part II, The Adjustment Potential of the Labour Market*, OECD: Paris.
Oosterhaven, J. (1993), 'Fiscale zones in Nederland?', *Economisch Statistische Berichten*, Vol. 78, No. 3911, pp. 454-457.
Oosterhaven, J. & H. Post (1993), 'Arbeidsparticipatie en werkloosheid in regionaal perspectief', *Tijdschrift voor Arbeidsvraagstukken*, Vol. 9, No. 4, pp. 378-383.
Pott-Buter, H.A. (1994), 'De bijzondere arbeidsmarktpositie van Nederlandse vrouwen', *Economisch Statistische Berichten*, Vol. 79, pp.352.
Scholten, H. & S. de Groot (1995), 'Integratie met behoud van specialisatie. Naar een nieuw model van arbeidsbemiddeling en sociale zekerheid', *Tijdschrift voor Arbeidsvraagstukken*, Vol. 11, No. 2, pp. 154-162.
Stanmeyre, S.G. (1990), *Een nieuwe opzet. Mogelijkheden van de nieuwe Arbeidsvoorzieningswet*, SMO-boek: Den Haag.
Stoffelsma, R.J. (1992), *Centrale overheid en regionale welvaart*, Stichting

Ruimtelijke Economie Groningen: Groningen. Proefschrift Rijksuniversiteit Groningen.
SZW (1990), *Rapportage arbeidsmarkt 1990*, Ministerie van Sociale Zaken en Werkgelegenheid: Den Haag.
SZW (1994), *Kwartaalbericht Arbeidsmarkt*, vierde kwartaal 1994, Ministerie van Sociale Zaken en Werkgelegenheid: Den Haag.
SZW (1995), *Kwartaalbericht Arbeidsmarkt*, eerste kwartaal 1995, Ministerie van Sociale Zaken en Werk-gelegenheid: Den Haag.
Teulings, C.N. (1994), 'Hoger minimumloon: meer werkgelegenheid', *Economisch Statistische Berichten*, Vol. 79, pp. 1112.
Teulings, C.N. (1995), 'Naschrift', *Economisch Statistische Berichten*, Vol. 80, No. 3391, pp. 16-17.
Thurow, L.C. (1975), *Generating Inequality*, MacMillan: New York.

7 Institutions and regional return to education in Sweden

Eugenia Kazamaki-Ottersten

7.1 Introduction

The 1990s of the Swedish labour market is entitled an era of change experiencing severe problems. These changes are induced by a sharp recession, by changes in industrial production and by growing structural deficiencies in the labour market constituency.

In most of the world, the former 'Taylor' production model, is gradually being replaced with high performance work organisations. Although there is no clear definition of what a 'high performance' workplace and work organisation is, several attempts have been made to describe the practices used within such workplaces and work organisations (Carnoy, Castells & Brenner, 1996). Among these practices self-managed teams, job rotation, total quality management, and quality control are most commonly cited. In Sweden many firms have undergone one or a mix of these types of changes to enhance production and raise efficiency in recent years. Part of these changes have been encouraged by public subsidies in the 1989 to 1995 period.

One outcome of organisational changes enhancing 'high performance' workplaces is that new markets for industrial products place higher standards on worker's performance which forces change on the entire training system. Increasingly training becomes a life time investment which takes place both at school and at the workplace. New patterns in recruitment policies are slowly established. Firms are as always selective in terms of labour quality in the hiring process, however, there is a growing emphasis on individual human and social capital endowments and individual ability to learn (Kazamaki-Ottersten, 1994a). These endowments are likely to be differently dispersed over regional labour markets.

Given the regional labour market differences in Sweden (Skedinger, 1993; Nilsson, 1995) we are interested in the regional dispersion of the return to human capital endowments. One argument is that the localisation of production is dependent upon the possibilities and restrictions given by technology bounds and by the availability of human capital endowments. The heterogeneity of the labour force in terms of education, skills and social capital defines the regions long-term development. Further, we assume that real wages determine how workers move between regions. The assertion is that workers move toward regions that offer high real wages. Then factor mobility interacting with a number of other variables such as for example moving costs can cause spatial economic structure to emerge and change (Krugman, 1996).

The goal of this chapter is to assess the return to education in different regions. The return to education is comprehended as a link between the market of labour and the market of education. First, in achieving competence the return to education is important. Second, in promoting and enhancing education in different regional areas the return to education is likely to be influential. Hence, because the wage will be influential and because the wage dispersion is small - notwithstanding growing over the past years - it is fruitful to study the regional return to education. Herein we find great regional differences in the return to education. Further, some regional patterns and trends can be tied to these differences.

Section 7.2 gives an overview of some Swedish labour market characteristics and section 7.3 assesses regional regularities. Section 7.4 briefly describes the extended human capital framework which is used to study the regional return to education. Section 7.5 presents the results from this framework. The last section 7.6 brings together some conclusions and identifies areas where future research is warranted.

7.2 General characteristics of the Swedish labour market

The Swedish labour market has for a long time been seen as the shining example concerning labour market systems, a competent labour force and vocational training. Full employment has been the major goal in the Swedish labour market (Edin & Holmlund, 1994). In its pursue extensive labour market policies, both supply and demand side measures, have been practiced. Figure 7.1 illustrates the development in unemployment and labour market measures during the period 1970-1994. There is a clear increase in both unemployment and the number of measures. The Swedish labour market has also been characterised by low mobility and a high degree of stability till the mid 1980s. Labour force participation in Sweden is high for both men and women. By international standards labour force participation for women, about 80 percent, is particularly high (Kazamaki-Ottersten & D'Agostino, 1993). Further, major regional labour market differences are present. The unemployment rate has consistently been higher in the northern forest counties of the country than in other areas as illustrated in Table 7.1. This suggests some structural problems in the Swedish economy.

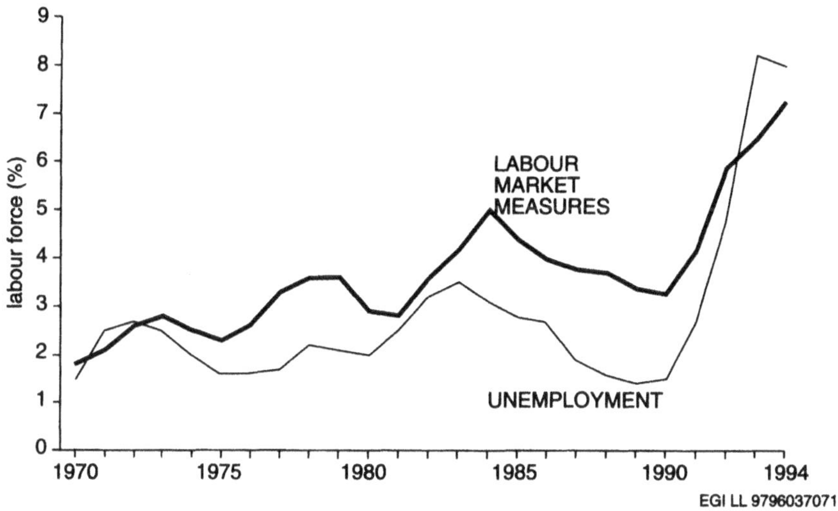

Figure 7.1 Development of unemployment and labour market measures in the period 1970-1994

The Swedish labour market is also highly institutionalised. First, it is a regulated market in terms of elaborate agreements between the agents in the labour market and law enforcement (Lindbeck, 1996; Rosen, 1996). There is an extensive labour market legislation. Many new laws were passed during the 1970s in order to improve the conditions of employment. The most well known among these and the one that can affect the labour market in terms of flexibility, mobility and unemployment is the 1974 Employment Act. This law stipulates 'employment till further notice' which means that an employment contract is valid until retirement. In addition, in cases of firing, dismissals and layoffs the 'first in last out principle' is to be followed (Kazamaki, 1991). It may be argued that the Employment Act adds to the cost of labour because the law does not discriminate between firms that may find it profitable to cultivate long-term relationships and firms that wish to operate more freely adapting short-term contracts in the labour market.

Secondly, unions have a long tradition and are influential in the wage setting which also makes the position of 'insiders' strong compared to the position of 'outsiders' in the labour market (Lindbeck & Snower, 1988).

Table 7.1
General characteristics and development of the labour market in different regions in Sweden

	Big Cities	Forest Counties	Other Counties	All Counties
1965-69				
U	1.4	3.0	1.6	2.0
Lmp	0.5	2.1	0.9	1.3
Wom	60.2	54.3	57.1	56.0
W	1218	1103	1061	1086
REP	168.3	78.2	84.5	90.6
1970-74				
U	1.9	3.3	2.0	2.4
Lmp	1.0	3.0	1.5	2.0
Wom	67.2	58.6	61.5	61.2
W	1887	1758	1698	1729
REP	227.5	122.6	141.8	142.8
1975-79				
U	1.4	2.8	1.8	2.0
Lmp	1.5	3.5	2.3	2.6
Wom	74.1	67.1	69.6	69.3
W	3198	3154	2983	3045
REP	438.2	255.1	282.7	287.1
1980-84				
U	2.2	3.9	2.9	3.1
Lmp	1.3	2.9	1.8	2.1
Wom	80.0	73.7	75.7	75.5
W	4878	4839	4614	4699
REP	595.9	351.8	364.4	383.4
1985-89				
U	1.6	3.0	2.0	2.3
Lmp	0.9	2.1	1.1	1.4
Wom	83.0	78.6	80.1	79.9
W	7140	7120	6829	6919
REP	895.3	441.2	474.7	501.4
1990-93				
U	3.8	5.3	4.1	4.5
Lmp	1.3	2.3	1.4	1.7
Wom	82.2	78.3	79.8	79.5
W	9821	9845	9439	9576
REP	1357.0	605.3	701.4	733.6

U: unemployment rate (percentage share of labour force), Lmp: number of individuals in relief work and labour market training (percentage share of labour force), Wom: female labour force participation, W: wages (öre per worked hour), REP: average price on owned houses (thousand krona).

Source: From different tables in Nilsson (1995)

A large fraction of the Swedish labour force is unionised including both white collar and blue collar workers. It is noteworthy that during the period 1968-1981 a positive union wage effect (declining during the period of study) is found (D'Agostino, 1992). Wage solidarity policies have been practiced leaving little room for large wage dispersion (Edin & Holmlund, 1992). However, the wage system has become more decentralised in recent years and it has always allowed for bargaining at different levels, including the local level with induced wage drift.

Thirdly, Sweden has an extensive practise of labour market policies. The aim and content of these policies have changed over the years and are constantly changing. However, the stylised philosophy of the Rehn-Meidner model which strongly advocates the use of active labour market programs (ALMPs) as the basis of labour market policies is still reigning ever since it was introduced in the late 1940s. The Rehn-Meidner model was concerned with stabilisation, structural (sectoral and demographic) and distributional policies. The purpose of the ALMPs was initially to secure jobs for 'all' individuals. In the seventies the goal was to keep existing jobs and avoid layoffs. The policies were demand-side oriented. In the late seventies wage subsidies, inventory support, and direct government orders to industries were directed to industries in need. ALMPs in the 1980s were targeted to groups that encountered problems in the labour market, e.g. teenagers. Since the 1980s the measures have in large continued to be targeted to groups and industries in need. More recent measures aim at creating provisional jobs. The most common measures have been temporary relief jobs and labour market training programs (see Table 7.1). During the late 1980s and in the 1990s temporary relief jobs decreased in number while individual and firm targeted measures increased. In 1994 the aims of the National Labour Market Board were to make use of and fill vacant jobs, to find new ways to work and cut the long term unemployment, and to provide jobs to immigrants and handicapped people. The first aim suggests that in the presence of vacant jobs these are not necessarily filled immediately even if there is a large pool of unemployed. This could be, for example, the case if people are not at the right places, and if the requirements asked for by employers are not met by unemployed. The second aim suggests a failure in the hiring process. Finally, the third aim suggests that some groups are more severely exposed to unemployment than others so that particular efforts are needed to provide jobs to individuals with specific labour market weaknesses. In 1992/1993 the labour market policies accounted for 5.5 percent of GDP, when considering the expenditure of Swedish labour market policies, including all policies and regional and temporary industrial policies (the two latter account for 0.5 percent of GDP) (Johannesson, 1995).

ALMPs have been given priority to unemployment compensation till the early 1990s. The consistently low unemployment rate, on average about 2 percent, until recent years has been interpreted as the success of these policies. A view that needs to be scrutinised. First, the programs are expensive and by the mid 1990s consume 3 percent of the GDP (payments for unemployment compensation not included). Second, there is little evidence as to the effectiveness of these programs (Calmfors

& Skedinger, 1995; Forslund & Krueger, 1995). Most such evidence is adhered to very specific microeconomic evaluations (Johannesson, 1995). It is noteworthy to mention that it is likely that ALMPs have prevented long-term unemployment.

On the other hand persistence in labour market measures also cause problems (Kazamaki-Ottersten, 1996a). Further, most studies on the effects of labour market policies share the same caveat in that the causal relationship between unemployment and labour market policies is not obvious. A problem seldom addressed in the literature. High unemployment induces increased labour market support. Meanwhile, the Swedish experience shows generous support even during peaks. Kazamaki-Ottersten (1992) found that labour market measures removed what appears to be little of the variation in the unemployment rate, and thus, we should be careful in relating low unemployment rates to extensive labour market activity. Evaluations of different policies deserve closer scrutiny and more studies are warranted. Finally, there is a pattern found between high unemployment - high number of labour market policies - low education - low mobility. This pattern is discussed in a later section.

Does Sweden still represent an exempt labour market? In 1995 the open unemployment rate reached 8 percent (average European Community 11 percent, US 5.7 percent), whereof 35 percent were unemployed for a period longer than six months, about 4 percent participated in labour market programs, and a growing number of individuals is found outside the labour force. 1996 has seen a slight deterioration of this development. The dramatic increase in unemployment contrasts previous experiences, for example, the 1.2 percent in 1990. The incidence to long-term unemployment has increased which suggests difficulties in hiring individuals. It should, however, be noted that the incidence to long-term unemployment in Sweden is low by international standards (Kazamaki-Ottersten, 1996a). This is in part explained by the fact that a large number of individuals are in labour market programs and hence not registered as unemployed.

The development in the Swedish labour market suggests a potential for unemployment to stabilise at a level higher than previous experiences. It further suggests that the Swedish labour market is becoming more similar to the rest of Western Europe (Lindbeck, 1996). However, in terms of its constituency the Swedish labour market is quite unlike other markets in that Sweden has a most unusual employment structure.

Could the deteriorating labour market situation been anticipated? This could be the case if more attention had been paid to the overall development in the Swedish labour market in the late 1980s. During this period the number of individuals outside the regular labour market, in different labour market measures, 'partially' unemployed, or 'latently unemployed' (hidden unemployment) started to grow despite low unemployment.[1] It is interesting to pose the question why some individuals are not hired despite a favourable labour market situation in terms of labour demand. This suggests a failure in the adjustment of prices in the labour market. It can also suggest a failure, as previously noted, in the endowments of human and social capital. The deteriorating labour market could also been anticipated in Sweden's unusual growth of employment vastly accounted for in local public sector employment. Most of this growth has involved women. The growing employment in the public sector has created an unusual employment structure which is sensitive to cuts in public expenditure (Pencavel, 1996). The cuts in public expenditure during recent years have resulted in increases in unemployment.

In concluding this subsection we suggest an alternative explanation to the previous experiences of low unemployment in Sweden. The rate of structural change, measured as shifts in employment demand in the economy, in the 1950s till the 1980s, was modest, resulting in a low unemployment rate (Kazamaki-Ottersten, 1994b). A hypothesis is that in the early 1990s the stability previously experienced has been broken most likely leading to higher levels of unemployment. This statement has to be qualified in future research.

7.3 Regional labour markets

Sweden is divided into 24 counties commonly classified into three types of regions: forest counties, big city counties and all other counties (see figure 7.2). The forest counties are situated in the northern part of Sweden, whereas the big cities are found in the middle, southern and south-west-part, Stockholm, Malmö and Gothenburg. The 'other' counties are widely spread over the south up to the north.

Substantial differences exist between and within the three regions. The southern part is characterised by agriculture while the north is characterised by forest areas where most of the mining, the pulp and wood, and the ship-yard industry is found. Further, Stockholm is a private and public service metropolis, while Gothenburg has many manufacturing firms. There is a concentration of high quality jobs to the big cities and some regional areas. During the past 20 years the concentration of individuals is to areas with an already large concentration of population. The regions play different roles in the Swedish production system even if GNP per capita is regionally quite evenly distributed. The similarities in GNP per capita is in part explained by the generous transfer system. Wage differentials are rather small between regions despite differences in productivity. This can be attributed to the influence of unions and solidaristic wage policies as previously noted.

In terms of production all industry sectors have increased their production during the period 1972-1991 (Nutek, 1995) with the exception of labour intensive production, which diminished slightly. The largest increase in proportional terms has taken place in R&D intensive production, that is in production that enhances education. The geographical pattern of production has been quite stable during this period. The regions with most production are with a few exceptions the same as 20 years ago. Production and consumption are evenly distributed in terms of population and Stockholm, Gothenburg and Malmö provide a relatively higher private service production than the other regions both relative to population and to total production.

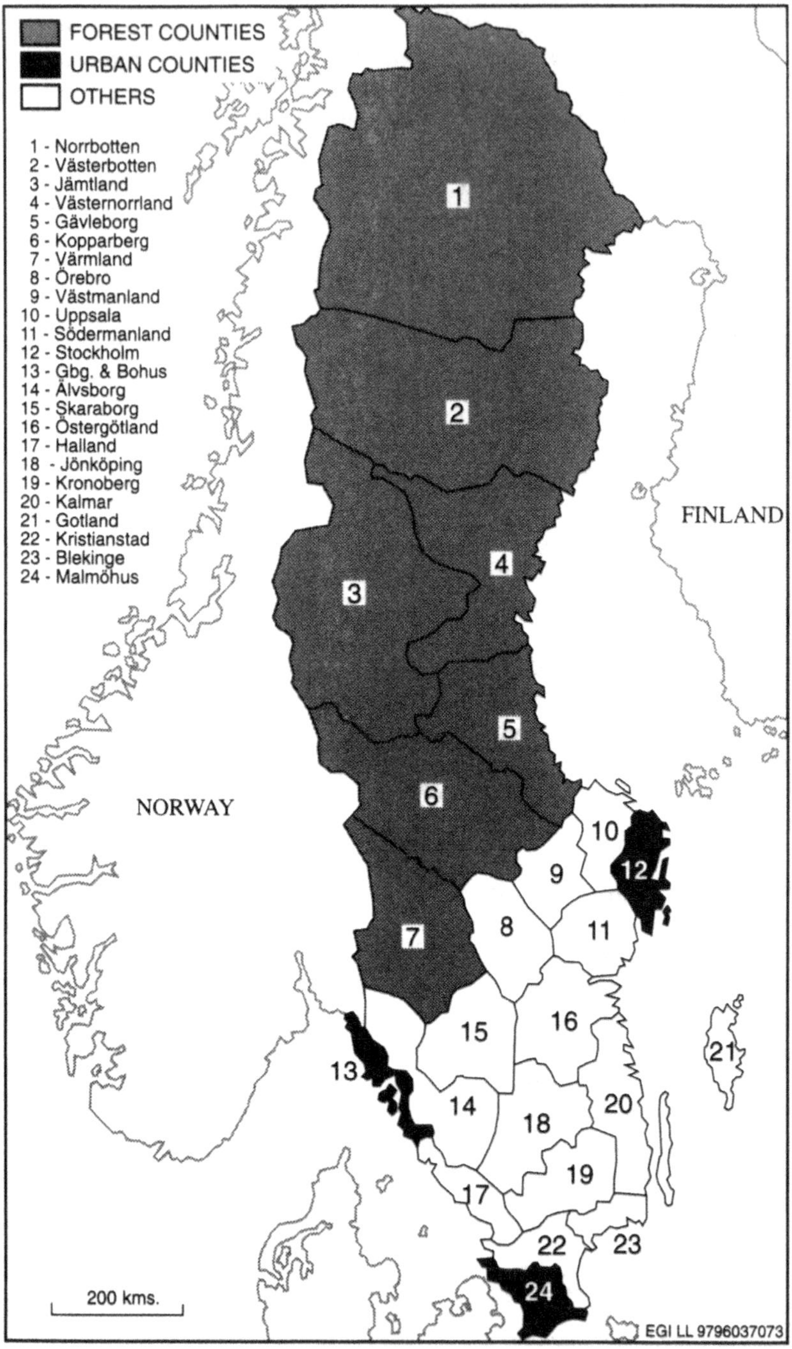

Figure 7.2 Regional classification in Sweden

The other regions, with the exception of regional centers, have a relatively high production of public services (Nutek, 1995). Labour intensive industry is found all over the country, whereas R&D intensive industry is concentrated to a few regional areas, in particular to Stockholm, large regional centers, and regional centers. The level of education differs between regions. In the big cities there a large share of the labour force, has at least three years of gymnasium (high school), including a large number of individuals with college degrees in comparison with the other regions. Table 7.2 shows the highest attained education in 1990 in the different regions using a somewhat finer regional division. The differences between the big city regions and larger regional centers in comparison to local and smaller regions are striking. Hence, there is a large degree of heterogeneity in labour, in terms of education. The pool of human and social capital endowments differs between regions. This difference is likely to affect the regions' development. New technologies and ideas most often emanate from regions with an industrial tradition and availability to individuals with qualified education.

Table 7.2
Highest attained education level in 1990 (percent)

	Pre High-school	High-school	College	Graduates PHDs
Stockholm region	30.7	47.9	22.4	0.9
Gothenburg region	38.0	42.4	18.8	0.8
Malmö region	38.1	43.0	17.9	1.1
Large regional centers	41.3	42.0	16.0	0.7
Regional centers	41.5	42.9	15.3	0.3
Local centers	46.3	41.4	12.2	0.2
Smaller regions	48.1	41.1	10.7	0.1
Small regions	51.1	39.3	9.4	0.1
All	40.0	42.9	16.5	0.6

Source: Nutek (1995)

The regional labour markets have shown stability up to the 1990s. The forest counties have overall experienced relatively high unemployment rates in comparison with other regional areas (Kazamaki-Ottersten, 1992). Many of the industries located in the forest counties were hit by supply shocks in the late 1970s. In a long-run perspective the difference in unemployment rates has remained robust, with the forest region experiencing an unemployment rate that on average has been 2-3 percent higher than the unemployment rate in Stockholm county until the early 1990s (see Table 7.1). In 1994 the unemployment rate was 7.5 percent in the big cities, 9.1 percent in the forest counties and 7.9 percent in other counties. With the sharp increase in unemployment during the past years there is some tentative evidence of smaller differences in unemployment rates between regional markets. This can in part be explained by the fact that there are proportionally more teenagers and immigrants in the big city areas and that the unemployment rates for these groups are high. Also unemployment among highly educated individuals has risen. Also these higher educaters more found in big city areas. The demographic distribution of the labour force differs in the three regional areas which also leads to differences in the endowments of education and skills available. The forest region has more retired individuals and few individuals in working age while the big cities have a larger demographic spread in the labour force.

An interesting question is whether there is unemployment persistence in some regions rather than others. During the 1964-1992 period, forest regions do not show higher persistence (measured as unemployment dependence on the unemployment rate) than other regions (Skedinger, 1993). ALMP have kept the unemployment rate low in the forest counties. In addition, the share of the long-term unemployed in the forest counties is relatively low in comparison with other counties that have been subject to persistence (Holmlund, 1993, Skedinger, 1993).

Table 7.3 shows the percentage of employees who belonged to a union by region in 1968, 1974, and 1981. Smaller regions are unionised to a higher degree than big cities. In addition, workers who live in Stockholm are less likely to join a union than those outside of Stockholm (D'Agostino, 1992). About 15 percent of the unionised workers live in Stockholm as compared to 24 percent non-unionised workers.

Let us next consider some other regional characteristics, as illustrated in Table 7.1. First, over the 1975-92 period there has been a drop for men in labour force participation in all regions, being sharpest in the Malmö region and in the small regions. For women we find an increase in labour force participation in all regions, particularly sharp in the smaller and small regions. Still, labour force participation is higher among women in big cities than in the rest of the country. This situation has been stable since the mid 1960s. Second, wages are quite equally distributed in the three regions, which in part can be explained by the solidaristic wage policy and by the influence of unions in the Swedish labour market (Edin & Holmlund, 1992).

Another important characteristic of regional labour markets is the supply of housing and the prices of real estate. Despite quite evenly distributed wages the prices of homes differ substantially between regions as shown in Table 7.1. The big cities show by far higher prices than the other areas, and the forest counties have had much lower prices. The market of housing and the market of labour are interrelated, although few studies have paid attention to this phenomenon. The Swedish housing market is quite regulated with controlled rents in government-own housing. This can lead to larger regional unemployment differences (Hughes & McGormick, 1987). In Sweden the housing system can fail to provide flexibility resulting in less mobility. The geographical mobility in Sweden has declined since the 1960s. At the end of the 1960s about 3 percent of the households moved to another county, at the early 1990s only 2 percent moved (Holmlund, 1993). In part this can be explained by the fact that in most households today two individuals work and thus moving costs are high. The tax structure and the economic situation in different counties are also likely to affect the moving behaviour.

Quite interestingly, despite low mobility between different regions, as in most other Western European countries, there are clear demographic differences in moving behaviour. Moving is affected by educational level, age and gender. Individuals with more than two years of college education attribute to one fourth of the mobility between regions in 1990. This ratio is four times as large as their ratio of the population (Nutek, 1995). These individuals clearly move to where the jobs are. Individuals in the age group 15-24 move to densely populated regions, either to find a job or to acquire higher education. Another group which has shown a great deal of mobility is that of the young low educated women. They have moved to a greater extent than the higher educated. During the second part of the 1980s this group of women moved to the big cities and to regional centers to take new jobs in public and private services. While women moved, low educated men remained in the regions with traditional industrial production. This suggests a concentration of young well educated men to the Stockholm region while well educated women are more spread over the country.

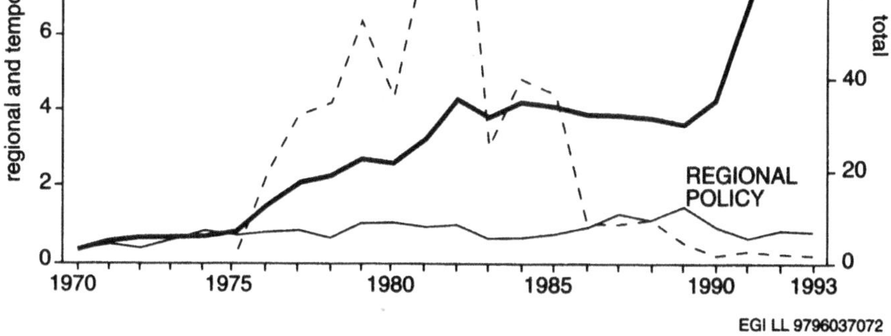

Figure 7.3 Expenditures on regional policy and temporary industrial measures (1970-1994; SEK)

Historically the forest counties have been subject to more labour market policies than other counties (see Table 7.1). A number of labour market policies have been targeted directly to different regions. Figure 7.3 shows the expenditures on directed regional measures over the years as well as of temporary measures. An increase in regional policies followed at the end of 1979. At the end of the 1980s most of the individuals involved in labour market programs were found in the forest counties. Although the aim and the type of measures have varied most measures are found in counties with higher than average unemployment rates. Persistence in labour market policies is suggested. Kazamaki-Ottersten (1992) found that the change in unemployment rates in the forest counties and in all other counties were rather synchronised with business cycle variations.

Given the regional differences the question arises whether policies have equated the differences and stimulated production towards lagging regions. Ever since the 1950s there has been a discussion on where to locate industries. Many industries since the 1960s have been located outside the big city areas in order to handle the expansion of the cities, as well as to provide and stimulate employment in less densely populated and less prosperous counties. In the 1980s parts of the public sector were moved from the big cities in order to equate regional differences. The National Labour Market Board gives rather elaborate recommendations to the county labour markets and money is distributed according to specific resource allocation tables (AMS, 1994/95). The National Labour Market Board outlines the general recommendations which are to be followed with some regional autonomy. However, the counties in large follow the general recommendations.

Table 7.3
Percentage of employees who were members of a Union in 1986, 1974 and 1981

Place of Residence	Stockholm	Gothenburg, Malmö and other cities >30,000	Cities <30,000	Rural areas
1968	59	73	76	69
1974	64	77	80	77
1981	75	87	87	84

Source: D'Agostino (1992)

In order to facilitate mobility, apart from the employment service administration, allowances have been paid to individuals in order to make geographical mobility economically feasible. This kind of program has varied over the years (Wadensjö,

1995). The 'getting-started' help, an extra amount as a pure incentive to move, has shown certain drawbacks. It has been argued that the grant is given to individuals who would have moved anyhow. The grant, introduced in 1959, was therefore abolished on July 1987. However, it was reintroduced in 1994. As with most programs the eligibility criterion has been that the individual concerned is either unemployed or risks to become unemployed. The individual should also be looking for a job in another region through the public employment service.

Finally, few studies have discussed the regional effectiveness of ALMPs and the results are quite diverse. For example, locking in effects are advocated in Nilsson (1995). Fredriksson (1995, p. 25), on the other hand, does not find that 'the provision of active labour market programs has prolonged adjustment by impeding migration flows in response to region-specific shocks'. Hence, more research is warranted in this area.

7.4 Human and social capital: three hypotheses

This non-exhaustive regional description suggests that Swedish regions clearly play different roles in economic activity. However, some regions are trapped in less favourable roles, as the northern forest counties. These regions show a number of weaknesses. It has a high unemployment level, and a low educational level, it is subject to excessive labour market measures and young individuals move to more prosperous areas. 'Brain-drain' can arise because the young and the more educated move. This may prevent a decent degree of technological and structural change in terms of enhancing required education and skills. Potential locking - in effects also leave the pool of unemployed with the less skilled and less attractive workers. In the long-run the forest counties' probability to attract highly educated individuals and high tech jobs is undermined. This scenario is aggravated if the return to education in this region is lower than in other areas.

The labour market is crucial for providing a healthy economic environment. Wages, education and skills are important factors in this market. The regional return to education may be a hard concept to define because individuals are moving from one region to another (even though less so in Western Europe than in the United States). For example, relatively more individuals have moved from the forest counties to other areas (except in the 1971-80 period). Interesting is that, despite a rather similar wage distribution in the country, large differences in educational trends exist. We believe that the return to education can shed some light on this. Further, the differences in the education trends most likely are also affected by social capital factors in the different regions.

It has long been recognised that individuals possess an endowment of human capital, most often made concrete in terms of number of years of schooling. However, also individual specific information about innate abilities and family background or, hereditary and environmental factors are important and should complement the information on economically oriented human capital. We call these kind of factors social capital (see also chapter three). Each individual possesses an endowment based on human and social capital. Social capital is embodied in an individuals relations to other individuals. In contrast to human capital which is an intra-personal concept, social capital is an inter-personal concept. Social capital can be seen as non-transferable advantages of birth, conveyed by parental behaviours, bearing on later-life productivity (Loury, 1977). In a broader framework social capital refers to properties of relationships among individuals, both ties based on kinship and other relations acquired or dissolved over the course of a lifetime.[2] Further, social capital can be viewed as an individuals personal social network (Burt, 1992). Briefly there are different dimensions of social capital, one relates to the number of relationships the individual has accumulated, another concerns the type of relationship and a third is related to the concept of time. In terms of the dimension that concerns the type of relationship we make a distinction between strong and weak ties (Granovetter, 1973). Strong ties are used to denote relations to, e.g., family members and close friends while weak ties can refer to acquaintances or distant relatives.

Finally, given the regional differences discussed, we expect some regional variation in the return to education. Three hypotheses we wish to examine:

1. The return to education is high in big cities, in university cities and in cities with substantial technological change. These regions have and attract a large number of educated workers.

2. The return to education is low in areas with low mobility and in areas where individuals in ALMPs are overrepresented like the forest regions. Areas with a large fraction of low educated individuals and difficulties in attracting individuals with higher education are subject to low return to education.

3. The effects of social capital on earnings are stronger in regions with established industrial traditions. The latter are based on strong social capital bonds. Hence, in regions with strong industrial traditions, social capital factors are influential.

7.5 An empirical analysis of regional returns to education

The empirical framework in this paper is based on an extended human capital approach.[3] Building on the notion of equalizing differentials by Adam Smith in 'the Wealth of Nations', the theory of human capital is predominant in the determination of wages. Important contributions in this area have been made by Jacob Mincer (1958, 1962, 1974), Theodore Schultz (1960, 1961), and Gary Becker (1962, 1964). In its most simplistic form, the traditional human capital equation can be specified as follows:

$$lny_i = lny_o + {}_{\beta}s_i + {}_{\beta}x_i + {}_{\beta}x_i^2 + u_i$$

In this model wage y is determined by schooling s and experience x. This specification has been extensively tested. Most of the human capital studies deal with US data. Applications related to earnings, education and the return to education are quite common (e.g. Freeman, 1975; Lydon, 1990; Pencavel, 1991; Psacharopoulos, 1985; Willis, 1986). A typical finding is that the return to schooling is substantially higher in developing countries than in developed countries. In the 1970s the average return to schooling was about 15 percent in developing countries and 9 percent in high-income countries (Psacharopoulos, 1985). A recent Swedish study shows that the income premium to schooling in Sweden has been declining during the period 1968-1981 from 7 to about 3 percent. Thereafter there has been a small increase in the return to education to about 5-6 percent (Björklund & Kjellström, 1993) (see also Edin, Fredriksson & Holmlund, 1994).

Recent studies have incorporated the effects of family background on earnings and returns to schooling and discussed the importance of unobservable worker attributes. A model of assertive mating developed by Lam & Schoeni (1993) supports that parental characteristics represent unobservable worker attributes. In an attempt to account for omitted variables, Kazamaki-Ottersten, Mellander, Meyersson and Nilsson (KOMMN, 1994) included social capital indicators into the human capital specification and found that these indicators significantly influence earnings, both directly and indirectly, through schooling. They further found that the return to education in Sweden is about 3-4 percent, and quite robust over the period 1984-1991.

The approach used in this chapter emanates from a traditional Mincer equation allowing for the effects of education, experience, tenure, and a number of control variables on wages. This Mincer equation is adjusted for three major problems.[4]

1. selection bias, which arises because in estimating earnings equations we are restricted to individuals receiving positive wages;

2. omitted variable bias. If some variables, which affect earnings and are correlated with education, are left out of the wage equation, this will induce a bias in the estimated return to education; and

3. measurement error. If there are random errors in the measure of education this will also bias the coefficient for education.

Lam & Schoeni (1993) show that the biases caused by omitted variables and measurement error can work in different directions. If an omitted variable is positively related to (true) schooling then the omitted variable bias will be positive while the bias arising from the measurement error in education will be negative.

To avoid the three pitfalls, we extend Leibowitz (1974). In this a recursive relationship between education and wage; education is determined by individual and family background characteristicswas postulated, whereas income is a function of education, other human capital variables, and individual and family background characteristics. This modelling framework makes it possible to address the second and the third problem. By recognizing that individual and family background characteristics may affect the wage directly, as well as indirectly through education, Leibowitz accounts for the problem of possible omitted variable bias, while education is explained within the model. In extending Leibowitz's framework we make use of social capital in order to account for omitted variable bias. This framework does not take the problem of selectivity bias into account, however. We remedy this shortcoming by including a selection equation. Further, in modelling the selection of individuals into 'wage earners' and 'others' we extend the common practice of considering only individuals in the labour force and include also some individuals outside the labour force, in particular, students.

The model sketched above is based on the human capital tradition, however, it also brings some sociological theory into this tradition by including the concept of social capital. Within this framework we assess regional differences in the return to education in the three regions: the big cities, the forest counties and the other counties.

7.5.1 Data and model specification

The data we use are from the Swedish Household Market and Non Market Activities (HUS) study (see Klevmarken & Olovsson, 1993). We make use of cross-section data for 1984, 1986, and 1991.[5] Our basic human capital variables are: schooling, working experience, and tenure, i.e. the period of employment at the current employer. All of these are measured in integer numbers of years. In addition, we use a dummy variable for the lack of experience, which is equal to one if the respondent's total working experience is less than three months and zero otherwise. The reason to include this dummy variable is to account for possible discontinuities in the wage-experience profile near the origin. For conformity between experience and no experience, experience is equal to one if the respondent's working experience exceeds three months.

Concerning the social capital variables, it is assumed that the individual's social capital varies over an individuals life cycle. To capture this variation we distinguish the social capital associated with childhood and youth from the social capital generated in the individual's adult life. In addition, we make a distinction between relational structures characterised by strong and weak ties, respectively. For the respondent's childhood and youth we include indicators of strong ties (family ties) and weak ties (community ties).[6] Among the family variables we consider the extent to which the mother stayed at home when the children were young, measures of the occupation of the respondent's father, and the father's and mother's education. Strong bonds between parents and children is a form of social capital which demands both physical presence of parents and their attention and involvement (Parcel & Menaghan, 1993). The social capital generated in the individual's adult life is partitioned correspondingly. Adult family ties are measured by marital status, number of children, etc. The indicators of community ties are measured by the time used by the individual in activities that differ with respect to the amount of external contacts (relations outside the family). On the one extreme there are activities that are characterised by no external contacts at all, like reading books. On the other extreme there are activities directly, focused on creating and maintaining external contacts, like entertaining quests at home and visiting friends. (Unfortunately, the data on adult life community ties are available only for the 1984 survey.)

7.5.2 Results

There are large differences in the regional return to education in Sweden. As Table 7.4 shows, these differences are robust over the study period. The return to education in the forest counties is lower than in all other counties. However, this result is not significant. For the two other regions the results on the return to education are significant on at least the 5 percent level, with the exception of the return to education in other counties in 1991 (note that there are fewer observations in 1991). Thus, the results on forest regions are highly tentative, while the results on big cities are robust.

Table 7.4
Regional differences in the return to education
(standard errors in parenthesis)

	Big Cities	Forest Counties	Other Counties
1984	0.0322	0.0176	0.0681
	(0.0181)	(0.0164)	(0.0153)
1986	0.0491	-0.00594	0.0541
	(0.0191)	(0.0255)	(0.0150)
1991	0.0600	0.0104	0.0103
	(0.0326)	(0.0281)	(0.0281)

A priori we expected the return to education to be highest in the big cities, in areas with a high level of education and in areas with a large amount of technical change. This is the case in 1991 for big city counties and in 1984 and 1986 for the 'other' counties which have the highest return in line with our expectations. The return to education in the big cities has varied between 3-6 percent and has increased over the years. In the 'other' counties the return to education was close to 7 percent in 1984 and over 5 percent in 1986, hence showing decreasing returns to education. Decreasing returns to education may be the case if the supply of individuals with higher education has grown large.

The results with respect to the social capital factors on earnings are quite interesting. There is not only a great amount of variation between the three regions over the period, but also within the three regions over the years. If we add the number of significant social capital variables over the years, the other counties and the forest counties are very close, whereas the big cities have few significant social capital indicators. Another phenomenon is that for the other counties the number of significant social capital variables has decreased drastically since 1984, whereas for the forest counties the spread of significant social capital indicators is quite even over the years. However, overall, for all regions there is a falling number of significant social capital indicators. In the forest counties the mother's and father's education has an effect on the individual's wage. The mother's and father's education turn up as significant variables in the other two regions as well.

The results from the 1984 time-use sample indicate that community ties matter in that being introvert - that is the extreme of external contacts - clearly affects the earnings negatively in both forest and big city counties, albeit the effect is small. The estimate for the other counties also turns up with a negative sign.

The low wage premium in the forest counties in comparison with the rest of the country raises the question of 'braindrain'. Individuals with a high level of education are not induced to stay in the forest counties, and so they will move. This aggravates the problems induced by the institutional system, which leaves areas with poor human and social capital endowments into the hands of more labour market policies and hence growing locking-in effects. In addition, a low premium to education does not give incentives to acquire higher education if one wants to stay in the region. Thus, the pattern previously stated in the descriptive part of this paper is sustained. A low return to education stabilises the pattern of high unemployment - high number of labour market policies - low education - and low mobility.

Given the above tentative results it is suggested that incentives to acquire higher education, wage adjustment to labour market changes, and fewer labour market programs, are likely to allow for structural changes. These can change fundamental patterns which impair on a healthy labour market constituency and by this achieve more flexibility in regional markets.

7.6 Conclusions

This chapter has provided some evidence that regions with a poor educational background, high unemployment and many ALMPs enhance lower return to education than other regions. The incentives to acquire education is low in such regions and individuals with higher education move to regions where the reward to education is higher. Such a pattern can induce 'brain drain' and 'new investment drain'.

Institutional factors may aggravate this pattern. Generous labour market support is likely to prevent or slow down the needed long-term structural change in problem areas. In a long-run perspective this development is fatal. Intentions to keep low unemployment in all counties at any point in time can result in long-run structural disturbances and labour market deficiencies.

The study also showed that social capital indicators affect earnings. The effects, however, differ between different regions during the 1984 to 1991 period. Social capital indicators affect earnings more in regions with stronger industrial traditions, like the forest counties and other counties, than the big cities. In making policy recommendations in different regions it is useful to consider both human capital and social capital endowments. In doing this, more research is warranted.

Notes

1. Individuals are 'partially' unemployed if they work less than they desire due to labour market conditions (less than 40 hours). Statistics Sweden defines 'latently' unemployed as those who wished and could have worked at the time of the interview but did not look for a job. These individuals do not fulfill the requirements on seeking a job but nevertheless assert that they want to work, for example, individuals that do not look for a job at the moment and individuals in vocational training. In 1993 336,000 individuals were partially unemployed and 140,300 were latently unemployed while 356,000 individuals were in open unemployment. See further Kazamaki-Ottersten (1996b).

2. There are many different uses of the term social capital in the literature, see: Granovetter (1973), Bordieu (1980, 1986), Coleman (1988, 1990), Putnam (1993, 1995), and Fukuyama (1995).

3. This section in large follows Kazamaki-Ottersten, Mellander, Meyerson and Nilsson (KOMMN, 1994). The empirical model briefly sketched in this section has been extended to account for regional return to education.

4. For a discussion on the shortcomings of the traditional human capital approach see, for example, Griliches and Mason (1972), Taubman (1976a,b) Griliches (1977, 1979) and Blackburn and Neumark (1995).

5. The 1984 data set is based on a sample of over 2100 Swedish households, identified by a stratified sample of Swedish speaking individuals aged 18-74 years. In each household with couples, either married or living together, both partners were interviewed. The response rate was approximately 74 percent, this yields 1564 households and 2795 individuals. The data contain information on, i.a., conditions during childhood, education, labour market experience, wages, and

family composition. The data were augmented with register information. In addition, in 1984 a time-use survey was conducted, based on telephone interviews.

In 1986 the data were partly updated by information from the personal interviews conducted in 1984 and partly by means of a new supplementary sample, directed to over 800 households. The individuals included in the supplement were asked approximately the same questions as in 1984. No time-use survey was conducted in 1986. For the 1986 panel the response rate was about 80 percent and for the supplement 60 percent, yielding total numbers of households and individuals of 1574 and 2724, respectively. The 1991 data contain slightly fewer individuals.

Individuals of age 65 or less, unable to work or retired, selfemployed, farmers, fishermen, and hunters are excluded. Remaining individuals in the samples are both members of the labour force and persons outside the labour force. According to the definitions used in the HUS survey, the labour force comprises those that are either gainfully employed or unemployed/laid off individuals that have looked for work within two months of the date of the interview.

The inclusion of individuals outside the labour force means that the population we analyse is more broadly defined than commonly; usually the samples used for the estimation of wage equations cover only individuals within the labour force. However, the relevant sample is determined by the variables that are endogenised. If the wage is the only endogenous variable the appropriate sample comprises individuals who want to work (members of the labour force). When schooling is also explained it is natural to include students as well. In addition, we include individuals that are potential labour force members or student. Both belong to the group which, in the HUS terminology, 'work in the home'. The potential labour force members are identified as working home individuals that have previous labour market experience and have responded affirmatively to the question if they want to work in the future. As potential students are designated working home individuals that were students during the previous year.

6. Numerous measures for the strength of ties have been used in the aftermath of Granovetter's 1973 article. The most common measure used has been the indicators 'closeness of a relationship' in which close friends are considered as close ties while acquaintances are weak ties. Other measures refer to the closeness of the two parties but also the source of the tie, such as relatives or neighbours. The lack of data in this study makes it necessary to use the type of relationship (family, community) as a proxy for the strength of a tie.

References

AMS, (1994/95), Uppföljning av länsarbetsnämndernas verksamhetsplaner, *Utredningsenheten*, 1995.

Becker, G.S. (1962), Investment in Human Capital: A Theoretical Analysis, *Journal of Political Economy*, 70 Supplement, Part 2, pp. S9-549.

Becker, G.S. (1964), *Human Capital: A Theoretical and Empirical Analysis, with Special Reference to Education*, National Bureau of Economic Research: New York.

Björklund, A. & C. Kjellström (1993), *Avkastningen på utbildning i Sverige 1968 till 1991*, (The Return to Education in Sweden between 1968 and 1991), mimeo, Institutet för social forskning.

Blackburn, M.L. & D. Neumark (1995), Are OLS Estimates of the Return to Schooling Biased Downward?, *The Review of Economics and Statistics*, 77, pp. 217-230.

Bordieu, P. (1980), Le Capital Social. Notes Provisaires, *Actes de la Recherche en Science Sociales*, 3, pp. 2-3.

Bordieu, P. (1986), The Forms of Capital, in: Richardson, J. (ed.), *Handbook of Theory and Research for the Sociology of Education*, Greenwood Press: Westpoint, CT.

Burt, R.S. (1992), *Structural Holes: The Social Structure of Competition*, Harvard University Press: Cambridge.

Calmfors, L. & P. Skedinger (1995), *Does Active Labour Market Policy Increase Employment? - Theoretical Considerations and Some Empirical Evidence from Sweden*, IUI Working Paper No. 429.

Carnoy, M., M. Castells & C. Brenner (1996), *What is Happening to the U.S. Labour Market?*, Manuscript, Stanford University.

Coleman, J.S. (1988), Social Capital in the Creation of Human Capital, *American Journal of Sociology*, 94, Supplement, pp. 95-120.

Coleman, J.S. (1990), *Foundations of Social Theory*, The Belknap Press of Harvard University Press: Cambridge.

D'Agostino, H. (1992), *Why do Workers Join Unions?*, Almqvist and Wiksell International: Stockholm.

Edin, P-A, & B. Holmlund (1992), *The Swedish Structure: The Rise and Fall of Solidarity Wage Policy?*, Working Paper 1992:13, Department of Economics: Uppsala.

Edin, P-A, & B. Holmlund (1994), *Arbetslösheten och arbetsmarknadens funktionssätt, Bilaga 8 till Långtidsutredningen.*

Edin, P-A., P. Fredriksson & B. Holmlund (1994), *Utbildningsnivå och utbildningsavkastning i Sverige*, (The level of Education and the Return to Education in Sweden), mimeo, Uppsala Universitet.

Forslund, A. & A.B. Krueger (1995), *An Evaluation of the Swedish Active Labour Market Policy - New and Received Wisdom*, SNS Occasional Paper, No. 65:

Stockholm.
Fredriksson, P. (1995), *The Dynamics of Regional Labour Markets and Active Labour Market Policy: Swedish Evidence*, Department of Economics: Uppsala.
Freeman, R.B. (1975), Overinvestment in College Training, *Journal of Human Resources*, 10, pp. 287-311.
Fukuyama, F. (1995), *Trust: The Social Virtues and the Creation of Prosperity*, Free Press: New York.
Granovetter, M.S. (1973), The Strength of Weak Ties, *American Journal of Sociology*, 78, pp. 1360-1380.
Griliches, Z. & W.M. Mason (1972), Education, Income, and Ability, *Journal of Political Economy*, 80, pp. S74-103.
Griliches, Z. (1977), Estimating the Returns to Schooling: Some Econometric Problems, *Econometrica*, 45, pp. 1-22.
Griliches, Z. (1979), Sibling Models and Data in Economics: Beginnings of a Survey, *Journal of Political Economy*, 87, Part 2, pp. S37-64.
Holmlund, B. (1993), *Arbetslösheten - konjunkturfenomen eller systemfel, Bilaga 12 till Ekonomikommisionens betänkande*, SOU 1993:16, Nya villkor för ekonomi och politik, Almänna förlaget: Stockholm.
Hughes, G. & B. McCormick (1987), Housing Markets, Unemployment and Labour Market Inflexibility in the UK, *European Economic Review*, 31.
Johannesson, J. (1995), Microeconomic Evaluations of Labour Market Policy Measures in Sweden, in Johannesson, J. & E. Wadensjö (eds.), *Labour Market Policy at the Crossroads*, EFA, Ministry of Labour: Stockholm.
Kazamaki, E. (1991), *Firm Search, Sectoral Shifts, and Unemployment*, Almqvist and Wiksell International: Stockholm.
Kazamaki-Ottersten, E. (1992), An Empirical Analysis of Unemployment by Region: a case study - Sweden, in Verhaar, C.H.A. & L.G. Jansma (eds.), *On the Mysteries of Unemployment*, Kluwer Academic Publishers: Dordrecht.
Kazamaki-Ottersten, E. & H. D'Agostino (1993), *Women, Jobs and Wages*, presented at ESPE, June 3-5.
Kazamaki-Ottersten, E. (1994a), Trends in Recruitment Practices in Swedish Companies, *Journal of Vocational Training*, 1, pp. 60-65.
Kazamaki-Ottersten, E. (1994b), Sectoral Employment Shifts and Unemployment, *Labour*, 8, pp. 377-394.
Kazamaki-Ottersten, E., E. Mellander, E. Meyersson & J. Nilsson (1994), *Pitfalls in the Measurement of the Return to Education*, IUI, Working Paper 414.
Kazamaki-Ottersten, E. (1996a), Combating Long-Term Unemployment in Sweden, Europäisches Forschungsinstitut Köningswinter, forthcoming.
Kazamaki-Ottersten, E. (1996b), The Labour Market Situation in Sweden, forthcoming, in Carlsson, B. (ed), Kluwer Publishers: Dordrecht.
Klevmarken, A. & P. Olovsson (1993), *Household Market and Nonmarket Activities: Procedures and Codes 1984—1991, Vol. I and II*, The Industrial Institute for Economic and Social Research and Almqvist & Wiksell International: Stock-

holm.
Krugman, P. (1996), *A Dynamic Spatial Model, Chapter 5*, Mimeo, Stanford University.
Lam, D. & R.F. Schoeni (1993), Effects of Family Background on Earnings and Returns to Schooling: Evidence from Brazil, *Journal of Political Economy*, 101, pp. 710-740.
Leibowitz, A. (1974), Home Investments in Children, *Journal of Political Economy*, 82, Part 2, pp. 5115-5131.
Lindbeck, A & D. Snower (1988), *The Insider-Outsider Theory of Employment and Unemployment*, MIT Press: Mass.
Lindbeck, A. (1996), *The West European Employment Problem*, IUI Working Paper, No. 466.
Loury, G. (1977), A Dynamic Theory of Racial Income Differences, Chapter 8, in Wallace, P.A. & A. Le Mund (eds.), *Women, Minorities, and Employment Discrimination*, Lexington Books: Lexington, Massachusetts.
Lydon, M. (1990), *Movements in the Earnings/Schooling Relationship 1940-86*, unpublished Ph.D. dissertation, Stanford University.
Mincer, J. (1958), Investment in Human Capital and Personal Income Distribution, *Journal of Political Economy*, 66, pp. 281-302.
Mincer, J. (1962), On the-Job Training: Costs, Returns, and Some Implications, *Journal of Political Economy*, 70, Part 2, pp. 550-579.
Mincer, J. (1974), *Schooling, Experience and Earnings*, Columbia University Press for the National Bureau of Economic Research: New York.
Nilsson, C. (1995), *Den interregionala omflyttningen i Sverige*, EFA, Arbetsmarknadsdepartementet: Stockholm.
Nutek, (1995), *Bilaga 5 till Långtidsutredningen.*
Parcel, T.L. & E.G. Menaghan (1993), Family Capital and Childrens Behavioral Problems, *Social Psychology Quarterly*, 56, pp. 120-135.
Pencavel, J. (1991), Higher Education, Productivity, and Earnings: A Review, *Journal of Economic Education*, Fall, pp. 331-359.
Pencavel, J. (1996), *Selected International Experience Concerning the Legal Framework for Collective Bargaining and Unionism*, Manuscript, Stanford.
Psacharopoulos, G. (1985), Returns to Education: A Further International Update and Implications, *Journal of Human Resources*, 20, pp. 583-597.
Putnam, R. (1993), *Making Democracy Work*, Princeton University Press: Princeton, New York.
Putnam, R. (1995), Bowling Alone: America's Declining Social Capital, *Journal of Democracy*, 6-1, pp. 65-78.
Rosen, S. (1996), Public Employment and the Welfare State in Sweden, *Journal of Economic Literature*, 34, pp. 729-740.
Schultz, T.W. (1960), Capital Formation by Education, *Journal of Political Economy*, 68, pp. 571-583.
Schultz, T.W. (1961), Investment in Human Capital, *American Economic Review*,

51, pp. 1-17.
Skedinger, P. (1993) *Hur fungerar de regionala arbetsmarknaderna?*, ur Tretton aspekter på regional utveckling: Nutek.
Taubman, P. (1976a), Earnings, Education, Genetics and Environment, *Journal of Human Resources*, 11, pp. 447-461.
Taubman, P. (1976b), The Determinants of Earnings: Genetics, Family and Other Environment - A Study of Male Twins, *American Economic Review*, 66, pp. 858-870.
Wadensjö, E. (1995), Effects of Labour Market Policy on Wages and Prices, in Johannesson, J. & E. Wadensjö (eds.), *Labour Market Policy at the Crossroads*, EFA, Ministry of Labour: Stockholm.
Willis, R.J. (1986), Wage Determinants: A Survey and Reinterpretation of Human Capital Earnings Functions, in Aschenfelter, O. & R. Layard (eds.), *Handbook of Labour Economics*, l, North-Holland Elsevier Science Publishers: Amsterdam, pp. 525-602.

8 Institutions and regional labour markets in Spain

Carlos Álvarez; José M. F. Polanco & Santos M. Ruesga[1]

8.1 Introduction

This chapter analyses the different behaviour in the regional labour markets of Spain, with special emphasis on how institutional variables affect them. Firstly, we analyse the institutional framework of the Spanish labour market, different aspects of the labour policies developed in the last decades, and the recent performance of the labour market. In section three, we study the basic characteristics of the regional labour markets in Spain. Following this, we analyse the existing disparities among the regional markets and their most recent changes. By using a logit method we establish a typology of regions. Finally, trying to understand further the regional divergences, we elaborate an explanatory model of the disparities between regional supply and demand with the help of structural and institutional variables.

8.2 The Spanish labour market

8.2.1 General characteristics of the institutional framework

The authoritarian political regime in Spain between 1939 and 1975 imposed a model of forceful intervention in labour relations: bargaining between employers and employees were suppressed and labour relations regulations originated from administrative acts. Both trade and business unions were illegal and strikes or lockouts were heavily fined. During this period there was a trade-off between low salary levels and high stability in employment. The structural labour surplus, obviously strong in the 1970s, was relieved by means of a mass-migrations to countries in northwestern Europe. The adjustment to demand fluctuations in the short term was by overtime work (Malo de Molina, 1984). This model of labour relations was particularly successful in the 1960s with a high level of economic growth. Although a crisis in the 1970s caused the first shock in the oil market, it was not until after the physical disappearance of the dictatorial regime that the old framework for the labour market was changed.

In less than two decades, three important legislative reforms have been made, which changed the labour market sharply (see Miguelez & Prieto, 1991). In 1980, the new Workers' Law implied the normalisation (democratisation) of labour relations, getting their institutional mechanisms closer to the rest of European countries with regard to workers' rights and collective bargaining. However, some tensions were still present and affected the labour market like the hiring, sacking, and movement of workers in firms. The first reform of Workers' Law was made in 1984, and fundamentally affected the manner of hiring employees. The use of temporary contracts was permitted to cover vacant positions, without any important restrictions concerning minimum periods or areas of activity, or the causes that justified it. Fourteen different ways of temporary hiring changed the Spanish labour market into a more flexible one. There was a second labour reform in 1994, which, while keeping most of the ways of temporary hiring, introduced changes intended for the inclusion of the young and, most important, rules for the possibility of more mobility and internal flexibility, both professionally and geographically. Another important change was the push for part-time hiring which so far was seldom used.

Moreover, the operation of Temporary Labour Businesses was set up. This improved the workings of the labour market by easing the adjustment between supply and demand. Also the monopoly of the National Employment Institute as an employment agency was removed. This opened the way for public or private companies to enter. Additional reforms were made concerning the working day, collective dismissal, salary structure and other matters, taking these to collective bargaining in order to reduce the labour administration's control. Reforms are still needed and should moderate the excessive use of temporary contracts, which obviously raises staff rotation. In some of these legislation reforms, the social agents, trade unions and employers, participated directly or indirectly.

The collective bargaining model in force today in Spain, is characterised by: a low rate of unionised workers, a deficient level of coverage of agreements among small businesses,[2] a high level of centralisation of the negotiations and a strong dominance of aspects related to salary over organisational and professional aspects, and those related to companies' productivity. Collective bargaining, although having enough ground to act on salary, productivity, mobility, etc., cannot modify the already established labour laws. Nevertheless, the above mentioned reforms imply a more important role for collective bargaining by deregulating several aspects of labour relations.

The trade union in Spain shows a large dispersion, reflected in a wide range of abbreviations. The two main unions are the General Worker's Union (UGT) and the Worker's Commission (CCOO). On a regional scale only ELA/STV achieves significant representation in the Basque country. While the national and regional trade unions operate all around a specific productive web, there are also plenty of unions of a professional nature. These perform their activities within the limits of a specific occupation and are often restricted to a single large company. Other organisations, such as Airlines Pilots' Union (SEPLA) or the Train Drivers' Union (SEMAQ), have acquired some relevance due to the singularity of their own activity. These organisations work at a national level but they have autonomy in respect to the confederations mentioned.

For the production units there is a double representation: a section of the confederation of professional trade unions and a labour committees' representative body elected by all the workers who legally have the privilege to negotiate and conduct collective bargaining (Ruesga, 1991). The union coverage is between 10 and 15 percent of the total number of workers. One of the lowest figures within the European Union. In explaining such a low union membership, quite in contrast with the high level of political representation, social and political aspects have to be taken into account. One of them is the role of work councils in negotiations and management of collective bargaining.[3] This reduces workers' interest in union-membership. Another aspect is the role that, in political terms, the trade unions have developed throughout the 1970s and 1980s in assuring a democratic regime in Spain. This implied important sacrifices - for example, wage restraints and resulted in a loss of credibility in the working class' view (Ruesga, 1986).

In contrast with the diversity of the trade unions, there is only one major employers organisation, called the 'Confederation of Spanish Employers' Organisation' (CEOE). Apart from this one, there are some smaller organisations, mainly in small and medium-sized companies.These co-operate with other social labour-related entities or self-employed collectives.

8.2.2 Labour policies

The labour policies developed in Spain in the last two decades can be analysed by distinguishing between institutional reforms, active and passive labour market policies.

1) Institutional reforms

There has been a continuous reform of the institutional framework which rules the labour market. This was based on three fundamental elements:

- *The gradual reduction of the government's intervention in labour relations.* The transformation of the political regime into a parliamentary democracy is reflected in the labour relations. Basically, there was a change from intervention in the labour market to a scenario based on social agents - workers and management - through collective bargaining.

- *Flexibility in the practice of labour relations.* Legislative reform affected fundamentally the ways of recruitment and made room for new practices of hiring, mainly related to temporary and part-time work. This was to improve the speed of labour adjustments and, particularly, the reduction of adjustment costs. Public administration labour policy has shown, like the general institutional reforms, a lower level of regulation of the labour market, searching for a greater flexibility of both employment and wages.

■ *Wage adjustment*. Between 1978 and 1986 collective bargaining, particularly on wages, took place in the framework of income policy. In this, besides social intermediaries, governmental entities were more or less active. The objective was to moderate the growth rate of nominal wages which was very high in the period 1973 -1978. However, the deficiencies and limitations of the collective bargaining model (Ruesga, 1991) implied many obstacles for the effective application of these agreements. This resulted in a nominal wage moderation significantly lower that the one expected and wished for by the social agents. This had large effects on the economy during the period from 1977 to 1985. It meant an adjustment in the labour market as a result of a strong reduction in employment levels and, consequently, increases in nominal labour productivity. The result was a large growth of unemployment and an expansion of wage adjustment and irregular mechanisms in the 'black economy' (Ruesga, 1988). Nevertheless, the added affects which arose from social agreements, institutional changes and employment policies, reflected an important fall in labour costs, even during the economic expansion between 1986 and 1991. The adjustments resulted in a recovery, macro-economically speaking, of corporate profits. This prepared the ground for an important growth of employment during late 1980s.

2) Active policies

Active labour market policies were developed in the late 1970s and extended later on. Many measures, intended to facilitate labour market adjustments, are essentially aimed at reducing labour costs. The following basic lines can be distinguished:

■ *Encouragement of temporary recruitment*. Before the beginning of the 1990s, some ways of temporary recruitment were allowed. From thereon a strong duality in the labour market between temporary and permanent workers emerged. Hiring for an indefinite time was allowed.

■ *Encouragement of recruitment of discriminated groups*. Actions were taken to foster the hiring of women, youngsters, disabled, long term unemployed and other groups who have difficulties entering the labour market. These programmes were co-financed by grants of the European Social Fund.

■ *Training of manpower.* In accordance with the policy of the European Community Structural Funds, actions to improve the quality of labour multiplied. The aim was the adaptation of labour supply to the constantly changing conditions of demand triggered by technological changes. In this, different institutions like the state, regions, town councils, chamber of commerce, and trade unions and business groups work simultaneously on the same topics.

■ *Improving the labour market operations.* The most important action was the ending of the legal monopoly held by the Employment National Institute (INEM) as a recruitment service. Labour reform, as referred above, made it possible in 1994 that private employment agencies work together with the INEM.

■ *Public employment.* The public sector was very active in the direct generation of jobs. The relative volume of employment has increased notably in the last two decades ; it changed from 14 percent of the total paid work in 1980 to about 18 percent in 1995 (see table 8.1). Changes between these dates show a clear anticyclical profile.

Table 8.1
Changes in public employment
(% public employees of total salaried employees)

Year	1981	1983	1985	1987	1989	1991	1993	1995
%	14.0	16.0	16.9	15.9	16.3	17.0	17.8	17.9

3) Passive policies

Although the activities developed in this field of labour policy, are not meant to influence the labour market directly, passive actions can affect it indirectly. On the one hand, the development of costs resulting from these activities, puts pressure - through quotation prices - on labour costs. The costs of passive policies gradually rose. Between 1980 and 1984, unemployment benefit costs increased at a rate of 1 percent as proportion of GDP. On the other hand, there was an attempt to relate unemployment benefits to job promotion programmes. For example, it was allowed to receive all the benefits at one time. By this, one can invest in new business generating new jobs.

It is complicated to valuate the efficiency. The problem is not only about contrasting the costs within the results in terms of balance reached in the labour market. It is also difficult to compare it with a situation without such labour policies. Because of this it is not possible to speak about important achievements.

Unemployment has kept going upward for twenty years and the balance in terms of employment volume is also not positive.

8.2.3 The recent performance of the Spanish labour market

Spain has a population of around forty million people, from which more than 80% are in the working age (over 16 years). About 36 percent of the latter is employed. A very low figure in comparison to the average of the European Union. This low level can be explained by the low level of activity in working age (60.1% compared to a 66.1% European average) and by the high level of unemployment rate (23% and 11% respectively).

The income per person, in comparison with the European average, has not shown significant changes in the last twenty years. It fluctuated between 75 and 80 percent of the European average. Productivity has increased at a rate of 2.2 percent in the period 1985 - 1994, and labour costs have shown an average rise of 1.2 percent. Unit labour costs have gone down on average 0.9% every year (see also Figure 8.1). This has resulted in an annual employment growth just below 1%.

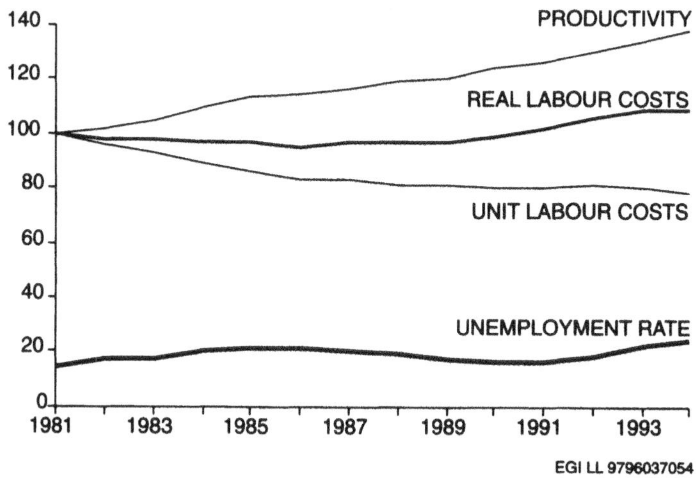

Figure 8.1 Changes in labour productivity and costs (indices; 1981= 100) and the unemployment rate (%) in the period 1981-1994 in Spain

Since the 1980s the Spanish labour market developed similar to other European countries, but was marked by a stronger duality between employment and unemployment. During the early 1960s, Spain had a high rate of agrarian productivity and an unemployment rate lower than 1%. During the 1970s and 1980s, the gradual industrialisation and internationalisation of the Spanish economy was parallelled by a significant growth rate. As table 8.2 shows, the Spanish unemployment in 1981 was 14.2%. The recession in the early 1980s lifted this rate to about 22% in 1985, the highest among the OECD countries. The strong growth of unemployment was caused by a rapid reduction of employment and a significant increase of an active youth population. During the late 1980s, Spanish economy reached the highest GDP growth rates in the OECD (between 4 - 6%), while the unemployment rate fell to 16.3% in 1991. Nevertheless, the important rise in employment did not result in a greater fall of unemployment due to an acceleration of the participation of women into the labour market (see table 8.2).

Table 8.2
Development of the activity and unemployment rate according to gender and age (1985-95)

Year	Activity rate				Unemployment rate			
	Women	16-19 years old	20-24 years old	Total	Women	16-19 years old	20-24 years old	Total
1981	26.6	44.7	59.9	48.1	16.2	43.0	29.6	14.4
1983	27.6	41.2	61.0	48.1	20.8	51.1	37.1	17.7
1985	27.6	37.5	60.9	47.4	25.4	55.9	42.2	21.9
1987	31.0	38.4	66.0	48.8	27.5	49.5	35.4	20.6
1989	36.8	16.2	67.2	49.1	25.4	38.2	32.8	17.3
1991	33.6	30.1	66.1	49.1	23.8	34.7	29.7	16.3
1993	34.8	28.5	63.0	49.0	29.2	50.3	40.5	22.7
1995	36.2	35.1	65.3	49.0	30.6	50.6	39.8	22.9

Source: Calculations by the authors and Ministerio de Trabajo (1995)

Between 1992-1994, however, the economic recession caused a rapid fall in employment, resulting in a unemployment rate of 24 percent.[4] During 1994 - 1996, the employment growth rate was moderate (around 2 or 2.5%) and unemployment stayed at 22%. Although statistical adjustments might reduce these high figures, the employment national average will not drop to 20%. It stays between 8 or 9% above the European average.

It is obvious that more flexibility in the Spanish labour market helps to make adjustments quicker in recessive stages of the business cycle. Similarly, the rise of employment in an expansive period would not stop because of expected high costs staff adjustments in the next phase. As a result of this, flexibility, the fluctuation in the volume of employment derived from the business cycle, was deeper compared to the situation in the previous decade (see figure 8.2). It is interesting to point out that, despite the changes in the unemployment rate, the activity rate experienced not only slight variations, although more significant in the last few years, but was the lowest among western countries. Fluctuations in the unemployment rate reflected directly the level of employment. In spite of serious imbalances in the Spanish labour market, its social-economic and productive system works without great stress. This is the result of a set of factors, like the increase in productivity and income levels in the last 15 years, a high public expenditures on social transfers - both on the individual and regional level -, the absorption of part of the negative effects of youth unemployment by family incomes and the development of the black economy (Ruesga, 1988).

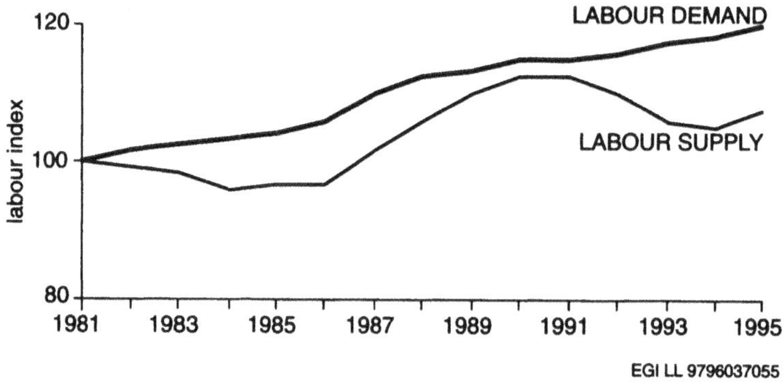

Figure 8.2 Development of labour supply and demand (1981 = 100)

Parallel to this development of employed and unemployed, a second duality emerged in Spain between the permanent and temporary employed. The Spanish labour market, which in the 1970s was one of the most rigid in Europe, turned to be one of the most flexible as far as different ways of hiring is concerned. The percentage temporary workers changed from 7 or 8 percent in the mid 1980s to 35 percent in 1995 (Figure 8.3). This atypical level of temporary recruitment, two or three times higher than in the rest of the European countries, can be explained not only by economic factors (strong presence of service-related employment), but also, and particularly, by the institutional changes and the strategy of flexibility. This resulted in much competition through low labour costs. The estimated average salary for a temporary worker is 35-40 percent lower than that of the average permanent employee.

Job creation was clearly limited because of the de-industrialisation related to the rise of foreign competition. This came from both European countries by competition via productivity, and the developing countries with lower labour costs.

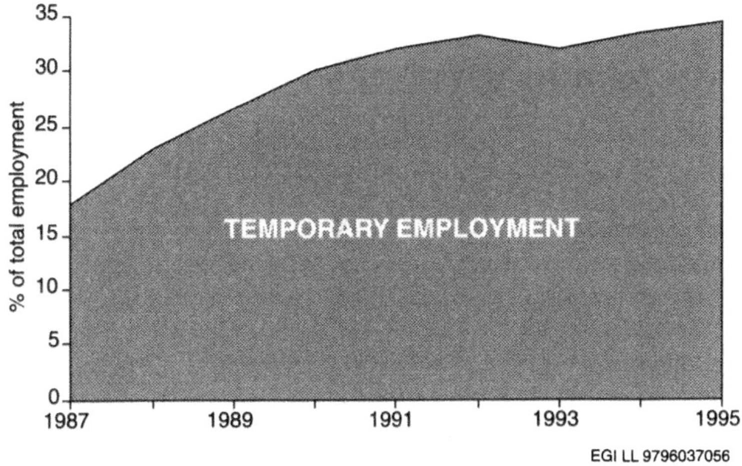

Figure 8.3 Development of temporary employment (% of total employment)

Employment growth was mainly in the service sector, which was less affected by external competition. Higher rates of economic growth seem to be limited due to the intensification of restricted macroeconomical policies linked to European Monetary Union. The development of the Spanish labour market in the next few years shows important uncertainties due to the expected increase of the female working population, a massive use of temporary recruitment and a rise of long-term unemployment. In this complex context, the inequalities between the different regional labour markets are another important and distorting element in the range of serious problems of the Spanish labour market.

8.3 Regional labour markets in Spain

8.3.1 The spatial framework

The Spanish state is divided from 1978 onward, into 17 autonomous regions (see Figure 8.4).[5] The Spanish constitution contains the basic principles of the territorial organisation. The procedure to become autonomous is also defined in this way, as well as the power of the regional governments (executive, legislative and judicial).

Figure 8.4 The territorial division of Spain

The distribution of political and administrative power between the state and regional governments (or autonomies) has the following order: 1) Authority of the state (foreign relations, defence, and economies that affect all the territories of the state, guaranteeing and preserving market unity; market, labour, fiscal legislation); 2) State authorities which can be transferred to the Autonomous Communities after agreement and precise definition of Autonomous statutes (working as regional constitutions); 3) Autonomous Communities exclusive authority, and 4) Autonomous Communities which, because their powers are not exercised as regional governments, are assumed by the Government. Two kinds of Autonomous Communities can be distinguished:

1) Comunidades 'forales' (foral communities)[6]

The Basque Country and Navarre are the two regions involved. They have, acknowledging the 1978 Constitution, certain privileges of self-government. It started during Franco's regime. Together with a set of other privileges, wider than the rest of autonomous communities, they are more self-financing than the rest of the regions. This allows for a larger capacity for programming their own economic and labour policies. The financing of the regional public sector is carried out within a regional self-government framework as far as management is concerned. Limited by a set of general principles, various fiscal and para-fiscal instruments are used. The finance relations with the state are regulated through an agreement in which is written down the contribution of these two autonomous communities to the state, in return for state services.

2) Comunidades de Régimen Común (Common law communities)

The rest of the autonomous communities have historic privileges when defining their access to self-government. Normally communities finance themselves through a system of taxes and other fiscal figures, or by transfers of the central administration. They also benefit from the state, as part of the state general budget is distributed among these communities, according to legally established criteria. Today, the system of financing autonomous communities is changing, giving way to a larger proportion of transferred taxes within their fiscal income scheme.

There are neither coordinating mechanisms among the autonomous communities themselves, nor with the state. There is only one institution with a decision-making character: the Committee on Fiscal and Finance Policy. This committee is in charge of following up the working of the autonomous financing mechanisms, and of modifying them, provided that the state and autonomous communities, come to an agreement. Problems emerged between the state and some autonomous communities about the interpretation of self-government rules and other laws, basically about financing, political and administrative responsibilities. These usually ended up in being resolved by the Constitutional Court. Since 1978, there is a constant trend towards decentralisation. This is reflected in the change of public expenditure among the different institutions, depending on the regional characteristics.

8.3.2 Regional disparities

Among the countries of the European Union, Spain and Italy have the most pronounced regional disparities. The Autonomous Community with the highest per capita income, the Balearic Islands, surpasses the least developed one, Estremadura, by more than 125 percent (see also table 8.3). For the differences in wealth, also a number of age-old historical factors, which have been shaping different attitudes among the economic agents of the various regions, are responsible. The map of relative development in Spain has not been substantially modified in the last two centuries. Traditionally, the highest degree of economic dynamism have been centred around the triangle Madrid, the Basque Country and Catalonia. Only recently in other regions, such as Ebro Valley, Balearic Islands and Mediterranean coast, development has been spreading. In contrast to this, the so-called Atlantic Axis, i.e., Cantabria, Asturias and Galicia, showed a backward development.

Table 8.3
Regional disparities in Spain

Autonomous Communities	GDP per capita (Spain=100)	GDP per capita (EUR15=100)		
	1995	1993	1994	1995
Andalucía	71.17	54.30	54.14	54.28
Aragón	109.08	83.47	82.94	83.12
Asturias	86.87	67.04	66.34	66.19
Baleares	159.83	114.90	119.57	121.87
Canarias	103.92	76.87	78.26	79.19
Cantabria	90.60	68.79	68.51	69.04
Castilla-La Mancha	84.05	65.69	64.75	64.05
Castilla y León	89.85	69.49	68.57	68.47
Cataluña	124.05	94.28	93.51	94.53
Comunidad Valenciana	100.92	76.61	76.67	76.90
Extremadura	68.94	53.52	53.40	52.53
Galicia	82.92	62.98	62.63	63.19
Madrid	126.64	98.74	96.92	96.50
Murcia	80.14	62.02	61.37	61.07
Navarra	118.36	87.78	88.69	90.19
País Vasco	109.77	82.11	82.35	83.64
Rioja (La)	111.96	83.31	83.59	85.31
Total Spain	100.00	76.30	75.90	76.20

Source: FIES (1996)

According to data from the three-year period 1989 - 1991, regional disparities in Spain (as measured by a simple indicator, regional maximum/minimum) is at the same level as in Portugal and Italy, but under that of Germany, France (including its overseas territories) and Great Britain. In this context of geographical economic disparity, internal redistribution procedures are very important, particularly those operating through the Social Security system. They dramatically reduce the disparities of the Gross Domestic Product per inhabitant.

8.3.3 Regional labour policies

In general, labour legislation is the state's responsibility. Therefore, the reforms take place at the level of the state. The ability to develop active economic - and particularly labour - policies by the governments of the Autonomous Communities depends on the degree of financial autonomy of each community and the kind of powers taken on by each community. In relation to this we come across two extremes in regional labour policies. On one end there are the privileged communities like the Basque Autonomous Community, which developed a wide range of measures, a great part of which complements the state's own labour policies. At the other extreme, there are the communities that exercise less power and have an inferior financial economy, such as Extremadura and both Castilles. In these regions, besides the region-specific state politics, labour policies are very closely connected to the use of European Community structural funds, primarily the European Social Fund.

The passive labour policy of subsidising unemployment is, for the time being, an exclusive state affair. Nevertheless, the so-called social salary should be noted. These are subsidies to persons who are unemployed and do not have a right to draw any unemployment benefits. This has been put into effect in almost all of the autonomous communities - of both privileged and ordinary status.

Within the regions, social partners define, usually as organisations to be consulted, regional economic policies in each autonomous community. This consulting usually takes place in the Autonomous Community's Social and Economic Councils. These are institutions of social representation whose consultation about social and economic projects carried out by the regional governments is obligatory by law. A similar institution exists at the level of the state. Unions and employers' associations mostly function as direct agents in carrying out some of the actions in labour policies, particularly concerning job and occupational training. Table 8.4 summarises the labour policies differentiated by the autonomous territories. We can note that a direct intervention by regional public administrations in the dynamics of the labour market is still low, but increasing.

Table 8.4
Labour policies and their management differentiated by territorial administrative regions

Policies	Actions	Main effect on	Area of application State	Area of application Regional or lower
Active Policies Supply-sided	• Legislative reforms			
	Reduce the retirement age	Labour Supply	X	
	Change in compulsory education age	Labour Supply	X	
	• Continuing and Professional Training		X	X
		Supply qualification		
Demand-sided	• Legislative reforms	Labour market flexibility /	X	
	Flexible contracts	Unit labour cost (UCL) /		
	Functional and Geographical mobility	Productivity		
		Labour Demand		
	• Employment Subsidies	Labour Demand / Labour	X	X
	• Employment Subsidies	market segmentation	X	X
	for specific collectives	Agrarian Labour Demand		
	• Rural Employment Plan	Labour Demand	X[1]	
	• Fiscal Incentives to	Disposable jobs		
	generate employment		X	X
	• Employment distribution			X
On labour costs setting	• Legislative reforms	CLU / Variable wage	X	
	• Social Security	CLU	X	
	Contributions	CLU	X	X
	• Fiscality on salaries			
On market behaviour	• Legislative reforms			
	Private employment	Frictional Unemployment	X	X
	services	Frictional Unemployment /		
	Temporary labour companies	CLU	X	X
Passive Policies	• Unemployment Subsidies	Unemployment Care	X	
	Professional			
	Social			
	• Agrarian unemployment	Unemployment Care	X[1]	
	Subsidy	Minimum income guaranteed	X	
	• Minimum guaranteed wage	Precarity situations Aid		X
	• Social Salary			

[1] With state resources, but applied to specific Regions

Source: Ruesga and Alvarez (1995) and own elaboration

Table 8.5
Basic characteristics of the regional labour markets

Autonomous Communities	Employ-ment rate (1994)	Activity rate (1994)	Unem-ployment rate (1994)	Regional unem-ployment rate minus national rate (1994)	Active popula-tion growth (1985-94) annual average	Employ-ment growth (1985-94) annual average	Unemploy-ment rate change (1985-94) annual average
a. **Régimen foral**							
Basque Country	38.0	50.6	24.9	+0.7	1.2	1.0	1.8
Navarra	40.9	48.0	14.7	-9.5	0.7	1.2	-2.0
b_1. **Régimen Común** (wider selfgovern-ment)							
Andalucia	31.0	47.4	34.6	+10.4	2.4	1.5	4.2
Cataluña	41.2	52.3	21.2	-3.2	1.7	2.0	1.0
Galicia	40.0	49.6	19.4	-4.8	-0.6	-1.5	4.1
Valenciana	39.2	51.9	24.6	+0.4	2.0	1.5	3.9
Canarias	37.8	51.5	26.7	+4.5	2.2	2.0	2.6
b_2. **Régimen Común** (narrow self-govern-ment)							
Aragón	39.1	47.8	18.1	-6.1	1.1	1.0	1.4
Castilla y León	35.7	45.3	21.3	-2.9	0.6	0.2	2.4
Extremadura	30.9	45.1	31.5	+7.5	1.2	0.5	2.8
Baleares	43.7	53.2	17.8	-6.4	2.2	1.7	5.0
Castilla-Mancha	35.5	44.2	19.5	-4.9	0.8	0.4	2.7
Asturias	33.1	42.7	22.5	-1.7	0.7	-1.3	1.5
Madrid	38.6	48.8	20.9	-3.3	1.6	1.8	1.0
Murcia	37.9	50.8	25.3	+1.1	2.5	1.7	5.1
La Rioja	38.5	46.5	17.0	-7.2	1.0	1.0	0.8
Cantabria	35.9	46.7	23.2	-1.0	0.6	-0.4	5.2
ESPAÑA	37.2	49.0	24.2	0	1.4	1.1	2.7

Source: Own calculation and INE (1995)

8.4 Changing regional imbalances in the Spanish labour market

8.4.1 General changes in regional unemployment

As table 8.5 shows, the difference between the region with the highest unemployment rate (Andalusia; 34.6) and the region with the lowest (Navarre; 14.7) was in 1994 19.9 percentage points. This means that, in relation to the average unemployment rate in Spain of 24 percent that year, the maximum and minimum regional unemployment rates were respectively 10 percent above and 10 percent below the national indicator.

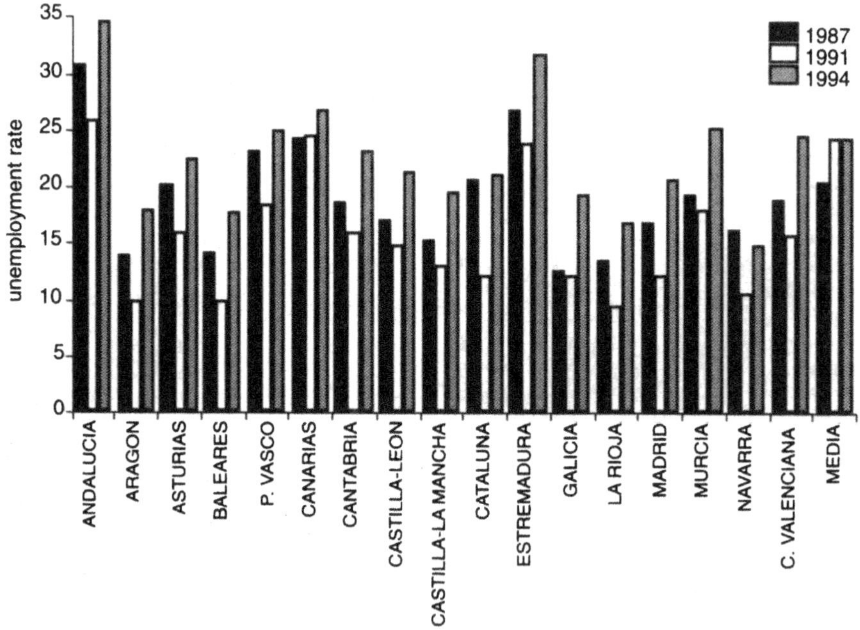

EGI LL 9796037057

Figure 8.5 Unemployment rates in the autonomous communities (1987, 1991 and 1994)

Several factors determined this situation. On the one hand, an exceptionally fast and uneven development throughout 1960s and 1970s gave rise to significant structural dissimilarities among the regions. In regions with less development, several factors have hampered job creation: a larger presence of the agrarian sector, deficiencies in infrastructure and productive capital formation, and the geographic distance from important European markets. On the other hand, some regions that showed high growth rates and a high standard of living have recently encountered a strong increase in unemployment as a result of a deindustrialisation of the non-competitive traditional sector. The increase in unemployment went along with a significant decrease in standards of living, and a drop in economic activity. In both kind of regions, the significant amount of public money directed at keeping up the purchasing power maintained a reasonable welfare.

In terms of the absolute dispersion of the regional unemployment index,[7] the lowest level of divergence was recorded in the early 1970s (see figure 8.6). From that time, this divergence grew progressively until mid 1980s, and since then it only slightly decreased until early 1990s. After that, it experienced another increase. Nonetheless, this observation is deceiving, since, in terms of relative dispersion index,[8] the results are very different, showing apparently an anti-cyclic behaviour.

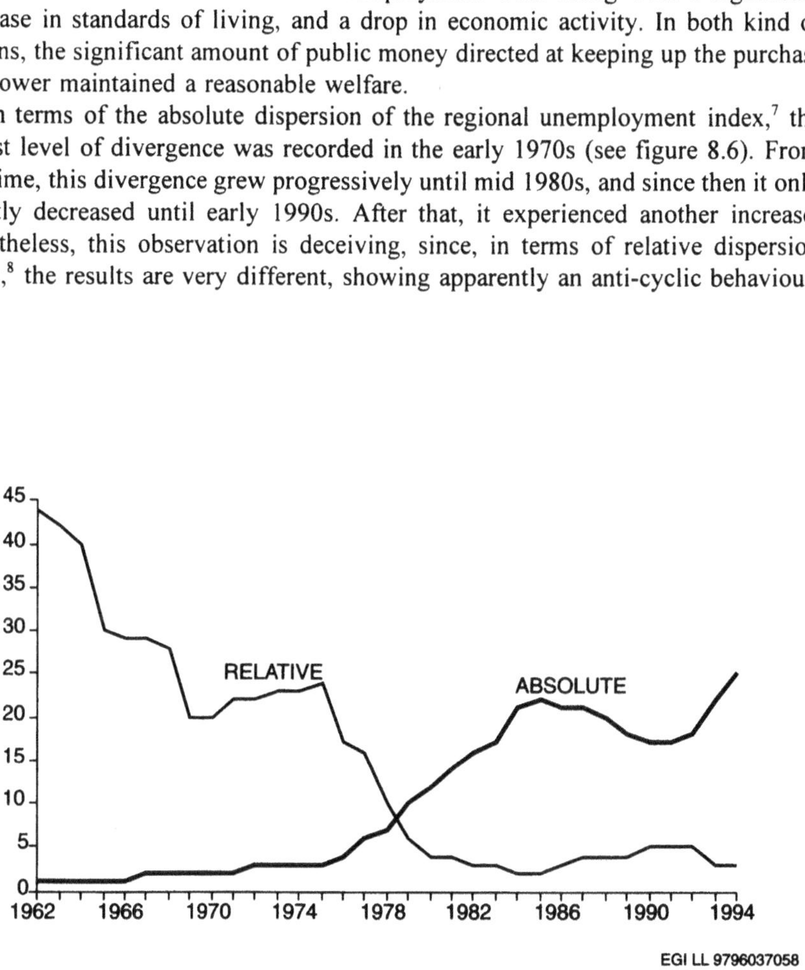

Figure 8.6 Change of the absolute and relative dispersion of the regional unemployment rates (%)

After an initial period of high relative, but decreasing divergence throughout the 1960s, there was a small increase during the first employment shock in the 1970s. Nevertheless, a sharp decrease occurred from the late seventies through the middle eighties, concurrently with the second shock (the most important in terms of the increase in unemployment). During the period of decreasing unemployment in late eighties, divergence rose again, to decrease once more with the new recession in the 1990s.

The Spanish regions do not behave significantly different from regions in other European countries. During periods of economic recession and increases in the national average unemployment rate, a reduction in the relative disparities among the regional unemployment levels is observed. In contrast to this, regional disparity increases in periods of economic growth. The convergence in periods of crisis is usually determined by the larger growth of unemployment in the most industrialised regions. The divergence in periods of growth is explained by the lower efficiency in creating employment in regions with fewer possibilities of investment and a lower presence of the service sector. This remarkable dynamic is confirmed for the last ten years by grouping regions, on the basis of the variation of annual unemployment rates in the most recent expansive and recessive phases (1985 - 1990 and 1991 - 1994, respectively; see figure 8.7).

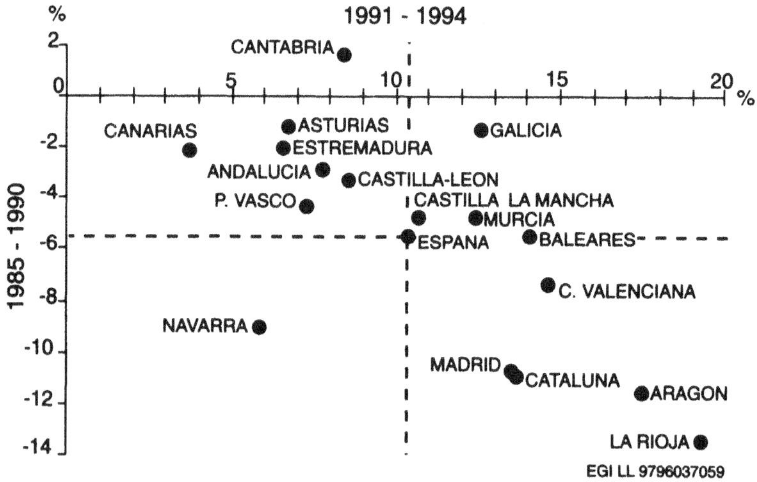

Figure 8.7 Relation between the annual growth rates of regional unemployment (1985-1990 and 1991-1994)

Throughout the first phase of strong employment generation (1985-1990), the regions with low unemployment rates (such as Aragon, Rioja, Madrid and Cataluña) showed the largest reductions of unemployment. In the phase of employment destruction (1991-1994) these very regions showed the largest yearly unemployment increases. In contrast to this, regions with larger unemployment rates (such as Andalusia, Estremadura, Asturias and Cantabria) experience more moderate variations during both phases of the business cycle.

The contradictory movements in the relative regional dispersion of unemployment throughout the period 1962-1995 have different origins. Its reduction, since 1960s through the mid 1980s, is determined by a considerable decrease of the dispersion in the activity rates. The increase in the regional dispersion of unemployment rates derives from a parallel increase in the dispersion of activity and occupation rates, although the increase in the dispersion of the activity rates stays at a higher level. From 1990 on, the reduction in the relative divergence of unemployment rates is more a result of a larger growth of the dispersion in the activity rate than of the change of the dispersion in the employment rates. This confirms Decressin and Fatás (1994), who state that a disparity in the regional unemployment rates is reduced by higher and lower numbers in the labour force. On the other hand, the relative dispersion in the unemployment rates shows an anti-cyclic development as earlier noted by Villaverde (1991), Ruesga & Álvarez (1992) and Toharia (1994).

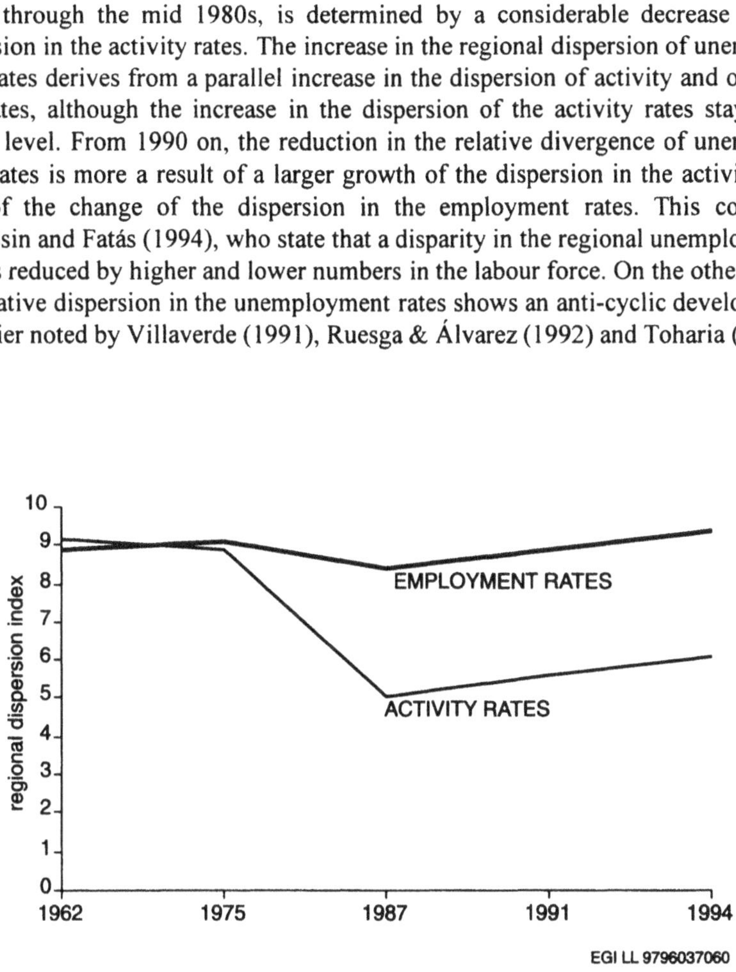

Figure 8.8 Index of regional dispersion of activity and employment rates

It can be concluded that Spain, like Italy (Bodo, D'Alessio y Signorini, 1993), shows a typical model in which both national unemployment and the regional disparities in unemployment are very persistent. In contrast, central countries in the European Union show persistence in their combined unemployment levels, whereas a lesser degree of persistence is found in their regional disparities. Meanwhile, the United States shows low persistence levels in both issues (Jimeno & Bentolia, 1995). This complex and contradictory development in regions with such diverse features complicates the adoption of common and clear-cut hypotheses about the causes of the divergence in regional labour markets in Spain.

8.4.2 *Analysis of inter- and intra-regional disparities in unemployment levels*

In an attempt to go more deeply into the causes of the regional differences, they will be analysed by defining the basic profile of regional labour supply. This to establish a typology of regions with homogeneous conditions. Use is made of an analysis of likelihood based on the logit method. We establish the inter-regional and intra-regional differences of being unemployed according to different characteristics of the active population. The initial data are micro-data from the Active Population Survey of the National Institute of Statistics for the years 1987, 1990 and 1994. In the logit model, the dependent variable has two possible values: wage-earning or unemployed. The likelihood of one of these situations depends on sex, age, education, civil status, relationship to the main person in the family and education. Data for the various years are homogeneous, centred on a term with low seasonality and have a high level of statistical significance. Results permit to establish both a static and dynamic analysis. The categories for the independent variables are: sex (male, female), age (16-19, 20-24, 25-29, 30-54 and 55 and over years old), civil position (single, married, other situation), relation to the main figure of the family (main person, spouse, child, others) and education level (no studies, primary school, secondary school, professional training, university studies).

The inter-regional differences in the likelihood of being unemployed reflect the regional differences in relation to the national average. The intra-regional differences in the likelihood of unemployment reflect the individual differences from a 'reference individual' within each region. This latter individual shows a very low unemployment rate and is an active, 30-54 year-old adult man with an average education. Those regions where individuals have a greater likelihood of being unemployed in relation to the national average (a high inter-regional index) usually have a lower internal dispersion of the probability of being unemployed among individuals (low intra-regional index). In contrast to this, the regions with a lower inter-regional index have a higher intra-regional index.

Table 8.6
Inter- and intra-regional differences in unemployment
(averages of index 1987-1990-1994 using logit probabilities)

	Interregional Index (1)	Intraregional Index (2)	Inter/Intra Index (2) / (1)
REG 1			
Canary Islands	173.0	127.5	0.74
Andalusia	182.8	149.1	0.82
Extremadura	154.9	143.6	0.93
Galicia	125.4	134.4	1.07
Murcia	120.7	146.4	1.21
Average	151.4	140.2	0.95
REG 2			
Valencia	108.5	146.1	1.35
Cantabria	115.3	158.0	1.37
Asturias	111.3	157.3	1.41
Castille-La Mancha	91.1	137.1	1.51
Basque Country	109.7	174.4	1.59
Average	107.2	154.6	1.45
REG 3			
Madrid	94.1	150.2	1.60
Balearic Islands	79.1	140.3	1.77
La Rioja	72.7	137.4	1.89
Catalonia	78.7	151.4	1.92
Average	81.1	144.8	1.79
REG 4			
Castille-León	82.5	162.1	1.96
Aragon	66.8	157.8	2.36
Navarre	68.8	182.9	2.66
Average	72.7	167.6	2.33

Source: INE and personal calculation based on a Logit Model analysis.
Ruesga, Alvarez, et al. (1997)

From these indexes, four groups of regions can be identified, having lesser or larger inter- and intra-regional differences (see table 8.6). Groups REG-1 and REG-3 correspond respectively to the least- and most-developed Spanish regions. The other groups, REG-2 and REG-4, are somewhat more heterogeneous, although in REG-2 regions have had more industry-related crises, whereas REG-4 are regions with the lowest unemployment rate. The results point out a higher homogeneity of the personal characteristics of the unemployed in regions with relatively higher unemployment rates. The regions with a more dynamic economy, and with lower unemployment rates, show up a higher dispersion of the possibility of having a job in relation to the individual features. Particularly, the educational level in the more developed regions is most relevant for explaining the access to a job. In contrast to this, in some of the less developed regions, people with a lower education have better possibilities compared to higher levels. Moreover, the analysis shows how differences in unemployment, as a function of labour supply characteristics, affects significantly the strong dispersion of the aggregated regional unemployment rates. Characteristics of the labour supply explicitly affects the regional dispersion in unemployment rates. Differences in the level of education level is particularly relevant in explaining, as a indirect index, the qualification level of the labour force.

8.5 Regional labour supply and demand in Spain: an explanatory model

The complex institutional framework described earlier, both at the national and regional level, influences substantially the regional labour markets in Spain. Therefore, we can interfere that the institutional approach, particularly at the national level, is important because it introduces new elements for analyzing unemployment/employment dynamics (Piore, 1973; Doeringer & Piore, 1975; Osterman, 1975; Sengenberger, 1981; Piore & Sabel, 1984; Appelbaum, 1989). Not only does it regard differences in productivity and qualification within labour supply, but it also takes into account the differences in the strategies of companies demanding labour. The main result is a segmented labour market characterised by workers with different salaries and labour conditions and of which some do not have institutional possibilities of competition (Bentolila & Dolada, 1990). Regional imbalances in the labour market can be analysed as the result of product market operations, to which both state and unions' strategies should be added.

The growing divergence among regions seems to be the result of the reaffirmation of previous situations. Endogenous problems and the lack of capability to attract new resources do not allow an equilibrium among the least developed regions. From this point of view, the labour market emerges as the final result of an interaction between various institutions and procedures. The distinctive aspects of such institutions and procedures depend on the social, technological and economic characteristics of each region or economic sector. This generates different types of institutions and procedures and produces different levels of employment and unemployment, labour stability and rotation, productivity, salaries and benefits. In this framework, conclusions differ on the effects of public expenditure, particularly unemployment benefits on regional unemployment. We can distinguish between those models which consider public expenditure as positive on regional unemployment divergences (Peters, 1983) and those which deny any efficiency of those programmes (Guccione & Guillen, 1982; Swales, 1982; Disney, 1984). The cause of this is rather economic, technological and social than related to the quantitative characteristics of the public expenditures. This means that the unemployment rate is to be understood in a wider sense as the result of an imbalance between supply and demand in a given labour market with concrete socioeconomic and institutional features. These explain better unbalanced (lacking of unemployment) or divergence situations (existence of unemployment) between demand and supply.

By identifying the factors and variables that determine labour demand and/or supply in a regional context, it is possible to explain the differences in unemployment rates. From this point of view, a causal model has been developed and applied to the regional context (van der Laan, 1992). The model relates a group of heterogeneous variables, according to different theoretical perspectives, to the regional labour market. By the use of principal components analysis, it is possible to evaluate the explanatory relevance of some theoretical concepts for which direct regional indicators are not available. The application of this explanatory model makes it possible to compose the Spanish framework in terms of theoretical concepts rendered in indexes (Aguado & Polanco, 1994). According to this modelling, the initial variables can be grouped in demand and supply factors as shown in table 8.7.

Before analysing the results of this model, it is necessary to note that this is a first step towards the identification of a wide group of variables taken a priori as explanatory. An explanatory model that allows us to arrive at some initial conclusions. It also clears the way for further research. There are some important limitations to the construction of specifications accurate enough for the theoretical and analytical assumptions. First, the model is for one year only. Given the fact that all variables used must refer to a regional context and also given the difficulties for obtaining data for such a specific level, 1991 is the most recent year where data for all Spanish regions are available. And second, the current availability of information restricts the quantification of some variables. The information does not necessarily reflects accurately the ex ante theoretical definition of the variable.

The results of the explanatory model are the following: The model explains 71 percent of the regional labour supply differences and 74 percent of demand. Chi-squared test verifies generic hypothesis of the model with a p-value of 0.162 for a confidence level of 95 percent. Residual goodness of fit tests (GFI and RMSR) support this. Variables that make up the *institutional regulation* did not reach an acceptable level of significance. This was mainly because there were large statistical problems in specifying some of the variables. Moreover, some variables behaved very erratically over time when sampled for one region. This distorts the analysis when applied to just one year. This happened, for example, with the variable that measures labour disputes. It mirrors the effect of the miners' strike in Northern Spain in 1991.

Table 8.7
Demand and supply factors explaining regional labour market performance

DEMAND:

a structural-institutional factor
* Productive structure
* Gross capital formation
* Gross Domestic Product per capita
* Productivity
* Inter-regional solidarity
* Education level (human capital stock)

a public sector factor
* Public expenditure
* Active population in the public sector
* Public investment

SUPPLY:

a migration factor
* Migratory balance

an institutional regulation factor
* Concentration of business firms
* Negotiation centralisation
* Labour disputes

a demographic factor
* Population growth rate
* Potential active population

a cost factor
* Average income
* Labour costs

The *structural-institutional* factor unites a group of variables that characterise the regional economic system. Both the explanatory power and the economic factors (Gross Domestic Product per capita, productive structure, specialisation level in services and agriculture, and labour productivity) behave as expected. There is less labour demand in the less developed regions. Investment - measured as a percentage of the Gross Domestic Product - has a negative value. This indicates that investment efforts are more intense in regions with a lower activity rate. Some of the variables included in this factor can be defined a priori as institutional variables. Nevertheless, it has been proven that its geographical materialisation is closely linked to the level of regional development. Therefore, while there is a positive relation between the human capital supply and the employment level, to be understood as an indicator of absorption of technical change, there is a negative relation between the latter and the level of inter-regional solidarity. This could indicate a compensatory activity on the side of the public sector regarding the amount of employment. This effect also becomes visible in the public sector factor.

The *public sector* presence - defined by the expenditure level - negatively affects regional labour demand. This could be interpreted as an ex post compensation. The public sector spends more in regions where labour demand is relatively lower. However, when public sector investment is measured by capital expenditure per employee, there is a positive relation with regional labour demand. It looks like the definition of 'public investment' conditions its sign. The relation between the public sector factor and the regional labour supply shows that labour demand conditions supply. This should be interpreted from an ex post perspective. Public sector activity is more intense in regions where demand is worse.

The factors representing the characteristics and behaviour of the general population show the expected relation to labour supply. The *migratory* balance (emigrants minus immigrants) contributes negatively to regional activity rates. Nevertheless, interregional migrations do not have a significant quantitative influence (Bentolila & Dolado, 1994). The same could be said about external flows, at least if only legal migrants are counted. The *demographic* factor correlates also positively with labour supply. Population growth has a positive influence on supply and a negative one on the potential labour force.

It is important to note that no significant empirical relevance has been found between *labour costs* and regional labour supply and demand. This result agrees with the research on the homogeneity in unit labour costs being in contrast with the high dispersion in the level of unemployment.[9]

8.6 Summary and conclusions

Besides the changing institutional and productive characteristics at a national level, different levels of regional autonomy, including labour issues, have developed in Spain in recent decades. These have contributed to larger disparities in labour supply and demand for every regional market and, consequently, in their unemployment rates. Empirical evidence, made visible in the initial descriptive analysis, is supported in this chapter by using different methods of statistical analysis. Firstly, a cluster analysis of the relationship between business cycles and annual variation in unemployment rates, establishes groups of regions showing up clearly different behaviour. In expansive periods, regions with low unemployment rates experience higher decreases that those regions suffering high unemployment rates. Therefore, increase in divergence slows down in recessions, showing different circumstances for creation and destruction of employment due to a different sectoral framework and levels of development.

Secondly, a logit-analysis of inter- and intra-regional divergences for the probability of being unemployed, has shown that different features of the labour supply, particularly the level of education, have a large influence in regions with relatively lower unemployment rates. Thirdly, the most important finding is based on a principal components analysis. This identifies the importance of structural, institutional and demographic factors for the adjustment of regional markets. We noticed the importance of the level of development and economic potential for the supply and, particularly, the decisions affecting job creation.

Although some statistical problems were found when specifying variables, the model has proven the effect of structural and institutional variables on the regional labour supply and demand. This reflects the diverse levels of development and, consequently, the economic potential of each region. The public sector presence emerges as an ex post explanatory variable that, simultaneously, conditions supply. It is suggested that it acts as a compensatory factor to social and economic effects derived from the labour imbalance level in each region. The lack of a significant statistical relation to some of the indexes is largely a result of the difficulties in the statistical definition of certain variables, as in the case of institutional regulation. Finally, we repeat the strong conditioning of the limited availability of statistical data. Accordingly, results obtained must be considered as tentative conclusions. Nevertheless, they offer an interesting approach to the explanatory potential using such an institutional perspective.

In conclusion, the singularity of the Spanish labour market in the European context, brought about by its high unemployment rates, disappears when the analysis is conducted in a regional framework. In this respect, imbalances in the Spanish regional labour market show a similar behaviour as in other countries of the European Union: an anti-cyclical component and a high persistence. In the Spanish case, the dynamics of regional disparities, in terms of unemployment rates, can apparently be better explained using labour demand rather than labour supply factors. According to this, the analysis of factors that condition the generation of employment within regions is essential for understanding the regional labour markets in Spain.

Notes

1. This research is been funded by the Comisión Interministerial de Ciencia y Tecnología (CICYT), an official agency of the Spanish state. Besides the authors, members of the researcher team were José Manuel García de la Cruz, Pablo Martín Urbano and Delfina Pérez Martínez.

2. Small and medium sized firms regulate their own labour relations, at the first stage, through sector agreements. These define a general framework. Bargaining at any specific business level virtually does not exist. This is a result of the automatic general alignment of sector agreements, whose contents are expanded

automatically to all firms in that sector (see Jimeno & Bentolila, 1995).

3. Spanish laws on collective bargaining give the agreements, once signed up, a universal application. That is, all employed in a firm or sector affected by the agreement are covered, whether belonging to the union or not.

4. However, administrative registration of unemployed, elaborated by the Instituto Nacional de Empleo, reduced that figure to 17 pe cent. For a general account on underestimation of employment in labour statistics, particularly in the Spanish Labour Force Survey (EPA), see Toharia (1995).

5. This spatial classification is similar to the NUTS-2 level of the European Union regional classification. Additional to these 17 regions, there are two townships, Ceuta and Melilla in Northern Africa, which operate as autonomous cities under the regulation of a special Territorial Statute.

6. 'Forales' is a special name for Basque Country and Navarre. There is no adequate english translation for it. The word originated about ten centuries ago and came from 'Fueros' indicating a kind of fiscal agreement between the Kingdom and a particular community.

7. It is the average of the deviations of regional unemployment rates with respect to the national value weighted by the percentage of active population in each region over the national total.

8. Measured by the half of the variance between different regional unemployment rates and national rate (Toharia 1994). For the purposes of the present analysis, this index is the most adequate given the important differences in the regional unemployment rates.

9. Rigidity (lacking of relation) is more obvious when regional wage dispersion takes occupational wage dispersion for every region into account (see Plaza, 1994).

References

Appelbaum, E. (1989), 'The Rise of Temporal Manpower in the United States', in Drago, R. & Perlmann, R., *Microeconomic Issues in Labour Economics*, New Approaches: Harvester Wheatsheaf.

Aguado, A. & J.M.F. Polanco (1994), *Métodos de segmentación basados en la*

aplicación combinada de técnicas estadísticas, en VI Encuentro de Profesores de Marketing, Editorial ESIC, San Sebastián.
Bentolila, S. & J.J. Dolado (1990), *Mismatch and Internal Migration in Spain, 1962-1986*, Working Paper No. 9006, Banco de España, Servicio de Estudios.
Bentolila, S. & J.J. Dolado (1994), 'Desajuste laboral y migración interior en España, 1962-1986', in Padoa-Schioppa, F. (comp.), *Desajuste y movilidad del trabajo*, Ministerio de Trabajo y Seguridad Social: Madrid, pp. 231-285.
Bodo, G., D'Alessio, G. & L.F. Signorini (1993), *Patterns of change in Italian regional labour markets: a multistep principal components analysis*, Applied Economics, nr. 25.
Decressin, J. & A. Fatás (1994): *Regional Labor Market Dynamics in Europe*, CEPR Discussion Paper 1085.
Disney, R. (1984), 'The Regional Impact of Unemployment Insurance in the United Kingdom', *Oxford Bulletin of Economics*, Vol. 46, No. 3.
Doeringer, P.B. & M.J. Piore (1975), 'Unemployment and the Dual Labour Market', *The Public Interest*, No. 38, National Affairs Inc.
FIES (1996), *Cuadernos de Información Económica*, Fondo para la Investigación Económica y Social, nr.68, May-June.
Guccione, A. & W.J. Guillen (1982), 'The Optimality of Labour Subsidies in a Regional Context. A Skeptical Note', *Regional Science and Urban Economics*, No. 12, pp. 381-386.
Instituto Nacional de Estadística (INE) (1995), *Encuesta de Población Activa.*
Jimeno, J.F. & S. Bentolila (1995) *Regional Unmployment Persistence (Spain, 1976-1994)*, Fundación de Estudios de Economía Aplicada, Documento de Trabajo 95-09.
Laan, L. van der (1992), 'Structural determinants of spatial labour markets: a case study of the Netherlands', *Regional Studies*, Vol. 26, No. 5, pp. 485-498.
Malo de Molina, J.L. (1984), *Mercado de trabajo y estructura salarial. El caso español: 1963-1975*, MTSS: Madrid.
Miguelez & Prieto (1991), *Las relaciones laborales en España*, Siglo XXI Editores: Madrid.
Ministerio de Trabajo (1995), *Boletín de Estadísticas Laborales*, December.
Osterman, P. (1975), 'An Empirical Study of Labour Market Segmentation', *Industrial and Labour Relations Review*, Vol. 28.
Peters, A.B. (1983), *Quantitative Impact Assesment of a Regional Oriented Labour Market Programme in Germany*, XXII European Congress of the Regional Science Association, Papers of the Regional Association, Vol. 52.
Piore, M.J. (1973), *On the Technological Foundations of Economic Dualism*, M.I.T. Cambridge Mass, Working Papers, No. 110.
Piore, M.J. & Ch. Sabel (1984), *The Second Industrial Divide*, Basic Books: New York.
Plaza, R. (1994), *Desempleo y salarios en España: diferencias interprovinciales*, Secretariado de Publicaciones, Universidad de Valladolid.

Ruesga, S.M. (1986), *Los sindicatos en España*, fascículo No. 35 de la colección Economía Española y de la CEE, tomo III: Barcelona, Orbis.
Ruesga, S.M. (1988), *Al otro lado de la economía*, Ed. Pirámide: Madrid.
Ruesga, S.M. (1991), 'La negociación colectiva', en Miguelez y Prieto 1991.
Ruesga, S.M. & C. Alvarez (1992), 'Desequilibrios espaciales en la distribución del desempleo y política de empleo' in Ruesga, S.M. (Coord.), *Economía y Trabajo*, Pirámide: Madrid.
Ruesga, S.M., C. Alvarez et al (1997), *An lisis estructual de los desequilibrios interrregionales del mercado de trabajo español*, Proyecto CICYT, SEC95-190, Madrid.
Sengenberger, W. (1981), 'Market Segmentation and the Bussines Cycle', in Wilkinson, F. (Ed.), *The dynamics of Labour Market Segmentation*, Academic Press Inc.: London.
Swales, J.K. (1982), 'The Employment Effects of a Regional Capital Subsidy', *Regional Science and Urban Economics*, No. 12, pp. 81-97.
Toharia (1994), 'La dinámica regional del mercado de trabajo', in Juárez M. (dir), *V Informe sociológico sobre la situación social en España*, Sociedad para todos en el año 2000, Fundación FOESSA: Madrid.
Toharia (1995), *How big is the unemployment in Spain ?*, paper presented to VIIth Annual Conference of EALE (European Association os Labour Economists): Lyon.
Villaverde, J. (1991), *Los desequilibrios regionales en España*, Instituto de Estudios Económicos: Madrid.

9 Labour market institutions and the North-South divide in Italy

Luigi Bonatti & Carlo Borzaga[1]

9.1 Introduction

The evolution of the Italian economy since the Second World War has not equally affected the twenty administrative regions into which the country is divided (see Figure 9.1). It has instead altered, but not removed, the regional disparities inherited from before the war. Until 1963, the sustained growth achieved by the Italian economy was largely confined to the northwestern regions of the country (Piedmont, Liguria and Lombardy), accentuating the divide between these and all the other regions. In the years that followed and until the end of the 1980s, a period in which the economy continued to grow - albeit weakly and more unevenly - the more dynamic regions were those located in the North-East (Veneto, Emilia Romagna, TrentinoAlto Adige and Friuli Venezia Giulia) and in the Centre (Tuscany, Lazio, Marche and Abruzzo). These regions saw a development of industrial districts based on export-oriented networks of small firms. The regions of the South benefited very little from this territorial extension of the productive base, despite policies introduced in their favour. Beginning in the 1980s, weak economic growth was increasingly concentrated in the already developed regions of the country, in particular those of the North-East and the Centre, while the southern regions achieved even less growth of income and, especially, of employment. As a consequence, the North-South divide widened even further.

This pattern of development has had a direct impact on the labour market, above all in terms of increasing gaps in employment changes and in unemployment rates. A contributory factor has indubitably been the manner in which the Italian labour market is organised and regulated. In particular, the propensity of the Italian institutions to protect those already employed (insiders) has interwoven with the different geographical distribution of insiders and outsiders, aggravating the initial disequilibria and altering their features.

Figure 9.1 Administrative regions of Italy

This chapter analyses the existence and evolution of this interweaving, restricting the discussion to the comparison between the Centre-North and the South.

Section 9.2 briefly summarises the development of the Italian economy since 1973, and the disparities between North and South. Section 9.3 concentrates on the evolution of the labour-market institutions and the North-South disequilibria determined by this. Section 9.4 examines the current situation of the Mezzogiorno and the factors hampering its development. Section 9.5 emphasises the need to rethink wage-setting mechanisms as a strategy to relaunch the economic development of the South.

9.2 Increasing North-South dualism

Until the early 1960s the core of Italian economic growth - the economic miracle - was located in the northwestern regions, which displayed the highest growth of income and employment. First, the mild recession of 1963-64, then the social unrest of the late 1960s, with an income redistribution in favour of labour, put an end to the period of high economic growth. The deterioration in terms of trade resulting from the first oil shock further compressed profitability and reduced the investment rate. Besides the rapid increases in real wages of the early 1970s, the Italian labour movement was able to restrict the employers' right to manage the labour force, especially in the large factories of the Northwest, giving greater rigidity to the utilisation of manpower and restricting the employers' freedom to select and fire workers. The response of the industrial system was to use small firms for relocating productive activities, with large companies relying more than in the past on outsourcing. This helped peripheral areas of the Northeast and the Centre to develop and integrate small firms into informal networks based on the efficient exploitation of complementarities and economies of agglomeration.

In the mid 1970s, nominal wages were fully indexed to the price index, thus creating the conditions for a cycle of devaluation and high inflation that characterised the second half of that decade. In the early 1980s, the shift to a tighter monetary regime characterised by a less accommodating exchange-rate policy triggered a wave of industrial restructuring in the Northwest. The job cuts brought about by this allowed firms to expel older unskilled workers from production. Hence, in the cyclical upturns that followed, firms were able to rejuvenate their workforce and upgrade their schooling levels. This process was made socially acceptable by the massive utilisation of CIG ('Cassa Integrazione Guadagni', i.e. special unemployment benefits for experienced workers on layoff) and early retirement schemes, which considerably reduced the number of redundant workers which otherwise would have been unemployed.

In the course of the 1980s, disinflation was made possible by convincing the unions to revise the wage-indexation mechanism, so that nominal wages became less sensitive to price movements. In contrast, the political class was unable to redress fiscal imbalances, thus giving rise to rapid growth in the public debt, although fiscal policy helped stimulate the expansionary cycle of the second half of the 1980s. Especially in the sectors sheltered from international competition, there were significant wage increases in this phase; given Italy's participation in the EMU, competitiveness of the manufacturing sector deteriorated and expansion was driven mainly by the growth of domestic demand.

In spite of the unfavourable exchange rate policy of this period, the industrial districts of the Northeast and the Centre were able to specialise their production during this cyclical upturn, exploiting new niches in international markets and successfully defending their market shares. This laid the foundations for the export boom achieved by these areas after the devaluation of the lira in 1992 and following years. Particularly in the North-East, the rapid export increase as a result of Italy's withdrawal from the EMU in September 1992, has considerably reduced the impact on GDP growth of the highly restrictive fiscal policy in recent years. In contrast to the 1970s, indeed, currency devaluation has not been immediately followed by increases in nominal wages, since in 1992-93 a new institutional framework for wage determination was agreed on by the government, the main unions and the employers' federations. This agreement dismantled the residual indexation clauses linking nominal wages to prices, and defined two levels of wage bargaining. At the national level, at which sectoral minimum wages must now be set linked to the targeted inflation rates established by the government for the following years. The second level is that of the firm, at which wage increases must be closely tied to indicators of the firm's performance. Even the opponents of neo-corporatist policy regimes recognise that, in a period in which both the nominal anchor provided by participation in an exchange-rate agreement and political stability were lost, pre-determination of the dynamics of the nominal wages was decisive in giving certainty to the Italian scenario. The end result was a fall in real wages and an increase of marginal profits that came about in the period 1993-95. Nevertheless, all the benefits of this export-led recovery were concentrated in the Northern and Central regions.

The reactions of the Southern regions to these changes in the Italian economy have differed from one period to another. Between the late 1950s and the mid-60s, mass emigration from the South to the Northwest depleted the rural population and reduced employment (mainly under-employment) in southern agriculture. Beginning in the late 1950s, public policies in favour of the South sought to industrialise the area by improving its infrastructure and, later, by subsidising the debt financing of private investment and thereby reduce the cost of capital. Moreover, the state invested directly in capital intensive industries (petrol-chemicals and steel) through state-owned enterprises. In 1968, also the 'fiscalisation' (partial relief) of the social security contributions paid by employers was introduced in favour of southern firms. This relief was extended in 1976 to full exemption for all new workers in manufacturing. The net effects of these subsidies on territorial differentials in terms of labour costs must be evaluated bearing in mind that, in 1969, the clauses in national labour contracts that established regional wage differentials ('wage cages') were formally abolished, consistently with the unions' principle of equal minimum pay for every region. These policies were able to reduce the differential in GDP per capita with respect to the rest of the country. The latter reached its all-time minimum in the first half of the 1970s (see Table 9.1).

Table 9.1
Per capita household consumption (HC), gross fixed investment (GFI), gross domestic product (GDP), disposable income (DI), and net disposable income (NDI)[1] in South Italy (North-Centre = 100): 1970-1995

	HC	GFI	GDP	DI	NDI
1970	68.8	86.1	59.1	63.8	54.8
1975	70.7	88.7	61.5	65.7	56.8
1980	70.2	72.0	59.3	62.5	54.1
1985	71.5	75.5	59.9	62.0	54.4
1990	70.7	64.7	58.8	61.5	53.0
1995	68.9	55.0	56.9	n.a.	n.a.

1 Per capita disposable income net of public redistribution
n.a.= figure not available

Source: SVIMEZ - Rapporto sull'economia del Mezzogiorno (various years); BANCA D'ITALIA

The oil shocks of the 1970s triggered the crisis for the basic industries on which state intervention in favour of the South relied: investment plans were drastically cut, while public funds previously committed to industrialisation were instead used to enable state-owned enterprises to continue in operation in spite of their heavy losses. During the 1980s, after long debates on its effectiveness, the public policy designed to foster the industrialisation of the South came to an end. Attempts to find a new development policy were not successful, and several different philosophies were discussed inconclusively. One of them was that the state should favour the spontaneous emergence of efficient networks of small firms (especially in the service sector) generating positive externalities. The hope was to replicate in the South the growth achieved by the industrial districts of the so-called 'Third Italy' (the Northeast and the Centre). The results were disappointing, particularly with regard to the quality of the newly born firms, with some important exceptions along the Adriatic coast. Furthermore, it was extremely difficult to attract direct investment and to induce firms external to the area to locate parts of their activity in the South.

As a result, the supply constraint arising from the inability of the southern economy to produce competitively tradable goods became even more binding in this period, so that local demand was increasingly met through net imports.[2] In the 1980s, indeed, the resources channelled to the South through the public budget were mainly transfers to support household incomes. These resources financed the structural trade deficit of the area, thus considerably reducing differentials with the rest of the country in terms of the disposable income and consumption that would have been justified on the basis of the differential in terms of output per capita (see Table 9.1).

That government transfers supporting household income were perceived as permanent helped to depress saving in an area still in need of a high investments. While in 1990 per capita consumption in the South was about 70 percent of per capita consumption in the Centre-North, per capita saving in the South was about 44 percent of that of the Centre-North. The low savings rate helped to perpetuate the South's dependency on external resources and fuelled increasing discontent among the northern population, since it was no longer possible to finance transfers in favour of the South by increasing the public debt. Moreover, this dependency gave great influence to the political and bureaucratic personnel who decided on the use of these resources, thus distorting the incentives and motivation of local southern entrepreneurs. In other words, the weight of public-sector on the southern economy opened up numerous possibilities for rent-seeking activities, creating an environment favourable for organised crime (Centorrino, 1990).

The insufficient international competitiveness of southern products and the importance of the public sector in southern income has made the economic activity of this area very sensitive to changes in Italian fiscal policy. When the latter became highly restrictive as a consequence of the financial crisis of 1992, in order to recover control on public debt, the South was hit by a deep and prolonged recession. Since exports represent a relatively small share of southern GDP, currency devaluation had weak beneficial effects on southern economic activity. For the first time in the post-war period, consumption fell. The construction sector, the traditional engine of the southern economy, entered a severe crisis. Indeed, the residential building industry slowed down as a result of the fall in permanent household incomes and of increases in real interest rates and in taxes on property; while public works practically came to a halt.

Since the mid 1970s, the process of convergence between the South and the rest of the country has been interrupted: the differential in terms of GDP per capita is currently larger than it was in the first half of the 1970s (see Table 9.1). The differential in the unemployment rate between the South and the other regions grew dramatically after the mid 1980s and is still growing in the 1990s (see figure 9.2). Nevertheless, increasing differentiation is under way among local areas within the South, which is certainly less homogeneous now that it was twenty years ago. Along the Adriatic coast (Abruzzo, Molise and parts of Puglia), especially, where the disruptive influence of organised crime was traditionally absent or weaker and the presence of the state industries (and the impact of their crisis) less salient, there are areas in which industrial districts emerge similar to those of the Third Italy. On the other hand, the areas in which the economy was more dependent on public resources, and in which the share of public jobs on total employment was more significant, exhibit lower growth rates (Trigilia, 1992). The three large regions of the Tyrrhenian coast (Campania, Calabria and Sicily) - those in which organised crime is more influential - are also those whose long-term performances in terms of growth and labour market indicators are more disappointing. In general, a self-propelled process of growth involving the entire South has not yet got under way.

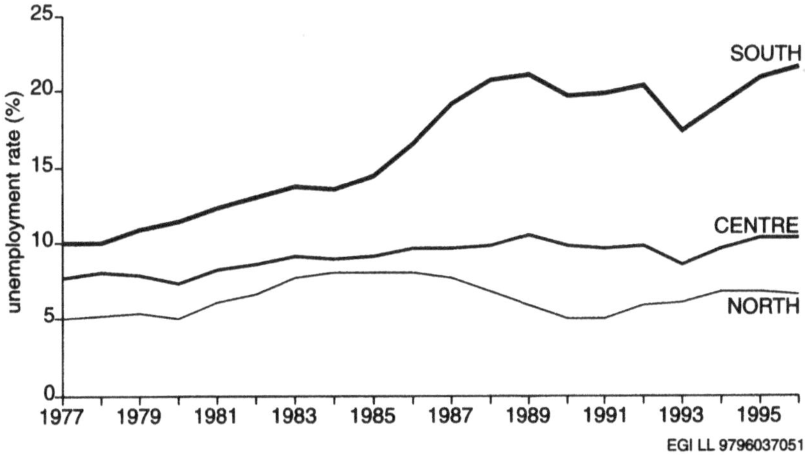

Figure 9.2 Regional unemployment rates*: 1977-1996 (percentages)

* Starting from October 1992 a different definition of job seekers has been adopted (standardised EUROSTAT) and individuals aged 14 are no longer included in the working age population.

Source: ISTAT - Rilevazione Trimestrale delle Forze di Lavoro

9.3 The polarisation of the labour market

The Italian labour market has often been described as highly regulated and institutionalised. The core of this institutional framework was formalised between the 1960s and the 1970s under pressure of the strong labour movement. The 'Statute of the Workers', containing a comprehensive set of rules for the protection of workers and their organizations vis-a-vis their private counterparts, was approved in 1970. The system intended to protect the representative union member of those years, that is, a male head of a household working full-time and normally for life - and possibly as the only bread-winner in his family - in a large firm, which was probably located in the North-West. The impact of the institutions across territorial areas differed according to their productive structure, endowment of resources and patterns of growth. In local environments in which the conditions for the development of flexible networks of highly productive small firms were already existent (as in the Northeast), the excessive rigidities limiting the growth potential of the traditional industrial heart of the country (the North-West) represented an opportunity to be exploited. In the more backward South characterised by a large agricultural sector and a fragile industrial sector, these tight regulations and rigidities ended up by exacerbating the polarisation of the labour market between 'insiders' employed in the state-owned enterprises and in a few - and subsidised - large private firms and the others (those precariously employed in low-productive small firms - often operating in the underground economy - or not working at all).

To understand the implications of the labour market institutions for regional disequilibria, the popular description of the Italian labour market as highly regulated should be considered in more detail. The aspects of the institutions regulating the Italian labour market most frequently emphasised are the rules restricting employers' control on hiring and firing, the availability of contractual forms permitting temporary work relationships, the process of wage determination in the primary segment of the economy, the system of income protection in the case of unemployment, the tax wedge due to the cost of pension schemes and to the CIG. According to some studies which compare industrialised countries in terms of the constraints and monetary costs inducing employers to layoff or fire their employees, Italy is ranked as the country with the tightest regulations (Emerson, 1988; OECD, 1994). This ranking has been recently contrasted with an international comparison of job turnover and workers' mobility across firms, which provides an approximate measure of the degree of rigidity of a national labour market. This shows that Italy more closely resembles the USA than do many other European countries (Contini & Rapiti, 1994; Boeri, 1996). Also international comparisons of job tenure, which orders countries by the degree of their labour market rigidity, confirm that the position of Italy at the top of the scale is not consistent with the stylised facts (CEPR, 1995).

However, it is possible to reconcile this contrasting evidence by observing that in all countries the job turnover rate is higher among small firms, whose employees represent a much larger proportion of total employment in Italy than in any other industrialised country. Firms with fewer than 100 employees employ almost 70 percent of workers in Italy, against 45-50 percent in the other OECD countries. Indeed, small firms display birth and mortality rates that are noticeably higher than those of larger firms. Moreover, they have greater opportunity to circumvent the most restrictive rules on hiring and firing, either legally (many rules do not apply to firms with fewer than 15 employees) or illegally. One could also argue that the legislation protecting the jobs of the employed workers is not neutral with respect to the peculiar size composition of the Italian private sector, since it may discourage small firms from raising their scale of production. At the other end of the size spectrum, large firms in Italy have had access to government schemes enabling them to shed redundant employees (temporarily or permanently) at low cost, by means of early retirements, special benefits for laid-off workers through the CIG, and other programmes. Not surprisingly, therefore, it are mainly medium-sized firms in Italy that exhibit a relatively low job turnover rate (see Table 9.2), since they face more obstacles and/or incur higher costs in manpower adjustment (Boeri, 1996).

Employment is concentrated within the small-firm segment particularly in the Southern regions: in 1993 about 35 percent of the southern workers registered for social security purposes and employed in the non-agricultural private sector worked in firms with fewer than 10 employees, and 75 percent in firms with fewer than 100 employees, against - respectively - 26 percent and fewer than 62 percent as the national averages.[3] These figures probably underestimate the share of workers employed in small and very small firms on total employment, since in 1993 about a third of the labour units in the South were irregular (against 18 percent in the rest of the country). Indeed, in the Northern and Central regions small firms have achieved performances which enable them to pay wages comparable with those paid by large ones, preventing the polarisation of the labour market characteristic of the depressed areas of South Italy. In these areas, the primary segment is relatively small and consists mainly of public and semi-public jobs (state-owned enterprises), and is coupled with a very flexible and extended segment of small and very small firms creating precarious jobs with low value added and productivity. On the other hand, it is the intermediate segment consisting of medium-sized firms that is particularly fragile in the South (Bodo & Sestito, 1991).

Table 9.2
Job turnover rates by firm size in selected OECD countries (as a per cent of employment)*

Country (years)	small firms <20	medium-sized firms 20<500	large firms >500	mean job turnover rate
Italy (1984-92)	35.3	14.2	12.1	23.0
France (1984-92)	n.a.	n.a.	n.a.	27.1
Germany (1978-90)	33.8	15.1	6.7	15.9
New Zealand (1987-92)	41.6	30.8	14.7	35.5
Sweden (1985-91)	44.8	22.5	18.6	29.1
United States (1973-88)	35.3	22.1	15.2	19.4

* Total job turnover; firm size in number of employees); n.a. = not available

Source: Boeri (1996)

Part of the secondary segment of the labour market is also characterised by irregular or informal work, especially in the South. A powerful incentive for the growth of the informal economy is the large tax wedge (including social security and national health service contributions), more than the legislation restricting employers' control on variations and use of their manpower. The Italian 'overall tax wedge' - defined as te difference 'between the cost of employing someone and the consumption which can eventually be financed from work' (OECD, 1994) - has constantly increased in the last two decades. In 1991 the amount of after-tax consumption which an employee can finance out of an additional amount in wages and social security contributions paid by his/her employer was about 38 percent of the employer's costs (OECD, 1994). Furthermore, this tax burden, by considerably increasing the labour cost incurred by employers, may be one of the reasons why a comparatively large share of total employment in Italy consists of self-employed workers, which is also a way to avoid and evade taxes. Among the major OECD countries, Italy has by far the largest share of self-employment in total employment. This share increased during the 1980s, and in 1992 it was above 22 percent (OECD, 1994).

That Italian labour-market institutions and policies have been oriented towards the protection of regular jobs in the formal segment of the economy, has discouraged any labour relationship different from the prototypical characteristics of a permanent position for a full-time worker. A consequence of this choice has been the small number of part-time jobs in Italy, which probably kept the female participation rate low. Among the major OECD countries, Italy has the smallest share of part-time work on total employment. This share remained approximately unchanged during the 1980s, and in 1992 it was about 5 percent (OECD, 1994). There are numerous signs that the figures for part-time jobs would be different if the informal economy was entirely taken into account. Under the pressure exerted by persistent massive unemployment, some measures have been approved during the 1980s and the 1990s to encourage the spread of contractual forms which allow the employers to hire workers on a part-time or temporary basis. Among these, the most widely used are temporary work-training contracts for young workers ('contratti di formazione e lavoro').

Another consequence of the tendency to protect those in regular employment is the lack of a generalised system of income protection for the unemployed. As mentioned above, the Italian provisions for redundant workers are extremely generous as regards to former employees of large firms, while unemployed workers without any firm affiliation or who worked in small firms are not eligible for an unemployment benefit, or for only a meagre benefit. Furthermore, the treatment received by the laid-off employees of large firms often depends on the ability of workers to exert pressure on the political authorities, since important aspects of this treatment are decided on a case-by-case basis, given the margins left to political discretion. Obviously, a system of this kind provokes strong resistance on the part of the unionised workers - those who enjoy the existing protections - against the spread of more flexible labour relationships. Moreover it increases the cost and the time required to adjust employment to sectorial or local shocks. Indeed, this makes it more difficult for the authorities to resist demands for subsidies in cases of structural crisis, slowing disinvestments within sectors in irreversible decline.

Institutions designed to protect employed workers by means of legal constraints and rigid regulations segment the labour market and create barriers between groups of workers with jobs for life, or at least with reasonably secure jobs, and the others. Data on job tenure indicate that, in Italy more than elsewhere, labour mobility is related particularly to a portion of workers subject to frequent job changes, while another group enjoys disproportionately long periods of job tenure. Particularly in the depressed areas of the South, this polarisation between groups of workers is marked, and it tends to coincide with the dichotomy between those with precarious jobs in the informal segment of the economy and those working in the primary segment. The presence of the so called 'wait unemployment' and queues for jobs in the primary segment of the economy are symptomatic for this.

Table 9.3
Female labour force participation rates, female employment/population ratios, and standardised unemployment rates in selected OECD countries in 1995

Country	participation rates[1]	employment/pop. ratios[2]	Standardised unemployment rates
Italy	43.2	36.1	12.0
southern Italy	**33.7**	**23.7**	**21.0**
France	60.0	51.6	11.6
Germany	61.3	55.3	8.2
United Kingdom	65.4	62.6	8.8
European Union	56.7 *	49.7 *	10.8
United States	70.7	66.7	5.6
Japan	62.2	60.2	3.1
Total OECD	59.2 *	54.4 *	7.5

1 Total labour force divided by the working-age population (15-64 year)
2 Total employment divided by the working age population (15-64 year)
* 1994

Sources: OECD - Employment Outlook, July 1996; Main Economic Indicators, March 1997; Italian data: ISTAT - Rilevazione Trimestrale delle Forze di Lavoro

The impression that one of the unintended effects of Italian labour-market institutions is the tendency to discriminate against specific groups of workers is reinforced when one considers the age composition of the unemployed,[4] which reveals the fact that first-job seekers have difficulties in finding employment in the formal segment of the economy. Institutions like the CIG exacerbate this, since during recoveries laid-off workers receiving a CIG benefit, have priority for re-employment. Consistently with this picture, a large share of the Italian workers who are in search of work are long-term unemployed. In January 1997 about two-third had been unemployed for at least one year. The low female employment rate in Italy, especially in the South (see Table 9.3), may be interpreted as further evidence that the Italian institutions are biased against some population groups.

The increased participation rate of women in the 1980s was the main reason why increased labour supply in Italy was only partially offset by an increase in labour demand. This was especially true in the South, where at the beginning of the 1980s the proportion of women actively participating in the labour market was still extremely low. The increasing unemployment rate among southern women was bred by the economy's inability to increase labour demand sufficient rapid to absorb the growing female labour supply. This inability has become even more marked in the 1990s, given that this growth has been close to zero, because the female participation rate has stopped rising. This in spite of the fact that the proportion of women belonging to the active workforce in the South is still much lower than in the rest of the country (see Table 9.3). The growing differences between women in the labour markets of the two macro-areas demonstrate that the territorial dimension of labour-market imbalances in Italy intersects with the polarisation of the Italian labour market between different segments and groups of workers.

The increasing regional imbalance did not result in internal migration flows. Moreover, there is some evidence that the persistently high unemployment rate of the South has not affected the wages set at the national level (see Bodo & Sestito, 1989). Nor should it be forgotten that in Italy the wages negotiated by the most representative unions must be paid to everybody (union and non-union members), ruling out the possibility for the unemployed to undercut the going wage rate. Even among small firms, where the union presence is quite weak, wages do not appear particularly sensitive to local labour market conditions (see Casavola, Gavosto & Sestito, 1995).

The above introduces the more general question of whether one of the costs of the excessive protection enjoyed by some workers is the low likelihood of the others in finding decent jobs. Under to this interpretation, the disappointing long-term performance of the Italian employment level can at least partially be explained in terms of a system that protects a portion of workers by keeping the labour cost high (mainly because of the generosity of both the pension system and the unemployment benefits for experienced workers on layoff); that determines rigid wage rates insensitive to local market conditions and productivity differentials; and that reduces the incentives for labour mobility across regions. In particular, high costs and insufficient flexibility, figure among the causes of the service sector's inability fully to exploit its potential for new job creation. Once one accepts this diagnosis, it should be recognised that without dismantling barriers to competition in the product market, increased labour-market flexibility can only redistribute monopoly rents in favour of profits, with tiny beneficial effects on employment. It is extremely debatable whether there would be sufficient social consensus to proceed along these lines.

Even informal institutions have adapted to a social equilibrium characterised by a low employment rate. The functioning of the family is a good example of this adaptation. Since those without jobs are mainly young people, it is obvious that the family - especially in the South - plays a crucial redistributive role. This certainly has to do with the tendency of Italian young adults to postpone the exit from their parents' homes and the formation of their own families. However, as the unemployment problem becomes more and more acute in the depressed areas of Italy, this social equilibrium may be about to break down.

9.4 The vicious circle perpetuating the disparities between the North and the South

The core of the North-South dualism is the persistent differential in per capita output between the two macro-areas: forty years ago GDP per head in South Italy was about 56 percent of GDP per head in the Centre-North. Now, forty years later, it is approximately the same. This despite the fact that investment in physical capital has been significantly higher in the South than in the North for a large part of this period, due to the state-owned enterprises and subsidised investments by private firms. Moreover, the South has failed to achieve higher growth rates, even though for the last quarter of this century the human capital endowment of this region (measured in terms of the share of working-age population with secondary school diplomas or university degrees) has been approximately the same as in the North (see Figure 9.3). A possible explanation for this persistent pattern is that the southern economy is trapped in a vicious circle which tends to perpetuate in time, causing a persistent inability to use existing resources efficiently and to create a system of competitive small and medium firms, thus reducing the productivity differential with the rest of Italy. The main factors contributing to the persistency of this 'trap' are the scarcity of infrastructures, the low quality of social capital, and the waste of human resources.

The historical backwardness of southern Italy in terms of *infrastructure*, especially in transportation and communication networks, and in water supply, could have been definitively eliminated in the last two decades, since there were sufficient public resources to do so. Unfortunately, the inefficiency and corruption of local authorities have squandered resources and prevented the existing funds from being used for the most necessary and urgent investment in infrastructure (Fabiani & Pellegrini, 1996; Ferri & Mattesini, 1996).

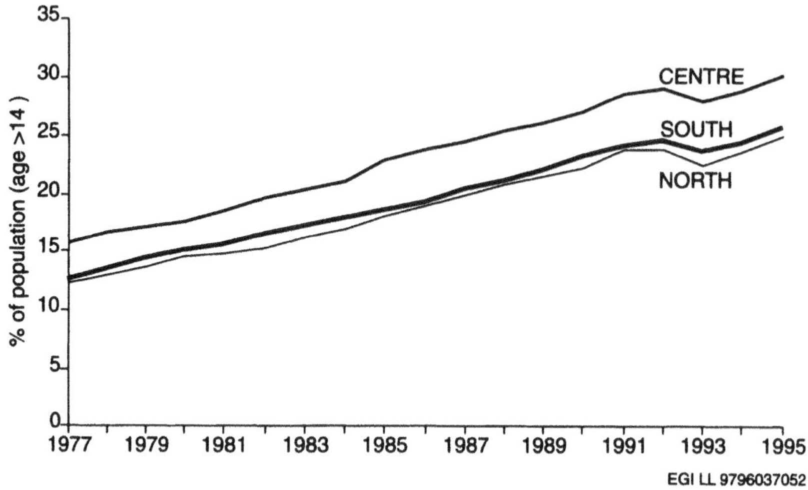

Figure 9.3 Most educated population[1] by region: 1977-1995 (percent of population aged 14 and over)[2]

[1] Individuals with 13 or more years of schooling
[2] See note to figure 9.2

Source: ISTAT - Rilevazione Trimestrale delle Forze di Lavoro

As a result, the lower infrastructural endowment of South Italy may be among the determinants of the systematic productivity differential between the Centre-North and the South (see figure 9.4). Furthermore, there are numerous indicators that the non-material goods known as *social capital* are in short supply in the South. The scarcity of this social capital can be traced to the traditional fragility of the southern society, to the fact that a consistent set of ethical values and informal institutions on which to found and reinforce universal rules and reciprocal obligations that transcend ties with one's relatives and friends have never been deeply felt and shared. This further hampers the functioning of both the market and the public administration, as institutions based on purely impersonal relationships. On the one hand, a public good like trust in the fulfilment of reciprocal commitments is in short supply in the South (Campiglio, 1993; Putnam, 1993) thus increasing transaction costs and creating an environment favourable to opportunistic behaviour seeking immediate gain and desinterest in building stable and long-term relationships.

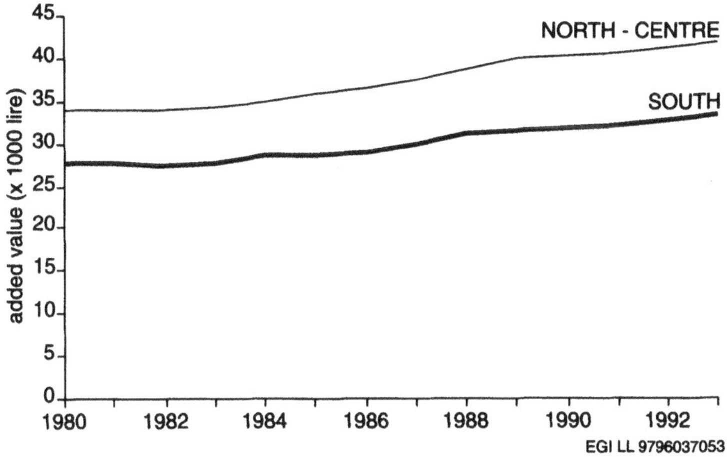

Figure 9.4 Value added (at factor cost) per labour unit by region: 1980-1993 (constant prices 1985: thousands lire)

Source: BANCA D'ITALIA - Relazione generale sulla situazione economica del Paese (various years).

On the other hand, it is precisely the dominance of precarious and unstable relationships that erodes the basis of an ethics which favours the establishment of a robust network of reciprocal obligations and the diffusion of respect for legality. This sense of precariousness and insecurity is reinforced in some areas of the South by the presence of organised crime, favoured in turn by the general climate of scant respect for legality. The differential in the interest on bank loans between North and South is another example of the operation of these reinforcement mechanisms. A differential, which reflects the greater riskiness and probability of default of southern debtors, but which also constitutes a serious competitive disadvantage for the growth in size and solidity of southern firms. The systematic *waste of human capital* is clearly evidenced by the fact that, in the South, only about one half of the population with secondary school diplomas was employed in 1994, against about two thirds in the North (see Table 9.4). Paradoxically, even in areas of Southern Italy affected by high unemployment rates, entrepreneurs complain about the difficulty of finding skilled workers (Banca d'Italia, 1995; Istituto G. Tagliacarne, 1996). This may signal that these areas are locked into an equilibrium path where (i) investment in machinery and sophisticated technologies (the 'good-firm' segment of the economy employing skilled labour) is discouraged by the shortage of adequately trained manpower, and (ii) individuals have little incentive to acquire the basic knowledge required by the good firms because local demand for workers in possession of these general skills is scarce. The persistence over time of this 'low-skill, bad-job trap' can be explained by the fact that learning-by-doing or training on the job are essential components of the process whereby the necessary skills are acquired, so that the availability of a sufficient number of skilled workers depends crucially on previous experience (Bonatti, 1996).

Table 9.4
Employment/population ratios[1] of most educated population,[2] by geographical area (1977-1995)[3]

	North	Centre	South
1977	65.4	58.3	54.7
1980	67.8	59.2	55.8
1985	66.0	62.3	56.2
1990	68.6	62.8	55.4
1995	65.0	58.5	49.3

1 Defined as total employment divided by population aged 14 and over
2 Individuals with at least 13 years of schooling
3 See note to figure 9.2

Source: ISTAT - Rilevazione Trimestrale delle Forze di Lavoro

Indeed, there is a complementarity between formal education and training on the job: to be hired by a good firm, an individual must have accumulated the requisite human capital, because without the appropriate basic knowledge and general training s/he will be unable to complete his/her training on the job.

The strategic complementarity between capital equipment and a skilled workforce may explain why local economies with different histories move persistently along growth paths characterised by differentials in labour productivity and per capita stocks of physical and human capital and which do tend to disappear. That the best educated represent more or less the same proportion of the working-age population in the North as in the South is consistent with the persistence of a 'low-skill, bad-job trap' in the South, if possession of a formal education is only one pre-requisite for the acquisition of the proper human capital required by the good firms. In particular it is consistent with the evidence that:

- the shortage of adequately skilled workers mainly concerns experienced workers with specific skills and specialisations acquired on the job;

- there is a mismatch between the basic knowledge and general skills required by the good firms and the types of school attended by the young people in the South; and

- southern job seekers are not willing to accept a relatively low entry wage in exchange for some training on the job because the lack of robust networks of good firms makes it less economically convenient to invest in the type of human capital required by the good firms.

In addition to the evidence provided by surveys showing that southern employers complain about the shortage of specialised workers, the qualitative mismatches affecting the labour markets of the South are quantitatively important. This can be found by contrasting the types of high school diplomas and university degrees predominant among those graduating in the South with those that prevail in the North. Indeed, a disproportionately large fraction of southern Italians obtain degrees related to the humanities, law and public administration, motivated to do so also by the traditional status enjoyed by the intellectual professions associated with these degrees in the South. By contrast, a larger proportion of students in the North opt for technical and scientific subjects (see Table 9.5).[5] An explanation for this difference is the attraction exerted in the South by public-sector employment in a context where the private sector can offer mostly precarious and badly paid jobs. A portion of the young people in the South who go on to higher education seem to aim at a public job, anticipating a long wait after school before they find such a job. During this waiting they may undertake some temporary activity in the informal economy, but without a real incentive to invest in a long-term relationship with their employers or to accumulate the kind of human capital required by the private sector.

The rationing on the demand side for jobs in the primary segment of the labour market dissuades many potential workers from even entering the active workforce. This structural discouragement particularly affects southern women, even those with secondary school diplomas, since only a fraction of this group participates in the labour market and a relatively small fraction is employed. In 1995, only 38.75 percent of the most educated women (at least 13 years schooling) were employed. It appears that their educational choices, oriented at the accumulation of human capital not demanded by good firms and in excess supply, are inspired by low confidence in their chances of finding jobs as a result of the investment in their own human capital. In other words, the decisions taken by many young people in the South concerning their education seems to respond primarily to the desire to postpone their official entry.

Table 9.5
Students enrolled in high school and universities by type per 1000 residents of the relevant age groups (1971-1991)

High school enrolment (15-19 years)

	Technical		Magistrale[1]		Scientific		Humanities	
	North	South	North	South	North	South	North	South
1971	211.50	181.75	42.34	58.86	78.30	71.41	51.37	56.15
1976	258.62	192.41	34.29	49.07	87.60	82.74	41.15	48.21
1981	248.32	205.15	36.90	55.76	75.74	73.63	40.23	50.24
1986	308.02	248.20	32.06	43.58	94.77	76.45	46.56	52.25
1991	298.59	299.27	33.89	46.45	121.79	93.41	51.47	57.87

University enrolment (20-29 years)

	Engineering		Economics		Law		Medicine		Language and Philosophy	
	North	South	North	South	North	South	North	South	North	South
1971	11.66	8.43	8.92	10.22	8.27	15.13	13.93	11.03	9.99	10.82
1976	13.68	9.59	7.66	7.86	11.87	22.70	24.55	20.95	4.56	14.58
1981	12.21	8.80	11.73	12.39	14.64	23.88	21.84	19.46	4.93	12.48
1986	18.03	8.21	17.20	13.27	17.91	23.19	14.15	10.74	8.35	10.40
1991	21.23	12.98	22.91	22.04	28.42	28.43	8.44	7.84	9.25	14.91

[1] Vocational 4-year-course for elementary school teachers.

Source: ISTAT

The scarcity of job opportunities also discourages active participation in the labour market by reducing the intensity of the search for a job. A low probability of finding a job tends to reduce search activity by southern women (Casavola, Gavosto & Sestito 1995). Moreover, the channels most widely used in the South to recruit personnel and to find jobs are typical of a labour market polarised between a public and semi-public segment and the informal economy. In 1995, 65 percent of southern job seekers sought jobs with private employers, against 86 percent of their northern counterparts. By contrast, 9.8 percent of young job seekers (15-29 years) in the South competed for public jobs, against 3 percent in the North. (See for the comparatively high propensity of italian job seekers to rely on family's and friends connections in their job-searching activities: Casavola & Sestito, 1995).

The southern labour market is characterised by a combination of the low probability of finding a job and a high reservation wage for those actively searching for employment in spite of the long period of time that will probably elapse before it is found. The relatively high reservation wage of southern job seekers is the rational response to a situation in which decent job offers are relatively scarce and the search for a job is expected to be a long process. In spite of the differences in unemployment rates between North and South Italy, in 1995 only 16.7 percent of southern job seekers were willing to accept a job offering a wage in the lowest bracket (in contrast to 26.7 percent of northern job seekers), while 31.9 percent were willing to accept a job only if the wage was in the highest bracket (18.1 percent in the North). The small number of good firms restricts the availability of career paths based on mobility across firms, which would allow workers to reap the returns on the investment that they made by accepting a lower entry wage (Becchi Collidà, 1993; Villa, 1993).

9.5 Policy implications

Several policies are required to break the vicious circle obstructing the development of the southern regions. Attempts are made to improve infrastructure and to create a more favourable environment for private investment, reducing the insecurity due to organised crime and improving urban areas. The competitiveness of southern firms should be boosted by making the financial institutions more efficient, thereby reducing the cost of capital and the rationing of credit. However, these policies alone are not sufficient: it is also necessary to improve the functioning of the labour market. Therefore, we discuss current efforts to introduce new and more flexible wage schemes reflecting the specific conditions of a depressed area and negotiated at the local level by the workers' and employers' representatives ('contratti di area', 'contratti di emersione', 'patti territoriali'). These make sense if, by allowing wage rates lower than the national minimum, they can help shift the equilibrium prevailing in a certain area toward a combination of lower entry wages and a greater probability of being hired.

Those opposing any such wage-reduction strategy argue that any labour cost reduction in the South would have only transitory beneficial effects on competitiveness and employment, because these wage cuts would not attack the productivity differentials between the two macro-areas (Capparucci, 1996; Cella, 1996; Giannola, 1996). This criticism is supported by the fact that wage differentials between North and South have already existed for a longer time (in 1993 the average wage in the South was approximately 90 percent of the average wage in the rest of the country) and have never helped to reduce the productivity differential between the two macro-areas. However, some of those skeptical about the beneficial effects of generalised wage reductions in the South recognise that these reductions may be necessary in the context of a purely defensive strategy, given that the partial fiscalisation of social security contributions in favour of southern employers has ended because the European Union vetoed its continuation. Notwithstanding this, the general 'philosophy' underlying the criticism of policies designed to increase wage differentials between the North and South emphasises that policies should instead seek to raise the productivity of southern firms.

In reality, the wage differentials between the Centre-North and the South largely reflect the different compositions by sector and firms' size of the two economies (Capparucci, 1996), with the larger weight of small and very small firms - and in general the informal economy - in the South. Combined with appropriate measures to remove environmental factors that depress the productivity and profitability of southern firms, territorial wage differentials for workers employed in the same sector and in firms of similar size may create a stronger incentive for southern firms to enlarge their scale of production (Faini, 1995; 1996). Moreover, these differentials may contribute to the 'emergence' of the underground economy. Moreover, they can stimulate external investors to locate part of their activity in South Italy, increasing the competitiveness of the southern economy in the production of internationally tradable goods (Acquino, 1996). Only by attracting substantial flows of private investment in competition with other depressed areas of Europe, can a virtuous circle be triggered in the South, giving rise to a cumulative process of increases in productivity and in workers' propensity to accumulate the 'right' human capital and to participate actively in the good-firm labour market.

If the objective of territorial wage flexibility is to make the wages of the good-firm segment more sensitive to the conditions of local labour markets, action can be taken primarily on the entry wages of newly-hired workers, so that the rent enjoyed by those lucky enough to find a good job in a depressed area will be reduced. For this, public jobs must become less attractive relatively to private sector ones, in order not to distort choices concerning education and labour-market participation. On the other hand, preserving the wage levels of experienced workers by means of collective bargaining guarantees sufficient returns for workers investing in the acquisition on-the-job of the skills required by firms.

One may wonder whether increasing territorial wage differentials might give rise to considerable flows of southern workers migrating to the North. Differentials in nominal wages would have to be quite large to translate into differentials in consumer wages, since there is a persistent and significant difference in terms of the cost of living between the two macro-areas (Campiglio, 1996). It is worth noting that in the 1950s and 1960s - the years of mass migration from southern Italy to the North - the differential in terms of lifetime expected labour income between a rural labourer living in the South and a worker employed in a large factory of the Northwest was very large, and induced the southern household to take the irreversible decision to move.

Table 9.6
Differences between employment/population ratios by age, 1977-1995

	20-24		25-29		30-59		average (total employment)	
	North	South	North	South	North	South	North	South
1977	63.39	37.01	73.19	55.56	64.48	60.24	49.83	41.95
1981	66.69	35.93	77.23	55.86	65.53	60.86	49.66	41.81
1985	59.78	32.65	75.64	51.87	65.25	60.65	46.87	40.59
1988	61.33	27.65	77.77	46.93	66.63	58.98	47.58	38.11

	20-24		25-29		30-49		50-59		average (total employment)	
	North	South	North	South	North	South	North	South	North	South
1989	63.65	28.73	78.37	47.26	75.86	63.01	48.36	49.31	47.65	38.08
1992	60.04	29.25	77.93	47.86	77.38	63.24	48.79	50.52	48.36	38.00

	20-24		25-29		30-39*		50-59		average (total employment)	
	North	South	North	South	North	South	North	South	North	South
1993	54.55	25.18	75.10	43.05	80.38	58.92	47.29	48.74	47.57	36.45
1994	52.17	22.40	73.28	40.75	80.40	56.81	45.53	48.01	46.80	35.19
1995	51.84	19.83	73.81	38.27	80.72	55.53	44.06	47.74	46.86	34.28

* Since 1993 more detailed information about employment status by age are available; here we show the marked difference regarding the group of employees aged 30-39, between North and South Italy.

Source: ISTAT - Rilevazione Trimestrale delle Forze di Lavoro

The compression of the differential in terms of consumer wages between the North and South in the last three decades is one of the factors explaining why migration flows from the South to the North have become negligible, even in years in which differentials in terms of unemployment rates have increased. In South Italy, the average annual net migration flow as a per cent of total population was -0.305 for the period 1982-'91 and -0.098 for the period 1992-'95. However, other factors have been at work too. During this period there have been prolonged phases with relatively low growth and high unemployment rates in the North as well, reducing the incentive to migrate from the South. Moreover, unlike the years of the Italian economic miracle when immigrants were mainly attracted by large firms offering employment for life in the most recent period, jobs have been mostly created by small firms, which cannot guarantee continuity of employment. Hence, emigration is perceived to be riskier than in the past. Furthermore, the inefficiency of the Italian services to job-seekers has serious consequences, since in the North vacancies are mostly in small firms. The lack of interregional information flows on vacancies hampers mobility as labour demand is more fragmented.

Other factors depressing mobility flows relate to increasing labour-market participation by women, who tend to be less mobile because of their family commitments, and - especially - to the high sunk cost of mobility due to government policies on housing (Attanasio & Padoa Schioppa, 1991). In contrast to this, recent findings show the less important role of government transfers for supporting southern household incomes as a factor deterring emigration flows among families whose young members are unemployed or in precarious employment (Faini, Galli & Gennari, 1997).

Considering the incentives and constraints faced by young males in the South, the choice of remaining at home and working precariously in the informal economy, while waiting for a good job nearby, used to be perfectly rational. Inspection of the employment rates by age, indeed, shows that these employment rates - as rough proxies of an individual's probability of being employed - are quite low for younger age groups and rise considerably among the people aged 30 and over (see Table 9.6). This may result in that job seekers become less selective as they grow older. It may be the case that some young workers - in precarious employment or with jobs that do not correspond to their desires or to the type of human capital that they possess - figure among those seeking regular jobs in the primary segment of the economy, but then resign and disappear from the unemployment figures as they grow older.

Also, as a consequence of shrinking job opportunities in the public sector, there are many signs that a deterioration in the chances of employment is under way in the South for older age groups (30-39) as well, with a relative widening of differentials vis-à-vis the North (see Table 9.6). It is probable that this renders the individual strategies used in the past less convenient, undermining the social equilibrium that has been established in the last three decades. However, as mentioned, there is no sign that this may trigger a new wave of migration from the South. In any case, it is highly questionable that new massive migration flows would be desirable, since in many respects it would be greatly preferable to induce the mobility of physical capital and of good firms to the South rather than move people and precious human capital away from that region.

9.6 Conclusion

The foregoing analysis of the Italian labour market and its institutions in the light of regional disequilibria has shown that they are incompatible with the sustainable growth of the economy and with a re-equilibrium of the labour market. The institutions have also influenced the evolution of regional disequilibria and, above all, they apparently enhance the ability of the northern regions to exploit expansionary phases more than they foster the growth potential of the depressed areas of the country. And yet it is in the latter regions that the disequilibria of the Italian labour market have become increasingly concentrated. The development of the southern regions therefore also requires a profound revision of the labour-market institutions in order to increase the flexibility, albeit contracted, of the labour market, in particular that of the southern regions.

Notes

1. Although this chapter is the result of joint work by the authors, sections 9.1, 9.2 and 9.6 can be attributed to C. Borzaga and sections 9.3, 9.4 and 9.5 to L. Bonatti. The authors wish to thank Fabrizio Povinelli for his valuable research assistance.

2. It is significant that the trade balance of the South (where imports and exports also include flows of goods and services between the South and the Centre-North) had been worsening over time. Indeed, the trade balance/GDP (%) of the South was -9.7 in 1951-60, -17.0 in 1961-70, -18.6 in 1971-80 and -22.5 in 1981-90 (Destefanis & Musella, 1997).

3. The source of these data, reported by Casavola, Gavosto & Sestito (1995), is the Istituto Nazionale della Previdenza Sociale (INPS), Osservatorio statistico sulle impresse.

4. In 1994 62.7% of the Italian unemployed belonged to the 15-to-29 age group. The unemployment rate of this group was 24.6%. Also international comparisons show the high incidence of youth unemployment in Italy: in 1995 youth unemployment (under 25 years) was 39% in Italy, against 21% in France, 13% in Germany, 31% in the UK, 35% in the US and 26% in Japan.

5. See for an econometric test on time series data for South Italy which supports the hypothesis that the prevalence of juridical and non-technical studies adversely affected the growth performance of the South: Paganetto & Scandizzo, 1996. On the waste of human capital caused in the South by the qualitative mismatches between the curricula and degrees of those who reach higher levels of schooling and the knowledge and stills demanded by the market see: Bodo & Sestito, 1991; Viganoni, 1992 and Capparucci, 1994.

References

Acquino, A. (1996), *'Aspetti analitici dei differenziali salariali territoriali'*, paper presented at the XII AIEL Conference of Naples, October.

Attanasio, O. & F. Padoa Schioppa (1991), 'Regional inequalities, migration and mismatch in Italy, 1960-86', in Padoa Schioppa, F. (ed.), *Mismatch and labor mobility*, Cambridge University Press: Cambridge.

Banca d'Italia (1995), *Bollettino economico*, No. 25.

Becchi-Collidà, A. (1993), 'Quali politiche per l'occupazione nel Mezzogiorno?', *Politiche del Lavoro*, No. 22-23.

Bodo, G. & P. Sestito (1989), 'Disoccupazione e dualismo territoriale', *Banca d'Italia, Temi di discussione*, No. 123.

Bodo, G. & P. Sestito (1991), *Le vie dello sviluppo*, Il Mulino: Bologna.

Boeri, T. (1996), 'La 'rigidità flessibile' del mercato del lavoro italiano', *Lavoro e Relazioni Industriali*, No. 3.

Bonatti, L. (1996), 'The Persistence of a 'Low-skill, Bad-job Trap' in a Dynamic Model of a Dual Labor Market', *Discussion Paper*, No. 3, Dipartimento di Economia, Università di Trento.

Campiglio, L. (1993), 'Le relazioni di fiducia nel mercato e nello Stato', in Zamagni, S. (ed.), *Mercati illegali e mafie*, Il Mulino: Bologna.

Campiglio, L. (1996), *Il costo del vivere*, Il Mulino: Bologna.

Capparucci, M. (1994), 'Il capitale umano come causa ed effetto dei divari di sviluppo del Mezzogiorno', in Brunetta, R. & L. Tronti (ed.), *Capitale umano e Mezzogiorno*, Il Mulino: Bologna.

Capparucci M. (1996), *I fattori dimensionali, tecnologici e di mercato nei differenziali retributivi delle imprese meridionali*, paper presented at the XII AIEL Conference of Naples, October.

Casavola P., A. Gavosto & P. Sestito (1995), 'Salari e mercato del lavoro locale', *Lavoro e Relazioni Industriali*, No. 4.

Casavola, P. & P. Sestito (1995), 'Come si cerca e come si trova un lavoro? Un quadro sintetico sull'Italia e alcune implicazioni macroeconomiche', in Amendola, A. (ed.), *Disoccupazione. Analisi macroeconomica e mercato del lavoro*, ESI: Napoli.

Cella, G. (1996), *Differenziare i salari: quante volte? Una nota su salari, produttività ed occupazione nel Mezzogiorno*, paper presented at the XII AIEL Conference of Naples, October.

Centorrino, M. (1990), *L'economia 'cattiva' nel Mezzogiorno*, Liguori: Napoli.

Centre for Economic Policy Research (CEPR) (1995), *European Unemployment: Is there a Solution?*, CEPR: London.

Contini, B. & F. Rapiti (1994), 'Young in, old out': nuovi pattern di mobilità nell'economia italiana', *Lavoro e Relazioni Industriali*, No. 3.

Destefanis, S. & M. Musella M. (1997), 'Domanda e offerta di tradables e determinazione delle importazioni nette nel Centro-Nord e nel Mezzogiorno (1951-1991)', in Costabile, L. (ed.), *Istituzioni e sviluppo economico del Mezzogiorno*, Il Mulino: Bologna.

Emerson, M. (1988), 'Regulation or Deregulation of the Labour Market: Policy Regimes for the Recruitment and Dismissal of Employees in the Industrialised Countries', *European Economic Review*, No. 32.

Fabiani, S. & G. Pellegrini (1996), *Education, Infrastructures, Geography and Growth: an Empirical Analysis of the Development of Italian Provinces*, paper presented at the VIII Villa Mondragone International Economic Seminar, June.

Faini, R. (1995), 'Stesso lavoro, diverso salario? Flessibilità, gabbie salariali e ruolo del sindacato nel Mezzogiorno', in Galambertini, F. et al (eds), *Le nuove frontiere della politica economica*, Il Sole 24 Ore: Milano.

Faini, R. (1996), *Flessibilità e mercato del lavoro nel Mezzogiorno: una terapia senza controindicazioni?*, paper presented at the XII AIEL Conference of Naples, October.

Faini R., G. Galli G. & P. Gennari (1997), 'An empirical puzzle: Falling migration and growing unamployment differentials among Italian regions', *European Economic Review*, (forthcoming).

Ferri, G. & F. Mattesini (1996), *Finance, Human Capital and Infrastructure: An Empirical Investigation of Post-War Italian Growth*, paper presented at the VIII Villa Mondragone International Economic Seminar, June.

Giannola, A. (1996), *Sviluppo economico ed occupazione*, paper presented at the XII AIEL Conference of Naples, October.

Istituto, G. Tagliacarne (1996), 'I problemi del mercato del lavoro', *Barometro delle imprese*, March.

OECD (1994), *The OECD Jobs Study*, Paris.

Paganetto, L. & P.L. Scandizzo (1996), *The Role of Education and Knowledge in Endogenous Growth*, paper presented at the VIII Villa Mondragone International Economic Seminar, June.

Putnam, R.D. (1993), *Making Democracy Work. Civic Traditions in Modern Italy*, Princeton University Press: Princeton.

Trigilia, C. (1992), *Sviluppo senza autonomia*, Il Mulino: Bologna.

Viganoni, L. (1992), 'Il ruolo del sistema formativo', in D'Antonio, M. (ed.), *Lavoro e disoccupazione del Mezzogiorno*, Edizioni della Fondazione Agnelli, Turin.

Villa, P. (1993), 'La disoccupazione in Italia: problemi di misurazione, contrapposizione delle analisi, inefficacia delle politiche', *Politiche del Lavoro*, No. 22-23.

Part Three
Eastern Europe

10 Institutions and regional labour markets in Bulgaria

Katia Vladimirova & Rossitsa Rangelova

10.1 Introduction

During the last years Bulgaria, as the other countries in Central and Eastern Europe, underwent a transition from central planning to market economy (Commander & Coricelle, 1995). This difficult and complex process is connected with significant reforms in the economic, social and political life. In a short period the country passed from an economy subjected to the principles of full employment, irrespective of economic effectiveness, to a situation where employment became dependent on the market economy based on competition and effectiveness. For Bulgaria this meant a change in one or two years from a situation marked by a significant lack of work force, i.e. hundred of thousands of vacancies, to the present situation of hundred thousands unemployed. This latter number is quickly rising along with a quicker cutting of jobs. The transition to a market economy, starting at the beginning of 1990, is connected with the abolishing of administrative methods and restrictions in the employment management, the abolishment of the forced movement of population as well as the establishment of a gradual development of the labour market institutions. Efforts were made to create the prerequisites for a transition to market economy and a new model of social relations and economic employment developed.

The development of the regional labour markets and their institutions was to a significant degree affected by the socio-economic development, the economic and political reforms and the development of other markets (commodity, capital, etc.). Employment and unemployment changes were close by related to the development of labour market institutions at various spatial levels. Bulgaria, among the smaller European countries, is divided into 9 districts (see Figure 10.1), 278 municipalities (communes), 5356 settlements, including 238 towns and 4444 villages. The capital of Sofia city has, excluding the suburbs, about 1.1 million inhabitants.

Figure 10.1 **Unemployment rates by districts (April 1996)**

This chapter analyses the regional labour market developments and institutions in Bulgaria. The next section outlines some main changes in the economic and institutional framework during the transition as a context for regional labour market developments. While the third section describes some changes on the labour market, the fourth section presents the establishment and development of labour market institutions. Section five studies the basic features of the employment policy and the labour market effects of the institutional changes. Finally some suggestions are made about the future developments of the institutional labour market framework.

10.2 The economic and institutional framework of the labour market

Since 1989 there is a drastic decrease of the gross domestic product (GDP). In the period 1989-1990 GDP decreased by 9.1 percent, in 1991 - by 16.7 percent, in 1992 -by 12.4 percent and in 1993 - by 6.2 percent. In 1994 for the first time after 1989 there was an increase by 1.2 percent, but it was followed again by a decrease of 2.5 percent in 1995. To a great extent the crisis in manufacturing and agriculture contributed to this. In contrast to this, the service sector increased in products from 30.5 percent in 1990 to over 50 percent in 1995, mainly as a result of finance, credit, insurance and trade activities. On the whole, however, Bulgaria was one of the Eastern European countries with the lowest economic growth during the first half of the 1990s.

With the economic reform the first steps for stabilising the Bulgarian economy and the creation of a new economic environment were made. The first stage of this reform was directed at anti-inflationary measures. The immediate objectives were the financial recovery of the economy on the basis of the control on money in circulation and the reduction of the budget deficit, change in the behaviour of the economic subjects towards the market economy and carrying out a coordinated budget, currency and commercial policy (Vladimirova, 1991). The starting conditions for the reform in Bulgaria were very unfavourable. This includes a centralised system of management with almost an entire state property of the means of production, an inefficient production structure and non-competitive products on foreign markets, an irrational employment structure, an unilateral foreign trade orientation and a considerable foreign debt and budget deficit. Moreover, the changing philosophy of the reform implemented by six different governments in six years caused additional difficulties. Restricted foreign financing and slow, inconsistent structural reform impeded the macroeconomic stabilisation. Six years after the beginning of the transition, Bulgaria's economy is still in its crucial stage, i.e. unknown dimensions of slow-down of production, employment, and investments.

The restructuring of the economy is strongly related to the development of the private sector. An essential characteristic of the transition is the institutionalisation of private property irrespective the fact that during the past years priority was given only to property restitution. The expansion of the private sector and its transformation led to an increase of its share in the total number of employed people and GDP. The share in the GDP reached to about one third in 1995 as compared to 7.2 percent in 1989.

The economic reform was also accompanied by the development of new legislation. Parliament adopted some basic reform laws, such as laws on Ownership and Use of Farm Land; laws on Transformation and Privatisation of State and Municipal Enterprises; the law on Foreign Investments and the Value Added Tax Law. They built the basis for the second stage of the reform, i.e. restructuring property and production and the establishment of a new economic environment.

In contrast to other Eastern European countries, the initial requirements for accelerating the restructuring did not justify the expectations in Bulgaria. It was extremely delayed as reflected in the delay of adopting the Law on Bankruptcy which, on its part, postponed large-scale laying-offs necessary for efficient and competitive production. There was not an increase of unemployment, but rather stagnation, i.e. there were no changes in inflows and outflows. Moreover the share of long-term unemployed increased which, in practice, also increased hidden unemployment. In the middle of 1996 only a real start of the structural reform was undertaken by the governmental decision for compulsory liquidation of 64 enterprises suffering losses, where over 25000 people were employed.

Nominal and real wages had an essential influence on supply and demand. The economic reform in Bulgaria started under for the centrally planned economy typical system of wage formation and regulation. Until 1989 there were only slight differences in intersectoral and regional wages. Wages ignored potential payment differences for specific jobs and qualifications. This lead to a decrease of the labour motivation. The first steps for wage-negotiating were made in 1990, but not until 1991 the negotiations started. The priorities were the definition of minimum wages and the compensation of the sharp decline in the real incomes after the initial price-jumps and liberalisation in the beginning of the economic reform. Regardless of the efforts of the Government and the strong pressure from the trade unions aimed at defending real wages, the real average wages in 1995 decreased by 52 percent as compared to 1991. The insufficient precision in the applied mechanisms resulted in a considerable opening of the 'scissors' between the average net wages of the employees inside and outside the budget sphere. The ratio between the highest and the lowest average net wages in these two spheres almost reached 1 : 3. The highest wages are in the financial, credit and insurance branches as well as in the different state-aided branches of manufacturing, such as the electrical production, the coal industry, metallurgy and ore output, transport, and communications. The lowest wages are in education, public health service, culture, etc.

The firm restrictive wage-policy in the state sector led to laying off of much of the work force as well as to voluntarily quitting of employees with higher and secondary education and professional qualifications. This decrease of the number of employed in the state sector was due to the repeated increase of fees for the compulsory social insurance (35-50% of the net wages) as well as for the unemployment risk (up to 5% of the net wages).

Unlike the state sector, the growing private sector of the economy does not conduct a policy of wages regulation. Here wage levels are determined by free negotiations. Although statistical information on the private sector is very poor and not quite reliable, studies show that the wages of the highly qualified personnel, of professionals and specialists, where unemployment is missing or very low, are two or three times higher than in the state sector. On the one hand, this attracts supply of labour to this sector and on the other hand, it exerts pressure on the wage level in the state firms.

10.3 Regional labour markets

10.3.1 Impact of demographics on regional labour markets

Before discussing in more detail the regional development of jobs and unemployment it should be stated that there are important demographic processes which influence the present labour situation considerably (People's Territorial Distribution, 1994). After 1989 an absolute decrease in the total population was observed. This decrease was stronger in some regions. In 1989 the total population was 8877 thousand and in 1995 it declined to 8385 thousand. An important factor for the decrease is the external migration that intensively began in 1989. More than half a million people emigrated, more than 80 percent of them being in the active age and with a good educational level and qualifications. Besides this, the natural population rate was influenced negatively by a gradual persistent decline in birth rates and rising general and infant mortality rates mainly due to the crisis in health care, deteriorating living standards and ageing of the population. The demographic situation for the various regions is presented in Table 10.1. Montana and Lovech are in the worst position. Lovech is among the districts with the biggest number of towns. Montana is the only district without a big town. Along with the decrease of the population, an intensive change of its age structure leads to quick 'ageing' and to an increase of the share of the elderly economically inactive. In contrast to this, the share of the under-working-age population decreased from 21.8 percent to 19.3 percent in the period 1989-1995.

The demographic processes as well as the increasing unemployment (see the next section) led to an increase of the pressure on the employed labour force. It has a strong regional aspect and turns into a negative factor in a number of towns, villages and municipalities, where ageing of population has reached crucial dimensions.

Table 10.1
Regional demographic indicators for Bulgaria in 1994 by district

district	national population share	per 1000 people		
		mortality	infant mortality	natural increase
Sofia city	14.1	11.53	12.06	-2.96
Bourgas	10.1	12.68	22.41	-2.28
Varna	10.8	12.61	16.49	-2.49
Lovech	11.9	15.85	16.22	-7.19
Montana	7.4	17.85	18.75	-8.96
Plovdid	14.4	11.66	13.21	-2.11
Rousse	9.0	13.84	18.11	-3.87
Sofia	11.6	13.24	15.83	-4.06
Haskova	10.7	12.19	16.56	-2.56

Source: Statistical Yearbook; National Statistical Institute, Sofia

10.3.2 Development of the regional employment

Most acute problems in Bulgaria during the first years of transition are the strong reduction of employment and high unemployment rates. The number of employed in the national economy was 4,365,900 in 1989 and decreased by nearly 1.3 million in 1995, i.e. by over 30 percent. In 1989 the share of employment of total population was 49.2 percent, whereas in 1995 it was only 36.2 percent. This, however, has a positive (alleviative) influence on the regional labour market, because it moderates the pressure of a lower labour supply. During 1990-1996 the labour market passed through several stages, characterised with different unemployment dynamics and structure, work force supply and demand, non-balance between labour supply and demand as well as the factors that determine this.

The reduction of production and employment, the demographic processes together with the payment of labour, population impoverishment, etc., had a large influence on labour supply. The economic reform, the abolishing of the existing institutions, the establishment of new political ones as well as the trade unions were decisive in labour demand. Regionally there is a trend towards an increase in the regional differentiation of the work force supply/demand ratio. According to table 10.2 the economic activity decreased all over the country. However, particularly due to demographics, the regions of Montana, Lovech, Rousse and Haskova have the lowest labour activity rate. The total employment rate stayed about the same in the period 1993-1995, and is particularly reflected in the regions of Bourgas and Varna.

Table 10.2
Labour activity, employment and unemployment rates in 1993 and 1995 by district (October)

District	Activity rate		Employment		Unemployment	
	1993	1995	1993	1995	1993	1995
Total	55.4	51.5	43.5	43.9	21.4	14.7
Sofia city	57.1	54.4	48.5	50.8	15.0	6.6
Bourgas	57.7	52.5	44.5	44.6	22.9	15.1
Varna	55.5	52.7	44.6	45.0	19.6	14.6
Lovech	54.4	50.0	43.3	42.3	20.4	15.4
Montana	50.8	45.8	39.6	35.4	27.3	22.7
Plovdiv	56.0	51.6	42.8	44.0	23.5	14.6
Rousse	53.1	51.1	39.4	42.3	25.8	17.3
Sofia	53.8	51.9	40.8	43.3	24.1	17.1
Haskova	57.9	51.1	47.2	43.3	18.5	15.2

Source: Employment and Unemployment. National Statistical Institute, Sofia, March 1996

The other districts can be divided in two groups: Sofia city, Plovdiv, Rousse and Sofia are mainly industrial centres with increasing levels of employment and Lovech, Montana and Haskova with inconsistent trends, but for the whole period decreasing levels of employment. Concerning the situation in towns and villages, Plovdiv, Rousse and Sofia have increasing, whereas Haskova and Montana have decreasing levels of employment both for urban and rural population (see also Table 10.3).

The reduction in employment in some regions went along with some basic changes in the economy of Bulgaria. The first change is related to the artificially maintained full employment under the conditions of centrally planned economy. In 1989 the state sector employed 94.5 percent of the total employed work force. At the end of 1995 this share went down to about two third. The number of the employed in the state sector decreased in the period 1989-1995 by 2 millions while the private sector increased only by 500 thousand. The decrease of 'overemploymen-t' in the state sector has not been balanced by a corresponding increase of the employed in the newly established private sector.

The second change in employment is related to changes in the branch structure of the economy. In 1989 almost two thirds of the employed (64.7%) had their job in industry, construction, agriculture and the forestry sector. At the end of 1994 this was about 59 percent. Most significant is the decrease in manufacturing. Employment went up in the service sector, mainly in trade, consulting and in the financial and credit system.

Table 10.3
Population over 15 years old by labour activity and district in 1993 and 1995 (October, %)

	Activity Rate				Employment/Population Ratio				Unemployment Rate			
	Urban		Rural		Urban		Rural		Urban		Rural	
	1993	1995	1993	1995	1993	1995	1993	1995	1993	1995	1993	1995
Total	59.9	55.6	46.2	43.0	48.2	48.4	34.0	34.7	19.5	12.9	26.3	19.3
Sofia city	57.1	54.3	56.6	54.8	48.4	50.9	50.8	47.9	15.2	6.3	10.1	12.5
Bourgas	63.9	56.3	45.0	44.6	50.9	48.2	31.4	37.0	20.4	14.3	30.1	17.1
Varna	60.4	55.6	43.7	45.5	49.8	48.2	32.1	37.1	17.6	13.3	26.6	18.5
Lovech	61.2	56.4	42.8	38.6	50.6	49.2	30.8	30.1	17.2	12.8	28.1	22.1
Montana	61.7	55.3	37.5	33.8	45.6	44.7	26.3	23.8	26.1	19.3	29.7	29.6
Plovdiv	58.7	54.5	51.1	46.2	45.8	47.2	37.5	38.1	22.1	13.3	26.6	17.4
Rousse	57.1	54.3	48.1	47.3	44.8	47.3	32.8	36.2	21.6	12.9	31.8	23.4
Sofia	58.0	57.5	47.8	43.6	44.5	47.6	35.6	36.3	23.3	17.2	25.5	16.8
Haskova	64.4	57.6	48.4	41.4	52.3	48.7	39.8	35.3	18.9	15.5	17.8	14.7

Source: Employment and unemployment National Statistical Institute, Sofia, March 1996

The third change in employment is related to the kind of labour contracts. The ratio between people working on temporary labour contracts and especially for those working without contract has changed. In 1995 about 90 percent of the total employed is hired labour and nearly 10 percent is self-employed. In the villages this ratio is higher mainly due to the self-employment in private agriculture. Compared to 1989, when employment was settled by labour contracts, in 1994 a kind of flexibility is apparent in the so-called 'civil' contracts or in the number of people without any contract. These forms of contracts are mainly characteristic of the private sector (close to 35 percent in 1995). In the state sector the dominant part of the employed (97.4 percent) are hired with labour contracts. Early in the 1990s employment in the various regions follows the common trends but with variations for individual regions, towns and villages. Most sensible was the decrease in the employment level in regions with large-scale firms in machine building, electronics and other manufacturing branches or productions being entirely orientated to the already non-existing markets of the east European countries (Vladimirova, 1991).

10.3.3 Development of the (regional) unemployment

In general, four stages are present in the transition of the labour market in Bulgaria (Vladimirova, 1995). *The first stage* begins with the initial official registration of unemployment as a reality in the middle of 1990, and continues until the start of the economic reforms (February 1991). Most characteristic of this stage is the significant number of still available vacancies and the change, only during a very short period, of a considerable excess of labour demand over labour supply to their balancing and the beginning of a supply excess. In five months only, the number of the registered unemployed doubled and the number of the free jobs decreased more than 2.6 times. At this stage the increasing labour supply is connected with the lay off of a great number of employed people from different social and political institutions (state and party machine, police, etc.), restrictions or stopping of activities related to ecological problems, conversion of the defensive industry, etc. Besides many women and younger people also employees with a higher education and professional training (i.e. engineering, technical, university, economic and other specialities) became unemployed. Laying offs were mainly connected with difficulties in providing resources for production, the existing shortage of energy, raw stuffs and materials, and financial and currency means.

The second stage in the transition of the labour market is mainly connected with the liberalisation of commodity and service prices, increase of the interest rate, and liberalisation of the exchange rates. One year only after the start of the reform in February 1991, the number of the unemployed increased almost 6 times. Up to now this period (1991-1992) has the highest dynamics in the increase of labour supply and decrease of demand. The laying offs changed the supply structure. The number of people looking for a job with a lower profession or without qualifications increased. The percentage of the unemployed with a good education and vocational training as well as that of women decreased but their absolute number kept on growing. Demand continued to decrease. The number of job searchers increased as did the number and the percentage of those leaving secondary and vocational schools, higher schools and universities. The unemployment level at the end of 1991 exceeded 11 percent of the economically active population in the country (Table 10.4).

Table 10.4
Unemployment structure in the period 1990-1995 (December)

	1990	1991	1992	1993	1994	1995
Unemployed (thousand)	65.1	419.1	576.9	626.1	488.4	23.8
Rate (percent)	1.7	11.1	15.3	16.4	12.8	11.1
Women (thousand)	42.4	228.4	302.4	302.4	265.4	235.6
Percent of total	65.2	54.5	52.4	52.4	54.3	55.6
Youth (up to 30) (thousand)	30.4	203.8	258.4	269.1	199.2	168.7
Percent of total	46.8	48.6	44.8	43.0	40.8	39.8
Education (percent of total)						
Elementary	21.9	34.5	45.3	47.3	52.6	56.6
Secondary	30.8	33.0	31.0	32.7	33.8	27.2
Specialist	27.7	21.4	15.4	12.8	9.0	12.0
Higher	19.6	11.10	8.2	7.2	4.6	4.2

Source: Monthly Bulletin of the National Labour Office

Unemployment during this period considerably varies by profession and region. At the end of 1991, the unemployment level of the agricultural workers exceeded 38 percent; for engineering and technical staff it was over 33 percent and in some regions it reached 40 to 62 percent. Data on these drastic changes by district are presented in Table 10.5. Within a year the ratio between the number of unemployed and vacancies dramatically increased. In Bourgas this was nearly 40 times, in Haskova about 30 times, in Plovdiv nearly 27 times, and in Varna over 25 times.

The development of small and private firms during this second stage was in its embryo phase and a small number of jobs were opened. The largest part of the privately owned firms established during this period belonged to services and regardless of their significant absolute number of jobs (24.5 thousand at the end of 1989, nearly 330 thousand respectively in 1993 and 413 thousand in 1994), the average number of the employed was small. To encourage private entrepreneurs and the development of the small firm sector, a special Decree of the Council of Ministers was adopted in 1991 as well as some tax concessions.

Table 10.5
Ratio between number of unemployed and vacancies by district (December)

district	1990	1991	1993	Jan.'96
Total	2.3	41.2	84	30
Sofia	2.7	48.3	23	6
Bourgas	1.3	50.9	125	45
Varna	2.1	53.4	60	28
Lovech	3.5	57.9	161	43
Montana	2.7	56.4	127	40
Plovdiv	2.7	72.7	147	42
Rousse	1.9	13.2	135	114
Sofia	3.2	64.5	70	23
Haskova	1.5	44.4	99	23

Source: Monthly Bulletin of the National Labour Office

The third stage in the labour market development is determined largely by the delay of the economic reform and particularly the property, production and foreign market restructuring. As a result, work force laying off was delayed as well as the establishment and opening of new kind of jobs. The number of people registered for the first time as unemployed and young people looking for jobs after completing their education continued to grow. Long-term unemployment (for more than one year) and the number of people in their active age needing social benefits was increasing. The slow development of the private sector and of the small- and middle-scale firms did not substantially increase the number of the vacancies. The unemployment level in some areas, towns and villages reached very high rates of more than 50 percent. Particularly the land reform caused this by the liquidation of existing organisational structures and a delay in the establishment of new ones.

The low labour demand in the period 1992-1993 is also related to a significant decline of the domestic market due to the intensive and large-scale impoverishment of the population and limited foreign markets. To be more specific, the economic crisis transformed into a market crisis. Production decreased and, related to it, lay-offs and/or irrational utilisation of the employed (time of waiting in unemployment, compulsory paid or unpaid leaves, etc.) increased. In 1993 the unemployment/population ratio exceeded 16 percent of the economically active population (see also Table 10.3).

The fourth stage of the transition began in the middle of 1993 and is still going on. It is characterised by the irregular development of labour supply and almost unchanged but strongly restricted labour demand. Dismissals considerably decreased due to the delay and still postponed implementation of the mass privatisation as well as the significant restructuring of production. Labour demand growth continued to be restricted because of the continuing economic crisis and narrowing of the commodity and services demand on the domestic market and the slow increase of the access to the foreign markets. The development of small firms and private business is restricted by the high interest rates of bank credits and the relatively small incentives. Unqualified labour supply increased considerably. The number of the unemployed with low education and without skills increased to more than half of the unemployed. The percentage of people receiving unemployment benefits and the number of long-term unemployed also increased. Those leaving the state institutional system, where they were registered as unemployed, grew in number. Looking for jobs they are desperate, discouraged, not believing and not expecting to be employed again.

A competitive market environment is impossible without high labour mobility (Angelov, 1994). In this framework it should be stressed that in Bulgaria labour mobility is very low. Causes for this are the insufficient education and training, underdeveloped infrastructure and housing, low income and lack of money for moving to another job in a different region.

In the middle of 1996 unemployment in Bulgaria consists particularly of the following categories:

- young people up to 30 years old (about 40 percent of their total number) and particularly those who appear on the labour market for the first time;
- women in their active age (16-55 years old) whose number among the unemployed, though fairly falling (66.7 percent of their total number in 1991), still exceeds half of the unemployed (53-54 percent);
- people with low education and without professional skills (nearly 55 percent of their total number);
- agricultural workers including those with higher education and vocational training; and
- engineering and technical staff.

Though hardly noticeable, demand is growing for skilled people with better education and vocational training. However, the employment contract changed under the continuing non-balance on the labour market. It became a common practice to employ people on term or civil contracts, without written contracts, etc.

The regional structure of unemployment shows a trend of convergence towards the national average. Montana remains the district with the highest unemployment rate, but some of the other districts have also depressed areas with unemployment rates of 40-50 percent or higher, for example Rousse, Plovdiv and others. Mostly these are uplands towns and villages with ethnic mixed population. Unemployment is taking enormous proportions among Gypsies and ethnic Turks in specific settlements in the Eastern Rhodope Mountains.

10.4 Labour market institutions

10.4.1 Labour offices, private job centres and other intermediates

Several measures were taken for an adequate legislation and for the creation of institutions for fighting unemployment (Vladimirova & Rangelova, 1995). Along with the first symptoms of employment destabilisation, at the end of 1989, the Council of Ministers adopted the special Decree No. 57 in relation to unemployment and particular the registration and social insurance of the unemployed. Thus, conditions were created for:

- registering the unemployed and available jobs;
- payment of a compensation to unvoluntary unemployed, mainly due to the liquidation of companies or structural changes;
- payment of benefits to young specialists and skilled workers registered as unemployed, and school leavers;
- establishment of a state system organising the reorientation, retraining, employing and paying of compensations and benefits. This system builds the National Labour Exchange, including a Central Office and offices in all bigger towns and villages;
- free of charge training and retraining of laid off workers and employees registered in the state labour offices (LO's); and
- establishment of a special fund for raising the professional qualifications of the unemployed (initially called 'Vocational Training and Retraining Fund' at present 'Vocational Training and Unemployment Fund').

Funds for these activities are raised by payments of employers as well as the state budget.

In the first period 1990-1991 mainly state institutions existed on the labour market which included the Central Labour Office Administration and 122 LO's in the bigger towns and settlements. Later on branches were established to some of these LO's. Although they have more limited functions compared than the LO's, they can give a more direct service. At present the number of the LO's affiliates is more than 150. Their functions increased gradually as well as the number of their staff. Their initial functions were to register the unemployed and the available jobs, and to pay unemployment compensations and benefits. Unemployed registered in the LO's only because of the possibility to get unemployment compensations and for young people, who are looking for jobs for the first time, to receive unemployment benefits. This function is confirmed by the mass refusal of the unemployed to register monthly in the LO's after the expire date for unemployment compensations and benefits. The LO's are now working on measures included in the active employment policy, i.e. training and retraining, temporary employment programmes for the long-term unemployed, etc.

In 1993 some LO's (9 of 122) changed into LO's for the corresponding municipalities and regional employment offices (REO's). The latter are responsible for the 12 or 16 LO's in their region. The basic principle is that they constitute the link between the Central Administration in the National Labour Office (NLO) and the LO's. The regional offices standardise and coordinate the work of the LO's, methodically and organisationally direct them, and assist in the fulfilment of the state employment policy including the qualifications programmes. Along with these activities they carry out analytic and forecasting studies for the corresponding regional labour markets. The Central Administration of the NLO uses the information coming from the regional offices for developing the national labour market policy and strategy (Rangelova, 1994).

As the basic labour market mediator the activities of the LO's developed and enlarged in scope during the past five years. During the first period 1990-1993 the payment of unemployment compensations and benefits and the registration of the unemployed and available jobs constituted over 90-95 percent of the work of the LO's. At present there are only few LO's where these functions are still basic or the only ones. The following activities related to a more active employment policy gradually developed in the LO's:

- informing the unemployed about jobs as well as about the possibilities to get qualified or trained;
- assisting in starting work, self-employing or inclusion in training and retraining;
- implementing programmes and other measures of the state employment policy; and
- controlling the labour legislation, the legality of the received compensations and benefits.

The intermediate, information and other services, carried out by the LO's for the unemployed as well as for the employers, are free of charge. This is also the case for the services of the other state institutions relevant to the labour market, like the specialist-clubs, the job-clubs, and the entrepreneurial consulting teams. The specialist-clubs at the LO's were built up along with the regional centres of the Scientific and Technical Unions and their objective was to motivate and help the unemployed with higher educational levels in their search for jobs or start their own business. They organise meetings between employers and unemployed, advise the unemployed when starting independent economic activities. The job-clubs have a similar function. They make the unemployed familiar with the jobs offered and techniques for searching jobs.

In developing these labour market institutions, especially the state institution (NLO) and the staff development, use has been made of countries like Germany, Belgium, Great Britain, the USA, France and international institutions as the ILO, the World Bank, the PHARE programme, etc. (Bulgaria and the European Community, 1993).

Besides the labour offices, also other channels have a, and sometimes more important role as intermediaries on the labour market, like the informal networks depending on the help and recommendations of colleagues, friends and relatives. Next to this, the mass media are important. Most of the available free jobs are filled by the informal networks and with the help of the media. In the second place, but a much lower level, are the state institutions (LO's), and on the third place stand the private and paid labour market institutions. A number of factors contribute to the still inadequate participation of the state institutions in filling the free jobs, such as:

- undeveloped state of LO's mediation services;
- insufficient contacts of the LO's with the employers and the local authorities;
- poor information for the employers about the potency of LO's; and
- formalism in the LO's work and employers' mistrust in the regional labour market institutions as a source of labour.

Moreover, in order to built the state employment policy and the corresponding labour market institutions, the Employment and Labour Market Department, functioning within the Ministry of Labour and Social Welfare, could develop more strongly national strategies, programmes, draft laws, labour market analysis and projects. A unit focusing on those activities is missing in the present structure of the Ministry, thus decreasing the coordination and effectiveness in the development and implementation of the state employment policy and the state interference in the labour market.

From the middle of 1991 onward it became possible through a special act, that the intermediary activity of informing and employing be carried out by private firms. At the end of 1995 about 70 such units were registered. They are located mainly in cities and bigger towns. Basically they can carry out three types of paid services: the first two are for those who search for jobs: informing about the jobs (working conditions, payment, social insurance, job requirements) and the help in signing a labour contract. The third one is for the employers, i.e. staff recruiting and selection. The activities of the private institutions on the labour market are, to some extent, supplementing those of the state institutions. They mainly offer services for employers demanding highly qualified workers and/or specific skills. Another important part of their work is the mediation in the 'work force export'. The private job centres diversify services in the labour market and expand competition there.

Up till now, the private institutions do not yet exercise a visible influence on the labour market. Potentially there is however a larger influence. Not only are their services paid (the maximum prices are regulated) but rather that many of them break the legal and financial rules. Experts suggest that state regulation of the private job centres should be codified and must ensure the replacement of the permission requirements by licensing in order to avoid unfair competition, fraud and other negative phenomena (Angelov, 1994).

10.4.2 Local authorities and tripartite cooperations

Other bodies and institutions that potentially could have close relations with the labour market are the local authorities and the structures of the National Council for Tripartite Cooperation. For the time being local self-government bodies and self-administration play an insignificant role on the regional and local labour markets. First of all they are not legislatively bound up with any obligations in the labour market policy. Furthermore, the necessary structures and staff are missing, as well as the understanding that the labour market is an important factor in their social and economic activity. However, due to an initiative of the LO's they became involved in the development and implementation of some of the unemployment programmes.

The national system for tripartite cooperation is a specific kind of labour market institution. It started in 1990, right after the establishment of the state system of labour market institutions. The social partners, with different intensity and consistency in time, separately or together, participate in the management and implementation of the labour relations during the difficult period of transition. In 1993 a National Council for Tripartite Co-operation (NCTC) was established as a body for carrying out consultations and cooperation between the Government as well as employees' and employers' organisations acknowledged as representative by the Council of Ministers. These organisations are: the Confederation of Independent Trade Unions in Bulgaria, the Podkrepa Confederation of Labour and the Organisation of Free Trade Unions as well as the Chamber of Commerce and Industry, the Industrial Association, the Union for Private Economic Enterprise and the Vuzrazhdane Union of Private Entrepreneurs. Two of these four last mentioned employers organisations represent the private sector, and the other two represent both state and private activities.

The NCTC was established on a national, branch, regional and municipal level.

Therefore it has a complicated vertical and horizontal structure. It has several standing committees like the one on labour force, on incomes, prices, and standards of living; or on collective labour contracts. The NCTC reflects a model of a centralised regulation of labour and social relations. During the past years different employment programmes, draft laws and other executive orders have been discussed and negotiated mainly at the national level.

Soon after the institutionalisation of the tripartite cooperation it got into a crisis and a long break of activities at the national level followed. The main problems are:

- the government's competence to determine the procedure of cooperation and consultations actually creates inequality among the partners and an advisory nature of the partnership. This leads often to a refuse of a dialogue on regulating industrial relations;

- both employers' and trade union's organisations are still in the process of formation and identification. Moreover, the organisations included in the Tripartite Cooperation do not yet represent the major part of employees and employers; and

- the tripartite cooperation works mainly on the national level. Branch and regional structures are not yet developed.

10.5 Employment policies

Characteristic of the employment policy during transition was ensuring the financial and institutional conditions for the increasing number of unemployed. Until 1996 there were no governmental policies directed at creating jobs by investments, restructuring of the economy and economic regulations (such intentions were clearly stated by the Government of the Democratic Left coming into power in January 1995). In the new labour relations model priority was given to legislative activities. Since the beginning of 1993 a considerably changed Labour Code is valid. A number of regulations have been developed, settling the compensations and benefits budgeting, supporting labour market institutions as well as measures of an active employment policy (Vladimirova, 1994).

The basic source for financing policy is the above-mentioned Vocational Training and Unemployment Fund. Funds for this are raised by employers' fees (until recently 7 percent of the workers' wages; now 5 percent). A small part comes from the state budget in order to pay compensations to the dismissed from the budget sectors. Thanks to the duly establishment of this fund, stability was created. Moreover, it was possible to finance passive and active employment policies.

10.5.1 Unemployment insurance and benefits

The Requalification and Unemployment Fund (RUF) has an important role in policy. It was established within the Ministry of Labour and Social Welfare. The fund is mainly used for three purposes:

- benefits for the unemployed;
- professional qualification and re-qualification; and
- encouraging employment by stimulating employers and the opening of new temporary jobs.

Persons laid off at the initiative of the employer through no fault of them, as well as persons whose labour contracts were ceased due to expiry of the contracted period, are entitled to benefits. Furthermore, it is necessary that a person during the last 12 months before the involuntary dismissal has worked on a labour contract for at least 6 months. This does not apply for young specialists and qualified workers who started working after their graduation and were laid off before they could acquire the 6 months length of service. The unemployed person has to confirm each month that he/she is not working on a contractual basis. Persons who have additional labour incomes, cannot receive unemployment benefits, regardless of the fact that they were laid off from their basic employment and were insured against the unemployment risk.

The unemployment benefits can be stopped before the fixed term if the unemployed refuses to accept the job offered, refuses to attend vocational training and retraining courses or wilfully stops attending such courses, starts working on a labour contract, works as a trader (employer) or as a cooperative member, works as an agricultural worker and his monthly earnings are more than the minimum salary, has acquired the right to retire, begins regular studies or joins the army. Unemployment benefits are also stopped (for a definite time) if the unemployed has found a job on a temporary or civil contract for a term shorter than 6 months.

Benefits are between 90 percent and 140 percent of the minimum salary for the country. For those employees having worked full time on a contractual basis benefits are 60 percent of the monthly average nominal salary, received the last 6 months before the dismissal. The latter applies to a comparatively small group of unemployed, mainly due to the delayed privatisation and structural reform. According to the present normative order (Government Decree No. 57 from 1989, amended and supplemented in 1993) unemployment benefits are paid in accordance with the length of service and the age of the unemployed. However, in the new Bill on Protection Against Unemployment and Employment Promotion, the term for paying benefits depends only on the length of service. New in this bill is the addition an unemployed gets if he or she is attending training or retraining courses.

Young specialists and young qualified workers can also receive social benefits. The amount is equal for all and 80 percent of the minimum salary. Help for long-term unemployment was normatively settled in 1994. Long-term unemployed are those who are registered in the LO's for more than 12 months. Their payment is 60 percent of the minimum salary. 'Help for inclusion' is 50 percent of the minimum salary and is paid 3 months to young people (up to 30 years of age), registered in the LO's as unemployed more than 1 year and included in motivation and orientation training courses organised by the LO's (Programme Encouraging Youth Employment). Persons who are registered in the LO's and do not receive benefits from the Professional Qualifications and Unemployment Fund and if the earnings per family member are lower than the minimum salary, can apply for social help. The unemployed receiving this kind of help can be included in the Temporary Employment Programmes as a priority. Territorial centres for social care selects the participants in the fulfilment of the different kinds of social activities.

The size and terms for receiving unemployment benefits are determined on the day of registration in the LO's. The LO decides on changes in the terms and size of the benefits. Unemployment benefits paid by the Vocational Training and Unemployment Fund increased over 4 times in the period December 1991 - December 1994. In particular the unemployment benefits in cash increased, but due to the increasing share of long-term unemployment, their proportion decreased from 95 percent to 90 percent. The social benefits increased over 10 percent and their share doubled in this period from 4.5 to 9 percent. The other benefits (children's allowances and other) increased over 10 times, but their share, because of the poor demographic situation is insignificant (0.5 percent in 1991 and 1.4 percent in 1994).

10.5.2 Active policies

Active policies started in the middle of 1991 and include:

- vocational training and retraining, professional orientation and motivation for labour market adaptation;

- encouraging an active search for jobs and in entrepreneurial activity through subsidies, tax and interest concessions; and

- stimulating employers to hire specific groups of unemployed (young people, disabled persons, long-term unemployed, etc.).

Along with the extension of the activities of the regional institutions in the Employment Programme, a Programme for Youth Development and a Programme for Vocational Rehabilitation of Disabled and People with Low Working Capacities will start. This will create opportunities for:

- the long-term unemployed to return to work for a given period of time, to receive labour income and better chances for permanent employment;
- young people to enter the labour market and to acquire adequate labour habits; and
- persons with low working capacities to return to active labour with more self-confidence.

Two of the programmes that started in 1994 in two regions will be spread to other regions: The Literacy, Qualifications and Employment Programme will operate in regions with an ethnically mixed population like the 'From Social Welfare to Employment' programme. This creates better opportunities for two very difficult groups of unemployed: the Gypsies and so called socially unadaptable risky groups. Regional programmes are expected to start with regard to people laid off from industries like the ore and coal industries. These programmes will be largely financed by the already mentioned Vocational Training and Unemployment Fund and for a smaller part by the state.

Most difficult is the insufficient understanding and participation of other institutions in the programmes and the passive behaviour of the unemployed themselves and of some of the LO's. The experience of other countries is used in the development of different employment programmes such as Germany, France, Belgium and Great Britain. However, when applying the experience of these countries, the national peculiarities, the behaviour of the unemployed and the different labour market institutions were not always sufficiently taken into account.

10.5.3 Effects of the institutional changes

The comparatively short period of existence of the labour market institutions (1990-1996) in a framework of undeveloped market relations did not permit them to develop entirely. In fact, two contradictory tendencies in the state labour institutions are present. On the one hand, a decentralisation of the greater part of the functions and on the other hand, a centralisation, in relation to the administration of the labour market institutions, development of strategy and the active employment policy.

The first and most important result, undoubtedly, is the establishment of a state labour market system which covers the full territory of the country, and registers and attends to all recorded unemployed. The second result is the securement of financing activities linked with the growing unemployment. This includes the payment of unemployment compensations as well as the institutions themselves and the implemented measures. The independence of the specialised funds from the strongly deficient state and regional budgets is also of importance here. Third, one could point at the development of an information system and studies on the labour market. These are directed at the regular informing of other institutions and the society about the situation of the national and regional labour markets, the measures and programmes, the labour demand on the part of the employers, etc.

The results of the active employment policy are up till now still insufficient. It are mainly intentions and projects that are prevailing, while the practical results are few. As a result, there exists mistrust and criticism in the abilities of the labour market institutions. Unemployed leave the system due to distrust.

At present there are no indicators which can measure precisely the immediate and long term results of the institutional changes. As a result of the LO's activities about 20,000 unemployed were trained in 1995, which is more than 13.7 percent compared to 1994. Figures for the number of unemployed who found a job after professional training clearly reflect the efficiency of the LO's. In 1994 over 5400 unemployed started working after training courses, i.e. 26.8 percent of the total number of trained unemployed. In Sofia city, where the level of unemployment is considerably lower than the national average, the number of trained and retrained unemployed, is quite high (nearly 24 percent in 1994). Particularly in comparison with the region surrounding Sofia which is about 6 percent or Lovech with 7 percemt. It is obvious that the well developed education network in the capital contributes to the good results. However, there is significant increase in the number of trained people living in small communities in comparison to big towns. In some of these larger towns, for example in Vratsa, Montana, Plovdiv and Pazardzik, there is even a decline.

There is also a preference for additional vocational training skills. People became more interested in tourist firms and family hotel business. This is connected with the intentions of some people to ground enterprises on their own. It should be stressed that only a small part of the trained unemployed, 3.3 percent in 1994, have assured contracts for future work. Basic reasons for this small number are the lack of clear perspective for the firm's development, the current financial instability of the firms and decreasing production.

10.6 Summary and future activities

The dynamics of the labour market in Bulgaria are clearly connected to the transition to the market economy. The transition is related to denationalisation and property privatisation, closing of unprofitable productions, enterprises and branches, reducing or stopping aiming at improving the ecology, restructuring of production, considerably decreasing the investments and the budget expenses, etc. The development of the high unemployment figures during this period was caused by the already existing level in the end of the 1980s, the low labour productivity, and connected with it, the hidden unemployment, the development of inefficient production as well as productions and structures not adapted to the requirements of the domestic and, particularly, the foreign market.

The economic and social reforms started and have been going on until now without a clear strategy on ending the crisis and structural adjustment of the economy. The involvement of the State was limited to the establishment of the NLO - including its regional units - regular wage bargaining and to measures deregulating industrial relations. The present state of the market bears the features of the model of reform. Mature institutions on the national and regional level are lacking. However on basis of already started or declared intentions of the relevant institutions the following further activities should be expected:

- In 1996 the Bulgarian Parliament voted for a 'Projection Against Unemployment and Employment promotion Law'. This regulates employer/employee relations in the event of unemployment - in particular in some regions - provision of employment services, occupational training and retraining, job security and job creation, mass redundancies, employment of Bulgarians abroad and foreigners in Bulgaria. These activities should be financed by the state budget. Along with this activity regional management and administrative programmes are expected to be elaborated. Moreover, programmes using local budgets are implemented.

- Further decentralisation of functions and activities of the state labour market institutions in the direction to the regional labour market units. In this respect it is necessary to develop private institutions as mediators of specific private labour markets.

- Specifying and activating the relations between the state and the other institutions (local authorities, trade unions, other non-governmental organisations, employers).

- A widening of the involvement of other institutions, like other ministries and organisations, state and local agencies in developing and implementing the employment policy and its financing.

- Reorienting the activities of the regional institutions from passive to active policies.

- Cooperation with other countries - including neighbouring - in working out and implement joint employment programmes, aiming at decreasing the tension due to excess labour supply of some professions particular in border regions.

References

Angelov, I. et al. (1994), *Economic Outlook of Bulgaria 1995-1997*, Institute of Economics, Bulgarian Academy of Sciences: Sofia.

Bulgaria and the European Community (1993), *The Transformation of the Labour Market and Social Policy. A View Towards Europe.* 'Ivan D. Danov' Publishing House: Sofia.

Commander, S. & F. Coricelle (1995), *Unemployment, Restructuring and the Labour Market in Eastern Europe and Russia.* Economic Development Institute of the World Bank, EDI Development Studies. The World Bank: Washington D.C.

Employment and Unemployment (1996), National Statistical Institute: Sofia, March.

Monthly Bulletin of the National Labour Office, current issues.

People's Territorial Distribution, Concentration and Urbanisation in Bulgaria, (1994), National Statistical Institute: Sofia.

Rangelova, R. (1994), *The role of the institutions in the transformation of economic systems of post-socialist countries: lessons and challenges.* Paper presented at the Third EACES conference 'Transformation of Economic Systems', Budapest University of Economic Sciences: Hungary, 8th-10th September.

Statistical Yearbook of Bulgaria (1994), National Statistical Institute: Sofia.

Vladimirova, K. (1991), *Restructuring of the Economy and Employment During the Transition.* Paper presented to the International Colloquium: Strasbourg, France, 9th-11th October.

Vladimirova, K. (1994), 'Labour Market and Employment Policy'. *Ikonomika*, No.4.

Vladimirova, K. (1995), *On Bulgaria's Labour Market: Unemployment and Alternatives of Employment.* University for National and World Economy. University Publishing House 'Stopanstvo': Sofia.

Vladimirova, K. & R. Rangelova (1995), *Institutions and Labour Market Developments in Bulgaria.* Paper presented at the 7th Annual EALE Conference, 7-10 September, Lyon, France.

11 Institutions and regional labour markets in the Czech Republic

Jaromir Gottvald & Milan Simek

11.1 The socio-economic background of the Czech labour market

For some years, the Czech Republic had a different unemployment experience than other countries in the Eastern European region. As figure 11.1 shows, unemployment remained remarkably low, lower than in neighbouring countries, but also lower than in most OECD countries.

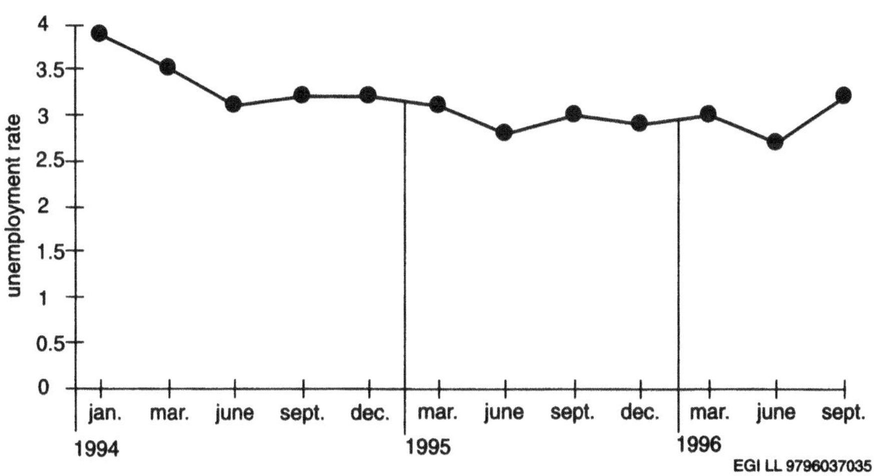

Figure 11.1 The rate of unemployment in the Czech Republic in 1994 and 1995 (%)

Source: Statistics of Ministry of Labour and Social Affairs

Considering that the decrease in output during the first years of transition has not been much different from neighbouring countries, the Czech labour market seems to be of major interest for comparative studies (Svejnar, 1992; Gottvald, Pedersen & Simek, 1994). A number of macro-economic indicators are shown in Table 11.1. The table shows no growth in real GNP for 1993 and a weak growth of 2.5 percent in 1994. Projections were about 4 to 5 percent for 1995. The splitting of former Czechoslovakia, the division of the Czechoslovak crown and the introduction of a value - added tax in 1993 had an important negative impact on the economy. The private sector has expanded dramatically through a voucher scheme of privatisation. Inflation declined below 10 percent. In contrast to some of the neighbouring countries the Czech Republic did not accumulate high foreign debts in western currencies before 1993. Table 11.1 shows that the balance of payments has remained in equilibrium during the years 1993-1994 and changed to a weak deficit in 1995. The general government budget has been balanced or had a small surplus and no major change was expected for 1996.

In the initial phase of the transition to a market economy a gradual reduction in labour demand took place. Even though lay-offs developed slower than the decrease in production, this resulted in a fairly sharp increase in unemployment in 1991. Until now major lay-offs, however, have hardly begun, as big firms until 1991 to a great extent could cover their losses by state subsidies. Bankruptcies as part of the privatisation process have not resulted in major shut-downs with massive lay-offs of workers. The lay-offs that took place have mainly affected working pensioners, youth without much experience, unskilled and female workers.

Table 11.1
Some macro-economic indicators of the Czech Republic

	1993	1994	1995
Change in Real GDP (%)	-0.9	2.6	4.8
Inflation Rate	20.8	10.0	8.9
Rate of Unemploment	3.5	3.2	2.9
Balance of Payments			
- current account (bill. USD)	0.3	0.6	-1.7
- capital account (bill. USD)	2.6	2.1	3.1
General Government Budget Surplus (% of GNP)	0.0	0.4	0.3

Source: Ekonom No.8, Finance a uver No. 4, Czech Statistical Office (1995)

A high absorption capacity in the private sector, especially in trade and services, resulted in a strong permanent demand for qualified workers. Labour mobility stabilised on 10 percent of total employment. Most of this mobility is among manufacturing. The future course of employment thus depends particularly on the restructuring of medium sized and big, formerly state owned, enterprises. The participation rate declined by 8 percentage points in 1994. This decline is stronger than in other East and Central European countries and could be a factor in explaining the low unemployment rate. The decline in the participation rate is much stronger for women, than for men.

The high unemployment rates in countries like Slovakia, Poland, Hungary or Bulgaria is the result of the introduction of the market mechanism (see also Horalek, 1993). If unemployment in other transitional economies is four or five times higher, it might be suggested that radical economic reform did not start yet in the Czech Republic. However, many analyses show the similarity of Czech transformation with the other countries in transition. Presumably there exist other factors influencing economic reform and which are connected with the historical development of the economy of a particular country. It would be a mistake to understand the Central and Eastern Europe countries as homogeneous. For example, the Czech lands were already high developed before the second world war. Capitalism and its industrial civilisation had developed and formed the cultural level as well as mentality and individualistic behaviour. A relatively strong middle class characterised by high cultural and qualification level, was typical for the Czech lands. This is difficult to find in other recent post-communistic countries. In comparison with the long historical period of 150 years, the relative short duration of communistic episode did not completely changed basic behavioral characteristic of the Czechs. Recovering of economic freedom and market conditions brought enormous spontaneous development of entrepreneurship and builds another reason for explaining the low level of unemployment.

Besides the decrease in participation and the growing entrepreneurship eight other main explanations have been put forward for the surprising Czech profile.

1. *A fast privatisation process and explosive growth of the private sector*
   The growth of employment in the private sector, from 1 percent in 1989 to 55 percent in 1994, was enormous. Private firms, and particular those which are not established by the voucher privatisation scheme, absorbed redundant workers from the state sector, public institutions and the co-operative sector. Mostly small and medium size firms hired new employees.

2. *Growth of the service sector*
   Heavy underestimation of this sector in the past and the sudden breaking down of barriers opened broad perspectives for the development of the service sector. Employment increased in services from 41.7 percent in 1989 to 50.6 percent in 1994.

3. *Low labour costs*
Individual labour costs are 15 percent lower in the Czech Republic than in Poland and about 25 - 30 percent lower than in Hungary (PlanEcon prediction). Labour costs are no more than 20 - 35 percent of the average labour costs in the European Union. This is not only a comparative advantage for foreign trade but also enables the employment of more labourers in firms. Labour hoarding is economically still acceptable, but labour - capital substitution is rather low.

4. *An active labour market policy and a restrictive unemployment insurance system*
A very active labour market policy is combined with an unemployment insurance system that is quite restrictive compared to neighbouring countries. To be eligible to benefits an unemployed worker must have been employed for more than 12 months during the previous 3 years. Tightening of eligibility rules in 1994 implied that the proportion of unemployed workers receiving benefits has declined from about 80 to about 40 percent. Benefit duration is, with six months, rather short. Benefit conditionality, i.e. willingness to take a job offer, is administered very rigorously.

5. *Labour market flexibility*
There are strong efforts to keep the Czech labour market flexible. The labour market successfully is defended against union pressure to increase the minimum wage level. Moderate wage bargaining from the unions and central wage regulation contribute to labour market flexibility.

6. *Liberal economic conditions*
OECD economic studies emphasise the significance to restrict labour market rigidity in order to increase employment. Nevertheless labour market deregulation mostly means an increase of the supply of lower paid jobs. If this deregulation is combined by a liberal economic policy then it also results in more skilled jobs. A liberal approach to international capital inflow and the removing of barriers for internal and external competition were important for labour force mobility.

7. *Economic growth*
There are many reasons to believe that the fall of the Czech GDP in 1990 - 1993 was lower than published in official statistical data. Causes for this are the existence of shadow economics, missing data for firms employing less than 25 employees and methodological statistical errors.

8. *The permanent high level of job creation*
This factor reflects some of the above mentioned factors. There were about 400 thousands newly registered unemployed in 1994 of which 80 percent found a job. In 1995 inflow was 352,221 persons and outflow was 365,660 persons.

Turnover in the labour market was higher because not all of them found their work by labour office activities. The growth of labour market turnover depends on the number of vacancies and on the level of job creation. There is a permanent increase of the number of vacancies from 1994 which resulted in a decrease of the ratio between unemployment and vacancies from 3.5 to 2.0 (see figure 11.2). This increase of vacancies even enabled the absorption of increasing labour supply due to a large population growth in the seventies.

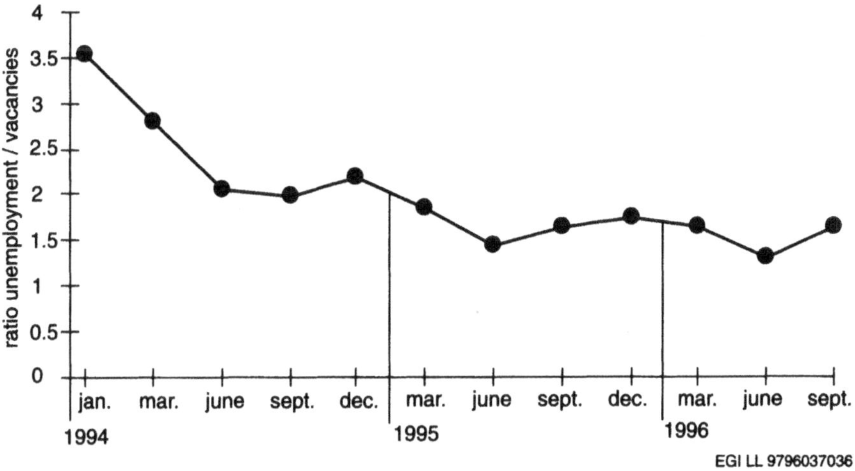

Figure 11.2 Ratio between unemployment and vacancies in the Czech Republic in 1994 and 1995 (persons)

Source: Statistics of Ministry of Labour and Social Affairs

11.2 The regional structure

11.2.1 Historical background

The regional set-up of the Czech Republic has developedin a very complicated way. During history it was created by a lot of regions of different significance. The Czech Republic can be considered as a natural region with the centre of Prague. Great Prague represents one seventh of the Czech population. Other big centres are Brno - previous capital of Moravia - and Ostrava. The latter arose during industrial revolution on the border of the two historical countries of Moravia and Silesia. These three centres create relatively closed subregions. We can identify moreover between seven to ten other regions (regions of the second level): the towns Ceské Budejovice, Plzen, Usti nad Labem, Liberec, Hradec Kralove, Pardubice, Olomouc a Zlin.

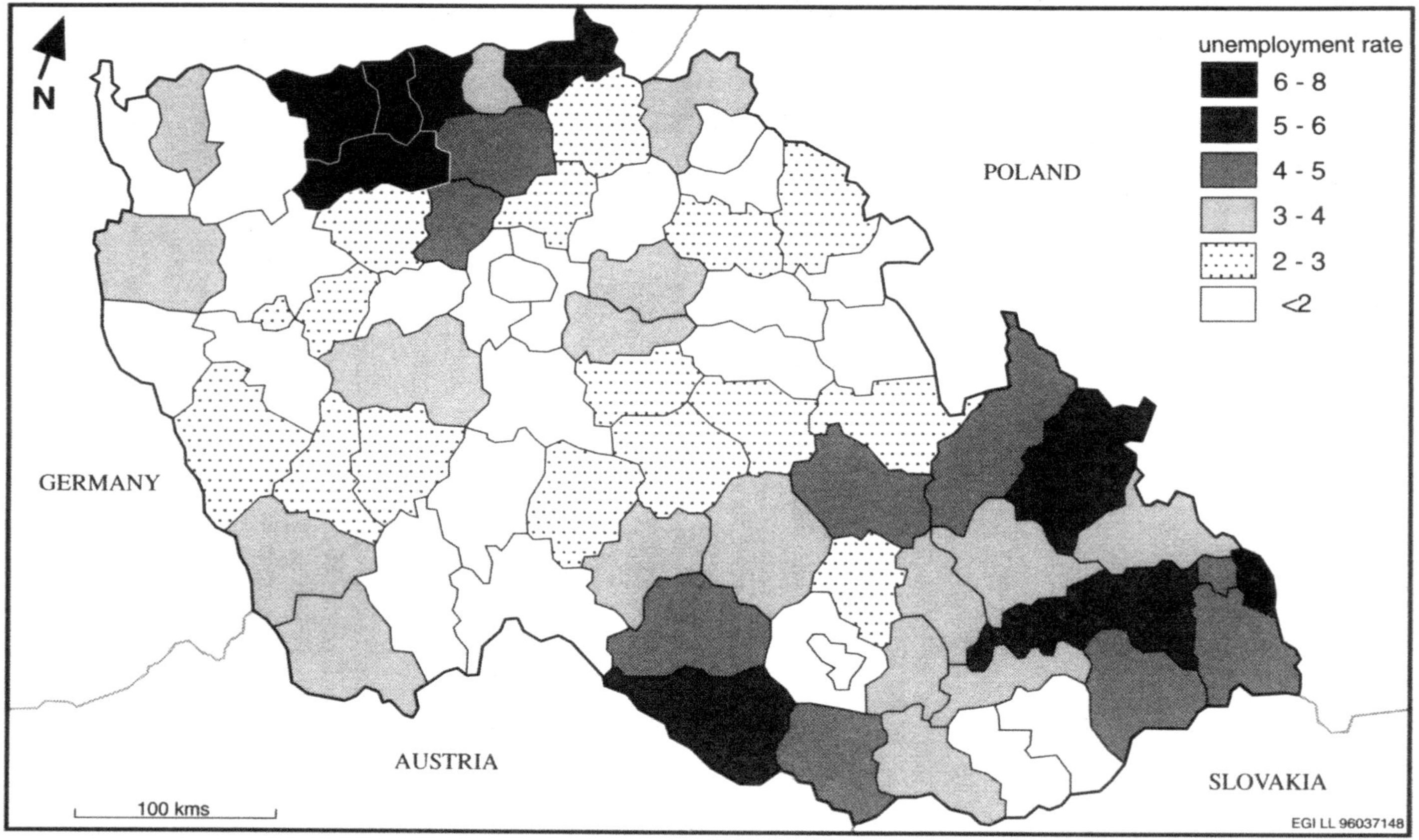

Figure 11.3 Administrative districts in the Czech Republic

(For Jihlava and Karlovy and Vary the regional position is somewhat controversial.) Up to the beginning of the nineties, facilities for citizens were developed in all of these centres. The economic power of these centres would have been weak if they were not centres of county's administrative bodies. The centres at the lower level were created by relationships with their immediate surroundings (commuting, technological relationships, lower administration functions). There are about 200 centres of such elementary regions. The present regional situation is the result of the regional set-up of the state in 1960. In the framework of former Czechoslovakia, the territory of Bohemia and Moravia was divided into the capital Prague and seven regions (Central Bohemia, Southern Bohemia, Western Bohemia, Northern Bohemia, Eastern Bohemia, Southern Moravia, Northern Moravia) and 75 districts. In the creation of the new districts, some unsensitive interferences with the 'natural' regional set-up were made. These still survive. Some important changes occurred, however, at the beginning of the 80's. Up to 1990 elected regional bodies existed in the Czech Republic (for the 7 regions and Prague, 5 in Bohemia and 2 in Moravia and Silesia). Their actual power was weak however. These bodies functioned like parts of the public administration. Regional bodies of this kind were abolished in 1990. Only some of them still exist as an organisational part of central bodies (regional departments of Ministry of Economy, Ministry of Environment, Czech Statistical Office). Labour market institutions on this regional level did not exist.

11.2.2 Administrative regions

The regional administrative structure is in the constitution and consist of municipalities (about 6200), and regions (definite number not constituted yet). According to the constitution the regions should have their own elected representatives, its own management and executive bodies and the authority to propose laws for the Parliament. It is discussed whether the regions will also have a task in public administration. The proposed regions will be probably large.

From the point of view of public administration the Czech Republic is divided, including the capital of Prague, into 76 districts (see figure 11.3). In each district there is one 'District Office'. Its activities are regulated by law. Public administration has its strict jurisdictions there. Here the special body 'District Assembly' controls the division of subsidies from the state budget. Besides the 'District Offices' there are other departments of the state in each district. From the point of view of the labour market 'Labour Offices' exist. They arose in 1990. Law regulates that Labour Offices are regional offices of public administration in the field of labour market and that the Labour Office districts are similar to the regional districts of District Offices. It is the jurisdiction of the labour offices to create branch offices (which administer all activities as labour offices) or detached departments (which administer only labour exchange activities). The establishment and activities of the branch offices and detached departments influences the development of the region. New, qualified labour jobs are created and citizens can administer their matters closer to their homes with lower costs. The visits at the offices are usually combined with using other services. In this way significant economic effects occur. The differences between the administrative areas of the various labour offices in relation to the area and population covered are indicated in table 11.2. The table shows that some small territorial units have been established based on a net of labour offices. The existence of small units is particular related to a higher number of inhabitants. Some territories with excess values are mainly administrative territories of larger cities where most demographical potential is present.

Table 11.2
Administrative areas of the labour offices according to the area and population covered

Area sqkm	Population (thousands)								Total
	2-5	5-10	10-20	20-50	50-100	100-200	200-500	1000+	
20-50				2					2
50-100		1	5	3	1				10
100-200	2	8	19	12	2	1 *			44
200-500	1	3	26	47	17	5	2 *	1 *	102
500-1000			2	15	22	5			44
1000-2000				2	3	2			8
Total	3	12	52	81	45	14	2	1	210

* towns = districts with no regard to the internal division

Source: Kovar, J. Territorial Structure of Labour Offices. Research report. VUROM. Ostrava (1994)

11.2.3 Main features of the regions

The existing regional differences in the Czech Republic are not only a result of different economic conditions but also of the demographic and geographic position of the regions. From the demographic point of view, the population in the eastern part of the republic (Southern Moravia, Northern Moravia) is younger than in the western part (Bohemia) (see table 11.3). Prague has the lowest number of children while the border areas have a high number. As a result of selective emigration, the older population is overrepresented in the countryside. The highest density of population is in Prague, Central Bohemia, Northern Moravia (Ostrava) and in the industrial parts of the Northern Bohemia. Border mountain regions have a low density (25 citizens/qkm and less).

Table 11.3
Basic features of regions in the Czech Republic (1991)

Regions	Area sqkm	Population (x 1000)	Density (citizens/ sqkm)	Age structure 0-14	15-59 (M) 15-54 (F)	60+ (M) 55+ (F)
Prague	496	1214.2	2248	19.2	56.9	23.9
Central Bohemia	11038	1112.9	101	21.1	57.5	21.4
Southern Bohemia	11345	697.5	61	22.2	58	19.8
Western Bohemia	10873	860.3	79	21.6	58.9	19.5
Northern Bohemia	7777	1174	151	22.4	59.2	18.4
Eastern Bohemia	11240	1233.2	110	21.9	57.4	20.7
Southern Moravia	15027	2049.3	136	22.1	57.3	20.6
Northern Moravia	11068	1960.8	177	22.6	59.2	28.2
Czech Republic	**78864**	**10302.2**	**131**	**21.7**	**58**	**0.3**

Source: Census from 1991

Table 11.4
Rate of economic activity and sector structure of employment in regions (%; 1995)

Regions	Rate of economic activity	Sector I	Sector II	Sector III
Prague	63.1	0.8	25.1	74.1
Central Bohemia	62.5	9.2	40.2	50.6
Southern Bohemia	64.3	11.0	41.8	47.2
Western Bohemia	64.9	9.7	40.5	49.8
Northern Bohemia	64.4	8.7	42.0	49.3
Eastern Bohemia	63.9	9.8	44.8	45.8
Southern Moravia	61.4	8.6	42.7	48.7
Northern Moravia	61.3	10.2	42.5	47.3
Czech Republic	**62.8**	**8.4**	**40.1**	**51.5**

I = agriculture, hunting, forestry, fishing, mining
II = manufacturing, production and network of electric energy
III = services

Source: Employment and Unemployment in the Czech Republic (1995) Czech Statistical Office.

As table 11.4 shows, there are no great differences among the regions in the economic activity rate. Still there are differences in the sectoral employment structure. The highest level of economic activity is in Prague and in its suburbs. Here is a concentration of top-level employment in the sphere of management, science and culture. The larger part of financial capital, foreign investment and foreign contacts are concentrated here as well. High prices and wage levels are characteristic. The rate of the economic activity in the Czech Republic was 62.8 percent at the end of 1995. Significant spatial differences can be seen in unemployment (table 11.5). For a long time the lowest rate of unemployment was in Prague including its suburbs (below 1 percent). Low rates of unemployment can also be found in Southern and Western Bohemia (about 2 percent).

Table 11.5
Registered unemployment and vacancies in the regions
(up to 31.12.1995)

Regions	Registered unemployment	Rate of unemployment	Registered vacancies	Number of unemployment per vacancy
Prague	1854	0.3	14432	0.1
Central Bohemia	14325	2.6	9892	1.5
Southern Bohemia	7362	2.0	8029	0.9
Western Bohemia	9671	2.2	8615	1.2
Northern Bohemia	29198	4.8	8723	3.3
Eastern Bohemia	14498	2.3	12377	1.2
Southern Moravia	29307	2.9	12382	2.4
Northern Moravia	46826	4.8	13597	3.4
Czech Republic	**153041**	**2.9**	**88047**	**1.7**

Source: Statistics of Ministry of Labour and Social Affairs

Higher values arose in Northern Bohemia and Northern Moravia (4-6 percent). A factor that accounts for the low unemployment in some districts is the greater ease with which their population can work in Germany and Austria. In summer 1995 nearly 17 thousand persons were employed abroad. Ten thousand of them (sometimes even 13 thousand) worked in Germany while 4 thousand have a job in Austria, commuting daily or weekly. The economic potential of these border territories is influenced by small distance travelling. These activities are missing in north-eastern and eastern parts of the country close to the Polish and Slovac borders. This, together with factors related to industrial restructuring and agriculture transformation explains the higher rates of unemployment here (see section 11.5; Svejnar & Terrel,

1994). Quite many Slovacs work in the Czech Republic. In 1995 it were approximately 53 thousand people and this number is still increasing. Most Slovacs work in Northern and Southern Moravia in mining, metallurgy, agriculture, construction industry and services. They commute daily. About one thousand Czechs have a job in Slovakia.

One of the important determinants for stable and low unemployment rates is the tradition of secondary education. The share of employees with secondary education in total employment is about 77 percent; 13 percent only have primary school and 10 percent are graduates. Thus the Czech Republic has the advantage of a highly qualified labour force. The greatest problem is the unemployment of people with primary school education only. Their rate of unemployment is 10.4 percent.

Population in the towns is less unemployed than those living in the countryside. The latter have the disadvantages of commuting and information barriers. According to the sector of last employment of the unemployed, the processing industry (from 23 to 45 percent) prevails in all regions. According to the kind of profession the situation is more diversified. In five regions (Southern Bohemia, Western Bohemia, Northern Bohemia, Eastern Bohemia, Northern Moravia) unqualified workers prevail, in Prague mainly technically and pedagogically educated people, in Central Bohemia employees in services and craftsmen in Southern Moravia. There are also regional differences in the number of the entrepreneurs per thousand inhabitants. Prague with 17 entrepreneurs per thousand inhabitants dominates. This is much higher than in Northern Moravia (about 9) and in Southern Moravia (9.5). Generally, entrepreneurship differs with the direction east-west and specific geographical positions.

11.3 Actors on the regional labour markets

The main actors on the regional labour market are the employers, households and the public administration. Their interaction influences the quality of the regional labour market. According to the law, advisory bodies are established, consisting of the representatives of trade unions, employers, co-operative bodies, labour offices and other experts. The purpose is to coordinate the state employment policy in districts.

There are direct links between the basic actors on the labour market and the institutions that represent their interests. For the employers the employer's and entrepreneur's unions exist. For the labour supply trade unions are present. Positive results are always expected from the effort to find a solution during bargaining and not only to press actions in order to gain more advantageous positions. The great success is that the process of transition is accompanied by social consensus. Trade unions are organised only in sectors. A regional type of representation does not exist. Not all actors on the regional labour market cooperate as much as possible. The reason for this is particularly the existing legislation. There is no collaboration between public administration bodies concerning labour market information exchange. It negatively influences the communication related with employment and the regional labour market.

Regional policy, as such, is very questionable in the Czech Republic. Government still denies all attempts to approve a state regional policy. Regional policy could monitor the social-economic situation of the districts. There is no effort to prevent larger regional differences and the latter are considered ex post only when they cause troubles to the whole society. Recently, the state gives more attention to the districts with higher rates of unemployment. Particularly small business is stimulated. As a result of the lack of coordination of the state and municipality interests, there is a room for the realisation of biased branch policies.

Labour offices performance in the districts is formally proper. But there are several functional problems. Seventy six labour offices are subordinated to the Ministry of Labour and Social Affairs. Barriers to communication have arisen and bureaucracy prevails. Another problem is the separation of labour offices from the district institutions. There is no legislative framework for their mutual relationships. Their co-operation depends completely on personal contacts. Moreover, the district level is not the appropriate level for labour market management. Real working relationships take place at a lower level. In some cases districts are small units. This concerns big cities like Prague, Brno, Plzen and Ostrava including their surroundings which are divided into independent village districts. The district level, however, in general does not reflect the complexity of the labour market. All districts offices and organisations stay within their regions counting the funds redistributed from the state budget. Cooperation across the boundaries of the district is sometimes very hard. For this reason a new perspective on regional problems is necessary. It is necessary to initiate institutional forms that are able to integrate the effort, material conditions, financial and human resources of the regions. The bodies should be capable to overrule the interests of the individual districts and to coordinate the use of resources. Without any doubt the establishment of larger regions is the most convenient solution to these requirements.

11.4 Employment policy

11.4.1 Basic objectives

Employment policy in the Czech Republic is aimed at the equilibrium between labour supply and demand, the efficient use of labour and the assurance of the citizen's right for being employed. State bodies responsible for the employment policy are the Ministry of Labour and Social Affairs and regional labour offices. Employment policy includes the following main activities:

- Permanent evaluation of the labour market situation, preparing of prognosis, and programmes for employment of workers who got unemployed due to large structural and organisational changes. The Ministry of Labour and Social Affairs is responsible for these activities at the national level, the labour offices at the district level.
- The provision of information and consultancy. These activities are carried out at the district level. They represent a main area of unemployment policy activities. They are not only provided for registrated unemployed but for everybody who is interested, including employers.
- The creation of subsidised and public jobs. The efforts stimulate both employers and unemployed for creating new jobs.
- The provision of requalification to citizens, consultancy for choice of the profession. The goal is to increase the mobility on the labour market.
- Ensuring that people apply for a job and within the period of requalification. Unemployment benefits are provided during unemployment or requalifiation.
- Measures for employment of disabled people.
- The registration of free jobs and citizens applying for jobs. This system has been developing since 1990. A problem is the insufficient developed network between labour offices making it impossible to look for jobs in the whole country.

11.4.2 Main policies

In the Czech Republic the intermediating of employment is considered as the most important kind of employment activity. According to the law, labour offices are responsible for intermediating of employment free of charge. For this purpose labour offices create databases of:

- Unemployed people containing information on qualification, labour experience, interest in certain jobs, personal and family situation.
- Registered free jobs containing basic characteristics of the jobs like the kind of work, requirements and wage conditions.

Particular attention is devoted to young people who have finished primary school and who do not prepare for a specific occupation, graduates of secondary schools and universities at their first job, disabled people, pregnant women, citizens taking care of a child younger than 15 years or disabled, unemployed people older than 50 years, unemployed people for more than six months, and socially nonadaptable people. When unemployed do not find a job up to 7 days from application and if registration and all other preconditions are fulfilled - previous employment lasting at least 12 months in last three years - then an *unemployment benefit* is paid. The amount is based on the average net income in the last occupation. The benefit is 60 percent of the income for the first three months and during the following three months 50 percent. Unemployed who are requalified receive a benefit of 70 percent of the average net monthly income in the last occupation.

According to the law another measure of employment policy is *early retirement*. This pension is lower than current pensions. The following conditions have to be fulfilled:

- the length of life employment is minimal 25 years;
- 180 days registration at labour office; and
- no more than 2 years from the necessary retirement age.

In the frame of employment policy *requalification* is realised. Requalification is considered to lead to new theoretical and practical knowledge useful for new jobs. There are two main forms:

- requalification of the unemployed offered and intermediated by labour office. It includes all costs, also these related with the participation in requalification process; and
- requalification of the employees where a part of total costs for the employers is paid from the funds of the employment policy.

Other employment measures are aimed at *young people*. It enables the employers to provide graduates with qualified praxis for further education. Costs related to these activities can be repaid - e.g. wage costs, contribution for the courses, etc. Financial means can be provided up to 12 months only.

Specific measures also help *disabled people*. Main attention is devoted to job rehabilitation. Job consultancy is very important, as is the preparation for the future occupation. It enables disabled unemployed to adapt gradually to future occupation at specialised working places. Some costs can be paid to unemployed. Under certain conditions employers can receive the contributions from employment policy for specialised working places. Labour offices can pay contributions to disabled unemployed who become an entrepreneur. There is an obligatory share of disabled on whole number of employees for the employers with more than 20 employees (4.5 percent and 0.5 percent for heavy disabled). A further measure is the support of creating new subsidised jobs. Labour offices can pay the costs related to this in case an unemployed decides to become an entrepreneur. In both cases there are several forms of support like direct subvences, loans without interest, and payment of bank loans interest.

Another form of employment policy is the *support of public jobs* - e.g. keeping parks tidy, infrastructure, etc. Labour offices, municipalities and employers submit an agreement and wage costs of unemployed can be paid for one year. Such jobs are short-term but they have to be newly created. A last kind of employment policy in the Czech Republic is the provision of subvences to employers for wages during the transition to new business.

11.4.3 Policy implementation

Employment policy in the Czech Republic is realised only at the district level by the Ministry of Labour and Social Affairs and the labour offices. Measured by the amount of funds, passive employment policy prevails. Unemployment benefits are about 62 percent of total spending. The rest builds the active employment policy (see also Polivka, 1994). Information on the programmes of active employment policy mentioned earlier are in table 11.6.

Table 11.6
Cost of active employment policy programmes and number of unemployed involved

Programmes	1992		1993		1994	
	mil CZK	persons	mil CZK	persons	mil CZK	persons
New subsidised jobs	968.6	82 277	217.9	12 250	241.5	9 874
Public jobs	223.0	25 503	159.6	11 760	183.7	12 927
Disabled jobs	55.7	1 308	48.7	947	61.6	746
Retraining	97.6	17 600	73.3	12 100	103.2	14 814
Young People	325.5	21 907	245.1	7 380	127.1	6 853

Source: Statistics of Ministry of Labour and Social Affairs

Active employment policy by the labour offices have caused a significantly dynamic on the labour market, particularly, a shift of employment to the private sector and an increase of employment in services. During the period 1993-1995 money was given to the different regions for active policy. Main criterion for funding was the development and rate of unemployment in the district. Depending on the labour market situation, active employment policy programmes were used in the districts differently (see also Vecernik, 1995).

Table 11.7 shows the results of the various programmes. It shows that active employment policy was directed mainly at the Southern and Northern Moravian regions, the eastern parts of the Czech Republic. Higher unemployment rates than the national average are registered here. Public and subsidised jobs are both significant for employment policy. The support of young people in employment has played an important role, too. Support of jobs for disabled people was less successful. Generally, we can say that employment policy has helped substantially to reach low rates of unemployment.

Table 11.7
Active employment policy programme in the regions in 1994

Regions	**Public Jobs**		**Subsidised Jobs**		**Young People**		**Disabled**	
	new jobs	located unempl.	new jobs	located unempl.	new jobs	located unempl.	new jobs	located unempl.
Prague	35	55	2	20	94	97	17	11
Central Bohemia	1099	1053	531	519	570	447	105	91
Southern Bohemia	952	927	289	267	245	246	51	47
Western Bohemia	494	519	187	321	167	167	105	26
Northern Bohemia	2434	3012	599	847	688	664	152	143
Eastern Bohemia	1400	1236	721	707	561	548	85	84
Southern Moravia	3042	2816	2763	2780	1958	1932	165	165
Northern Moravia	3976	3309	4341	4413	2738	2724	171	179
Czech Republic	13432	12927	9433	9874	7021	6825	851	746

Source: Statistics of Ministry of Labour and Social Affairs

At the beginning of 1994 the government decided to help regions with very high unemployment. There were 4 districts: Bruntal, Novy Jicin (Northern Moravia), Znojmo (Southern Moravia), Louny (Northern Bohemia). The aim was to create a model for solving similar situations. The measures were realised at several levels:

- *Wider support of small business.* There are many programmes supporting small business in the Czech Republic. Some of them are applied in the particular regions only. Subvences were strengthened in the districts with high unemployment.

- *Support of infrastructural development.* Infrastructure is usually very bad in problem regions (transport, telecommunications, etc.). It prevents the development of business in these territories. A part of funds was directed to this sphere by public administration bodies.

- *Active employment policy.*

All tools of active employment policy were reinforced in specific districts in crisis. Some were assisted by international funds.

11.5 Future developments of labour market policies and the institutional framework

A stable labour market situation accompanies the transition of the Czech economy. There is a good choice of applied approaches and programmes of employment policy. Employment policy measures were critically judged and some of them are ready for small adaptions. New programmes are introduced, too. A new attitude to employment policy should result in a widening of the possibilities of existing tools. The main changes in the programmes of the active employment policy are:

Preparation for future occupations. With regard to job mobility and effects of increased education, it is suggested to provide preparation for occupation even for (still) employed people. It is proposed that the measure will be fully financed from the employment policy funds for those employees who will loose their job for organisational reasons.

Subsidised jobs. New jobs will arise based on agreements between employers and labour offices. We can expect substantial changes here. The creation of new jobs by employers will be restricted. Despite good effects of this measure there was much deadweight. Creation of new jobs will be limited to regions with a high rate of unemployment and with a need of a quick economic revival. Subsidised jobs will be used to support employment for a shorter period than a working week. It is suggested to create or to reserve public jobs for long-term unemployed and for less qualified people. In order to support labour mobility in regions without transport links, it is proposed to pay the cost of transport for those employers who admit unemployed people.

Support of employers starting new small firms. It is suggested to pay to the employer a contribution for the wages when he is unable to secure work for a working week due to the change of his business plan.

Projects for the regional revival of employment. This programme aims to increase the employment in regions with long-term unemployment, decreasing number of jobs and a small number of new jobs. This tool is not directed at the unemployed but to the effective use of the employment policy funds. It is proposed that citizens can apply for intermediating of jobs wherever in the Czech Republic.

Public administration of the Czech labour market is managed at two levels. The central (Ministry of Labour and Social Affairs) and the district level (labour offices). The microregional level (level lower than district) is covered by a network of administrative areas of labour offices and their branches. It is difficult to influence the labour market situation in regions larger than a district because of the non-existence of 'higher regions'. The question is how public administration will provide for these supra-regional problems. There are two possibilities. The first is that a major part of public administration will be transferred to the regions. This means the creation of regional labour offices. However, it is not a problem of labour offices only, but it concerns all public administration. The second possibility is that the main functions of public administration will be provided at the district level while the system of employment services will not be changed. The first version looks more rational. An optimal decision is to create regional institutions with the goal to influence regional labour market globally and to co-ordinate not only employment policy activities of a larger territory but other actions as well. The basic intermediating activity should be ensured by a network of about 200 functioning 'microregional labour offices'. This approach requires an information net with online connections with all offices in the Czech Republic.

Decentralisation, however, is not the present goal of government. The problem seems to be political. Problems of public administration are not regarded. There are speculations about the size of future regions and it is not clear which territorial unit would be optimal for internal state management. The only existing agreement of experts is that the number of units should not exceed 25 or 30. Decentralised management is still influenced by various regional and local interests. A reasonable number of new regions is between 8 or 14 including Prague.

References

Employment and Unemployment in the Czech Republic (1995), Czech Statistical Office: Prague.

Gottvald, J., P. Pedersen & M. Simek (1994), *The Czech Market in Transition - Descriptive Analysis of a Micro Data Set*. Working Paper 94-9, CLS, Denmark.

Horalek, M. (1993), *Employment and Unemployment in the Czech Republic 1991-1993*. Research project of Friedrich Ebert Foundation: Prague.

Kovar, J. (1994), *Territorial Structure of Labour Offices*. Research report, VUROM: Ostrava.

Polivka, M. (1994), *New Active Labour Market Policy*. Ekonom No. 8, Prague.

Statistics of Ministry of Labour and Social Affairs (various years).

Svejnar, J. (1992), *Labour Markets in Transitional Economics*, World Bank Annual Conference 1992: Washington.

Svejnar, J. & K. Terrel (1994), *Explaining Unemployment Dynamics in the Czech and Slovak Republics*. Working paper 60, CERGE-EI: Prague.

Vecernik, J. (1995), 'The Emergent Labour Market and Job Projects in the Czech Republic', *Economic Paper*, Vol. 1, Prague.

12 Regional labour market institutions in Slovakia

Magdaléna Hiadlovská

12.1 Introduction

The main problem of the transition of the labour market in Slovakia is the adjustment to a new structure of the economy. The modernisation of the allocation and structure of production and labour is a task for the state, regions and municipalities. Regions play an important role in implementing the state policy and in developing regions with regards to their endogenous potential. To combat structural unemployment, regional authorities can use their power within their region to organise or support activities for attracting new firms, products or industries, helping people to start new firms and improve the matching of the labour force with the needs of new jobs. The growth of small firms is important as a part of the solution for the high unemployment levels.

In order to highlight the possibilities of institutions for influencing regional labour markets, in particular time aspects are considered hereafter. Ex ante and ex post approaches are distinguished. The aim of the ex post or curative approach is to decrease the number of unemployed and is represented mainly by labour market policies implemented by central and regional authorities. The aim of the ex ante or prevention approach is to avoid unemployment by solving the economic ills which increase the risk of unemployment in a region. This is a task for macroeconomic policies as well as regional and local development policies.

12.2 The general socio-economic setting of the labour market

After the Second World War, the labour market in Slovakia existed under a central planning regime which was aimed at full employment. In traditional rural regions new industries were established, including heavy and armament industries. Production was oriented at energy-intensive industries demanding also large inputs of raw materials. Everybody was employed. However, unemployment in Slovakia has been growing from 1990 onwards, when the transition of a centrally planned economy to the market economy was introduced, and mainly from 1991, when the liberalisation of prices started. The collapse of the trade with the CMEA countries caused a substantial reduction of the traditional markets for Slovakian production and significant job losses. The reduction of GDP during the first three years of transition was 23.7 percent (Statistical Yearbook, 1994). As figure 12.1 shows, the growth of unemployment was particularly large in 1991 - a rise by 10.2 percent-points - and was determined by the liberalisation process. After a stabilisation in 1992, in 1993 the unemployment rate grew again by 4 percent-points because of the splitting of Czecho-Slovakia. At the end of 1995, unemployment rate decreased to 13.1 percent (333,291 people).

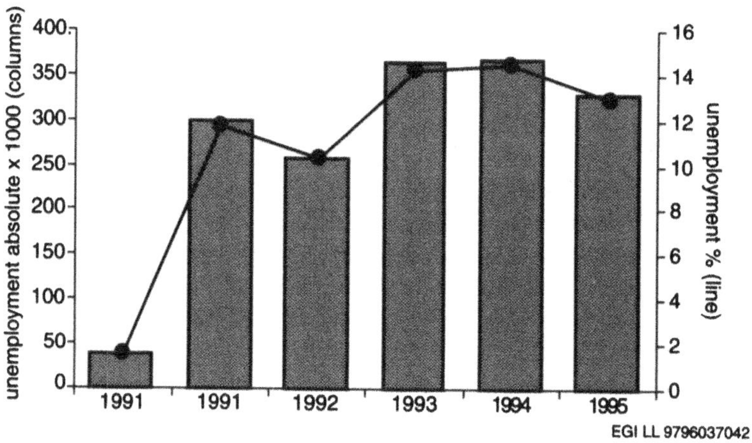

Figure 12.1 Development of unemployment 1990-1995

The largest job losses in the first two years of transition occurred in agriculture (25.3 percent and 9 percent in 1991 and 1992 respectively), construction (5.6 percent and 30 percent) and manufacturing (12.1 percent and 11.2 percent). While employment in these sectors decreased, employment in the service industry increased. From 1991, the number of employees in services increased by 21.8 percent (Statistical Yearbook, 1995). The share of services increased from 43.4 percent in 1991 to 57 percent in 1994, while the share of construction and manufacturing decreased. Agriculture showed a stable pattern (Statistical Yearbook, 1995). The relative development of employment in the various sectors is shown in figure 12.2.

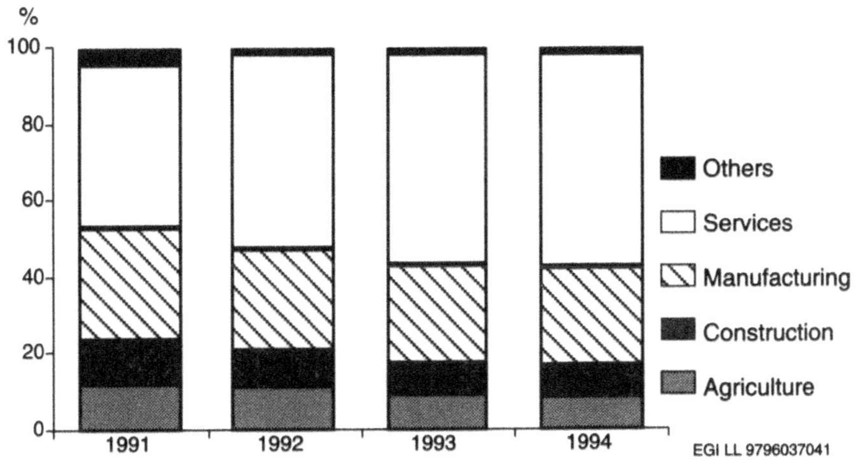

Figure 12.2 Changes in the sectoral employment structure (1991-1994)

From 1989 to 1993 the number of employees in the private sector rose by 79.3 percent. At the same time, the public sector dropped by 36.6 percent. In other forms of ownership this number has risen by 158.2 percent. 59.4 percent is employed in the public sector, 36.3 percent is the private sector and 4.3 percent in the other sector (Statistical Yearbook, 1994). Part-time employment is not high and comprises only 2.5 percent of total employment. Of the 56,200 part-time employed, 9 percent cannot find a full-time job and 22 percent cannot work full-time because of an employer decision (Data from Statistical Office).

Long-term unemployment (more than 12 months) has been growing too. Its share of unemployment has risen to 54.1 percent in 1995. The ratio of short-term unemployed (up to 3 months) was 16 percent. The number of unemployed school-leavers grew from 5,726 in 1990 to 39,235 in 1991 and to 49,474 in 1993 (Statistical Yearbook, 1994). At the end of 1994, the share of schoolleavers of unemployment was 14.5 percent, and 14.6 percent in 1995. Women unemployment was 49.9 percent at the end of 1995 (Data from Employment Services Administration). Unemployment in relation to job vacancies has been growing from 37 unemployed job seekers for 1 vacancy in 1991, to 48 in 1993. At the end of 1995 it was at the level of 22 (Data from the Slovak Ministry of Labour, Social Affairs and Family and Employment Service Administration, 1991-1995). However, this number may be an underestimation as not all vacancies are reported to the employment offices.

A distinction can be made between two periods of transition (Ochotnichý, et. al., 1995). In the first two years of the transition (1990-1991) unemployment started to grow, having frictional and structural features. There were spatial and professional mismatches on the labour market, which could be solved by labour mobility schemes, providing information on labour market, training, etc. In 1991, unemployment started to have classical features - determined by a high level of real wages, or/and a low level of aggregate demand. The mismatch between the number and structure of unemployed and vacancies rose considerably. Hence a change in the policies and instruments applied are necessary. Besides labour market measures, systematic macroeconomic policies leading to economic growth and restructuring of the economy should be implemented.

The main policy goal during the transition period was to adjust to the transition shock and to avoid high inflation. The employment policy consisted of active and passive labour market policies. However, after 1993 employment policy was not updated towards a more comprehensive policy with connections to other macroeconomic policies (Ochotnický, et. al., 1995; Homola, 1995a; Ševcech, 1995). Besides labour market policy, there is also no comprehensive restructuring policy, neither at the central, nor regional level. The State Budget of Slovak Republic for 1996 aimed at a wider implementation of public works, regional policy measures and construction growth which should result in a decrease of unemployment. The Central Government expects stronger multiplier effects from public investments, mainly highways, water constructions and construction of houses.

12.3 The regional differentiation of the socio-economic setting

There have been strong geographical concentrations of vertically integrated industrial complexes under the centrally planned economy in Slovakia. This resulted in a low degree of product diversification, hence higher vulnerability to exogenous shocks and divergent patterns of demand as soon as industrial subsidies were phased out (OECD, 1992). There are substantial regional differences of social potential, infrastructure, territorial possibilities for development and dynamics of modernisation (Búšik, Smetana & Rajčák, 1995). Many regions have been dependent upon one or few big employers belonging to the old industrial or agricultural sectors.

In 18 of the 38 districts, unemployment rates are higher than 15 percent (see Figure 12.3). Those 18 regions have been typical agriculture areas or/and areas with strong concentration of one or two types of industries - mainly machinery, chemical, metallurgy, foodprocessing, woodprocessing and shoemaking industries. They are situated in the east and south of the country. 14 are border regions. Regions with some larger central cities (Bratislava, Trenčín, Liptovský, Mikuláš, Banská Bystrica, Košice) have considerably lower unemployment levels and have a more diversified regional production structure and situated at main railways or roads. The difference in the unemployment rate between regions with the highest and lowest unemployment rate within Slovak districts has grown considerably (see figure 12.4). These differences have a similar regional pattern since the start of the transition.

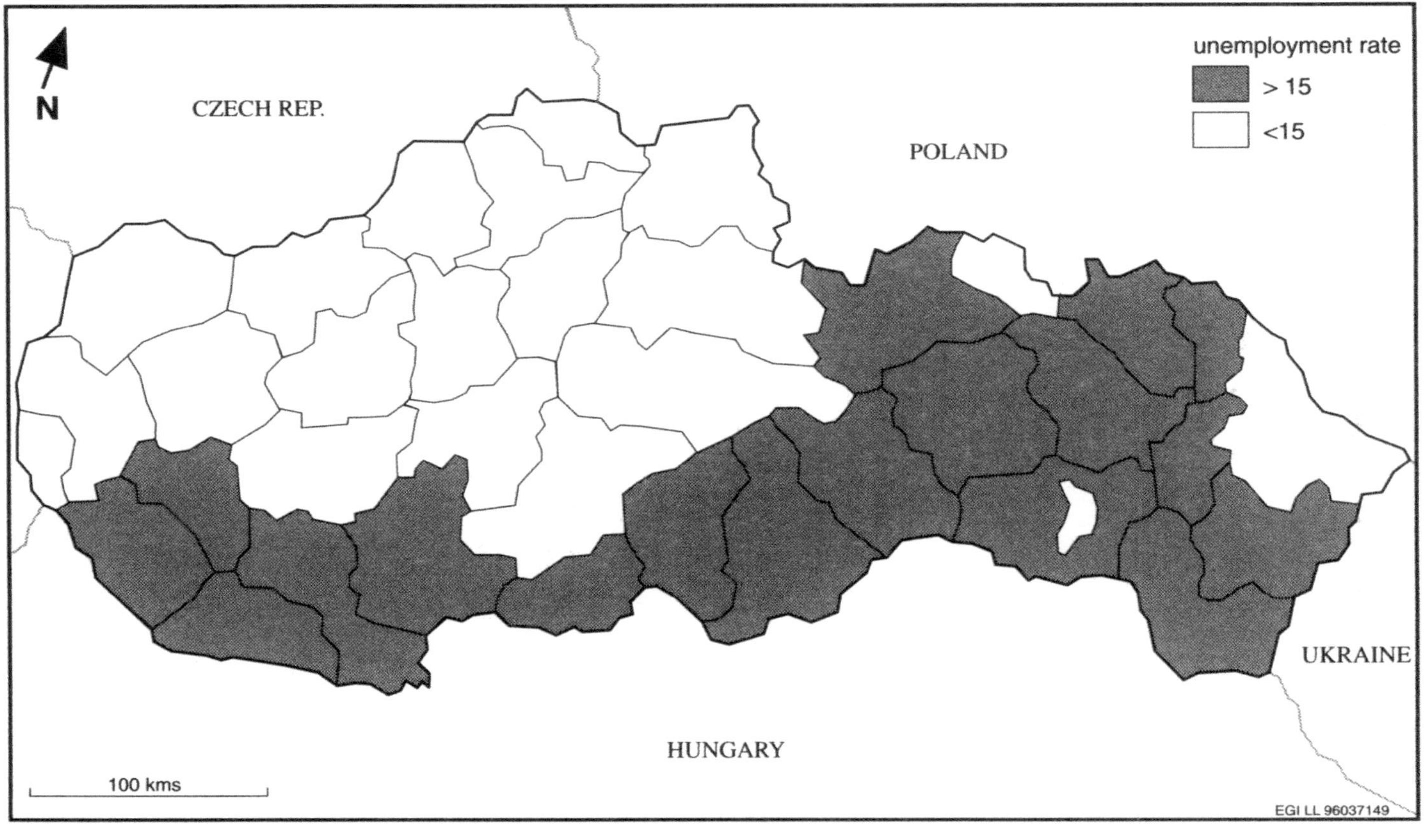

Figure 12.3 **Regional variation in unemployment rates in Slovakia (1995; Employment Services Administration)**

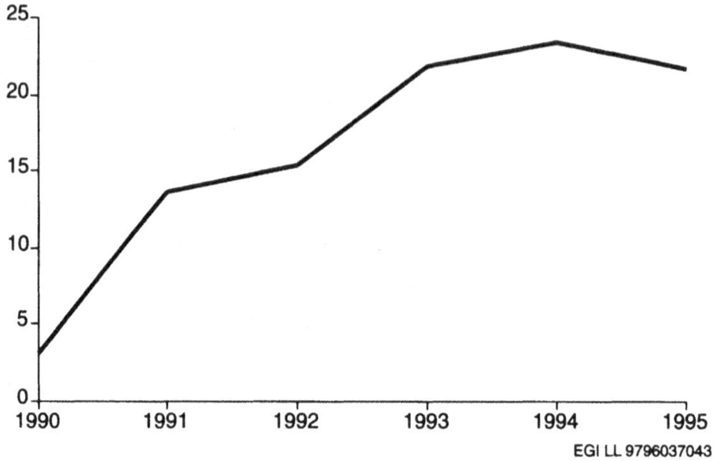

Figure 12.4 Development of the regional difference between the highest and the lowest unemployment rate in Slovakia, 1990-1995 (districts)

The growth of the new private sector, mostly as small and medium-sized enterprises, is highly concentrated around the urban areas where skills and experience are more diversified. The ratio of entrepreneurs per 100 working population across regions differs from 6.7 to 19.4 percent.

Generally, as far as the economic structure and unemployment rate are concerned, regions in Slovakia can be divided into four groups (Ochotnický, et al., 1995).

- Regions with a diversified economic structure and with prosperous enterprises. The centres of these regions are well accessible by road or railway. They are very well equipped by technical and social infrastructure. Unemployment rate is lower than the national average.

- Regions with a homogeneous economic structure, oriented at only one activity (branch, enterprise). Mostly suffering from the restructuring of production. Unemployment rate is about the national average.

- Regions with several smaller enterprises belonging to branches suffering highly of the recession. There is not much regional co-operation. The regions have an inadequate infrastructure. Unemployment rate is much higher than the national average.

- Regions where agriculture is the leading sector. They have a good potential for agriculture production. Unemployment rate is just a little higher than the Slovak average.

With the closure of many enterprises and the deepening of sectoral and regional structural change, a major relocation of labour from declining to expanding regions would be required. However, the Slovakian economy nowadays faces housing shortages which, together with high costs of transport, results in low levels of internal migration and commuting.

12.4 Actors on the labour market

There are various institutional actors on the labour market in Slovakia. Most important are the governmental organisations at various spatial levels, the employer's organisations, the trade unions and some independent employment services. Some of these actors work together like in the Slovak Board of Economic and Social Agreement which represents the government, trade unions and employers. It was founded in 1990 as an independent institution. The conclusions and opinions of the Board have an advisory character for the Government and the Parliament. The first Slovak General Agreement between Slovak Government, trade unions and employers was made in 1991. What are the characteristics of the various actors on the labour market?

12.4.1 Governmental organisations

There are three main central governmental labour market institutions in Slovakia:

- Ministry of Labour, Social Affairs and Family;
- Employment Fund; and
- Employment Services Administration.

The *Ministry of Labour, Social Affairs and Family*, starting in 1990, proposes and implements labour market policy instruments and measures, monitors the allocation of the labour force, provides assessment of labour market situation, draws labour market prognosis, manages and controls the Employment Service Administration and manages an information system on employment (Act No. 319/1993).

In 1993, the *The Employment Fund* was established to raise funds and finance unemployment benefits and active labour market policy. The Fund is controlled by employees, employers and the state and has its tripartite boards in each of 38 administrative districts (Act No. 10/1992, Act No. 319/1993). The Fund raises money from employers (3 per cent of payroll wages or 4 per cent from the stated basis for self-employed) and employees (1 per cent of gross wages).

The *Employment Services Administration* (ESA) was established in 1994 to control employment services provided by district labour offices. ESA is controlled by the Ministry of Labour, Social Affairs and Family. ESA implements the objectives of labour market policy and submits proposals for labour mobility. It controls district labour offices, administrates state financial resources for labour offices, conducts the monitoring of the labour market, analyses regional labour markets and creates an information system of the labour market. It established Advisory Committees in administrative districts with representatives of employers and employees (Act No 319/1993).

There are overlapping responsibilities (e.g. labour market analysis, active labour market policy, information system, handling complaints) of the three central labour market institutions. This increases administration costs and has a detrimental effect on the impact on the labour market (Homola, 1995a; Ševcech, 1995; Šipöcz, Marek & Tegtmeyer, 1995).

District labour offices implement instruments and measures of labour market policy. They analyse and provide information on labour markets, advise, train, support job creation and relief works, pay unemployment benefits and provide and organise support for disabled unemployed. They draw programs on creating jobs for those who have become unemployed as a consequence of structural changes. They co-operate with other state administration offices in a region and with other institutions. They coordinate sub-district offices (Act No 83/1991; Act No 319/1993). District and sub-district labour offices provide labour market services free of charge. Sub-district offices provide information on job and training opportunities, number of unemployed and vacancies, help to find jobs, decide on eligibility of unemployment benefits, collect information from employers on their intentions in laying-off employees and their employment prospects, provide district offices with information on current labour market situation and its prospects, propose job creation and relief work policy in co-operation with local governments and implement support for the handicapped (Act No 83/1991; Act No. 319/1993).

The labour market policy in a district is financed by two resources. One is created by the legal claims of unemployed. The financing goes from the ministry of labour, via the ESA, towards the District Offices (see figure 12.5). The second part is based on various criteria, like the rate of unemployment, receipts from the respective region distributed through the Employment Fund, and the effectiveness of expenditures paid out for active programmes in the past.

12.4.2 Employer's organisations

The Slovak Association of Employers' Associations was created voluntary in 1991. It involves 24 members, employing 1.3 million of people in almost all branches.

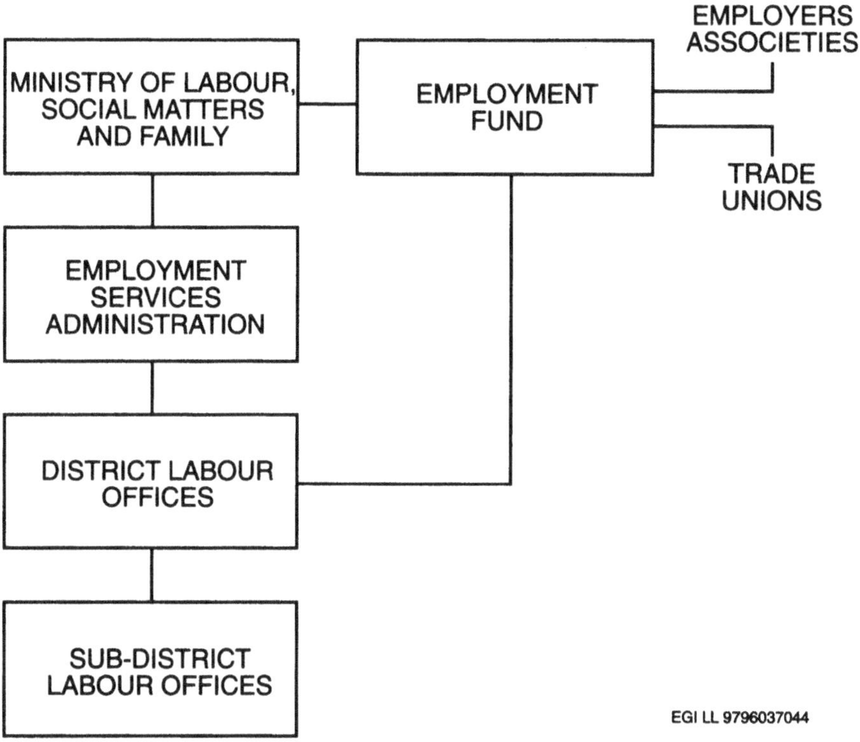

Figure 12.5 Relations between labour market policy institutions

Their objective is to create a positive business climate. They support the development of regional tripartite structures. The Association of the Slovak (Private) Entrepreneurs was established in 1990. The Association actively participated in new legislation for small and medium-size enterprises (SME), in tripartite negotiations and is a representative body for entrepreneurs towards other public economic agents. It is the most important association of entrepreneurs in Slovakia and has 60 offices within the country.

12.4.3 Trade unions

Agreements of the ILO in relation to the freedom of creating associations, collective bargaining, safety and health of workers, employment policy, discrimination, and protection of wages were ratified in Slovakia during the period 1964-1990. After 1989, a new organisational structure of the trade unions was created. Unions activities have changed towards more independence in negotiating. By this they got more importance. They take part in creating the new social system in Slovakia. Act 2/1991 and the Labour Code brought the legislation for collective bargaining. They define basic regulations on collective agreements in which wage and employment regulations are agreed. They can be prepared at the organisation level as well as between associations of trade unions and employers.

The Confederation of the Trade Union Associations was established in 1990 and involves professional associations of trade unions. It is the largest group of unions in Slovakia. They aim at full employment, suitable wage and pension policies, a low inflation rate and facilitating the impact of the transition on the standard of living. In November 1995, 42 Trade Union Associations were involved.

Trade union membership declined from 2.4 million in 1990 to 1.2 million in 1995 (Data from the Confederation of the Trade Union Associations). The decline is a result of political, social and economic changes, and the growth of private business.

12.4.4 Independent employment services

There were several independent employment services established in Slovakia after 1990. They are mainly concerned with solving unemployment in a region or community. They are established as associations like the associations of local government, local enterprise releasing a considerable number of people, associations of entrepreneurs and regional trade union associations. The employment services can also be foundations or other types of non-governmental organisations. They do not cover a large part of labour market, but help in solving unemployment in the communities by implementing new measures and local co-operation.

12.5 Governmental labour market policies

In 1992, total expenditure for labour market policy was 5.52 mld Sk (Czechoslovak koruna). This is about 3.4 percent of GDP. Of this amount 69 percent was spent for active and 31 percent for passive labour market policies. In 1993, total expenditures were 3 mld Sk, but the shares of active and passive policies changed dramatically: now 36 percent was spent on active and 63 percent on passive policies. In 1995, however, it again changed. 5.98 mld Sk was now spent on labour market policy (1.58 percent of GDP), but - 63.5 percent was spent again on active labour market policy (Data from the Ministry of Labour, Social Affairs and Family of Slovak Republic and Employment Fund).

As far as the *passive* policy is concerned, an unemployed person is entitled to get a benefit of 60 percent of his/her average net wage of the previous job during the first three month of unemployment, and 50 percent of the wage during the following months. The highest sum eligible is 150 percent of minimal wage. The duration of the unemployment benefit depends on the age of the unemployed: 6 months for 15-29 years and up to 12 months for 50 and more years old. Hereafter an unemployed is eligible to get a social benefit and is not registered anymore at the labour office.

The main *active* policy measures in Slovakia are the support of job creation, relief work, training, counselling, sheltered workshops and shortterm work schemes for handicapped and youth employment support. They are aimed mainly at unemployed job seekers. Training is aimed also at those in a risk of unemployment. Job creation is supported by loans and subsidies to employers who create a new job for at least two years and to those who start up a new business. There is subsidy available for employers who employ a person for relief work, up to his or her total wage. This support is eligible up to 9 months. New opportunities for employing people on relief works were defined by the Central Government in April, 1995. Many more branches became eligible to utilise this measure than before. Disabled people can get special counselling and short-term work schemes from the labour office. Sheltered workshops are organised for disabled who cannot work in other organisations (Government Regulation 251/1993). There are no special programmes for long-terms unemployed.

An important governmental objective for the creation of new jobs is the support of SME. In 1993, the national government approved the Complex SME Support Programme for 1993 and subsequent years. In the Programme, financial, institutional, and legislative instruments of the state assistance to the SME were identified. Financial instruments involve a system of direct and indirect support to the SME growth. The aim was to create a legal background to the SME state assistance and to guarantee an efficient business environment. The instruments include a system of organisations like the National Agency for Supporting SME which was created to co-ordinate financial, international, regional and local SME support facilities. The main measures of the Agency are:

- financial support programmes;
- analyzing the business environment and legislation;
- advice and education;
- dissemination of information; and
- institutional help to associations of entrepreneurs.

These schemes were supported by the central Government, banks and the European Union. The National Agency has been coordinating the European Union support for small and medium entrepreneurship (PHARE Programme). In December 1995, the PHARE Support Programme was agreed for 1996-1999.

In May, 1995 the Act on the state support of small and medium size entrepreneurship was passed (Act No.100/1995). The main aim is the further development of SME. Programmes with a wide range of objectives are eligible to get support: the creation of new jobs; employing graduates of secondary schools, universities and high schools; employing handicapped people; science and technology development and its commercialisation; environmental protection; exports; tourism development; and business growth in the regions most hit by restructuring of industries and unemployment. Special eligibility conditions for particular programmes are notices by Ministries where applications for support have to be submitted. The Slovak Ministry of Economy co-ordinates programmes for SME development and reports once a year to the Central Government and National Parliament on the results.

A main network for helping people to start or develop their own business consists of the business innovation centres, regional advisory and information centres, entrepreneurship centres and regional development agencies. These centres/agencies were established with the help of foreign assistance. The assistance includes mainly know-how and information transfer. There are seventeen Business Innovation Centres (BICs) and Regional Advisory and Information Centres (RPICs) working in one third of all (38) districts. All of them are non-profit and locally controlled. They are sponsored by the National Agency for SME. Each has a board of directors representing various businesses and municipalities of the local community which partially fund the operation. Their primary goal is providing business information for new entrepreneurs as well as existing SME. The second goal is training (Siegel, 1995).

In three central cities in Slovakia, Entrepreneurship Centres are founded by the Central Europe Institute (Washington, D.C.), providing one-to-one counselling for SME on business plans, marketing and management issues (Búšik, Smetana & Rajčák, 1995). Scientific-Technical and Innovation Parks have been established in four cities to introduce new innovative and high-technologies. Seven Regional Development Agencies were established in areas with a higher concentration of manufacturing and foreign investments, where local players are more active.

Moreover, to promote the development of enterprises, the Slovak Guarantee Bank was created by the Ministry of Finance. The Ministry of Economy delegates power to the Bank to manage the financial instruments and the development of programmes to provide finance for, for example, the programme for development of tourism. Next to banks, which have allocated their loans mainly to SMEs, there are several foreign (European and American) programmes supporting business growth, labour market restructuring and regional development (PHARE, Know-How Fund, USAID, EII). They have supported business innovation centres, regional development agencies, restructuring of large enterprises, innovative active labour market measures, the creation of labour market information system, etc.

12.6 Regional actors and policies

12.6.1 Regional state administration

In Slovakia, the state administration is decentralised to the 38 administrative units (districts; see Figure 12.3) and 121 sub-districts. In all the (sub-)districts, there is a state administration office and labour office districts. The number of inhabitants in each district varies from 44,700 to 235,000. The density of population differs from 52 to 169 inhabitants per square kilometre. Slovak districts are smaller than comparable regions in Europe (from 847 to 2075 square kilometres).

There is a regional development department at each district administration office. They have an obligation to foster economic development and co-ordination of local governments. The activities of the district administration offices are:

- the approvement of regional development programmes, some of them in the form of the action plans;

- running business advisory centres, some of them are transformed to BICs (Business Innovation Centres) or RPICs (Regional Advisory and Information Centres);

- monitoring the development of a region for the central state. The information is used for evaluating the employment situation;

- communicating with local governments, specialised district administration authorities and main local firms and agencies on economic development. This to cooperate and create projects or partnerships; and

- attempting to create regional development agencies in regions with financial and professional help from abroad.

Incentives for projects of regional development are stimulated by the district state administration, which mediate assistance from bilateral or international sources (Búšik, Smetana & Rajčák, 1995). As the administration itself is not a member of business community, its role is limited to that of an initiator. Moreover, the frequent changes in central government have had an impact on the leadership of the district state administration, and slows down the continuation of creating new ideas to cope unemployment.

12.6.2 Local government

Local governments in Slovakia function at the municipal level and are responsible for technical infrastructure, social and health care, recreation and sports, environment, physical planning, regulation of economic activities, give obligatory position to investment and entrepreneurial activities in the municipality (Act No.481/1992). These responsibilities give local governments significant powers to influence local labour markets. However, there are large differences between big cities and towns and villages in their possibilities to combat unemployment. There are high unemployment rates in many villages and towns which were dependent on just one employer. Creating new jobs in this situation is difficult. The tax system does not give much financial power to implement all responsibilities given by the Act for the majority of 2853 local governments in Slovakia, from which only 72 have more than 10,000 inhabitants (Čapková, 1994; 1995). There are 1964 municipalities with less than 1000 inhabitants in Slovakia. Possibilities are larger in cities with more technical, professional and financial resources: local fees, subsidies and loans, supply of municipal property at a low rent, temporary rent-fee lease of municipal premises, advisory and consultancy activities, information services, business incubators units, training, promotion, infrastructure improvement and the establishment of municipal companies (Čapková, 1994).

When considering the number of measures and types of involvement available, local governments in Slovakia have more possibilities to combat current unemployment than district administration offices. Nevertheless, the opportunities to bring down unemployment are smaller for local governments because an evaluation of market trends and promotional activities is more difficult at this low spatial level. This should be more a task for regional government - which yet does not exist in Slovakia - or/and for regional administration. There is no regional level having financial resources and regulation power to administrate the state regional policy in the regions.

12.6.3 Regional policies

Regional policy as part of macroeconomic policies has an important impact on the unemployment of particular regions. The state regional policy for the transition period of Slovak economy is framed by the 'The Basic Values of Regional Policy' dating from 1991. This was further developed in 1992 (Resolution of Slovak Government, 1991; 1992). It stated the position, role and responsibilities of local governments, districts and the central administration in regional policy. The aim is an effective utilisation of resources and a balance between the various economic and social functions of regions taking into account sustainable development. Eleven districts and later also fourteen areas within other districts, where negative effects of transition have accumulated, were identified as aid areas. The aid areas basically cover those hit by highest unemployment levels (see Figure 12.3). The initial activities of the state regional policy were: an obligation of each district to make a programme of development, to establish business centres at each district, to advise starting-ups of small businesses and monitor the social-economic situation in the districts. Regional boards with an advisory role were established in districts. Then, further government support programmes were approved like the special support to particular regions.

Regional policy had no legal status until 1995: no ministry was responsible for its implementation. There were only some departments and later on the Centre of Strategic Studies; an advisory central state institution. To foster and introduce the regional development policy, the Slovak Regional Development Strategy was elaborated in January 1994 by the Centre of Strategic Studies (Slovak Regional Development Strategy, 1994). In 1995, the Centre was transformed to the governmental Office for Strategy of Social, Science and Technical Development.

12.7 The results of the labour market policies

Within four years, a legal basis for a set of labour market policy instruments has been established in Slovakia. Also, more institutions are aware of the need to cope with the rise of unemployment. In responding to these problems, a considerable dynamism can be observed at the local and regional levels. However, introducing the legal framework of a labour market does not necessarily enable economic agents to act efficiently. Therefore, policies should be devised which allow the involvement of more institutions. Having said that, the rest of this section discusses the effects of the passive and active labour market policies. Slovakia spent in 1995 2,181 mld. Sk on *passive* labour market policies; 1,600 mld (73.4 percent) of this was spent on unemployment benefits. The difference between minimum pay, unemployment benefit and social benefit to unemployed is not large. This does not stimulate parts of the unemployed to return to work (Homola, 1995b, Ochotnichý, 1995). Estimations about the number of unemployed who do not want to return to work varies from 10 to 50 percent (Homola, 1995b).

The main part of *active* labour market policies deal with job creation. In 1995, 71 percent of all active measures was spent on this measure and 42,871 jobs were created (which was by 40 percent more than in 1994) (Data from Ministry of Work, Social Matters and Family). On relief works, 20 percent of active measures was spent and 33,310 persons were employed (which is more than 123 percent in comparison to 1994). In the first half of 1994, 609 people worked in sheltered workshops (Ochotnický, 1995).

There is a debate on the impact of active labour market measures. They have affected only 6-12 percent of the total labour market in 1991-1993 and, in the first half of 1994, only 2 percent. Also there has not been a direct relation between active policy measures and changes in unemployment. There are regions with a high share of active measures and low unemployment as well as high unemployment. In other regions unemployment is low, although they implement fewer active measures (Homola, 1995b). Although the provision of measures is limited by the lack of resources, they could be more effective by focusing on groups which are hardest hit by the unemployment like longterm unemployed, handicapped, gypsies and young people. To strengthen the impact of active measures, the targeting in each region could be improved by regionally determined criteria in addition to those set centrally. The mix of all active measures implemented by employment offices should be more coordinated with measures and activities of other regional institutions - employers, employees, regional state administration and local governments (see also Homola, 1995a, 1995b; Ševcech, Haško, 1995; Ochotnichý, 1995).

In 1995, The National Agency for Supporting SME provided six thousands consultations, five hundred new enterprises were established with its support and 1,600 new jobs were created. The measure of entrepreneurial activity (MEA) shows the share of entrepreneurs in the working population. At the end of 1994 the MEA for Slovakia was 9.2 percent. This was 11.9 percent at the end of 1993. The highest values were in the cities Bratislava and Košice and in 1993 in western Slovakia. In the districts hit hardest by unemployment the MEA was lowest (Búšik, Smetana & Rajčák, 1995). Growth of entrepreneurship should be supported mainly in underdeveloped regions. However, it should not be the only remedy for unemployment.

12.8 Future developments

This section discusses shortly the future development of the spatial institutional framework. The development of unemployment will depend on the speed of adjustment to structural changes. Possibilities for better functioning regional labour markets could be found in creating comprehensive macroeconomic policies taking into account causes of unemployment, regional disparities and their causes as well as stimulating regional policies and initiatives. The first steps have been taken. The joint initiative of the Slovak Confederation of Trade Union Associations and the Slovak Employment Fund to assess the labour market and to analyse macroeconomic issues of employment and problems in implementing the policy, resulted in a study 'Analysis of Labour Market' released in June, 1995 (Ochotnichý, et al., 1995).

To enable a more efficient implementation of labour market policy, there is a proposal to establish national labour offices by merging the Employment Fund and the Employment Services Administration, while the conceptual task of the Ministry should be strengthened (Ševcech, 1995). Legislation on regional development was prepared in order to deal with jurisdictional issues and a range of economic tools to stimulate and promote regional development. The guidelines for regional development employment programmes were distributed in all the 38 district labour offices.

As the resources for active labour market policy are not sufficient, long-term policy is even more needed and should be created through the co-operation between regional authorities and regional development policies. A more decentralised approach to labour market policies is needed and a better targeting is required for those groups most at risk of long-term unemployment and those regions most hit by unemployment. More agencies should be established in regions, mainly in peripheral and rural ones, and those already established should be supported in human management or/and funding. The growth of SMEs will play an important role for new jobs. However, regional development in Slovakia should strongly emphasis a broad multisectoral policy and avoid a narrow focus on small enterprise development only (Frost, 1995). A shift in the focus of public institutions from individual efforts to co-operation and actual implementation of those projects already enroled would be helpful.

The Resolution of the Slovak government No.755/1993 has approved the reorganisation of the concept of the local and regional government in Slovakia, and the Slovak government in its Action Programme, passed by parliament in January 1995, has confirmed the decentralisation of the state administration and further strengthening of local government. As a first step, the second-tier of regional state administration authorities will be established. There are several proposals by different authorities, which differ in the number of counties (second-tier regional authorities) and districts (first-tier regional authorities). At the time of writing, there was still no agreement about the new territorial and administrative arrangement of the Slovak Republic. Questions about the geographical, and financial aspects and responsibilities of a future authorities were still present.

References

Act. No. 83/1991.

Act. No. 10/1992.

Act. No. 481/1992.

Act. No. 319/1993.

Act. No. 100/1995.

Búšik, Smetana, & M. Rajčák (1995), *Specific Outlooks of Economy Transition Impacts on Slovak Regions*, Report from Centre for Strategic Studies: Milan, January.

Čapková, S. (1994), 'Basic Information on Local Governments in Slovakia', in *Local Governments in the CEE and CIS*, Institute for Local Government and Public Service: Budapest.

Čapková, S. (1995), 'Local Authorities and Economic Development in Slovakia', in Coulson, Andrew, et al., *Local Government in Eastern Europe*, Edward Elgar.

Data from the Slovak Ministry of Labour, Social Affairs and Family, and Employment Services Administration , 1990-1995.

Frost, M. (1995), 'Local Economic and Employment Development Programme', in *Local Solutions to Unemployment*, Conference Proceedings, IROMAR EF UMB: Banská Bystrica.

Government Regulation 251/1993

Homola, A. (1995a), 'Aktívna politika trhu práce a možnosti jej regionálneho využitia', in *Zborník z konferencie Riešenie nezamestnanosti v politike obcí, miest a regiónov*, IROMAR EF UMB: Banská Bystrica.

Homola, A. (1995b), 'Politika trhu práce a dlhodobá nezamenstnanosť', *Sociológia*, 27, 1-2, pp. 51-54.
Ochotnický, et.al. (1995), 'Analýza trhu práce', *Trend*, No. 23.
OECD (1992), *Employment Outlook*. Paris: OECD.
Resolution of the Slovak Government No. 755/1993.
Siegel, H. (1995), *Regional Development Update, Pace Corps Today, Newsletter for Slovak Peace Corps Volunteers*, January, No. 4.
Slovak Regional Development Strategy (1994), Centre for Strategic Studies of the Slovak Republic: Bratislava.
Statistical Yearbook of the Slovak Republic 1994 (1995), Statistical Office of the Slovak Republic: Bratislava.
Statistical Yearbook of the Slovak Republic 1995 (1996), Statistical Office of the Slovak Republic: Bratislava.
Ševcech, J. & V. Haško (1995), 'Úloha Fondu zamestnanosti pri riešení problémov nerovnováhy na trhu práce', in *Zborník z konferencie Riešenie nezamestnanosti v politike obcí, miest a regiónov*, IROMAR EF UMB: Banská Bystrica.
Šipöcz, T., A. Marek & H. Tegtmeyer (1995), 'Súčasný stav a perspektívy informačného systému trhu práce a jeho úloha pri riešení nezamestnanosti v SR', in *Zborník z konferencie Riešenie nezamestnanosti v politike obcí, miest a regiónov*, IROMAR EF UMB: Banská Bystrica.

13 Institutions and regional labour markets in Rumania

Constanta Partenie, Dorin Jula,
Daniela Constantin, Cornelia Pârlog
& Calin Dinga

13.1 Introduction

This chapter offers an instrument for the analysis of the institutional labour market policy in Rumania during the transition to the market economy. The labour market is an institutionalised economic system ordered through norms regarding labour protection, participation and promotion. In this market the largest institutional strength evidently belongs to exchange transactions. This is because at the moment of negotiations the actors have only a presumptive existence in which the parts claim contractual stipulations regarding mutual protection. In fact, the entire philosophy of the labour market revolves around positive cooperation. Partners meet on the labour market to negotiate a future transaction i.e. a modality of positive cooperation which is subsequently developed. This is based on mutual confidence, understanding and solidarity. The rules of the negotiation game on the labour market require a triple normative - institutional determination i.e. a) rules and institutions enabling the organisation of actors according to their interests like trade-unions or companies; b) rules and institutions meant to define the role of each part, legality of strikes, negotiation forms and formal procedures as well as governmental arbitration; c) rules and institutions meant to establish ways for social partnership and for arrangements between the parts, including penalties.

These brief theoretical notes illustrate the complexity of the institutional renewal in the transition economies. The novelty of these changes, the lack of institutional experience of a free labour market and the necessity to develop during an extremely short period a true avalanche of new regulations, lead to an overproduction of rules, norms and organisations. Meant to ensure the operation of a hybrid economic system between a command economy insufficiently dismantled and a market economy still insufficiently regulated, this institutional abundance appears to be a syndrome of inconsistency. Under these circumstances Rumania, similarly to other Central and East-European countries, has not yet defined a clear-cut option for a certain socio-economic and regional European model of the labour market i.e. British, German, French or Mediterranean. Similar to other Central and East-European countries Rumania is interested to join the European Union. The efforts of these countries to build a new institutional labour market system is based on a mixture of parts from each model. Presently, as Europe itself is concerned with defining its own socio-economic model able to compete with the American and Japanese models, the zonal labour markets of East-European countries will probably continue to develop their reforms in the next decade. This will result in large changes in the institutional and regional organisation of labour markets.

For a long time the differences in economic potential and labour force between different geographic regions of the country will continue to exist. This will give a local touch to economic development. In accelerating the Program for Economic Reforms, especially in the area of privatisation and implementation of Rumania's Plan for Joining the European Union, this heterogeneity will gradually fade away. Particularly the fragmentation of labour market in the two property forms i.e. state and private, acting as 'mobility barriers' will gradually be reduced at the both the national and the local level.

13.2 Socio-economic conditions of the labour market

Rumanian labour market reform includes two main objectives. The first is the creation of socio-economic conditions necessary for the operation of labour market mechanisms which allow employers and employees to negotiate. The second is the establishing of an institutional system to enable the labour market administration to assist unsuccessful job seekers with minimum strains and within a legal framework. Socio-economic conditions generating a specific behaviour of entrepreneurs and social actors on the Rumanian labour market are strongly bound to the four rules of the economic game characterizing transition and reform i.e. rules related to: 1) prices; 2) enterprises; 3) credits (monetary-financial) and 4) foreign trade. Priorities connected to the implementation of these rules - as objectives of the Economic Reform Program - are the integration of the economic policy instruments and their implementation and the creation of room for feedback reactions from the real economy.

The complex and completely new shift from the command economy to the market economy is conditioned by the evolution of the whole socio-economic system. A conditioning which results from the inertial character of the still insufficiently dismantled centralised system and also from the still insufficiently regulated market economy. Therefore, the labour market deviates from an aggregated market and, collecting all latent strains of transition, it turns into a permanent source of macro-economic instability. Although theoretically the labour market has a derived character as compared to the market of goods and services, Rumania's transition economy is characterised by three phenomena brought about by the reform programme. These changed this market into a source of primary causal disfunctions for the other markets. These phenomena are, firstly, the coming out of hidden unemployment, which induced a bubble-type unemployment with no direct connection to the actual labour demand. Secondly, there is the rapid and chaotic restructuring of organisations without being accompanied by a corresponding privatisation process or by a coherent reform of enterprises both state-owned or under cooperative ownership. Thirdly, there is a lack of finalisation of the economic reforms, with the result that an exploring-type operation is applied.

These phenomena also have effects on the labour market and gives it specific features. Firstly, there are the inertial effects of the centralised economy. Employees are still highly dependent on the state. This results from the concentration of property in the state's hands and from the slow development of a free labour market. The private sector generates still insufficient jobs capable to absorb the unemployed resulting from the decline of traditional activities in the state-owned industrial sector. Besides this, private firms are mainly small with a few or no employees. The private sector companies, which developed on the basis of various privatisation procedures like the renting system, the Management-Led Employee Buy Out (MEBO) method and sales by auction, implemented especially in the areas of trade, tourism or services, all have less than 50 employees. Privatisation of the labour market induced by the Governmental Program for Privatisation is not significant. According to this program 30 percent of the social capital of the previous state-owned enterprises were converted into joint stock companies and freely distributed to the population as certificates of ownership. As long as the real conversion process of these value coupons in proper shares is obstructed by the extremely slow development of mass privatisation and by the absence of stock exchanges, their unique economic effect is to contribute to the increase in susceptibility to institutional reform.

Secondly, there is the extremely low level of initiative among the unemployed reflected in a small rate of new entrepreneurs among the laid off and especially among the discouraged job seekers. This could reveal that the unemployed keep on expecting that they will be assisted by the social protecting system. Furthermore, this also contributes to the increase in the number of unemployed people who, after the period of social assistance, do not benefit from any kind of social allowance.

Next to the features dating back to the 'old system' there are also three main labour market features brought about by the development of the market economy. A first one is the break in the correlation between economic growth - according to production growth, labour productivity growth, return on capital - and nominal wage level (see Figure 13.1). This break started in 1990 and induced a rapid inflation by increasing costs and, alongside with other negative effects like price liberalisation, reduction of the number of working hours/week and decrease in the output, generated a reduction of the real wages and all other categories of real income. The real wage still remains at a much lower level as compared to 1990. It attracted government's attention who looked for counteracting solutions such as those included in its *second best* policy.

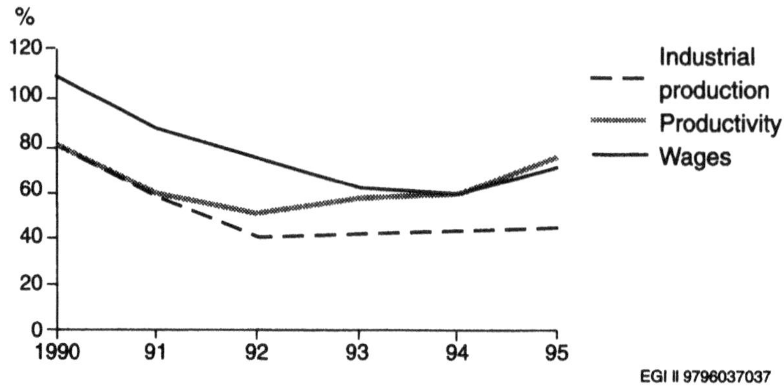

Figure 13.1 The change in industrial production, productivity* and wages**

* industrial production per worker
** deflated

These *second best* intervention measures represent the second aspect of the labour market due to the economic reforms. It is indirectly conditioned by measures aiming to alleviate the undesirable effects of the reforms. These measures are directed at the diminishing of the *cost-push* inflation spiral through limiting the increase of individual wages and subsequently of total wage by applying additional taxes. Although it was considered that limiting the wage increase will result in a small pressure on prices, it nevertheless proved to be useful (see Figure 13.2). Further measures were directed at the restoring of the correlation between wage and labour productivity by restructuring state-owned enterprises and providing material incentives to employees. This was an expected reaction of the government to the wage indexing system as a function of increases in price of the main products and services involved in the cost of living. Another measure was the reduction of excess demand of consumption goods. This derived from the disequilibrium and under-production crisis affecting the economy as a result of the excess of liquidities owned by the population. In turn, this was the result of the wage increase resulting from bargaining and from an indexation without a real increase in production. Gradually implemented in the period 1991-1994, and mainly focused on effects regarding improvement of wage costs and preventing future increases, these *second best* governmental steps have not been effective in their short-term objectives in relation to costs or to the long-term goals regarding labour market restructuring.

The third feature of the labour market, generated by implementation of economic reforms, is the defensive role of the state in wage policy and generally in income policy. Being highly marked by an extra-economic touch i.e. political and electoral in nature, this policy did not succeed in activating structures connected to a free labour market as was expected on the basis of its strategic goals regarding price liberalisation. Moreover, it disturbed the mechanisms of labour market control through wages.

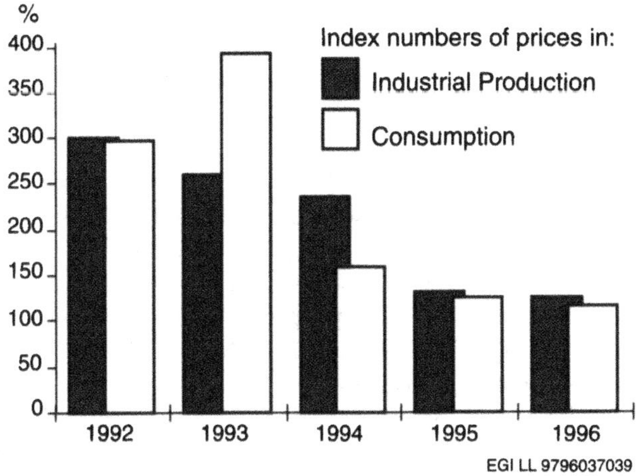

Figure 13.2 The change of the index numbers of prices in the industrial production and consumption (1992-1996)

13.3 Institutional reform and labour market policies

A substantial number of studies about the transition to the market economy note three specific features of the general economic policies:

- overestimating political motivation as against the arguments of economic rationale in macro-economics decision making. This makes it impossible to disconnect the economic analysis from a political background;

- difficulty of using a clear cut separation between state and market. This means the state is regarded as almighty in implementing economic reforms, or the market is considered as a self sufficient system requiring no control; and

- focusing the objectives and instruments of macro-economics policy mainly on the market of goods, services and the money market without providing for a supervision of the labour market in relation to the capital market.

Also the various institutional reforms on the labour market in Rumania reflect these features. The newly established labour market institutions can be grouped in two categories: 1) institutions involved in regulation of labour market legislation; 2) organisational institutions regarding actors and roles on the labour market. Impact of these institutions on the strategic behaviour of actors on the labour market and respectively on the face to face meeting of labour demand and supply is characterised by a high degree of employee's dependence on the state, a low level of entrepreneurial initiative among the unemployed and a defensive role of the state as against an offensive role of trade-unions in wage policy. This offensive role disturbed the mechanisms meant for regulating labour demand and supply ratio through wages.

Rumania's wage and social protection policy was not changed according to a well developed strategy synchronised with other developments like privatisation, price liberalisation, monetary and fiscal policy, investment policy, financial policy, etc. Most often, it took the shape of an urgent reaction to strains generated by the trade-unionist offensive movement. Having not a well defined place in the hierarchy of government's priorities, the labour market collected all the strains of transition and so itself became a source of instability.

In 1990, under the pressure of repeated calls for strike, the government agreed to increase substantially the wages of some professional groups in branches occupying a key position in the economy such as coal mining, railways, and air and sea transport. In 1991, due to the increase of the economic problems, the government adopted a double system of wages. A unique wage differential with all state-owned enterprises was implemented and accepted by all trade-unions in the country. Considering that no criteria were available for differentiating between enterprises on the basis of their real outputs, this system brought about some differentiation possibilities. This was the only moment of nation-wide social agreement. It expressed a consensus of opinions and solidarity in order to change to the market economy in an ordered manner.

The wage system was further amended in 1992, owing to some extremely unfavourable economic and social conditions on the labour market which resulted in a strong increase in the unemployment rate (see Figure 13.3). Under these circumstances the main priority of government's economic policy was the labour dismissed from the state-owned enterprises. Having to reduce their economic activity under the pressure of chain insolvency, as well as due to the lack of orders from the potential users of their products, but especially due to scarcity of the capital necessary for implementing new technology and economic relaunching, the state-owned enterprises were forced to large scale dismissals.

Moreover, there was a liberalisation of wages in the private sector. As this sector proved to offer extremely limited job opportunities, the government applied new solutions. Legislative and administrative steps were taken with the aim to persuade state-owned enterprises to create job opportunities for the unemployed.

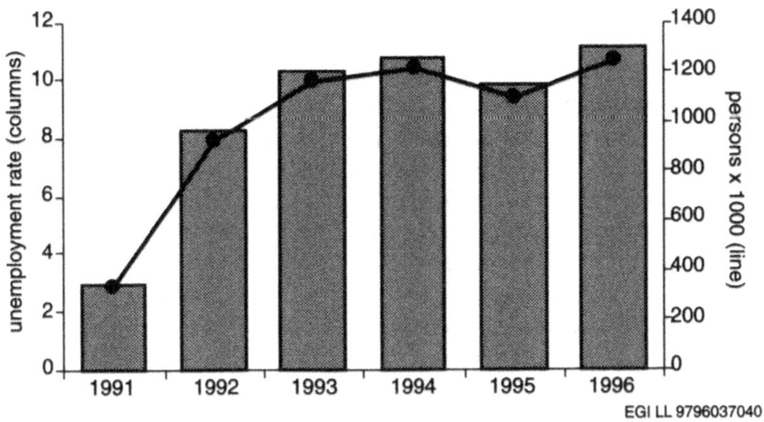

Figure 13.3 The change in unemployment in the period 1991-1996

The state control over wage and social protection policy shifted its focus from the norms regarding wage level to norms regarding the total wage fund. Establishing a maximum ceiling on the wage fund, calculated by the multiplication of employees by the gross average wage, enabled state-owned enterprises to become more flexible in employing supplementary labour. An excess of the maximum ceiling was taxed considerably higher. As there were no guarantees for the payment of the minimum gross wage, it was up to the enterprises to redistribute the maximum wage ceiling to a higher number of employees with payments under the minimum wage. Starting with May 15, 1993 when the minimum gross wage was established - as a result of negotiations carried out by trade-unions with employers' associations and state-owned enterprises - the paying of salaries under the minimum level was suppressed. Because of this firms had to layoff a large part of their labour force. This affected not only wage and social protection policy but also budgetary and fiscal policies.

The minimum gross wage, as a basic element applied in the reform strategy, and as a special instrument in the wage and social protection policy, proved to be a permanent source of labour market distortion. It increased unemployment and its duration. The minimum gross wage was implemented in a period when the so called 'hidden' unemployment of the centralised economy became evident. Unemployment was officially registered in Rumania since February 15, 1991 after the passage of

Law No.1/1991 regarding social protection of unemployed and their professional re-integration and retraining. This law made visible the accumulated unemployment of the centralised economy. Up till then unemployment was hidden by a formal job. It got the shape of underutilisation of working time, labour utilisation in activities requiring a lower qualification degree as compared to its own qualification and leaves without payment for people dismissed in practice but for which no legal unemployment provisions existed. As a result of this quasi-determined labour legislation, not only people having a precarious statute resulting from their layoff were registered as unemployed at the local offices of the Ministry of Labour, but also others who were either job seekers or simply considered the opportunity to take advantage of this law. The biggest share of unemployment was represented by people working in the construction-industry who came mainly from rural areas being qualified on the spot. Suspending investment in constructions and closing of many construction sites resulted in a mass layoff of labour. An important number of other categories were also registered as unemployed, such as: classes or correspondence schools, graduates of universities, secondary schools or vocational education schools. On the background of this phenomenon, the high level of layoff which followed the payment of a minimum gross wage resulted in, what was wrongly called, technical unemployment. Labour was assumed to be in leave without payment in view of a potential assimilation of new technologies.

In exercising its control over the wage fund, government changed the wage negotiation system which, starting with 1992 is conducted at the level of enterprises. This manoeuvre was aimed to:

- maintain control over wage-increasing pressures and cost-push inflation;
- shift the economic problems from macro- to micro-economic level; and
- individualise wages through giving enterprises the possibility to differ the wages as a function of their output.

None of these targets was attained. Nevertheless, certain problems arose within trade-unions which found themselves in the position of not being able to solve the wage distortions which appeared between self-administration authorities, commercial companies using state-owned capital and units budgeted by the state. Wage differentiation in the state sector did not result from the economic output of enterprises, but from their oligopoly in the national economy and by the power of trade-unions. Under these circumstances the highest wages were obtained not by the people working in the most profitable enterprises but by those in the enterprises occupying a key position in the economy. For example 'The Regie Autonome of Electricity' - RENEL - which had the lowest level of labour productivity per employee, offers its employees the highest wages. Employees in this branch appear to be most protected from inflation as compared to other professional groups. Making a very rapid change from the policy of grant aided energy price to price liberalisation according to international market, RENEL adopted a rather asymmetrical strategy regarding the energy-consuming units in the economy. RENEL penalises any delay in invoice payment, finally disconnecting the respective units from the supply network. This is the reason why RENEL is often claimed to act as a bankruptcy law, which law itself was postponed by the government due to its antipopulist character.

With all these distortions occurring in wage and social protection policy it can be claimed that the process of wage differentiation has already started. The development of the private sector is expected to result in wage differentials according to criteria of profitability of firms as well as to the individual merits of employees. Wage differentiation policy was based in Rumania mainly on the increase of the difference between minimum wage and average wage. Social protection policy was meant to result in changes at the level of wage incomes and nominal incomes as well as to modify their structures. Keeping in mind the share of different income sources to the total nominal income of employees' families, the pensions were subject to the most pronounced erosion. Among pensioners the category most unfavourable affected are the retired peasants. As a consequence, all the social costs of the transition to market economy, brought about by price liberalisation, inflation, unemployment, bankruptcy of state-owned enterprises, and a dramatic fall of the industrial production and especially those costs enhanced by the lack of a coherent policy on labour and wages, are exclusively beared by the population.

In the meantime, other phenomena appeared on the labour market, such as:

- a change in the unemployment structure by age particularly by the increase of young labour supply entering the labour market;
- a change in the unemployment male/female ratio. Women were overrepresented in the total and in all age groups; and
- a change in the ratio between the number of tax paying employees and the number of people getting social benefits. For example the number of employees per person receiving social protection, 1.9 in 1993, dropped to 1.6 in 1994. A further decline of this coefficient will result in less job seeking and a division of the population in two categories: the active population who pays taxes and those who do not work and expect support from the state.

13.4 The negotiation game

With a strong economic destabilisation affected by cumulating crises and disbalances and by an increase of unemployment and inflation at the background, the social partners were involved in negotiations. As under any circumstance of uncertainty, it is easy to understand that relationships between negotiators do not always belong to the area of positive cooperation. The policy of wages and social protection as well as the rules of negotiation are insufficiently substantiated by legislation. Together with the gap separating the social partners, due to differences between obligations and abilities, this is a barrier in cooperation. Moreover, their representativeness differs substantially. There is only some overlap of interests in certain areas and along certain, well determined time periods. Consequently, under the economic conditions of transition, the government, trade-unions and employers do not 'de facto' negotiate on wage and social protection policy in the sense of reaching an agreement in which each obtains a result. According to the market economy this should be established in such way that having a winning part does not necessarily mean that all others are losers. On the contrary, through successive negotiations the partners should agree upon the distribution of their risks, advantages and inconveniences according to labour legislation. The relationships between social partners develop in reality like an oligopolistic game: each partner anticipates his 'rival's' move in order to establish his own, best actions.

In order to study how decisions regarding wage and social protection policy are taken during transition period we can make use of game theory. A game involves a situation in which decisions are necessarily interdependent. Strategy is an ordered plan of rules describing the sequence of tactics applied by the player in every conceivable situation along a well determined time period. For maximising its payoff each player must choose a strategy. For example, a good poker player sometimes bluffs, cleaning up a bad hand provided his opponents misread it for a good hand. Having bluffed in the past and repeatedly caught he may use this situation and persuade his partners to keep betting even when he has a terrific hand. This has certain similarities with economic games. In this sense the best strategy of a player depends on his capacity to anticipate the strategies of other players. With wage and social protection policy, equilibrium might occur when each player choose its best strategy, given that the strategies are followed by other players - i.e. Nash equilibrium. To reach such a situation no ambiguous moves are allowed by the rules of the game, the partners being aware that breaking the rules results in penalty and disqualification.

Arbitration and control of the social negotiation game are indispensable in order to solve the dilemma: agreement or cheat. A possible solution could be the establishment of pre-commitments by all partners. In the game of negotiations between the social partners i.e. government, trade-unions and employers, an important role is played by labour legislation. This in relation to the strategy chosen by each of the partners and of the manner the wage and social protection policy is drawn up and - especially - implemented. According to the economic changes in Rumania, this policy went through successive changes and several drafted laws are still subject to debates in Parliament. A part of the old Labour Code of the centralised economy is still in force. An example is the legal provisions regarding cancellation of an individual labour contract. Evaluating the reactions of trade-unions on a national level as reflected in labour conflicts, negotiations and strikes, we could state that this game of social negotiations renders evident all latent problems of transition. Such a situation - which becomes clear when negotiation tactics in wage and social protection policy come to action - consists of the fact that social partnership does not really include the government, trade-unions and employers, but only two partners i.e. government and trade-unions.

The Rumanian's transitional wage and social protection policy appears as a game simultaneously played by government, on the one side, with several other partners on the other side. Among these partners, the trade-union includes a broad range of employees involved in activities budgeted by the state such as health care, education, culture, training, etc. Having in view that each movement made by any participant changes the configuration of the game, it can be noted that government's wage and social protection policy meant to solve pre-established objectives cannot cope with the situation, except for a very short time period. This policy pendulates from one urgent matter to another, using extremely contradictory instruments which can only give a provisional solution for a specific social-economic problem.

In this strategy game the state makes use of its political power and of its legislative and economic prerogatives. Firstly, the state practises its direct, formal and institutional self representation as an arbitrator and mediator of labour conflicts which develop on a national scale. Secondly, the state makes, as a partner in negotiations, use of an indirect representation through the State Ownership Fund. Administering the major part of the capital of the former state enterprises (70 percent), converted in Joint Stock Commercial Companies or in Self Administration Authorities, the state actually becomes an employer. It makes use of the commissioned authority principle exercising its right to appoint the managers of these firms. According to the privatisation strategy, the state is, in compliance with the Governing Program, responsible for these enterprises. The position of this 'employer' is rather doubtful as none of the enterprises is able to identify its affiliation to a known economic system. They are not regarded as part of the centralised economy because the state retracted its direct role as official in charge (while maintaining its administrative duties), but they do also not belong to the market economy because they escape the competition game as well as the bankruptcy law.

Although the Private Ownership Fund administers 30 percent of the share capital of the state-owned enterprises, distributed to the population as Private Ownership Certificates, these shares are still ambiguous from the viewpoint of their owners' representation in the game of negotiations between the social partners. The employers acting in the private sector achieved neither the necessary economic power nor the real interest to act as a countervailing power in the trade-unionist fight which became very strong and offensive. The reason for this is very simple: trade-unions are not involved in contractual relationships with private employers. This does not necessarily mean that employers in the private sector are extremely generous or that the wages and social protection of their employees couldn't generate labour conflicts. On the contrary, there is an ever increasing number of actions at law against employers, of letters and petitions addressed to the Ministry of Labour and Social Protection by citizens, institutions, firms, trade-union organisations, etc. Under these circumstances labour conflicts arise because labour legislation is still insufficiently substantiated. Consequently institutional renewal bears the touch of the too often conjuncture situations marked by uncertainty and by a provisorial state.

After several years of transition and reforms, the Rumanian market is still insufficiently settled. Although the overall view shows a relatively organised market, it is still hybrid in character. Although its external appearance is organised according to the new institutions involved in regulation and organisation, it is still marked by a confuse mixture of trends specific to the old system of the centralised economy.

13.5 Regional disequilibria of the labour market

From a regional point of view the labour market is fragmented. Analyses carried out on different geographic areas showed that it needs at least three decades to equalize economic differences induced by investment disequilibria accumulated along 45 years of centralised economy. After mass-privatisation it is possible that investments of both internal and foreign capital will be made in economically lagged areas especially if the state will implement a regional policy. In this an important role is played by the local administrative authorities which should increase their involvement in urbanisation and the development of communication infrastructure. The institutional apprenticeship will gradually change into a true meso-economic labour market arena such as to act as a binder, connecting the micro-economic level with macro-economic structures. The local labour markets will become integrated and pass towards a socio-economic model enabling to implement Rumania's plan meant for joining the European Union. The eclectic character of the institutional renewal of the Rumanian labour market will fade away.

At this moment though, labour market disequilibria exist in all areas of the country. This occurs with on the background a relatively high national level of the unemployment.[1] At the end of 1991, the unemployment rate was 3 percent. It rose up to 8.4 in 1992, to 10.2 in 1993, and to 10.9 percent (more than 1.2 million persons) at the end of 1994. Territorial discrepancies between the unemployment rates are relatively high in Rumania, their amplitude ranging between a minimum level of 4.1 percent (Gorj) and a maximum of 24.7 percent (Vaslui). Earlier in this chapter we already discussed some of the general causes of this situation. The unemployment rate by county at the end of 1994 is presented in Figure 13.4. It shows that the national area is relatively polarised. Unemployment rates are lower in the West - South West of the country, including the counties of Bihor, Gorj, Mehedinţi (respectively 8.1 percent, 4.1 percent and 8.0 percent). Higher rates are present in the regions located in the East - North East part of the country, where unemployment rates have values as high as the already mentioned 24.7 percent of Vaslui, 18.1 percent in Botoşani and 17.3 percent in Neamţ and Iaşi.

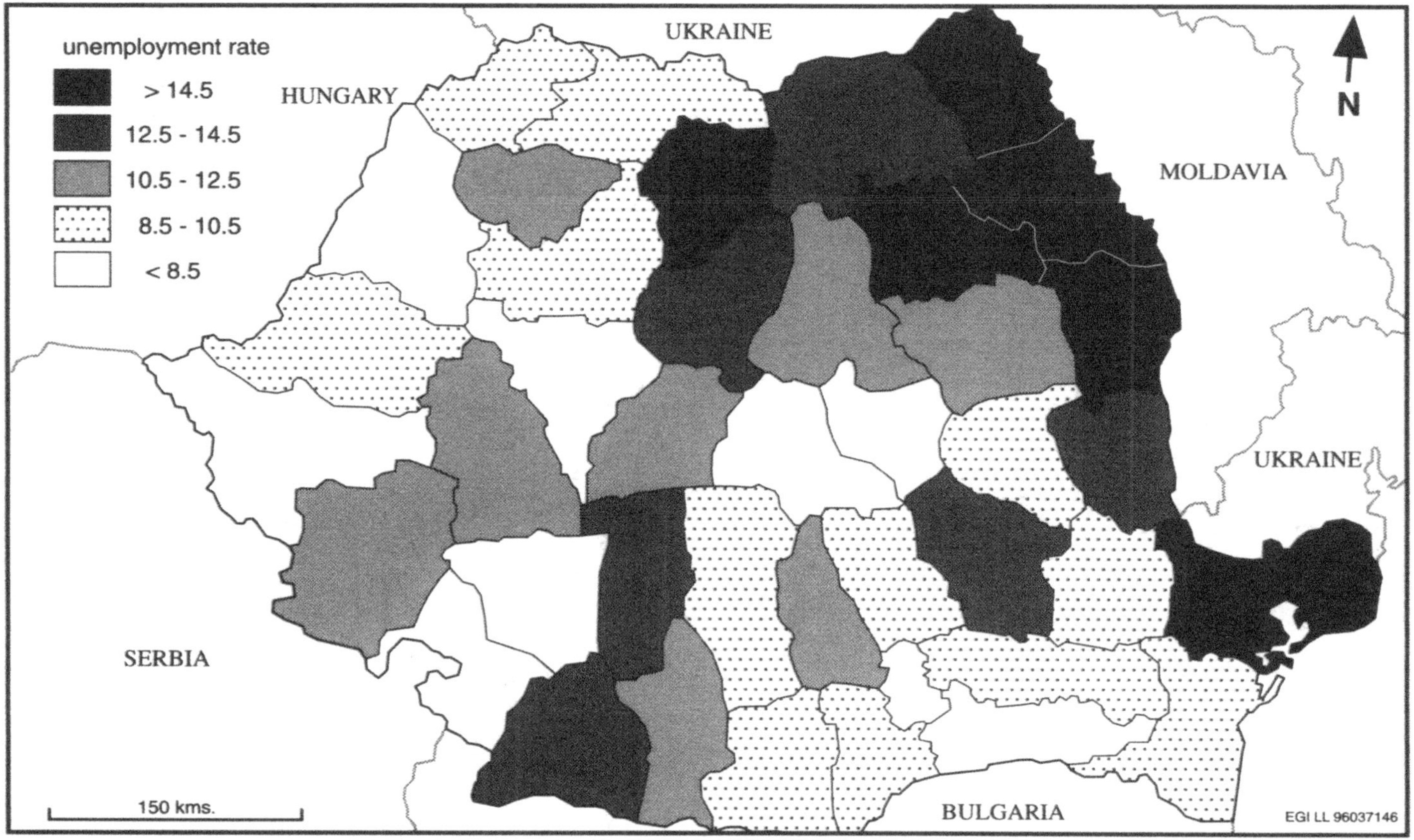

Figure 13.4 Regional unemployment by December 31, 1994

A third area, situated between the previous mentioned, is located in the middle of the country and comprises also the South - South East (the counties Braşov - Prahova - Bucureşti - Călăraşi - Constanţa). The lowest unemployment rates were recorded in the areas where the economic activity is concentrated in powerful self-administrated authorities. These are organised as state monopolies of national interest (electric power, mining, transport). Considering their key position held within the economy, their trade-unions represent real pressure groups. They succeeded, given the considerable subsidies from the budget, to obtain job-security and wage-increases.

Next to unemployment rates, unemployment duration reflects the persistence of labour market disequilibria. At the national level 46.1 percent of the unemployed were more than 270 days unemployed. Figure 13.5 shows the regional variation in unemployment duration. In the counties of Timiş and Neamţ more than two-thirds of the unemployed exceed the 270 days, while in Hunedoara only 25 percent of the unemployed persons are in a similar situation. In 18 counties, more than half of the unemployed exceeds 9 months. There is, however, no regional correlation between the unemployment rate and the share of the long-term unemployed. Distribution of these indicators is almost symmetrical in the national territory. Thus, in 15 of 23 counties, where long - term unemployment exceeds the national average, the unemployment rate is below the average. In 18 counties where long-term unemployment is below the national average, the unemployment rate is symmetrically distributed: the unemployment rate in nine counties is below the average and in the other nine counties it is above that average. Hence, the interdependency ratio between the two indicators (Yule-Kendall) is very low: 0.2.

Labour market accessibility represents another typical feature of regional labour market disequilibria. It is measured as the share of persons that apply for their first job in the total of the registered unemployed. One can notice a large variety of situations, with values ranging from 31.2 percent (Vâlcea) to 0.1 percent (Buzău) as compared to the country average of 8.1. At the same time, there is also in this case a poor correlation between the territorial distribution of labour market accessibility and the unemployment rate (-0.06) and the long-term unemployment (-0.04). Negative correlations show a propensity of the youth to delay their claims for a vacancy, given the long-term unemployment.

The educational level of the population can also be related to regional labour market disequilibria. There are substantial regional gaps in the professional training of the labour force. The share of graduated persons of the total population aged 12 and over is presented in Figure 13.6. Counties where important academic institutions are located (Bucureşti, Cluj - Napoca, Timişoara, Braşov, Iaşi, Craiova, Constanţa, Sibiu) as well as the regions in their proximity, are mostly favoured. Academic graduates are concentrated around Bucharest. This is mainly because of the attraction exerted by the capital upon high-skilled labour force.

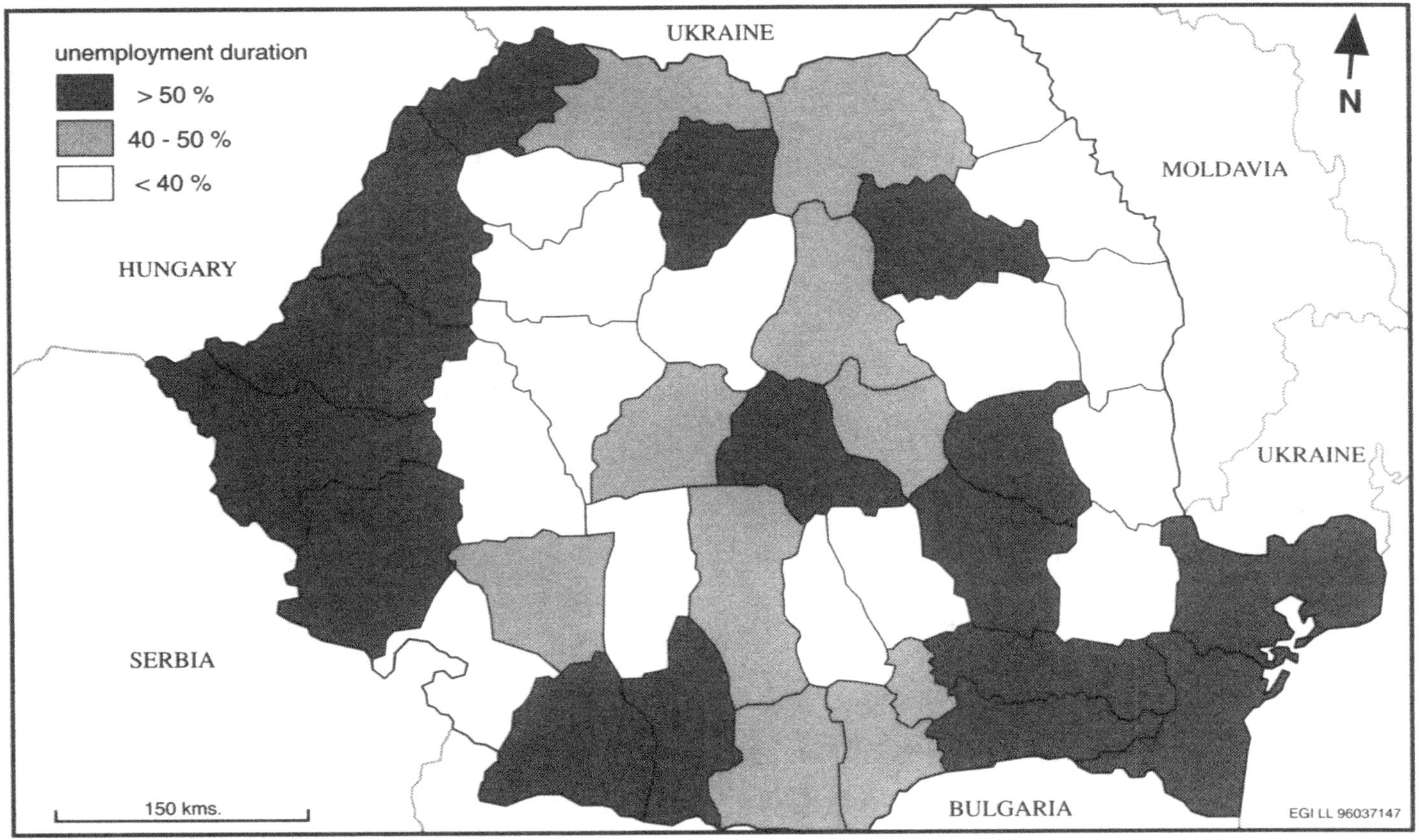

Figure 13.5 Unemployment duration (share of the unemployed longer than 27 days unemployed)

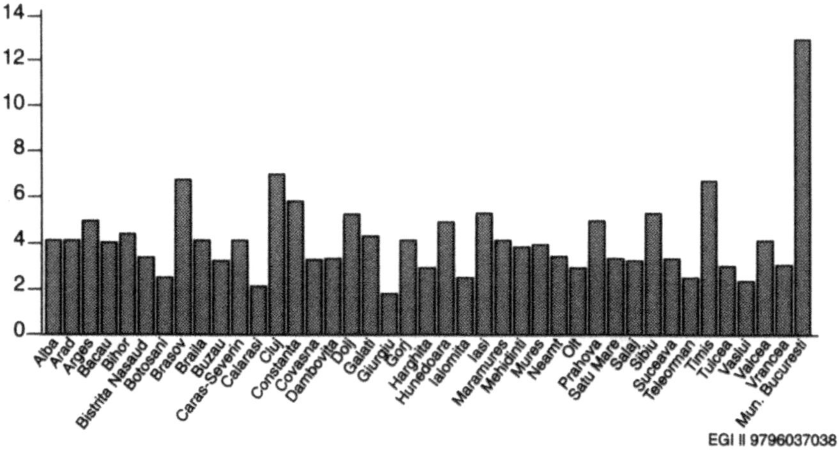

Figure 13.6 Share of academic graduates in total population aged 12 and over (1992)

Mitigating existing disequilibria in the economic and social development of regions is a prior condition for internal cohesion. This implies a balanced distribution of infrastructure and the awareness of unity and common destiny. It is obvious that, given the major regional gaps that persist in the social conditions and quality of life, internal cohesion can hardly be attained (Jula, 1995). The existence of regional disequilibria in general economic development and the labour market may bring about a cumulative growth of inequities (Myrdal, 1957). This can happen because of the higher innovation ability and competitional capacity of the developed areas, which may induce a permanently polarised development. Such processes clearly lead to the widening of gaps, but are also the result of the incoherence of a strategy aimed at mitigating these disequilibria. Moreover, the filtering down of activities could lead to the persistence of regional disequilibria. The developed regions always accrue important valuable elements, passing towards other areas those activities that become undesirable such as: declining activities or those implying rough, tiresome and low-skilled work, obsolete technologies, standardisation and so on (Planque, 1983). This distribution towards less developed areas may sometimes occur not only as a result of economic performance or competition, but also for ecological reasons.

Similar issues occur in relation to demo-economic processes. By removing all barriers to inter-regional migration of the labour force, economic restructuring can be accompanied by major population flows. These flows, as a rule, result from jobseeking and are directed from the less developed towards the developed regions, and concern young and middle aged persons, mostly highly skilled. The developed regions exert a backwash process on the less developed regions. The consequences are reflected in depopulation, mainly in qualitative terms of less developed areas, in a change in the demographic growth and in an increased process of ageing. All lead to a decline in the 'competitiveness' of these regions.

A combination of the filtering the activities to and the declining 'competitiveness' of the less developed regions, may cause a spatial bipolarised economy. This may perpetuate the contrast between the developed regions (with greater innovation abilities, highly skilled and productive labour force, and as a consequence, with higher incomes) and the rest of them, where economic growth and a employment increase (at a relatively low - skilled level) is mainly achieved, by the spreading from the developed areas. Such a situation can be alleviated through a higher general development of the whole area. If a higher level of development is reached, the probability for new activities to be located in lagging areas will increase, even though territorial planning policies are still not intensive.

13.6 Regional unemployment

As discussed, Post-War Rumanian economy saw it's largest decline in employment during the period 1990-1992. This decline occurred mainly in manufacturing (over 810 thousand persons) and transport (nearly 112 thousands). The number of lost jobs of 922 thousand in these two branches is comparable with the total unemployment figure of 929 thousand in this period. Employment decline was somewhat diminished by new job creation, mainly in agriculture (306 thousand) and trade (215 thousand). These dynamics might point at a strong negative regional correlation between industrial output and unemployment. However, a relatively poor correlation between the industrial output and the unemployment rate shows up for the period 1990-1992 (correlation coefficient = 0.24). Undoubtedly, the fall in output by 37 percentage points, represents a major explanation for the growth of unemployment at the national level. Yet, looking at the above-mentioned correlation, this explanation of regional disequilibria is not satisfying. It means that other factors are important for the regional unemployment level. Particularly the growth of new job-searchers and the migration of the unemployed can be mentioned.

13.6.1 New job-searchers on the labour market

At the national level the decline of employment was about 381 thousand jobs during the period 1990-1992. Over the same period, unemployment rose by 929 thousand persons. Thus, in absolute terms, employment decline can explain just over 40 percent of unemployment growth. For the whole period 1990-1994, employment dropped by 570 thousand persons and unemployment increased to 1224 thousand persons. Thus, 46.6 percent of the size of unemployment can be explained by job losses. This means that unemployment is also the result of new labour supply, not yet included in the active population at the beginning of this period, like individuals under training, housekeepers, etc. The active population increased by almost 650 thousand persons during this period, thus attaining a global activity ratio of nearly 49.9 percent.

Similar changes have been recorded at the regional level. Excepting Caraş-Severin county, where the active population considerably dropped and the counties of Arad, Mehedinţi, Tulcea and Sibiu, where the active population slightly decreased or remained constant, in all the other regions, new job-searcher widened the gap between demand and supply. As far as persons that claim their first job are concerned, their share in total unemployment ranges between 44.3 percent in Vâlcea county and 0.1 percent in Buzău county. The county average is of 12.7 percent.

The increasing number of job-claims represent a normal phenomenon for two reasons. On the one hand, the existence of unemployment benefits generates additional supply. On the other hand, if changes in income not related to work are negative, which seems to be natural in a highly inflationary environment, the income effect on total work-time supply of individuals leads to an increase of job-claims on the labour market. This is influenced particularly by the regulations on retiring and pensioning, the duration of the working-week, of holding more than one appointment, and so on.

13.6.2 Regional migration of the unemployed

Regional migration of the unemployed affects its spatial distribution but also its general level. Labour mobility reduces the aggregate level of unemployment, if the labour force migrates towards areas with labour force deficits. In turn, this leads to a decline of the pressure upon the labour market with a surplus. For Rumania, migration flows of the unemployed are oriented in two main directions: (1) from the areas with labour force surplus towards the areas where job opportunities are greater and/or there are better social conditions for the unemployed, and (2) from the industrial areas towards the regions of birth. The first flow reflects the well-known push/pull model. The second one occurs as a result of the implementation of the Land Law. Without coming into details, we remark only that this law reconsidered land ownership by individual owners, by restoring the land seized during the collectivisation process in the sixties. However, it leads also a re-orientation of a part of the unemployed from the industrial centres towards their regions of birth, which were abandoned during the '60-'80 period. As a result, a shift in the migration after 1990 can be noticed, even if the traditional rural - urban flow remains stable. Before 1989 the ratio between the number of individuals coming to town and those leaving peaked in 1981, when this ratio was 3.6 to 1; later on this ratio was kept on around 3. In 1991, a major internal migration process occurred, with values being slightly lower than the cumulated migration in the four years before. The village - town migration in 1990, however, includes a large number of individuals that had already their residence in towns without a legal status. This as a result of residential restriction regulations applied. So, the migrate figures partly reflect the regulation of a legal status.

Following 1990, a reduction of the migration towards urban areas can be noted. For each 17 individuals coming to town, 10 persons left. An opposite tendency is manifested in the migration towards rural areas. For the whole period 1980-1990, for each 10 persons leaving the rural areas only 3 persons were returning, after 1990 the latter figure rose to 6. Obviously, as a historical, long-term trend, this reversed phenomenon in traditional migration from rural areas to urban ones would not expand, so that on short- and medium-term this trend could be again reversed.

When the unemployment figure was nearly reaching one million in the period 1990-1992, internal migration amplified the unbalanced territorial distribution of unemployment. In this perspective, the case of Vaslui can be mentioned. In the past, this county was one of the major sources of job-searching emigrants towards expanding urban labour markets located in its proximity (Braşov, Iaşi, Galaţi) or even more distant ones (Constanţa, Timişoara). The return of parts of the laid - off active population from these towns, as an result of the economic depression, caused the rise of the unemployment rate in Vaslui county to the highest in the country. Yet, out of 58 thousand unemployed, only 18 thousand can be explained by the employed reduction in this county, while 40 thousand are the result of recent applicants. Taking into account that the number of persons that claim for their first job in that area is insignificant (91 persons, or 0.2 percent of the unemployed), it means that most unemployed came from other areas.

13.7 Regional policy and the labour market

As noted in section 13.5, the persistence of regional disequilibria may cause in the future negative economic effects. Next to 'autonomous' processes, also the incoherence of a strategy meant to cope with these disequilibria plays a role. Besides the already mentioned effects of the regional labour market disequilibrium and the inefficiency of the non-interventionist policies, it is useful to stress that not economic growth as such results in a decrease in regional disequilibrium (Jula, 1993). This implies the necessity of an active involvement in regional policies of both the national and local public authorities. This in accordance with the overall economic policy and strategies regarding the national area development (Constantin, 1992). Taking into consideration the tendency to decentralisation, the emphasis is to be put on the local level of the regional policy and should focus on using the advantages of the local economies, according to endogenous development requirements. In this the labour market becomes one of the most important issues.

As other countries' experience also show, even though regional policies have their own objectives, measures are adopted only as a result of labour market difficulties. Hence, they can be classified as measures focusing directly or indirectly on the national employment and unemployment policy. This means that, generally speaking, a consensus can be reached between labour market and overall regional policies, about the targets, actions and instruments. This does not exclude the possibility that conflicts between targets may occur. A major conflict may occur between the targets concerning overall economic development and the growth of general competitiveness of the region (as a general regional policy target) on one side, and the targets aiming to attain a higher level of employment, eventually that of full employment on the other side.

Regional policies with an impact upon the labour market can support the improvement of infrastructure, stimulate the development of small and medium - sized businesses, encourage private entrepreneurship and the demonopolisation of the economy. The improvement of the infrastructure aims to increase the regional standard of living, the stabilisation of the population and increasing region's attract-iveness for investors. Among the direct effects of infrastructure and other capital asset investments upon employment, one can point at the creation of new jobs required for their construction, operation and refurbishment. There are also indirect positive effects upon employment, considering that a decrease in transport costs, as well as that of the required investment in performing certain utilities, generates private investments. Stimulating the development of small and medium-sized business, can generate new jobs and bring about a diversification in the activities performed in the region. Thus, actions aimed at directly stimulating private invest-ments, as far as regional development is concerned, can have a major role in the Rumanian economy.

Concrete actions and measures that could bring about the achievement of the mentioned targets are classical in territorial planning practice, and create financial opportunities like low-interest loans, guaranteed credits, and other incentives. The main beneficiaries of these incentives can be private or public companies. A direct involvement of the public capital in the achievement of these targets can be envis-aged, eventually sharing partnership with private capital. As far as the instruments of regional policy is concerned, the discussions concentrate on conditions of aid allocation, regions, activities and type of projects that could benefit from financial assistance. Apart from the 'classical' mechanisms, usually concentrating on firms in difficulty, supporting ineffective economic structures in the lagging regions, propo-sals related to positive structural adjustment favouring economic activity diversifica-tion should also be considered (Waddley, 1986). These discussions occur in the context of the transition period with scarce financial means and constraints emerging from privatisation and structural adjustment.

Note

1. The official size of unemployment by county, is presented at regular intervals in the Bulletin of the National Commission for Statistics, directly subordinated to the Rumanian Government. The real size of the unemployment is hardly to be assessed, considering the growth of moonlighting in the past years. It is assumed that most of shadow labour market is concentrated in construction, agriculture, trade and services. No estimations about the size of this market exist, but only partial information that could help an assessment on the expansion of this phenomenon. Therefore, there are periods when about 20 - 25 percent of the persons that have unemployment benefit rights do not cash them. Informal reports are mentioning that during farming -work seasons, employers are exerting pressures to take advantage of 'technical unemployment', that means temporary job-loss due to economic depression, without ceasing the labour relations between the company and employee. As far as the real economy is concerned, according to some estimates the size of the shadow economy is about 30 percent of the Gross Domestic Product (Albu, 1995).

References

Albu, L.L. (1994), 'Probleme teoretico-metodologice ale abordarii economiei ascunse', *Probleme Economice*, No. 42/1994, Centrul de Informare si Documentare Economica, Institutul National de Cercetari Economice: Bucuresti.

Constantin, D.L. (1992), *Previziune si politici regionale*, Buletin No. 8/1992, Comisia Nationala de Prognoza.

Jula, D. (1993), 'Dezechilibre in dezvoltarea economica din Rumania si Spania', *Probleme economice de perspectiva europeana,* Academia Romana, Academia Regala a Doctorilor in Stiintedin Barcelona: sept. Bucuresti.

Jula, D. (1995), 'Consecinte ale dezechilibrelor regionale asupra proceselor de integrare economica', *Analele Institutului National de Cercetari Economice, anul V, Vo. 15, No. 1-2/1995,* Centrul de Informare si Documentare Economica, Institutul National de Cercetari Economice: Bucuresti.

Myrdal, G. (1957), *Economic Theory and Underdeveloped Regions*, Duckworth: London.

Planque, B. (1983), 'Une nouvelle organisation spatiale du developpement', *Le developpement decentralise. Dynamique spatiale de l'economie et planification regionale,* LITEC: Paris.

Waddley, D. (1986), *Restructuration regionale*, O.C.D.E.: Paris.

About the Authors

Carlos Álvarez
Faculty of Economic Sciences
Castille-La Mancha University
Albacete, Spain

David Armstrong
Northern Ireland Economic Research Centre
Belfast, the United Kingdom

David H. Blackaby
Department of Economics
University of Wales
Swansea, the United Kingdom

Luigi Bonatti
Department of Economics
University of Trento
Trento, Italy

Carlo Borzaga
Department of Economics
University of Trento
Trento, Italy

Daniela Constantin
Department of Economic Forecasting
Academy of Economic Studies
Bucharest, Rumania

Calin Dinga
Department of Economics
Polytechnic University Bucharest
Bucharest, Rumania

Jouke van Dijk
Faculty of Spatial Sciences
University of Groningen
Groningen, The Netherlands

Jaromir Gottvald
Faculty of Economics
Technical University of Ostrava
Ostrava, The Czech Republic

Andries de Grip
Research Centre for Education and the Labour Market
University of Maastricht
Maastricht, The Netherlands

Magdaléna Hiadlovská
Institute for Municipal and Regional Development
Banska Bystrica, Slovakia

Dorin Jula
Institute of Economic Forecasting
Bucharest, Rumania

Eugenia Kazamaki-Ottersten
Industrial Institute for Economic and Social Research
Stockholm, Sweden

Lambert van der Laan
Erasmus Centre for Labour market Analysis (ECLA) and Tinbergen Institute
Erasmus University
Rotterdam, The Netherlands

Cornelia Pârlog
Department of Economic Forecasting
Academy of Economic Studies
Bucharest, Rumania

Constanta Partenie
Department of Economics
Polytechnic University Bucharest
Bucharest, Rumania

José M.F. Polanco
Departamento de Administracion de Empresas
University of Cantabria
Spain

Rossitsa Rangelova
Institute of Economics
Bulgarian Academy of Sciences
Sofia, Bulgaria

Carlos Resa-Nestares
Faculty of Economic Sciences
Autonomous University of Madrid
Madrid, Spain

Santos M. Ruesga
Faculty of Economic Sciences
Autonomous University of Madrid
Madrid, Spain

Milan Simek
Faculty of Economics
Technical University of Ostrava
Ostrava, The Czech Republic

Katia Vladimirova
University for National and World Economy
Sofia, Bulgaria

For Product Safety Concerns and Information please contact our EU representative GPSR@taylorandfrancis.com Taylor & Francis Verlag GmbH, Kaufingerstraße 24, 80331 München, Germany

Batch number: 10725991

Printed by Printforce, the Netherlands